Internet
Sex Offenders

Internet Sex Offenders

MICHAEL C. SETO

American Psychological Association • Washington, DC

Published by
American Psychological Association
750 First Street, NE
Washington, DC 20002
www.apa.org

To order
APA Order Department
P.O. Box 92984
Washington, DC 20090-2984
Tel: (800) 374-2721; Direct: (202) 336-5510
Fax: (202) 336-5502; TDD/TTY: (202) 336-6123
Online: www.apa.org/pubs/books
E-mail: order@apa.org

In the U.K., Europe, Africa, and the Middle East, copies may be ordered from
American Psychological Association
3 Henrietta Street
Covent Garden, London
WC2E 8LU England

Typeset in Goudy by Circle Graphics, Inc., Columbia, MD

Printer: United Book Press, Baltimore, MD
Cover Designer: Naylor Design, Washington, DC

The opinions and statements published are the responsibility of the authors, and such opinions and statements do not necessarily represent the policies of the American Psychological Association.

Library of Congress Cataloging-in-Publication Data

Seto, Michael C.
   Internet sex offenders / Michael C. Seto.
      pages cm
   Includes bibliographical references and index.
   ISBN-13: 978-1-4338-1364-1
   ISBN-10: 1-4338-1364-5
   1. Online sexual predators. 2. Sex offenders. 3. Child sex offenders. 4. Sex crimes—
Prevention. I. Title.
   HV6773.15.O58S48 2013
   364.15'3—dc23
                                              2013001882

British Library Cataloguing-in-Publication Data

A CIP record is available from the British Library.

Printed in the United States of America
First Edition

http://dx.doi.org/10.1037/14191

For Meredith, who inspires me to be a better human being, scientist, and clinician, and Oliver, who reminds me every day why I have chosen such an unusual career path. I also want to dedicate this book to the children who have been victims of the crimes described within it; I hope you can grow up healthy, safe, and loved. Last, I want to acknowledge the perpetrators who have shared their stories with me in my clinical work and in the research that is represented in this book: You are not only your crimes, and you can lead a better life.

CONTENTS

PREFACE

This volume follows my recent book on pedophilia and sexual offending against children, also published by the American Psychological Association (Seto, 2008). After that endeavor, which took almost 3 years to complete, I thought I would take a break before assuming the (satisfying) challenge of writing another book. But after a plenary talk on online offending I gave at the 2009 Association for the Treatment of Sexual Abusers (ATSA) conference in Dallas, Texas, a colleague, Jean Proulx, asked me why I was not writing a book about this topic, given the demand for knowledge about this emerging problem. That was a good question. It was clear that there was a great deal of demand because of the increasing number of cases seen by law enforcement and by clinicians; it was also clear that there was a lack of research.

I was also motivated to write this book by a long-standing fascination with online technologies, beginning with reading *Neuromancer* (Gibson, 1984) as a high school student, with its description of cyberspace (a term that Gibson purportedly coined) and its crypto-dystopian view of the impact of online technologies on human freedom, capacity, and behavior. As someone who learned to create very basic computer programs using punch cards and then a teletype device connected to a university mainframe, I remember well the emergence of the World Wide Web, when websites were numbered in the hundreds rather than the hundreds of millions.

My enthusiasm for writing this volume was also spurred after participating in a series of national and international meetings on online sexual offending: a roundtable meeting sponsored by the National Center for Missing and Exploited Children in February 2009; a G8 Ministers of Justice symposium at the University of North Carolina at Chapel Hill, organized by Kurt Ribisl, Ethel Quayle, and Roberta Sinclair in April 2009; an international child protection meeting in June 2011 in Toronto, hosted by the Ontario Association of Children Aid Societies and organized by Tink Palmer; and the Attorney General of the United States' summit on child exploitation and abuse in October 2011. I also had the privilege of testifying before the United States Sentencing Commission regarding federal child pornography sentencing guidelines in February 2012. In addition, training workshops from 2007 to 2011 gave me many opportunities to speak with law enforcement and clinical professionals regarding their experiences and questions about online offending. I cannot name them all, but I appreciate the suggestions and directions they gave me in pursuing this work.

Reflecting the fact that this book is about the way that the Internet can facilitate sexual offending, I rely heavily on online resources. Though I try to use permalinks whenever available, links can change over time; the documents might still be found, however, using search engines when links are no longer active. Also reflecting the nonlinearity and linkages of the Internet, this book includes footnotes and appendices that do not follow the main narrative but provide additional information and context about the content in the corresponding chapter. One can treat them like links or pop-up boxes while reading.

Research that I have been involved in and that is reported in this book has been funded by the Ontario Mental Health Foundation, Social Sciences and Humanities Research Council, U.S. Department of Justice, Centre for Addiction and Mental Health, Royal Ottawa Health Care Group, Norwegian Ministry of Child and Family Affairs, Swedish Ministry of Health and Social Affairs, and the Swedish Research Council. I am very grateful for their financial support. I am grateful as well to the Royal Ottawa Health Care Group and my university affiliations (University of Toronto, Ryerson University, Carleton University, and University of Ottawa) for their support of my work and my students. The views expressed here do not necessarily reflect the views of these organizations.

There is increasing international attention and collaboration to address this problem, reflected in international law (United Nations Protocol), law enforcement (e.g., Virtual Global Task Force), advocacy work (ECPAT International), and research. These efforts are international in scope because the

Internet transcends (or ignores, depending on one's politics) national borders. Child pornography may be produced in the United States, distributed via servers based in Europe, and downloaded by users in Canada. Reflecting the international nature of online offending, I have had more opportunities for international collaboration as a result of my involvement in this area. With such a wide network, I cannot name everyone, but I would particularly like to thank Klaus Beier, Ray Blanchard, James Cantor, Angela Eke, Sandy Jung, Eva Kimonis, Niklas Langstrom, Mike Wood, Janina Neutze, James Ray, and students Kelly Babchishin, Chantal Hermann, Elisabeth Leroux, Anita Lam, Lesleigh Pullman, Lesley Reeves, and Skye Stephens. I would also like to acknowledge the invaluable assistance of Cathy Maclean and Susan Bottiglia, librarians at the Royal Ottawa Health Care Group, who aided me in locating hard-to-find journal articles and books while writing this book.

I have benefited greatly from the helpful criticisms and suggestions of Angela Eke and Grant Harris, who read the entire book in draft form. They are fantastic colleagues, and any errors or omissions should fall solely on my shoulders. I am very grateful to the editorial team I worked with at the American Psychological Association—Susan Reynolds, Tyler Aune, Erin O'Brien, Ron Teeter, and Anna DeVault—for their support during the development and production of this book.

In the interest of disclosure, I am currently a member of the prevention policy committee of the National Center for Missing and Exploited Children (http://www.ncmec.org), have consulted pro bono with the Thorn (formerly DNA) Foundation's Tech Task Force (http://wearethorn.org), and I am a member and former elected board of directors representative for ATSA (http://www.atsa.com). I am an associate editor for the ATSA journal, *Sexual Abuse: A Journal of Research and Treatment* (http://sax.sagepub.com) and the *Archives of Sexual Behavior* (http://www.springer.com/psychology/personality+%26+social+psychology/journal/10508). I am also on the editorial board of *Law and Human Behavior* (http://www.springer.com/psychology/psychology+%26+law/journal/10979). I have no financial interests in any of these organizations. I will earn royalties for the sale of this book, so please buy this copy or encourage your library to do so (now you know where I stand on intellectual property rights). I occasionally provide consultations or give training workshops on the topics covered in this book for a fee.

Internet
Sex Offenders

INTRODUCTION

My pictures that are on the Internet disturb me more than what Matthew did because I know that the abuse stopped but those pictures are still on the Internet.
    —Masha Allen ("Sit Down With a Molestation Survivor," 2006)

IMAGES

I vividly remember the most recent (and, I hope, last) time I viewed child pornography. As part of a research study involving case files from a large number of police services, my colleague Angela Eke and I sat down with one of the investigators to review a sampling of images that had been seized by police during their investigations. Most of the images on the computer screen were clearly of young children before or anticipating puberty. Some were alone or in sexually suggestive poses, but many images depicted the children involved in sexual acts with other children or with adults. Some of the children were clearly distressed, with frightened, tearful expressions on their faces.

I do not know whether I saw any images from the best-known child pornography series that have been identified by international and national bodies, including Interpol, the National Center for Missing and Exploited Children (NCMEC) in the United States, the Canadian Police Centre for

http://dx.doi.org/10.1037/14191-001
Internet Sex Offenders, by M. C. Seto

Missing and Exploited Children, or the Child Exploitation and Online Protection Centre in the United Kingdom. Some of the older, well-known series, including the KG, KX, and Helena (aka Hel-lo) series, are described by Jenkins (2001) in his landmark book on online child pornography. According to Jenkins, the KG ("kindergarten") series depicted very young girls, estimated to be between the ages of 3 and 6. This KG series had hundreds, possibly thousands, of images of these girls in the nude. The KX series showed the same girls engaged in fellatio or masturbation of adult men. Helena was a girl who appeared to be 7 or 8 years old, shown in multiple series with a peer-aged boy or with an adult man. The Misty series is a more recent well-known sequence of images recording sexual abuse perpetrated against a girl, Amy, between the ages of 4 and 9 by her uncle. Her victim impact statement as an adult was posted online ("Document: Victim Impact Statement," 2009; J. Schwartz, 2010).

It is a devastating thought that these children, now adults 20 or 30 years later, continue to have their images circulated online. Children were exploited to create these images, and many of these images record acts of child sexual abuse. Consumption of child pornography creates a market for this content. Out of the thousands of children who have been exploited in this way, only a small proportion have been identified. In the United States, those who have been identified have the option, under the Crime Victims Right Act (2004), to be notified every time one of their images is introduced as evidence in trial so that they can become aware of the suspect's custody status, submit a victim impact statement, and learn about future court proceedings. Under other legislation, child pornography victims have the right to pursue civil claims against child pornography possessors, as Amy did. Some victims opt out, however, not wanting to anticipate regular notices as their images are used over and over again in court trials.

Possibly the most well-known identified child pornography victim is Masha Allen. As a young girl, she was adopted from the former Soviet Union by Matthew Mancuso, who subsequently sexually abused her for years and posted images of her on the Internet. She was identified through the efforts of an international investigation led by Detective Bill McGarry of the Toronto Police Service. It turned out that the perpetrator had already been convicted of child sexual abuse and was serving a prison sentence at the time. Masha Allen was willing to be identified by name and testified before the United States Congress about the impact these crimes had on her. Other victim identification efforts by the Toronto Police Service, one of the international leaders in this arena, are described by Julian Sher (2007) in his book, *One Child at a Time*. A particularly horrible example is that of Jessica (a pseudonym), a young girl who was repeated sexually abused by her father, which was documented in a series of 400 images taken over a 2-year span. These pictures included images of her in a cage with her hands and feet bound and tears streaming down her cheeks. She was eventually identified by a small international network of agents, including the Toronto Police Service, FBI, and NCMEC (Sher, 2007).

These victim identification cases are complex: Jessica's father had made efforts to blur his face in images that were posted online, but the Toronto Police Service found an image that showed his face from the side, providing some clues to his identity. Another clue came from a close-up of a wristband the girl was wearing in several images. A police investigator was able to recognize most of the letters and determine it was for a chain of amusement parks that operated in five American states. Other images showed the girl in a Brownie uniform; though the offender had blurred images of the troop badge, the first two troop numbers were somewhat legible. Investigators determined there were several hundred troops with the same first two numbers, but only some of these troops overlapped with the states where the amusement park chain operated. Detectives realized there were three amusement parks in the area around Raleigh, North Carolina, and three Brownie troops with the same starting two numbers in the area. There was another clue: The girl was wearing a simple green dress in some images, which looked like a school uniform. Taking a guess, investigators contacted a school uniform manufacturer in the Raleigh area and found that the dress was used in only two schools in North Carolina, both in Raleigh. A picture of the girl was sent to the local FBI special agent, who went to the schools and showed the picture to the principal, who immediately identified the girl. Amazingly, this detective work took place only 33 hours after the investigation began.[1]

OTHER ONLINE SEXUAL OFFENDING

The use of online technologies to promulgate child pornography is only one form of online sexual offending (see Chapter 2). The typical child pornography offender seeks out sexual depictions of children, sometimes spending hours a week in this activity and likely masturbating and fantasizing about these images. Another form of online sexual offending involves the use of communication technologies to sexually solicit minors in the form of engaging them in sexual chat, exchanging pornography, creating child pornography (e.g., by convincing a minor to create and share sexually explicit images

---

[1]Because of news stories about these kinds of successes in victim and perpetrator identification, there has been an arms race with offenders hiding their faces and attempting to "sterilize" images to avoid any potential clues in clothing or background. Similarly, there has been an arms race in the use of technology to hide child pornography activities online.

of themselves), and by suggesting real-life meetings where sexual activity can take place (see Chapter 3). For example, an adult may send instant messages to youths who are participating in online chat rooms, message boards, or social networking sites such as Facebook or Myspace. Online technologies can also be used to facilitate other kinds of sexual crimes, including juvenile prostitution, sex tourism, or sexual trafficking, and solicitations of adults that lead to sexual assaults (see Appendix 1.2 and Resource A).

PUBLIC REACTIONS

The public's reactions to online offending have paralleled its reactions to stories about child sexual abuse and pedophilia more generally. There is, understandably, fear and anger about threats to children's well-being, safety, and physical integrity. The reaction may even be stronger because the scenes depicted in child pornography are unambiguous and can be more emotionally evocative than victim and witness testimony for jurors and judges, no matter how honest and eloquent the testimony. There are also fears about the unanticipated consequences of online offending. While I was working on this part of the manuscript, the sad story of Amanda Todd was frequently in the news (e.g., Dean, 2012). Amanda Todd was a 15-year-old girl who committed suicide after a downward spiral that was greatly influenced by the bullying she received when an adult man who solicited her online distributed a topless image of her (captured from a webcam interaction) after she refused to create and send more images to him. She posted a poignant YouTube video about this experience shortly before she killed herself (https://youtu.be/vOHXGNx-E7E).

In the early 2000s, colleagues and others—clinicians, prosecutors, and police investigators—began contacting me to ask about what was scientifically known about child pornography offenders. Given my long-term research interests on pedophilia and sexual offending against children, studying child pornography and other online offenders and their crimes seemed like a natural evolution in this work, especially with the increasing power and access to Internet and related technologies through the 2000s.

Child pornography and sexual solicitation of minors have been around a long time, well before the arrival of the Internet (as I discuss in Chapters 2 and 3). However, the Internet has clearly facilitated these forms of sexual offending. There were (and are) many central, unanswered questions about online sexual offenders and their offenses:

- Who are the offenders? Most are familiar with computers and related technologies; most child pornography investigations involved digital content. They seem to be different from the "typical" sex offender. If so, how are they different? Do these differences matter with regard to risk, treatment, or supervision?

- What motivates these individuals to seek child pornography? The most obvious candidate reason is pedophilia (i.e., sexual attraction to prepubescent children), but are there other motivations? What about individuals who seek images of older children or carry out online sexual solicitations?
- Some individuals have claimed they viewed pornography because of an Internet, pornography, or sexual addiction. Is this plausible?
- What is the risk that a child pornography offender poses for sexually offending against a child? What is the risk that a child pornography offender will seek out child pornography again?
- What are the treatment and supervision needs of these offenders? What could be done to reduce their risk?

These questions motivated me to seek out answers, searching the social scientific literature and talking with colleagues. But there was little empirical research addressing these questions. I started a child pornography offender follow-up study with Angela Eke, thinking that we might do a few studies on this population before moving on to other research. But 8 years later, I am still actively involved in research on this population, partly because the results have been so fascinating and partly because it is clear that a much stronger empirical foundation is needed to guide policies and practices in this area.

WHY THIS BOOK

Though the number of online sexual offense cases is still a tiny fraction of real-world child sexual exploitation and abuse cases (Wolak, Finkelhor, & Mitchell, 2009), I believe it is worthy of a book-length treatment for several reasons. First, much less is known about online sexual offending than conventional sexual offending. There have been a number of recent books on online offending, but none that have focused to the extent that I do in this volume on the practical questions this offender population raises about risk to reoffend, clinical and correctional management, and intervention. Second, online sexual offending is likely to continue to increase, in contrast to the decline in conventional sexual offending against children, as more of the world goes online and these technologies become more and more a part of everyday life. Third, new policies and practices are being implemented as a result of concerns about online sexual offending that affect everyone who is online, not only parents who might be concerned about the safety of their children and the professionals who work with perpetrators or victims. Proposed laws such as the Protecting Children from Internet Pornographers Act of 2011 (H.R. 1981) in the United States and the Investigating and Preventing Criminal Electronic Communications Act of 2012 (Bill C-30) in Canada—which place greater restrictions and reduce privacy online by requiring Internet service providers to retain data for longer periods of time (thus making them available by subpoena without individual notification)—are presented as legal mechanisms to combat online sexual offending.

There have been several major legal and policy initiatives that have reflected and amplified concerns about this class of crime. Focusing on the United States, inarguably the world leader in identifying online sexual offending as a priority, these include federal laws targeting online sexual offending—for example, Congressional directives to increase sentence severity for child federal pornography offenders in the Prosecutorial Remedies and Other Tools to end the Exploitation of Children Today (or PROTECT) Act of 2003; the G8 Global Symposium for Examining the Relationship between Online and Offline Offenses and Preventing the Sexual Exploitation of Children, held in 2009[2]; the U.S. Department of Justice first National Strategy to address child sexual exploitation, published in 2010; and the U.S. Attorney General's summit on child exploitation and abuse, held in fall 2011. Hamilton (2012) summarized the dramatic shift in resources that have been put toward online child sexual exploitation investigations.

THIS BOOK'S BLUEPRINT

In this volume, I address these issues, particularly the risk posed to children but also including perpetrators' risk of further online offending; effective assessment and management; and policy and practice implications of emerging research on child pornography offenders and their crimes. In Chapter 1, I set the context for this book, discussing the development of the Internet and its ramifications for sexual offending. I focus on the question of whether the Internet has created a new kind of sexual offender or has facilitated actions by individuals who might not have acted without online technologies. In Chapter 2, I discuss the history of child pornography, the impact of the Internet on its availability, review what we know about child pornography content, and discuss the continuum of culpability in child pornography offending, ranging from possession to distribution to production. In Chapter 3, I review and discuss what we know about the solicitation of minors for sexual purposes,

---

[2]The G8 ministers' declaration can be found at g8italia2009.it/static/G8_Allegato/Ministerxs_delaration_on_child_pornography,0.pdf

variously called *luring, traveling,* or *grooming* offenses. I review theories about the etiology of online offending in Chapter 4, focusing on how they are similar to and different from theories of contact sexual offending against children. I then review, in Chapter 5, research on the characteristics of online offenders, particularly studies that have compared online and contact sex offenders to see how online offenders are similar versus different on theoretically and empirically important variables. In Chapter 6, I examine the central question of how pornography use is related to sexual behavior and how child pornography use might be related to contact sexual offending against children. In Chapter 7, I discuss risk assessment and how online offenders can be prioritized according to the risk they pose to reoffend, either by committing contact offenses against children or by committing further online offenses. In Chapter 8, I discuss intervention, covering not only treatment but also criminal justice sanctions and prevention efforts. I conclude with a final chapter summarizing what we know, identifying future directions for research, and making evidence-based suggestions for policy and practice.

1

OVERVIEW OF ONLINE SEXUAL OFFENDING

Younger readers of this book will not remember a time when the Internet was not a constant part of their lives, at home, school, and work. However, older readers will remember the emergence of the Internet and its related communication technologies, beginning in the early 1990s. There was a headiness and excitement about this idyllic frontier, emerging first for most users as e-mail, then as bulletin boards and newsgroups, and then text-based web surfing using the National Center for Supercomputing Applications Mosaic browser. Early in the Internet's history, there were few pages and few users.[1] Since then, the number of computers connected to the Internet and the number of sites have increased exponentially. There are now over two billion users (see Figure 1.1 on Internet usage). E-mail, instant messaging,

---

[1]This book is not about the history of the Internet. For interested readers, more information is available at Internetsociety.org/Internet/Internet-51/history-Internet/brief-history-Internet. For an entertaining, nostalgic look at early pages, see the Internet Archive's Wayback Machine: http://www.archive.org/web/web.php

http://dx.doi.org/10.1037/14191-002
Internet Sex Offenders, by M. C. Seto

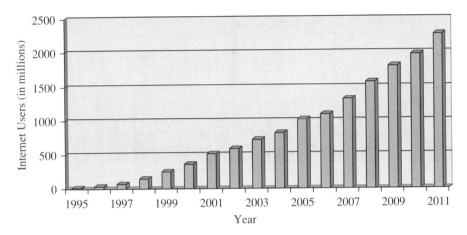

Figure 1.1. Number of Internet users globally (in millions), 1995 to 2011. Data derived from various sources, estimated closest to end of year. Retrieved from http://www.internetworldstats.com/emarketing.htm

Internet telephony, and videoconferencing have transformed the way we communicate with each other. Social networking sites such as Facebook and LinkedIn have transformed how we connect to others. The vast repositories of knowledge available through search engines and dynamic collaborations such as Wikipedia (a user-generated online encyclopedia) have changed how we learn and use knowledge. The portability of Internet-connected devices such as smartphones and tablets has only increased our connectedness.

The transformative and pervasive power of the Internet for communication and other social benefits has also been true for criminal behavior as well, with increasing concerns about cybertheft and fraud, online harassment, and the digital distribution of illegal pornography, particularly child pornography. Reflecting these trends, law enforcement agencies have developed specialized units, such as the Internet Crimes Against Children Task Force in the United States (http://ojjdp.gov/programs/progsummary.asp?pi=3), the FBI's cybercrime unit (http://fbi.gov/about-us/investigate/cyber/cyber), and local and state cybercrime units.

Pornography, including child pornography, has always changed as a result of technological advances in photography, film, and then video. But the Internet has surpassed these earlier technologies because its prevailing culture, set by the academics and progressive thinkers who established the first protocols, is one of (perceived) anonymity, personal freedom, and disregard for laws (as demonstrated by the widespread pirating of music, movies, and software). This culture is well represented by the Electronic Frontier Foundation (https://www.eff.org/), with its promotion of anonymity, privacy, and online freedom. This cyber-utopian vision is described well by John Perry Barlow, the lyricist for the Grateful Dead, in his rather florid *Declaration of the Independence of Cyberspace* (1996):

> Governments of the Industrial World, you weary giants of flesh and steel,
> I come from Cyberspace, the new home of Mind. On behalf of the future,
> I ask you of the past to leave us alone. You are not welcome among us.
> You have no sovereignty where we gather. (para. 1)

There is an inherent tradeoff, however, between this vision and human nature. The same technologies that allow political dissidents to challenge authoritarian government efforts to censor or silence them can allow others to engage in crimes such as the transmission of child pornography and sexual solicitation of minors. In some ways, in the past 20 years the Internet has operated like the old Wild West. And like that frontier, it is now becoming more governed, with increasing regulation and oversight, such as the approval of a new top-level .XXX domain by the Internet Corporation for Assigned Names and Numbers to demarcate an adults-only area for legal pornography businesses and also by the establishment of the Virtual Global Taskforce in 2003, an international collaboration of police forces to combat online child sexual exploitation (http://www.virtualglobaltaskforce.com). Efforts to regulate and police the Internet are a response (or, at least, justified as a response) to public alarm about the widespread availability of (child) pornography on the Internet, the potential effects of exposure to this content on minors, and the safety of children and youths as they are increasingly active online, both in becoming involved in child pornography (e.g., being convinced to produce sexually suggestive or explicit images of themselves in the nude or semi-nude) and being solicited by adults for sexual purposes.[2]

To date, most prosecutions of Internet-facilitated sexual offending have been for child pornography offenses, but more people have been prosecuted for sexual solicitation of minors since the implementation of laws criminalizing communication with children through the Internet for the purpose of committing a sexual offence (e.g., Criminal Code of Canada, R.S.C. Sec 172.1; 18 U.S.C. § 2422 [1985]; see Table 1.1). National arrest estimates show that the number of child pornography cases tripled from 2001 to 2009 (Wolak, 2011). There are similar data in other jurisdictions. The number of online luring cases has also increased during a similar time period, both in Canada (Loughlin & Taylor-Butts, 2009) and in the United States (Wolak, Finkelhor, & Mitchell, 2008). Though the total number of online sexual

---

[2]These points are relevant for other online arenas, including noncriminal sexual behavior (cybersex between consenting adults, infidelity, legal pornography use), nonsexual behavior (e.g., gambling), and militarization in the creation of cyber warfare divisions by the U.S. government and allegations of government-initiated hacking of other nations (Clarke & Knake, 2010; Morozov, 2011).

TABLE 1.1

Child Pornography and Solicitation (Luring) Laws in the Countries Where Most Online Offender Research Has Been Produced

Country	Child pornography law	Solicitation (luring) law
Australia (federal law)	Sexual depictions of persons who are under age 18 or who appear to be so as judged by reasonable persons in the community (Krone, 2005).	Criminal Code Act 1995 sections 474.26 and 474.27 prohibit the use of a "carrier service" to communicate with the intent to procure a person under the age of 16 or expose such a person to any indecent matter for the purposes of grooming.
Canada	Sexually explicit visual content of someone under age 18 or depicted as under age 18; written or visual depictions that counsel sexual activity with someone under age 18. Exemption for artistic, educational, scientific, or medical merit. (Criminal Code of Canada)	Electronic communication with a person believed to be a child for the purpose of facilitating the commission of sexual offences. Depending on the offence, the requisite age (real or believed) of the intended victim varies from 14 to 18 (Criminal Code of Canada).
United Kingdom	Depictions of persons under age 18. Sentencing Advisory Panel distinguishes between five types of child pornography content, based on the COPINE[a] typology: (a) images depicting nudity or erotic posing; (b) sexually explicit without adult, for example, masturbation or sexual interactions between children; (c) nonpenetrative acts between adult and child; (d) penetrative acts between adult and child; and (e) depictions incorporating sadism or bestiality.	In England and Wales, sections 14 and 15 of the Sexual Offences Act 2003 make it an offence to arrange a meeting with a child, for oneself or someone else, with the intent of sexually abusing the child. The meeting itself is also criminalized. The Protection of Children and Prevention of Sexual Offences (Scotland) Act 2005 introduced a similar provision for Scotland (http://en.wikipedia.org/wiki/Protection_of_Children_and_Prevention_of_Sexual_Offences_%28Scotland%29_Act_2005).
United States (federal law)	Sexually explicit visual content of someone under age 18 or depicted as under age 18; obscene fictional depictions of someone under age 18 unless there is "literary, artistic, political or scientific value." Viewing child pornography without actively downloading and saving the image is illegal under federal law (PROTECT[b] Act of 2003).	Luring a minor to cross state lines for sexual purpose or using electronic or other means to transmit contact information regarding minor. Traveling to meet the minor met online would also violate federal law if one of the computers involved was in a different state. (Sexual Exploitation of Children Act)

Note. [a]COPINE = Combating Paedophile Information Networks in Europe. [b]PROTECT = Prosecutorial Remedies and Other Tools to end the Exploitation of Children Today.

offense cases is still small compared with real-world child sexual abuse and solicitation cases, they represent a growing proportion of sexual offenses as more and more time is spent online. In the United States, online cases represent about 10% of the total number of sexual offense cases, probably reflecting political and law enforcement priorities. The percentages are smaller in other jurisdictions, such as Canada, Australia, and the United Kingdom (Choo, 2009; Loughlin & Taylor-Butts, 2009; Nicholas, Kershaw, & Walker, 2007).

WHAT IS SPECIAL ABOUT INTERNET OFFENDING

In our introduction to a recent special issue on Internet-facilitated sexual offending in the journal *Sexual Abuse: A Journal of Research and Treatment*, Karl Hanson and I asked the fundamental question of whether Internet offenders were special (Seto & Hanson, 2011). In other words, does distinguishing offenders who use the Internet to commit sexual offenses make any more sense than distinguishing offenders because they used a car or another technology to commit their crimes? We suggested there were two prevailing views. One view considered Internet-facilitated sexual offending to be an extension of conventional offending, just as Internet banking, for example, could be construed as an extension of banking in the real world and thus online theft akin to real world theft. This view can be tested by comparing the characteristics and offenses of online offenders to those of conventional offenders; the patterns of similarities and differences can reveal the extent to which Internet-facilitated and real-world offending resemble each other.

The second view of Internet-facilitated sexual offending holds that individuals who had never sexually offended might become involved because of distinctive properties of the Internet. In this view, these individuals would not have committed sexual offenses if the Internet did not exist as a facilitator. A. Cooper (1998, 2002) suggested, for example, that Internet-related sexual behavior (which might include accessing illegal pornography and online solicitation) was facilitated by a "Triple-A engine," reflecting accessibility, affordability, and (perceived) anonymity.

- *Accessibility*. Sexual content, including illegal sexual content, is readily available, certainly more so than before the Internet became a regular part of our lives. The same is true for potential interactions with minors.
- *Affordability*. The cost of high-speed access to images, video, and real-time interaction is much cheaper than it was in the days of actual magazines, books, pictures, and films; the cost of 1 month's access, and all the activity that can represent,

is comparable to the cost of a single magazine or book in the 1970s, in today's dollars (Jenkins, 2001). A person motivated to solicit minors can approach hundreds—or more—individuals for free if they use publicly available computers and free online services such as e-mail and social networks.

■ *Anonymity.* One surfs the Internet alone, and there is a sense that, with so many other users and usernames or e-mail addresses not directly linked to one's name and identity, online activity is anonymous. It is not truly anonymous, however. Except for the most privacy-minded and technologically sophisticated users, our online activity leaves digital traces, but the common perception is that no one is aware of what we are doing online.

As is discussed further in Chapter 4, online sexual offending appears to be a "hyper-male" phenomenon, with more than 99% of large online offender samples being male (Babchishin, Hanson, & Hermann, 2011; see also Appendix 1.1). According to clinical and criminal justice data, this is an even higher percentage than for contact sexual offending, where 90% to 95% of offenders are male (Center for Sex Offender Management, 2007; see also Denov, 2003; T. Peter, 2009). The percentages are lower when focusing only on offenders with child victims, and self-report data indicate the gender difference is not as large as criminal data suggest. Nonetheless, the large majority of sexual offenses are committed by men (which is why I use the male pronoun throughout this book), with offenses committed by women receiving less political and empirical attention (however, sexual abuse by a female perpetrator seems to have a strong association with male perpetration; see Denov, 2003).

There is almost no information on female online offenders. Martellozzo, Nehring, and Taylor (2010) reported on two female online offenders identified over a 5-year period. Both were deemed to have been compelled by a male co-offender. One of these women claimed that she had been coerced by her partner to participate in downloading child pornography and in creating pornographic images. The second woman created images of her own children but minimized her responsibility for this, claiming that she was pressured by a boyfriend she met online through a social network (and had never met in real life). She also claimed she was unable to end the online relationship, though she had ended several real-life abusive relationships. In another small case series, Elliott and Ashfield (2011) described four female online offenders: Ms. A, who groomed an adolescent male online, engaging in sexual chat; Ms. B, who produced child pornography using her children for a male co-offender who asked her for this content; Ms. C, who used peer-to-peer software to download child pornography and communicated with individuals who were sexually interested in minors online; and Ms. D, who sexually abused her children with her husband and produced and distributed recordings of these crimes. In my follow-up research with Angela Eke, less than 1% of online child pornography offenders were female (Seto & Eke, 2005). Basic research on sex differences in sexual response suggest that the relationships between sexual interest, sexual arousal, and online sexual behavior differ for men and women (Chivers & Bailey, 2005; Chivers, Rieger, Latty, & Bailey, 2004; Chivers, Seto, Lalumière, Laan, & Grimbos, 2010).

PUBLIC ATTENTION

Online sexual offending is increasingly in the public eye, with regular news stories about child pornography and solicitation arrests, take-downs of national and international child pornography trafficking rings, and sensational stories of Internet-related sexual assaults and even homicides. Child pornography and solicitation cases appear regularly in the news media, along with stories about child sex tourism or juvenile prostitution (see Appendix 1.2). As in many other areas, celebrity involvement garners more attention. Gary Glitter, known for his glam-rocker fame in the 1970s and as a singer–songwriter, was arrested for possession of child pornography in 1997 after taking his computer in for repair ("Glitter Jailed Over Child Porn," 1999). He was also subsequently convicted for child sexual abuse in Vietnam involving two girls, aged 10 and 11 (though other girls also came forward), and served a 3-year prison sentence as a result. As this book goes to press, he has been arrested following allegations made in the wake of the Jimmy Savile scandal in the United Kingdom, in which this famous celebrity television host allegedly had sex with hundreds of underage girls, including handicapped and hospitalized girls he met through his charity work (Quinn, 2012).

Pete Townshend, a guitarist for The Who, was cautioned by police as a result of Operation Ore, for using his credit card on a single occasion to access a child pornography website ("Who Star Cautioned Over Child Porn," 2012). A forensic investigation indicated he did not possess any illegal images, but he was cautioned that possession of child pornography was prohibited for any reason. The explanation he gave in media accounts was that he was curious about the problem of commercially available child pornography, in light of his own childhood sexual abuse. As a final example, American singer R. Kelly was indicted in 2002 on 21 counts of child pornography possession following the identification of a videotape depicting him having sex with a teenaged minor ("R. Kelly to be Tried," 2007). He was acquitted in 2008 after the identity of the girl could not be proved. Kelly was also charged with 12 counts of child pornography possession after police found pictures of a nude and clearly underage girl, with some of the pictures

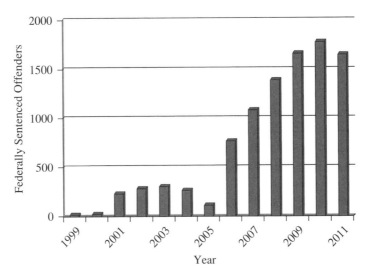

Figure 1.2. Federally sentenced child pornography offenders, 1999 to 2011. Data from U.S. Sentencing Commission Annual Report and Sourcebook of Federal Sentencing Statistics: http://www.ussc.gov/Data_and_Statistics/Annual_Reports_and_Sourcebooks/index.cfm

showing him having sex with her. The charges were dropped when a judge ruled that the police had seized the pictures illegally.

Motivans and Kyckelhahn (2007) described a steady increase in the number of federal child exploitation prosecutions involving child pornography in the United States, such that child pornography offenders represented one of the fastest growing groups in the federal system and two thirds of all child exploitation cases. This trend has only continued, as shown in a compilation of the number of federal (American) child pornography offenders extending to 2011 (see Figure 1.2). The estimated number of arrests for child pornography offenses in the United States tripled from 2000/2001 to 2009 (Wolak, Finkelhor, & Mitchell, 2011). It is hard to obtain more precise estimates in the United States, however, because there is no national system for tracking Internet offenders at the state level.[3]

The U.S. Attorney General, Eric Holder, announced the first national strategy on child exploitation prevention and intervention on August 2, 2010. This included a threat assessment regarding child pornography, online luring, and commercial sexual exploitation of children. The U.S. Department of Justice (2010) reported that for the years 2000 to 2010 there were substantial increases

[3]Some, but not all, states require Internet offenders to be placed on sex offender registries, but problems and troubling questions about the efficacy of these registries have been reported (Schram & Milloy, 1995; Tewksbury, 2005; Zgoba, Witt, Dalessandro, Veysey, 2008).

in multiple parameters, including complaints received, investigations launched, and prosecutions. For example, the FBI Innocent Images Initiative opened 113 cases in 1996; this had increased 20-fold, up to 2,443 cases, by 2007.

The phenomenon of increasing online offending cases is not unique to the United States. Middleton, Mandeville-Norden, and Hayes (2009) reported a five-fold increase in child pornography cases from 1999 to 2005 in the United Kingdom, with child pornography cases now representing more than one fifth of all sexual offense cases and one third of probation cases. Similarly, Dauvergne and Turner (2010) noted a sharp increase in child pornography cases in Canada, with approximately 1,600 cases of child pornography offenses reported in 2009, compared with 2,600 cases of sexual offenses against children (the latter could include online solicitation cases). In other words, over a third of sexual offenses pertaining to children in Canada involved child pornography in 2009. Reflecting these criminal justice trends, clinical referrals have similarly increased as offenders are referred for evaluations or treatment. Figure 1.3 shows the number of child pornography offenders referred to the Sexual Behaviour Clinic of the Centre for Addiction and Mental Health from 1996 to 2005, during the time I was employed there. Bates and Metcalf (2007) reported a similar increase in clinical referrals in the United Kingdom.

The National Juvenile Online Victimization Project, now repeated three times in the 2000s, has estimated that the number of arrests in the United States for Internet sexual crimes tripled from 2000/2001 to 2009 (Wolak, Finkelhor, & Mitchell, 2011). Approximately two thirds of the Internet crimes involved possession or distribution of child pornography. Looking only at federal cases, there has been an exponential increase in the number of child pornography cases, far exceeding federal prosecutions for contact sexual offending (Motivans & Kyckelhahn, 2007). This strong upward trend is important to understand because sentences are getting longer for comparable child pornography offenses. Wollert, Waggoner, and Smith (2012) examined U.S. Sentencing Commission data for federal child pornography sentences and found that the average sentence was approximately 3 years in the late 1990s; a decade later, the average sentence length was approximately 10 years, comparable to the average sentences received by those who had committed contact sexual offenses. As a result, Internet offenders will be in prison longer and will require longer terms of supervision than they did in the past if eligible for probation or parole (Wolak, Finkelhor, & Mitchell, 2009).[4]

---

[4]The much longer average sentences for federal child pornography offenders, even with increasing downward variances by federal court judges, is due to a mandatory minimum sentence of 5 years for receipt of child pornography and sentencing enhancements that apply in almost all cases (e.g., enhancement for having any image of a child under the age of 12, having 600 or more images). The guidelines can be retrieved from ussc.gov/Guidelines/2011_Guidelines/Manual_HTML/2g2_2.htm

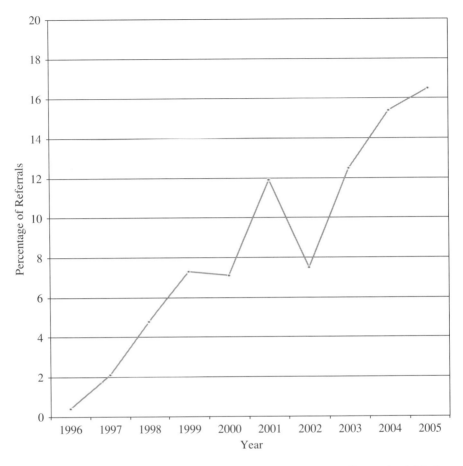

Figure 1.3. Clinical referrals to the Sexual Behaviour Clinic at the Centre for Addiction and Mental Health, 1996 to 2005.

TIP OF THE ICEBERG

Krone (2005) emphasized that the total amount of child pornography (and child pornography activity) is unknown because we have little information about nondigital content or personally produced collections that are never traded, unless they are discovered by someone accidentally (e.g., a roommate, a computer technician). Child pornography possession is mostly identified now because of online activity, so we know more about child pornography offending as a result of the Internet. There is good reason to believe these numbers are only the visible tip of the iceberg.

The amount of peer-to-peer network trafficking in known child pornography files far exceeds the number of individuals who have been identified by police investigators (e.g., bit.ly/ecfibF). The U.S. Department of Justice (2010) noted that two law enforcement operations (Fairplay and Roundup) identified over 20 million unique Internet protocol (IP) addresses accessing known child pornography files on peer-to-peer networks, using 120,000 to 170,000 child pornography files on their watch lists. This result does not mean that 20 million people were accessing child pornography, because individuals using different devices would register multiple IP addresses, individuals logging in with dynamic IP addresses through a particular Internet service provider might be recorded as different unique IP addresses, and some of the peer-to-peer activity could be unwitting or inadvertent (e.g., if someone downloaded a large batch of pornography files, unaware that some of those files contained child pornography). Nonetheless, the implication is that there are many more individuals accessing child pornography than have ever been identified. Slightly less than half of the unique IP addresses were American-registered addresses.

Independent computer science studies indicate child pornography, though uncommon, is readily available through peer-to-peer networks (Prichard, Watters, & Spiranovic, 2011; Steel, 2009). BitTorrent (http://www.bittorrent.com/) is currently the largest peer-to-peer network, with a decentralized structure that precludes analysis of queries and downloads in the way that the Gnutella peer-to-peer network (https://en.wikipedia.org/wiki/Gnutella) could be studied by Steel (2009). Prichard et al. (2011) analyzed the top 300 publicly accessible search terms in isoHunt (http://www.isohunt.com), an internationally popular peer-to-peer network search engine, and concluded that three of the top terms referred to child pornography (*pthc*, for pre-teen hardcore; *Lolita*; and *teen*). I dispute the last term because 18 and 19 year olds are also teenagers and depictions of them would be legal. The term *teen* might instead be interpreted as the "barely legal" genre of mainstream pornography, though an analysis of online searches of large data sets indicated that content depicting 16 year olds is the number one age-related search (Ogas & Gaddam, 2011). However, images of teens ages 13 to 17 would be illegal. The first two terms studied by Prichard et al. (2011), *pthc* and *Lolita*, are unambiguous. This analysis does not tell us how many users entered these terms or how often users entered these terms.

Whatever the explanations for this increasing demand, it is clear that the number of potential investigations already far exceeds law enforcement resources.[5] Many law enforcement agencies have not dealt with the backlog

---

[5]Many online offenders remain undetected. For example, most of the Riegel (2004) sample had never been charged, though 95% admitted they had viewed child pornography at some time in their lives (some quite frequently), and three quarters of the child pornography only offenders in Neutze, Seto, Schaefer, Mundt, and Beier (2011) had no official criminal record.

of cases arising from major international police operations begun in 1999 (Krone, 2005). The most famous and largest was Avalanche, which followed the discovery and prosecution of the owners of Landslide Productions for brokering sales of child pornography through its member websites. Avalanche was paralleled by major investigations in Canada (Snowball), the United Kingdom (Ore), and elsewhere. Though resources for law enforcement in this area are increasing, the reality is that only some cases will be thoroughly investigated and prosecuted.

IMPETUS FOR THIS BOOK

Why are lawmakers, professionals, and the public so concerned about Internet-facilitated sexual offending? In part, Internet sexual offending is connected to broader concerns about child sexual exploitation and sexual abuse. Production of real child pornography involves exploitation of a child, even if no contact sexual abuse takes place, because the images are used for sexual gratification, can be distributed widely, do not deteriorate, and the child cannot legally consent.

Part of the concern is clearly driven by the risk posed by Internet offenders to commit contact sexual offenses. It is intuitively appealing that someone who is sexually interested in children and accessing child pornography or engaging in online communications with children is more likely to commit contact offenses than someone with no such interests. This in turn ties into the fear, anxiety, and stigma associated with pedophilia, reflected in public perceptions of online offenders (Lam, Mitchell, & Seto, 2010) and of sex offenders more generally (Levenson, Brannon, Fortney, & Baker, 2007). Levenson et al. (2007) found, for example, that the public believed that sex offenders were homogeneous with regard to risk to reoffend, that they were highly likely to reoffend, and that they were unlikely to improve with treatment.

Another plausible reason for the strong reaction to online offending is the "realness" of images, videos, and online communications (e.g., the texts from online chats and instant messages). These digital data can be used in prosecutions of online offenses as hard evidence of the sexual interests and intentions of the perpetrators. In many contact offense prosecutions, in contrast, the evidence is often circumstantial, and even in cases where there is no doubt that offenses took place, there may still be uncertainty about what happened and, for perpetrators who deny the offenses or refuse to talk about it, their intentions. Many of the offenders I have assessed who have committed crimes against children have denied pedophilia and claimed that the sexual offense they committed was an aberrant reaction to exceptional stress and negative life circumstances. This can be contrasted with an online solicitation offender whose e-mails provide explicit details about what kinds of sexual acts he wants to engage in and his sexual desire for a particular minor.

With child sexual abuse cases on the decline since the early 1990s (Finkelhor & Jones, 2006; Jones & Finkelhor, 2001; Mishra & Lalumière, 2009), more law enforcement and child welfare resources have become available for online sexual offending cases. From a law enforcement perspective, these cases are a good investment because they produce high conviction rates (95% or higher; e.g., Motivans & Kyckelhahn, 2007). A difficult and controversial question is whether the increase in child pornography offending helps explain the decline in child sexual abuse cases because of a cathartic effect of having access to this content as an outlet for masturbation and fantasy in lieu of sexual contact with children. This question is discussed in Chapter 6.

CURRENT ONLINE OFFENDING LAWS

Child Pornography Laws

In the United States, the first federal child pornography law was established in 1978, and only two states had specific child pornography laws in 1977. Before these laws came into effect, child pornography crimes were covered by obscenity legislation. The Federal Sexual Exploitation of Children Act in 1978 prohibited the manufacture or commercial exploitation of obscene material involving persons under age 16. This resulted in child pornography no longer being available in adult stores. The 1984 Child Protection Act finalized it by making any depiction of sex involving a minor automatically obscene and outside of First Amendment protection. This 1984 act also raised the legal age from 16 to 18, without concomitant changes in the legal ages of consent for sexual intercourse. Canadian, U.S. federal, British, and Australian child pornography laws are specifically described in Table 1.1; much of the research on child pornography offenders has come from these four countries.

How should child pornography be defined (see Gillespie, 2010)? Is an image of a nude or semi-nude child sufficient to be deemed pornography? In the United States, the Dost test outlines six considerations that needed to be considered at trial (*United States v. Dost*, 1986): (a) whether the focal point of the visual depiction is the child's genitals or pubic area; (b) whether the setting of the visual depiction is sexually suggestive (e.g., lying down on bed); (c) whether the child is depicted in an unnatural pose or in inappropriate attire, considering the child's age; (d) whether the child is nude or clothed; (e) whether the visual depiction suggests sexual coyness or a willingness to engage in sexual activity; and (f) whether the visual depiction is intended or designed to elicit a sexual response in the viewer. These criteria are not expected to be relevant to pictures of children in the bath or nude at a public beach. Yet these nonexplicit images can also be sexually arousing, just as photographs of nude women or men can be sexually arousing in the absence of any emphasis on the genitals or any depiction of sexual activity. Attempts to codify child pornography and what Lanning (2001) and Taylor and Quayle (2003) have described as "indicative" materials are described in Chapter 2.

Solicitation Law

Solicitation laws prohibit the use of electronic means to communicate with minors for the purpose of facilitating a sexual offense—for example, engaging in sexual contact with someone under the legal age of consent (see Table 1.1). Some laws on solicitation have origins in laws regarding communicating with minors for sexual purposes. For example, in Canada, the criminal charge of "invitation to sexual touching" applies if an adult invites a young person under the age of 16 to touch himself or herself or the adult for a sexual purpose. Thus, someone could have been charged for invitation to sexual touching for asking a young adolescent girl through a webcam interaction to touch herself, even though no physical contact ever takes place.

LEGAL GAPS

Several authors have pointed out contradictions or gaps in online offending law (Gillespie, 2010; Seto, 2010). For example, the age of consent for sexual activity is 16 in Canada and the large majority of American states, usually with exemptions to avoid criminalizing sexual relationships between similar-aged minors. Yet the child pornography or solicitation laws just mentioned include the involvement of any minor under the age of 18. Thus, a 17-year-old male could legally have sex with his 16-year-old girlfriend in Canada (or in Illinois or Washington state), yet he could be criminally prosecuted for possessing or producing digital images of his girlfriend in a sexually explicit pose (Wolak, Finkelhor, & Mitchell, 2012). This behavior is of social concern because adolescents may not realize or appreciate the significance of such images being distributed to others—but should it be criminalized?

Online offending laws do not include the same age-related exemptions to avoid criminalizing peer interactions, though some states are beginning to recognize this gap by changing the laws so that adolescents are treated differently. It is also the case that police and prosecutors are taking age into consideration when they have discretion, issuing a caution or warning rather than pressing a criminal charge. In their study of "sexting"—involving adolescent production, distribution, or possession of sexually explicit images of themselves or their peers using mobile technologies—Wolak et al. (2012) found that the majority of adolescents involved in sexting cases were not criminally charged.

As I discuss in further detail in Chapter 2, sexting does occur among adolescents. An early survey reported in 2008 suggested that this activity was endemic, with approximately a fifth of teens having sent or posted nude or semi-nude photos or videos of themselves (see the Sex and Tech Survey; The National Campaign to Prevent Teen and Unplanned Pregnancy, 2008). However, this study has been criticized for including the reports of 18- and 19-year-old teenagers (for whom sexting activity is legal, if not prudent) and for including photos that would not constitute child pornography (e.g., pictures of a minor in a skimpy bikini or in underwear). Surveys using more cautious operationalizations have produced sexting prevalence estimates ranging from 1% to 4% (Lenhart, Ling, Campbell, & Purcell, 2010; Wolak et al., 2012).

WITHOUT BORDERS

One of the challenges in responding to online offending is the transjurisdictional nature of the Internet and the crimes it can facilitate. The International Centre for Missing and Exploited Children (2010) in a legal review found that half (95) of 184 Interpol member countries in the world did not have specific child pornography laws, and others had laws that were deemed inadequate. Though some of the remaining countries prohibit all pornography or cover child pornography under existing obscenity laws, child pornography is not illegal in all countries. Thus, someone could legally have a computer server containing child pornography images in a country where child pornography is not illegal, yet others accessing those particular images would be engaged in criminal conduct according to their home country's laws. Moreover, the laws vary across countries; for example, written descriptions of sex with children are legal in the United States, protected by the First Amendment, but not in Canada. It is a cliché—but a cliché built on some truth—that the Internet does not respect national borders. Computers involved in a single child pornography trading ring can be located across multiple countries, making investigation and prosecution more complicated than many real-world crimes.

SUMMARY

Strong upward trends in criminal justice and clinical cases indicate there is a pressing need for a better understanding of online offenders. This volume presents a theoretical and empirical framework for understanding online child pornography and solicitation offenders and their crimes.[6] I then proceed to a review and discussion of practical implications of emerging research on online offenders, in terms of their assessment needs, risk to reoffend, and interventions.

Concerns about online offending can be connected to a general wariness about the Internet's prominence in our lives and accompanying broad social changes. Exposure to online pornography from a young age and sexual networking through online technologies may represent the largest natural quasi-experiment in sexuality that we have ever engaged in. The Internet is approaching omnipresence in the developed world, and the increasing numbers, technicality, and international nature of this offending all suggest this is a complex issue. Moreover, the observed increases in Internet sexual offending cases have been paralleled by a substantial decrease in the number of child sexual abuse cases, and sexual or violent crime more generally (Finkelhor & Jones, 2006; Mishra & Lalumière, 2009). This suggests that Internet sexual offending is a new phenomenon that may not be influenced by the same factors as other kinds of sexual or violent crime. Internet sexual offending requires systematic research and policy attention.

---

[6]There is essentially no research available on the use of the Internet to commit other kinds of sexual offenses, such as online solicitations of adults for encounters that will result in sexual assault or rape or online exhibitionism, or the related social problems of child sex tourism and juvenile prostitution and the impact of the Internet in these areas (see Appendix 1.2 and Chapter 3 of this volume).

APPENDIX 1.1
PREVALENCE OF PEDOPHILIA OR PEDOHEBEPHILIA

I have previously suggested that the upper limit of the prevalence of pedophilia in the general male population was 5%, on the basis of surveys of men recruited from the community, with the true prevalence being unknown in the absence of epidemiological research (Seto, 2008). These surveys produced upper-limit estimates because the researchers asked about sexual fantasies or masturbation to fantasies about sex with children but did not ask questions about frequency or duration that would be needed to identify pedophilia (e.g., Briere & Runtz, 1989). An individual who had thought about sex with children on a few occasions only, or who thought about sex with children on rare occasions, would probably not meet the criteria or the proposed revisions to the criteria of the American Psychiatric Association's (2000) *Diagnostic and Statistical Manual of Mental Disorders* (4th ed., text rev.; *DSM–IV–TR*) or the World Health Organization's (2010) *International Classification of Diseases* (10th rev.; *ICD–10*).

Additional studies with data relevant to the population prevalence of pedophilia have appeared since my 2008 book. These studies are listed in Table 1.2. One study in particular is described in more detail here. Santtila et al. (2010) conducted a survey of 1,310 men (average age in the late 30s).

TABLE 1.2
Prevalence of Pedophilia Redux

Study	Sample	Potential pedophilia prevalence
Ahlers et al. (2011)	367 German men	9.5% had sexual fantasies about children
		6.0% had masturbation fantasies about children
		3.8% had sexual contact with children
Beier et al. (2009)	373 men	4% had sexual contact with a child
		9% admitted to having fantasies about children
		6% admitted masturbating to child fantasies
Crépault & Couture (1980)	94 men	62% fantasized about sex with a young girl
		3% fantasized about sex with a young boy
Fromuth, Burkhart, & Jones (1991)	582 college students	3% had sex with child when respondent was age 16 or over
Seto et al. (2013)	1,978 Swedish young men	4% viewed adult-child sex
Templeman & Stinnett (1991)	60 college students	5% expressed interest in sex with a girl under age 12

Sexual interest in or sexual activity with children aged 12 or younger was reported by 0.3% of the sample, with the concomitant value for children ages 15 and younger being 3.5%. The study suggested a 3% upper limit for pedophilia plus hebephilia and 1% for pedophilia proper.

In the proposed *DSM–5* criteria (American Psychiatric Association, 2012), pedophilic disorder can be diagnosed if an individual exhibits an equal or greater sexual interest in prepubescent or early pubescent children, compared with adults, over a period of at least 6 months; has acted on this interest or is experiencing clinically significant distress or impairment as a result of the interest; and is at least 18 years old and 5 years older than the children of interest. The sexual interest can be expressed in thoughts, urges, fantasies, sexual arousal, or behavior. Diagnostic specifiers include whether the person is sexually attracted to prepubescent children (Tanner Stage 1 of physical development), early pubescent children (Tanner Stages 2 or 3), or both prepubescent and early pubescent children (see Blanchard, 2010a, 2010b, 2010c; for a description of Tanner Stages, see http://en.wikipedia.org/wiki/Tanner_scale); whether the attraction is for boys, girls, or both; and whether the pedophilic disorder is in remission or being evaluated in a controlled environment. The last point addresses the challenges of evaluating the diagnosis in an environment where the person is not exposed to children or to child stimuli (e.g., in a secure hospital unit or correctional facility), just as an individual may have a substance dependence disorder that is not manifested in a controlled environment but that could emerge if there was ready access to drugs or alcohol.

The *ICD–10* definition of *paedophilia* (F65.4) is simpler than the definitions provided in *DSM–IV–TR* or *DSM–5*: "A sexual preference for children, usually of prepubertal or early pubertal age." It differs from the *DSM–IV–TR* definition by not specifying a minimum time period, frequency, or intensity (Criterion A); not requiring action or distress (Criterion B); and not requiring a minimum age or age difference (Criterion C). The *ICD–10* definition also differs by including children of early pubertal age. In the clinical literatures, *pedophilia* has usually been defined as a sexual interest in prepubescent children. *Hebephilia*, however, has been defined as a sexual interest in pubescent children, that is, children in the midst of pubertal changes.

CHILD PORNOGRAPHY USE AND DIAGNOSIS

Research on child pornography adds to our knowledge of the prevalence of pedophilia and hebephilia because it is a relevant indicator of sexual interest in prepubescent or pubescent children (Seto, Cantor, & Blanchard,

2006). In fact, child pornography use can be a better diagnostic indicator than having sexual contact with children, because some of the men who have contacts are nonpedophilic; these contact offenders are antisocial or opportunistic offenders who do not sexually prefer children but who are still capable of sexually interacting with them. A recent analysis of a different sample of offenders suggested that having a child pornography charge is comparable to having two child victims (Blanchard, 2010c). Thus, the proposed *DSM–5* criteria describe child pornography use as one of the behavioral indications of pedohebephilia. I (Seto, 2010) discussed some nuances about considering child pornography offending, particularly the age and gender of the children depicted in the child pornography content.

PEDOPHILIA AND HEBEPHILIA

There is great controversy about the proposed inclusion of hebephilia in the *DSM–5*, beginning with an empirical article by Blanchard et al. (2009) that suggested that hebephiles have a sexual response pattern that is distinct from pedophiles or from teleiophiles, which was followed by a series of commentaries and responses (Blanchard, 2009; Franklin, 2009; Green, 2010; Plaud, 2009; Seto, 2010; Zander, 2009). Blanchard (2010a) further responded to these initial commentaries and then letters addressing specific points that were raised.[7]

Research on hebephilia has been ably and helpfully summarized by James Cantor (http://individual.utoronto.ca/james_cantor/page19.html). The controversy hinges on the scientific question of whether hebephilia represents normative sexual interests in young adolescents or whether it represents serious psychopathology (Blanchard, 2009, 2010a; DeClue, 2009; Green, 2010; Plaud, 2009; Tromovitch, 2009; Zander, 2009). Much of the heat and opposition to the addition of hebephilia in the *DSM–5* seems to be driven more by policy and practice concerns about the use of hebephilia to expand the potential scope of sex offender civil commitment in the United States rather than by concerns about the peer-reviewed science behind the concept of hebephilia, even though the objections are often posed in scholarly journals using scientific language (Franklin, 2010).

---

[7]Ray Blanchard is the chair of the paraphilias sub-work group and therefore centrally involved in the revision process. Ken Zucker is the chair of the sexual disorders work group and is therefore responsible to the *DSM–5* steering committee for the paraphilias and other sexual disorders. Both are long-time colleagues; I worked with them at the Centre for Addiction and Mental Health, and I have coauthored work with both of them. I am not formally involved in the *DSM–5* revision process, except to provide information about my relevant research and to have written a commentary in the *Archives of Sexual Behavior* (Seto, 2010).

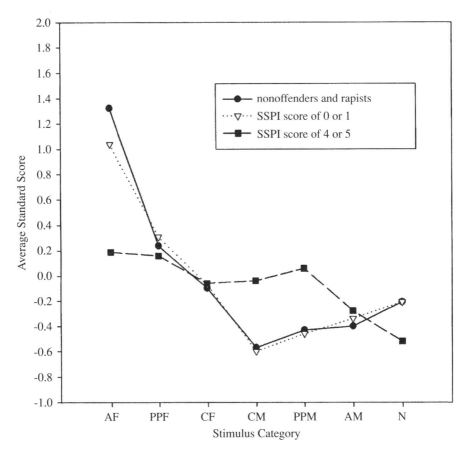

Figure 1.4. Sexual response gradient shown by heterosexual nonpedophilic men (nonoffenders or rapists). Strongest arousal to adult females (AF), followed by prepubescent females (PPF), and very young female children (CF). AM = adult males; CM = young male children; N = neutral stimuli; PPM = prepubescent males; SSPI = Screening Scale for Pedophilic Interests. Reprinted from "A Brief Screening Scale to Identify Pedophilic Interests Among Child Molesters," by M. C. Seto and M. L. Lalumière, 2001, *Sexual Abuse: A Journal of Research and Treatment, 13,* p. 22. Copyright 2001 by Sage. Reprinted with permission.

Science does not exist in a sociopolitical vacuum; research can (and should, in my opinion) influence policy and practice. But to criticize the scientific examination of what I also consider to be a distinct sexual interest in pubescent children, because it might be used in a way that the critics do not like, is an unpalatable idea.

It is likely there are more hebephiles than pedophiles, given the sexual response gradient in men, where nonoffending men respond most to depictions of adults, followed by adolescents, and then prepubescent children (Blanchard et al., 2012; Seto, Lalumière, & Kuban, 1999; see Figure 1.4).

From a Darwinian perspective, interest in pubescent children is less of a departure from the normative interest in sexually mature persons than is an interest in prepubescent children (Blanchard, 2010b; Buss & Schmitt, 1993; Seto, 2008). An interest in infants or toddlers, if it exists as a distinct age interest, would be the rarest of all (Greenberg, Bradford, & Curry, 1995). Hebephilia should be more common than pedophilia if the sexual response gradient idea is correct, even though prepubescence encompasses a wider age range than the relatively narrow window of pubescence.

The following quote from Holt, Blevins, and Burkert (2010) is illustrative in this context (anecdotally illustrating the importance of puberty as a liminal event in pedophilia, something that I emphasized in my book on pedophilia; Seto, 2008)

> Little girlfriends are hopeless causes because they grow into big girls in short order and then are unattractive. That is why it is rare I know a girl for more than a few months or years. Once they grow into puberty, we slide apart and go our separate ways. (p. 11)

APPENDIX 1.2
JUVENILE PROSTITUTION, SEXUAL TRAFFICKING, AND SEX TOURISM

The United Nations and many international nongovernmental organizations (NGOs) recognize juvenile prostitution, sexual trafficking of women and children, and juvenile sex tourism as international human rights problems, but the scope and severity of these problems are unclear. Data collection is extremely difficult, given the secretive and criminal nature of these activities and the expectation that these activities are more likely to thrive in jurisdictions where systemic data collection is difficult. Prevalence estimates of these problems vary widely and often appear to depend more on the source of the estimate than on any reliable data collection. Government agencies tend to be more conservative than NGOs, which in turn tend to be more conservative than advocacy groups (cf. Estes & Weiner, 2005; Hughes, 2000; International Labour Organization, 2006). The International Labour Organization (2006) estimated that 1.8 million minors were involved in prostitution or pornography globally in 2000.

The demand for juvenile prostitution and sex tourism may be a response to increasingly punitive sanctions for sexual behavior involving young adolescents and younger children in the industrialized world, the misguided belief that children are less likely to transmit HIV, and a fetishizing of virginity. It is likely that situational or opportunistic offenders are more common than pedophilic or hebephilic offenders in juvenile prostitution and sex tourism, because data on the average ages of juvenile prostitutes have suggested that most of the activity involves adolescent girls, both domestically and internationally. Demand for juvenile prostitution and sex tourism creates economic incentives for sexual trafficking of minors.

I think these topics belong in this book because online technologies are increasingly involved in juvenile prostitution (online escort advertisements), juvenile sex tourism (information is posted and discussed about where to go and how to arrange trips), and trafficking (illicit communication). For example, there has been sustained criticism of Backpage.com for advertising escorts in the adult classifieds that could easily include trafficked or pimped juveniles (https://www.nytimes.com/2012/03/18/opinion/sunday/kristof-where-pimps-peddle-their-goods.html). I believe that future research on the online aspects of these criminal and antisocial activities is needed to better understand these phenomena, which represent a potentially large and uncharted range of commercial sexual exploitation. As I previously mentioned, one of the advantages of studying online behavior is that digital evidence can be analyzed, unlike the secretive and unobserved behavior that takes place every day in real life. Interested readers are directed to Resource A for more information.

APPENDIX 1.3
PSEUDO CHILD PORNOGRAPHY, PSEUDO LURING, AND THE IMPORTANCE OF PUBERTY

PSEUDO CHILD PORNOGRAPHY

Dines (2008) and other writers have commented on the proliferation of sexual content that could be described as *pseudo child pornography* because it plays on the idea that the persons who are depicted are minors—for example, sites that advertise "schoolgirls," "innocent teens," "first-timers," and "petite girls." Dines also commented on the popularity and commercial success of *Hustler*'s "Barely Legal" series and its subsequent copycats. Some have argued that the complete or near-complete absence of pubic hair on pornography actors (except for the niche genres of "hairy" or "natural" models) and the fashionable uptake of pubic denuding in the general population is also related to this eroticization of youthfulness (Herbenick, Schick, Reece, Sanders, & Fortenberry, 2010).

Mainstream culture has also pushed (and/or reflected) social norms about the eroticization of even younger children, including the recent appearance of prepubescent girls in full make-up and fashionable attire in a French *Vogue* photo shoot, with a 10-year-old model on the cover (bit.ly/yf2OOh); lingerie for young girls from major retailers such as La Senza and Abercrombie and Fitch; and child beauty pageants, as shown in television programs such as *Toddlers and Tiaras*, in which young girls are dressed up in swimsuits and gowns in a grotesque caricature of adult beauty pageants.

Related to this idea, I ran a Google Ngrams analysis of the frequency that words appear in a large set of scanned books; the results show that the mention of *pedophilia* began before the mention of *child pornography*, but it has since been supplanted by the greater appearance of *child pornography* in the past 25 years (see Figure 1.5).

PSEUDO ONLINE LURING

Pseudo online luring involves fantasy role playing between adults in online forums. For example, a CNET article described the controversial presence of age-related sexual role play in the early years of Second Life, a virtual world that has since dwindled in popularity (cnet.co/yMVNxw). There may continue to be fantasy role playing in other online venues as well—for example, when adults engage each other in private chat rooms, with one of them pretending to be a minor. This is behavior that has likely

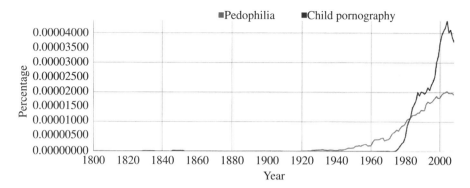

Figure 1.5. Google Ngrams for the terms *child pornography* and *pedophilia* created spring 2012. Google Ngrams analyze the frequency with which particular words or phrases appear in the more than 5 million books (published between 1500 and 2008) that have been digitally scanned by Google Labs. The Ngram algorithm and database are described by Michel et al. (2011).

occurred in many private bedrooms, but now the stage is much larger. How does one prove that the behavior is fantasy only, as opposed to driven by an actual interest in meeting and sexually interacting with minors online? The distinction matters in terms of prosecution decisions, but does it matter in terms of public policy and the potential risk to minors of sexual exploitation? I discuss the distinction between fantasy-driven and contact-driven solicitation offending in Chapter 3.

THE IMPORTANCE OF PUBERTY

In my writing on this topic, I have repeatedly made the important distinction between child pornography depicting prepubescent or pubescent children and pseudo child pornography and illegal pornography depicting older adolescents under the age of 18 (in Canada and the United States). The former content is suggestive of *pedophilia* (sexual interest in prepubescent children) or *hebephilia* (sexual attraction to pubescent children), whereas the latter is not indicative of a paraphilia, and in fact is normative given that many adult men are sexually attracted to sexually mature teenagers, even if they are under the legal age of majority or under the legal age of consent for sexual activity (16 in Canada and in many American states; Seto, 2008; Seto & Lalumière, 2001). Similarly, solicitation offenses committed against older adolescent minors is illegal, but the greater social concern is for sexual solicitations of prepubescent and pubescent children, which again may be indicative of pedophilia or hebephilia.

Pubertal status is the critical, nonarbitrary delineator between nonnormative and normative sexual interests. As I discussed in more detail in my previous book, legally defined age of consent is arbitrary in the sense that it varies from jurisdiction to jurisdiction and is not obviously linked to reliable measures of cognitive or emotional development (Seto, 2008). In contrast, puberty reflects objective and biologically relevant changes in appearance and reproductive status, as indicated by changes in the appearance of genitals, breast development (in girls), axillary and pubic hair, and changes in body size and shape. These distinctions can be reliably made, though they can be fuzzy at the boundaries.

The age ranges spanning prepubescence and pubescence may surprise you. The average age of onset for puberty has gone down steadily in the past century in developed nations, especially for girls and even more so for African-American girls (Herman-Giddens et al., 1997; Thomas, Renaud, Benefice, De Meeüs, & Geugan, 2001). Many North American girls now show signs of secondary sexual development by the age of 12, including breast budding, shifts in waist-to-hip ratio, and so forth. Though the laws described here are defined on the basis of age, which can be objectively determined through available records, the critical distinctions from a sexological or psychological perspective are biological status.

As an example of how pubertal status, chronological age, and legal status can conflict, child pornography laws specify depictions of persons under the age of 18. Yet images of an 18-year-old woman who was petite, thin, and who had small breasts and narrow hips and otherwise looked like a young adolescent girl would be legal, as long as she was not presented as someone under the age of 18 (in Canada). Wolak and Finkelhor (2011) described the case of a statutory sexual offense where a 12-year-old girl convinced a young adult man that she was 19 on the basis of her photos. Though this is a sensational example, minors are occasionally mistaken for adults sufficiently often to manifest in popular culture, including the fetishizing of schoolgirl uniforms (e.g., Britney Spears's record cover and music video for "Hit Me Baby, One More Time"), the slang term *jailbait* to refer to someone who is sexually attractive but below the legal age of consent, and the eroticization of youthfulness in fashion and media to the point that the Council of Fashion Designers of America had to specify that model ages should be checked to make sure models are at least 16 years old for runway shows (http://cfda.com/the-latest/health-initiative-guidelines-updated-by-the-cfda), in part because the models may be topless or appear in sheer or otherwise revealing clothing during these appearances. To repeat, being sexually attracted to sexually mature adolescents is frowned on and illegal to act on if the adolescent is below the legal age of consent, but it is common among men and it is not indicative of psychopathology or paraphilia.

2

CHILD PORNOGRAPHY

Gillespie (2010) discussed the challenges in developing legal definitions of child pornography, including how a *child* is defined, what kinds of content are covered (e.g., depictions of fictitious children), and the boundary between sexually explicit content that would clearly be deemed pornographic by a reasonable person and images that might still be used for sexual purposes but that fall outside the scope of current child pornography or obscenity laws (e.g., images of children in underwear or swimsuits, images of nude children in which there is no sexually explicit or suggestive posing or behavior).

The definition of child pornography is further complicated because laws typically do not distinguish between developmental age categories. Laws in Canada and the United States define *child pornography* as any sexual depictions of persons under age 18, which means that images of sexually mature persons under the age of 18 who are at or above the legal age of consent for sex are legally considered to be the same as images of young adolescents, pubescent-aged children, or prepubescent children. Child age is sometimes

http://dx.doi.org/10.1037/14191-003
Internet Sex Offenders, by M. C. Seto

reflected in sentencing; for example, federal sentencing guidelines in the United States view images of prepubescent children as an enhancement factor, resulting in an increased recommended sentence length.

Another complication for the definition of child pornography is that the law should define the sexual content threshold. There is likely high agreement about depictions of sexual activities or images emphasizing the anogenital regions of children, but what is the threshold for sexually suggestive content? What about defenses of artistic, educational, or other merit, as in the case of artistic photographs of nude children without explicit sexuality? Yet, despite these questions, the large majority of child pornography images identified by police are unambiguous. They depict sexual activities, focus on the anogenital region, and are of prepubescent children, particularly girls. This set of images seized by police does not represent all child pornography, however, as there are undoubtedly selection effects: Only cases involving unambiguous child pornography content will lead to arrest and prosecution and thus the inclusion of these images in police databases. Someone who has images exclusively of older adolescents who may or may not be 18 or older or someone who has a set of artistic photographs of nude children or who has innocuous-looking photos of their children in the bath might be investigated by police but is unlikely to be prosecuted and convicted.

What are the critical age cues that underlie the sexual valence of child pornography? I raised this question in my 2008 book in discussing the physical and psychological cues that elicit pedophilic sexual responding. Focusing on the physical cues, the leading candidates include: (a) small body size; (b) waist-to-hip ratios close to one; (c) high head-to-body ratio; (d) low fat distribution; (e) neotenous facial features; (f) smooth, hairless skin; and (g) immature appearance of the genitals. Jim Pfaus (personal communication, June 1, 2010) pointed out to me that these cues can be arranged from those that are distal to those that are proximal, with body size being more obvious from a distance and then shape (waist-to-hip ratio and head-to-body ratio), whereas one has to get close to someone to see skin texture, presence of axillary hair, and genital anatomy (Buss, 1994; Connolly, Slaughter, & Mealey, 2004).

HISTORY OF (CHILD) PORNOGRAPHY

Pornography and technology have been intertwined throughout human history. According to the tangible evidence—because oral stories leave no trace—there is a rich history of erotic artifacts, including the earliest known artistic expressions in Paleolithic cave paintings and carvings of fertility symbols such as phalluses and Venus figures. There is historical and cross-cultural evidence of child pornography, including stories about sex with children from a Chinese sex manual from the 1400s called *The Admirable Discourses of the Plain Girl* (described by Tannahill, 1980), other Chinese literary references to sex between men and effeminate boys (Ng, 2002), and Arabic literary references to sexual relationships involving men and male youths (Schild, 1988). Of relevance to the distinctions raised in Chapter 1 about the important demarcation of pedophilia, pubertal status is relevant to attractiveness in this literature; for example, Ibrahim Ibn Sahl (1212–1251 CE) wrote: "Oh you of tender pale cheeks, you were light until the beard came to smudge your beauty. I think of the candle, its wick blackening as the flame goes out" (translated by Lane, 1977; p. 11).

More recent examples include anonymously produced Victorian novels describing explicit sexual scenes involving children (Anonymous, 1890, 1898). Some writers have argued there was a different sensibility in the Victorian era regarding the notion of sexual innocence in childhood and the erotic meaning of nude images of children (Ariès, 1962; Boas, 1966). Taylor and Quayle (2003) described the arrest in 1874 of Henry Hayler of London, who was found by police to have an estimated 130,000 photographic glass plates depicting child pornography images. Charles Dodgson, better known as Lewis Carroll, the author of *Alice's Adventures in Wonderland*, is also notorious for his friendships with young girls, especially Alice Liddell (the inspiration for the title character in *Alice's Adventures*), and his long-standing interest in photographing nude or semi-nude girls and collecting similar photographs and sketches. Because other photographers also had nude or semi-nude children as subjects, some have argued that this enthusiasm was aesthetic and normal for the time (Lebailly, 1999). Others have expressed suspicion that Dodgson was a celibate pedophile who was sexually attracted to young girls but never acted on this interest beyond taking photographs (Cohen, 1996).

With the advent of modern photography and then film, child pornography became available in the form of photographs, magazines, books, and films. Jenkins (2001) wrote about the history of child pornography in the 20th century and suggested there was a "golden era" for nondigital child pornography in the 1970s, with more liberal sexual norms and a flourishing commercial trade in child pornography films, magazines, and books in pornography stores (e.g., with titles such as *Nudist Moppets*, *Lollitots*, and *Bambina Sex*). Most of these magazines and books were of European origin, many produced by Denmark's Rodox/Color Climax. Public opinion eventually turned against the increased availability of child pornography, however, emerging with lurid media claims about the scope and profitability of child pornography. Jenkins (2001) described a 1977 NBC television news story that implausibly claimed 2 million American youths were involved in child pornography, that child pornography generated revenues of $5 billion per year, and that children were abducted, raped, and killed in *snuff films* (recorded killings for profit). To put these claims in historical context, this was also the same decade when extraordinary allegations were being made of pernicious ritual sexual abuse rings; few cases of ritualistic child sexual abuse have ever identified, however, and there are no known snuff films depicting the rape or murder of children (e.g., Jenkins, 1998; Nathan & Snedeker, 2001).

The public backlash against the availability and impact of child pornography led to the emergence of specific child pornography laws in 1978 and increased law enforcement, setting the stage for the current era, in which child pornography has been identified as a top priority. In regard to the subsequent difficulty in obtaining child pornography in the years before the Internet, Howitt (1995) interviewed 11 adult male pedophiles who reported that they infrequently used child pornography. Instead, they created their own pornographic materials using images from catalogues, magazines, and other freely available and legal sources. Other studies from the 1980s and early 1990s also suggested pedophilic sexual offenders had infrequent access to child pornography (e.g., Marshall & Barbaree, 1988).

THE DAWN OF ONLINE CHILD PORNOGRAPHY

The Internet and its related technologies have contributed to an explosion in the availability and distribution of child pornography. Before the Internet era, individuals interested in child pornography had to contact commercial distributors or individuals (e.g., through classified ads placed on the back pages of adult pornography magazines) to purchase or trade content, or they had to produce their own content. Each contact or production of child pornography might have led to detection and arrest, with the concomitant loss of reputation, employment, and friendships, not to mention the legal consequences (see Jenkins, 2001; Lloyd, 1976; O'Brien, 1983). Moreover, the content consisted of photographs, films, magazines, or books that would deteriorate with age, were challenging if not impossible to copy with high fidelity, and that could be interdicted during distribution by law enforcement officials. There were only so many physical objects, and distribution required time and money. Criminalization and prosecution drove this activity further underground, and thus the costs grew, reflecting supply and demand. Some individuals could not afford child pornography or could afford only a small amount of the material (Jenkins, 2001).

Beginning in the mid-1990s and exploding through the 2000s, the production and distribution of child pornography has become much easier and cheaper with the rapidly increasing access and concomitantly decreasing cost of digital cameras and related technologies. These digital images rarely deteriorate (files can become corrupted as they are copied, but this is rare, and there are often multiple copies) and can continue to be distributed long after the children in the images have become adults (recall Amy's and Masha's stories from Chapter 1). Sadly, there is so much child pornography content available that police cannot stem the flow.

As mentioned in Chapter 1, the Internet has facilitated child pornography offending because of accessibility, affordability, and anonymity (see A. Cooper, Delmonico, Griffin-Shelley, & Mathy, 2004). The Internet provides 24-hour access every day of the week. Digital images and videos can be duplicated ad infinitum, with essentially no deterioration in quality. Thus, the supply of child pornography has exploded. Child pornography content is also much more affordable: Two magazines containing a few dozen photos might have cost $40 in 1980, according to Jenkins (2001), whereas the same amount of money could provide Internet access to thousands of images. Last, the Internet gives the illusion of anonymity and reduces the perceived risk of detection and consequences. It also can reduce the actual risk of detection, because of the sheer number of Internet protocol (IP) addresses involved in peer-to-peer trading and the easy availability of software that can erase histories, encrypt files, and anonymize interactions.

In his social history of child pornography, Jenkins (2001) joined online message boards relating to pedophilia and child pornography in 1999 and 2000 and observed members who were early Internet adopters who traded child pornography (see Appendix 2.1). Some members boasted about being involved in digital child pornography activities 20 years earlier, well before the arrival of a public World Wide Web (one can therefore infer the user was affiliated with an academic or military institution at the time). These message boards operated before the more intense law enforcement scrutiny of recent years, so users were bolder about posting images purporting to be child pornography. Jenkins was confident that the images did in fact depict child pornography because any false images were quickly flamed and derided in subsequent posts.[1]

Jenkins's (2001) technical analysis is now dated because public and private message boards have been surpassed by peer-to-peer file-sharing networks as distribution systems (Prichard, Watters, & Spiranovic, 2011; Steel, 2009). Nonetheless, his book provides a fascinating glimpse into this online subculture and the technological and sociocultural challenges facing law enforcement and other efforts to stop child pornography offending. Though the technologies have changed a great deal in the subsequent decade, the subcultures have not changed as much (see Appendix 2.1).

---

[1]Jenkins (2001) stated that he protected himself from inadvertently possessing child pornography, which could have led to his prosecution in the United States, by disabling image loading in his browser and analyzing only the texts of messages and picture descriptions.

Two themes become clear in reading Jenkins's (2001) book. First, child pornography has been digitally available for many years. For example, one respected user (Kindred) on the Maestro message board wrote, "Where were most of you twenty years ago? It was an exciting time online" (Jenkins, 2001, p. 25). Second, law enforcement efforts are more likely to catch naive or technologically unsophisticated child pornography offenders, because savvy offenders are less likely to be detected. Sophisticated child pornography offenders can turn to a variety of methods—file encryption, steganography (hiding data within other digital files), anonymous e-mail services, anonymizing proxy servers, and so forth—that make them more difficult to detect and track.[2]

The back-and-forth between child pornography offenders and police investigators creates an ongoing technological arms race, wherein police investigators and forensic computer analysts have to be sufficiently technologically savvy to investigate users effectively, whereas users may become more sophisticated in turn as law enforcement efforts increase. One can compare the situation in the late 1990s, when Jenkins was doing his research, and the sophisticated takedowns of child pornography trading rings described by Sher (2007).

AVAILABILITY OF CHILD PORNOGRAPHY ONLINE

The prevalence of child pornography content that is available on the Internet is unknown. Early surveys suggested that child pornography images represented only a small proportion of the total pornography content. These early studies could not, however, have included content that is invisible to researchers (e.g., through encrypted, strong password-protected servers intended to be available only to members of a private child pornography trading ring), and it did not include text or audio files. Mehta (2001) examined 9,800 randomly selected images that were posted to Usenet newsgroups (an older form of publicly accessible message boards that allowed images and other files to be distributed freely) between July 1995 and 1996 and found that 4% of the images depicted prepubescent children and 11% depicted pubescent children. Mehta, Best, and Poon (2002) analyzed 507 randomly selected video clips obtained through the Gnutella peer-to-peer

---

[2]As part of my research for this volume and for my previous book (Seto, 2008), I occasionally read the Girlchat and Boychat message boards. Both are publicly accessible pro-pedophilia forums. It was notable that Girlchat has a section devoted to security and countersurveillance measures. I have half jokingly stated in presentations that much of what I first learned about online security and countersurveillance came from these pages and links. This second theme suggests that technological support and ongoing training will be a critical issue for law enforcement efforts.

file-sharing network and found that 4% of the clips depicted children in sexual situations. Hughes, Gibson, Walkerdine, and Coulson (2006) examined searches and traffic patterns on the same peer-to-peer network and estimated that 1.6% of search traffic and 2.4% of response traffic was related to child pornography. There was evidence of child pornography trading communities in this analysis, because 57% of peers that shared illegal pornography shared no other content, and the majority (83%) of these peers had illegal content traffic of 50% or more.

Steel (2009) identified some of the limitations of the analysis by Hughes et al. (2006), including the small sample of queries (approximately 10,000) and the use of human judges to classify queries, which could miss search terms that seem innocuous but are in fact code words for child pornography content. Steel conducted a new analysis of 235,513 queries and 194,444 query hits from the same Gnutella network, using automated search algorithms. Gnutella carried approximately 40% of all peer-to-peer traffic and was the most popular file-sharing service at the time. The most prevalent query and the top two filenames were child pornography related. This does not mean, however, that child pornography was prevalent. A total of 1% of all queries and 1.4% of all query hits (based on unique filenames) were related to child pornography.

Prichard et al. (2011) found that child pornography search terms placed in the top 300 search terms on isoHunt, one of the major search engines for peer-to-peer networks. These results are consistent with those reported by Hughes et al. (2006), and they suggest that the relative prevalence of child pornography has gone down since the 1990s. At the same time, Operations Fairplay and Roundup in the United States have identified over 20 million unique IP addresses involved in the peer-to-peer distribution of known child pornography files on their respective watch lists (United States Department of Justice, 2010).

Other evidence also suggests that child pornography is less readily available than it used to be. Child pornography could be accessed through publicly available websites in the 1990s, but no images could be found by Bagley (2003) when he looked in 2002. Increased law enforcement scrutiny and highly publicized arrests have driven child pornography activity further underground, making it more likely that individuals will use security techniques such as anonymous e-mail services, cloud storage (storing data remotely rather than on one's computer), and programs designed to hide their browsing activities.

At the same time, the absolute amount of child pornography has undoubtedly gone up, as old content continues to be copied and circulated and new content is uploaded. The fact that child pornography content represents a smaller percentage of query hits in the late 2000s than surveys of public newsgroups in the later 1990s, approximately a decade earlier, obscures the fact that there has been a tremendous rise in the total amount of pornography available online, both through free and paid channels.

INTERNET AND RELATED TECHNOLOGIES

I have already discussed how the Internet can facilitate child pornography offending through increasing availability, affordability, and (perceived) anonymity. The Internet is also transnational, making government regulation and policing that much more difficult. These points also apply to other online sexual offending, including sexual solicitation of minors, juvenile prostitution, sexual trafficking, and sex tourism. Related technologies have also played a role, particularly the increasing availability of digital cameras, to the point that high-quality photos can be taken with mobile phones, and the low cost and high capacity of memory devices, from a few hundred kilobytes on the floppy disks (a now obsolete storage medium) of the 1970s to the gigabytes possible on flash memory drives no bigger than one's thumb. A large child pornography collection consisting of many thousands of images and hundreds of videos can be saved on a single highly portable and easily hidden device. One of the ideas to be explored in this and later chapters is whether the current emphasis on Internet-facilitated sexual offending is capturing individuals who, before the advent of the Internet, would have never accessed child pornography by trying to contact someone to purchase photographic prints or videotapes (see Appendix 3.5).

Jenkins (2001) commented on the predominant Internet culture, which values communication, anonymity, and privacy over intellectual copyright and legal regulation of content and activity. Jenkins observed that someone who would never steal from a store may think nothing of downloading pirated music, movies, and software. This is a topic that I come back to again in this book, because the structure, security, and surveillance of Internet activity have direct relationships to the incidence and risks of Internet-facilitated sexual offending. There is an uneasy detente between these conflicting visions of the Internet. Is the Internet a public place, subject to legal jurisdiction and privacy rights; a marketplace, where corporate interests reign supreme; or an extra-legal landscape that is not subject to any nation's laws?

CHILD PORNOGRAPHY CONTENT

It is my contention that the pornography content that one seeks and repeatedly views reflects a person's sexual interest. Even in the absence of any self-reports or collateral information (e.g., sexual offending history or sexual relationship history), knowing what kind of pornography someone regularly accesses and views tells us something about their sexual interests. This is especially true if the content is rare, difficult to find, or comes with the risk of severe consequences, as in the case of child pornography. Given all of the adult pornography of many variations that is readily available online, often for free, it is diagnostically informative that someone would still access child pornography.

Possession of child pornography in itself, however, is not enough to determine the sexual interest of users. Important parameters to consider include the total amount (having 10,000 images is more indicative than having 10 images), ratio of a particular pornography category to other categories of pornography (having 80% of pornography on a hard drive being child pornography compared with 8% is suggestive), and frequency and recency of access (more frequent and recent access is suggestive). Other parameters include the age and gender of children depicted in child pornography, because research on pedophilia has suggested that individuals who engage in behavior involving young boys are more likely to be pedophiles than those who engage in behavior involving young girls only (Seto, 2008). An additional consideration is whether the sexual content includes other indicators of atypical sexual interests, such as sexual violence, bestiality, and fetishism: Someone with a range of different content might plausibly argue a general interest in unusual pornography, whereas someone with a pornography collection that predominantly features young children would be less persuasive making this claim.

The potential diagnostic significance of pornography preferences is complicated by the fact that some offenders will view but not save pornography that is interesting to them, taking great care to permanently delete evidence of their online viewing; some offenders will collect pornography that is not of interest to them but might be useful for trading (see Appendix 2.3 and Appendix 4.1); and the high-volume trafficking made available by peer-to-peer file-sharing systems means much larger (and noisier) collections. It can be more convenient for a child pornography user to download all 10,000 images that come up following a particular keyword search to find the subset of images that are truly sexually arousing, even though most of those images might not be of interest to him. If the user does not go through and delete uninteresting images (which he might not, given the number of files to be reviewed and the low cost of memory storage), then stored content is less directly related to sexual interests than if a user organizes and manages the pornography they obtain online. In such cases, forensic analysis of file access is even more valuable. The person might have many nonrelevant images, but he is likely to view and re-view those images that are of most interest to him. These ideas are discussed by others, including Glasgow (2010, 2012) and Seto (2010).

CHARACTERISTICS OF CHILDREN IN CHILD PORNOGRAPHY

Analyses of several large data sets regarding child pornography images have produced consistent results (Baartz, 2008; Oosterbaan & Ibrahim, 2009; Quayle & Jones, 2011; Wolak, Finkelhor, & Mitchell, 2011). The majority of seized images are of prepubescent children, of girls rather than boys, and depict sexually explicit activities. From their experience with the Combating Paedophile Information Networks in Europe (COPINE) database and interviews with child pornography offenders, Taylor and Quayle (2003) claimed that "a common characteristic of child pornography is that the subject is generally smiling; it is rare to see pornographic photographs of a child in distress" (p. 22). Research has suggested that only a small minority of child pornography offenders might be interested in depictions of distress or suffering. In the National Juvenile Online Victimization Project, for example, approximately one in five child pornography offenders had any child pornography content depicting bondage or sexual violence (Wolak, Finkelhor, & Mitchell, 2005). In my police case file study with Angela Eke, approximately 10% of the child pornography offenders had pornography content that was considered to be suggestive of an interest in rape (based on reliable rater judgment); approximately 20% of offenders had content suggesting an interest in sexual sadism, defined as images where the person showed distress, was bound, or was being physically abused (Eke & Seto, 2012; Seto, 2009). Larger percentages of the offenders had some images in these content categories, but we were focused on those collections that had images that were described, organized, or in sufficient numbers to suggest a specific sexual interest. An individual might download 1,000 images from a peer-to-peer network, for example, and unwittingly download some images depicting sexual violence. Having many such images, having organized these images into their own folder, or having descriptive file names was considered to be evidence that the offender was aware of the specific image content and chose to keep it.

Knowing whether someone detected using child pornography is also interested in other kinds of sexual content is potentially important because research on contact sex offenders has suggested that those with multiple paraphilic interests pose the greatest risk of sexually reoffending (Hanson & Morton-Bourgon, 2004, 2005). Evidence of multiple paraphilic behavior is not uncommon, with studies showing that sizable minorities of sex offenders with child victims have also engaged in exhibitionistic or voyeuristic behavior or have sexually assaulted adults as well (Abel, Becker, Cunningham-Rathner, Mittelman, & Rouleau, 1988; Bradford, Boulet, & Pawlak, 1992).

CONTENT TYPOLOGIES

Before the popular advent of Internet child pornography, now former FBI agent Ken Lanning (2001) suggested there was a meaningful distinction between types of child-related images, ranging from indicative images (e.g., images of clothed or semi-clothed children that, in context, suggest a sexual interest in children) to indecent images of nude children, to obscene images depicting sexual activity involving children. Drawing from Lanning's distinction, Taylor, Holland, and Quayle (2001) presented the COPINE scale of severity of child pornography content, ranging from legal but indicative (of sexual interest in children) content to content depicting child pornography in conjunction with other paraphilic (sadistic or zoophilic) content. Taylor et al. suggested additional considerations of child pornography content including (p. 40) the following:

- Size and organization, both reflecting amount of involvement. Complex categorization may also indicate active involvement in trading.
- Presence of new or private material, which indicates contact with producers or production oneself.
- Addition of suggestive text or exaggerating suggestive qualities of the image.

The COPINE scale purposefully includes nonchild pornography content and ranks images according to judgments about the degree of victimization portrayed. The scale was rationally created; there was no empirical evidence at the time to suggest that individuals with more severe images were more paraphilic, caused greater victim harm, or posed a greater danger of recidivism than those with images less severe on the scale. The U.K. Sentencing Advisory Panel has adapted the COPINE scale to distinguish between five levels of severity: (a) nudity or erotic posing; (b) solo masturbation or child–child sex; (c) nonpenetrative adult–child sex; (d) penetrative adult–child sex; and (e) presence of other paraphilic content, such as bestiality or sadism. Though severity influences sentence length (presumably to reflect the sentencing goals of deterrence and punishment), one study suggested that COPINE severity is not related to risk of recidivism (Osborn, Elliott, Middleton, & Beech, 2010). This was not a strong test of this question, however, because the sample size was small and there were no new sexual convictions during the follow-up period, precluding prediction of new sexual offenses.

In the United States, federal sentencing guidelines recognize severity or culpability through increased penalties for having images of children under the age of 12, depictions of sexually explicit activity, and content depicting sadism or violence. The determination of sadism or violence has a low threshold that is not consistent with clinical definitions, however, because case law considers any penetration of a young child to be evidence of sadism, on the assumption that any such penetration necessarily causes physical and/or psychological suffering.

CHILD PORNOGRAPHY USE IN THE GENERAL POPULATION

What is the prevalence of child pornography use in the general population? In other words, how extensive is the problem of child pornography exposure or use? A few relevant studies have been conducted, but none has been the kind of large, representative survey with sufficiently precise questions to lead to epidemiologically valid estimates. We instead have to rely mostly on surveys of convenience samples, as is true for our knowledge about the prevalence of pedophilia (see Appendix 1.1). Nonetheless, these surveys are useful.

First, an early and relevant study did not look at child pornography exposure or use, but did look at potential interest in such content. Bogaert (2001) surveyed a group of 160 university men about their pornography interests by asking them to make choices from hypothetical pornography film titles and brief descriptions. For depictions of child sex, the choices were: "On My Lap. XXX. Little Sally is the tender and sweet age of seven, but she knows just what to do to turn on her man! It all starts by sitting 'on his lap.' Explicit sexual behavior" and "The Younger the Better. XXX. She's only eight and still in grade school, but she is well-schooled in the ways of sex! See this little dynamo do her stuff! Explicit sexual behavior" (p. 37). Six percent of the young men selected the child sex titles as those they would most like to watch from the selections that were available, which included a wide range of mainstream and unusual pornography content.

Bogaert (2001) found that the selection of the child sex titles was predicted by scores on measures of antisocial personality traits, low social desirability, pornography experience, and *erotophilia* (positive interest in sexuality) but not by sexual experience or intelligence. Self-reported sexual arousal to the proposed content was significantly related to pornography title selection. In other words, the men who selected the child sex titles also reported greater sexual arousal to the idea of child sex than other men, further supporting the idea that pornography choices are related to their sexual value (see Seto, Maric, & Barbaree, 2001). Self-reported sexual arousal to child sex content was a stronger unique predictor than the other factors reported previously; only antisocial personality traits and low social desirability continued to be significant predictors of title choice. This latter finding is consistent with the idea that antisociality factors best explain whether an inchoate sexual interest is expressed in behavior, ranging from selection of pornography content to sexual contacts with persons (see Seto, 2008, and Chapter 4 on the motivation–facilitation model of sexual offending).

Seigfried, Lovely, and Rogers (2008) surveyed online pornography users and found that, of the 307 respondents who completed all the measures, 30 (approximately 10%) admitted using child pornography. This finding was unexpected because Seigfried et al. did not make efforts to protect the IP addresses of the respondents, even though they assured anonymity and randomly assigned unique identifier numbers (see Ray, Kimonis, & Donoghue, 2010). (A court subpoena could have allowed police to access electronic data that would allow them to identify IP addresses and then trace those addresses to the respondents.) Those who reported using child pornography scored higher on two measures of antisocial personality traits. The two groups did not significantly differ, as predicted, on any of the Big Five personality dimensions (i.e., Extraversion, Neuroticism, Agreeableness, Conscientiousness, Openness to Experience).

Another unexpected result in the Seigfried et al. (2008) survey was that 10 of the 30 child pornography users reported they were female, a higher percentage of females than in the subset of nonchild pornography users. Assuming the responses were honest, which is always an assumption for anonymous online surveys, this suggests that women are relatively more likely to use child pornography than men, which is not consistent with what is known about gender differences in general pornography use, other sexual behavior, and sexual offending (Petersen & Hyde, 2010). It also suggests that criminal justice investigations have been unable to successfully detect female child pornography users, because most detected child pornography users are men. For these reasons, I am skeptical about this specific result.

Seto, Kjellgren, et al. (2010) reported results of an analysis of two large population-representative samples of Swedish and Norwegian male high school students ranging in age from 17 to 20 years. In both samples, approximately 4% reported viewing pornographic depictions of adult–child sex. This is a conservative estimate of the prevalence of ever viewing child pornography because the study operationalization was stricter than many laws; sexually suggestive or explicit depictions of children alone (or child–child sex) would constitute child pornography in many jurisdictions but would not meet the study definition of this item. In a subsequent analysis of the Swedish sample data, we found that child pornography viewing was significantly predicted, in the expected directions, by the following variables: self-reported likelihood of having sex with a minor age 14 or younger, having friends who think sex with children is acceptable, having friends who have viewed child pornography, frequent pornography use, and watching violent pornography. These variables seem to be psychologically meaningful in the sense that they fit with explanations that have been provided about child pornography offending. As I discuss in further detail in Chapter 5, these explanations include pedophilia (self-reported likelihood of sex with children), peer influences (having friends who think sex with children is acceptable or who have viewed child pornography themselves), and problematic pornography use (high frequency, use of violent pornography).

In a recent study involving online offenders, contact offenders, nonsex offenders, and community volunteers, Prentky et al. (2010) reported that 2% of college-aged men and less than 1% of college-aged women reported they had viewed pornography that depicted prepubescent children. A higher proportion of these samples (14% of men and 4% of women) had viewed pornography that appeared to depict younger adolescents who seemed to be between the ages of 11 and 15. Similarly sized minorities of their samples reported viewing other atypical pornography, including depictions of bondage and sadism, rape, and urophilia or coprophilia. More extreme pornography viewing was predicted by self-reported delinquency.

Ray, Kimonis and Seto (in press) surveyed 227 mainstream pornography users and found that 42 (18%) admitted viewing child pornography. Child pornography users and nonchild pornography users were then compared on personality and behavioral measures: The two groups were similar on loneliness, attachment, and some personality factors; child pornography users, however, were higher on openness and sensation seeking and were more likely to report interest and experience in sexual contacts with a minor (cf. Seto, Lalumière, & Quinsey, 1995; Shim, Lee, & Paul, 2007). These results do not suggest that almost one in five mainstream pornography users have viewed child pornography, because the survey was posted on websites addressing problematic pornography use and pro-pedophilia forums.

Altogether, these studies are consistent with the idea that approximately 2% to 4% of men have viewed child pornography, which is again consistent with the upper-limit estimates of pedophilia suggested in Chapter 1. Not all respondents would have repeatedly viewed child pornography or would have accessed this content because they were sexually aroused by it, but the subset who did repeatedly view child pornography and who found it sexually arousing would be expected to have pedophilia (Seto, Cantor, & Blanchard, 2006). These estimates do not include the higher prevalence of adolescents who have engaged in so-called sexting, which involves the production and distribution of child pornography content through nude or semi-nude images of underage persons (see Appendix 2.4).

CHANGES OVER TIME

The University of New Hampshire's Crimes Against Children Research Center has completed important studies of child pornography offenders through detailed telephone surveys of cases investigated by over 2,000 law enforcement agencies across the United States and resulting in arrest (Wolak, Finkelhor, & Mitchell, 2011). In the National Juvenile Online Victimization (NJOV) Project, the cases were drawn from all Internet Crimes Against

Children task forces, half of the agencies with officers who had received specialized training prior to early 2000, and a random selection of all other local, county, and state agencies in the United States. Three waves of NJOV Study data collection have now been completed, in 2000/2001, 2006, and 2009. The resulting research reports and articles from this research group, led by David Finkelhor, Janis Wolak, Kimberley Mitchell, and Michelle Ybarra, are cited frequently in this volume. Because their NJOV Study data set now includes three waves, and their Youth Internet Safety Survey consists of multiple waves as well, the Crimes Against Children Research Center is in the unique position of providing an empirical lens on trends over time in online offending, including characteristics of the offenders and their crimes, the nature of child pornography content or of online solicitations, and corresponding youth behavior while online.

Wolak, Finkelhor, and Mitchell (2011) examined trends over time in the characteristics of child pornography offenders and their collections on a subset of 429 cases from Wave 1 and 605 cases from Wave 2. Child pornography possession cases were considered to be Internet-related if they involved a proactive police investigation of online activity—for example, if child pornography was received or distributed online or arrangements to share child pornography were made online or child pornography was found on a computer or removable storage device. Using a complex weighting scheme, Wolak, Finkelhor, and Mitchell found the number of arrests for child pornography crimes had doubled from Wave 1 (estimated 1,713 arrests) to Wave 2 (estimated 3,672 arrests). The latest data indicate the number of arrests tripled from Wave 1 to Wave 3.

To keep this in perspective, Wolak, Finkelhor, and Mitchell (2011) noted that the total number of arrests continues to be a small percentage (less than 10%) of the corresponding number of arrests for contact sexual offenses against children. In 2009, there were approximately 4,900 arrests for online offending in the United States. A greater proportion of these online arrests were generated by proactive police investigations (47%) compared with previous waves, suggesting that policy changes and resulting greater law enforcement efforts have contributed to the increase in numbers of cases; that is, the increase is not simply an expression of more online offending. The number might be stable, or even in decline, but more cases are being identified through greater police attention. In 2009, 70% of online offending cases involved child pornography only, with no concomitant charges for solicitation or contact offending. The corresponding values were 59% in 2006 and 45% in 2000/2001, suggesting again that proactive investigations are differentially identifying child pornography cases.

Analyses are still underway for the 2009 NJOV Study wave. Offenders were similar between Waves 1 and 2: Almost all offenders were male, a large majority were Caucasian, and they were similar in income and education (with wide ranges for both). Few had any prior arrests and few had histories of mental illness, substance use, or violence. There were two sociodemographic differences: A higher proportion of offenders arrested in 2006 were young adults between the ages of 18 and 25, and even after controlling for age, fewer offenders in Wave 2 were employed full time.

Examining the seized content, the majority (70%) in both waves had images mostly of girls, with approximately 15% having images mostly of boys and 15% having images of both sexes in similar numbers. Most offenders in both waves had sexually explicit images depicting adult–child sex or the sexual penetration of a child; a minority of offenders had any sexually violent child pornography images. There were some differences over time: A larger percentage of offenders in 2006 had images of very young children (babies and toddlers appearing to be less than 3 years old), consistent with anecdotal observations from police that more child pornography images of younger children were being seized. Moreover, a larger proportion of offenders in Wave 2 had only images of children who appeared to be younger than 12, collections of a thousand or more images, videos, and computer-generated or morphed images.

Wave 2 included questions about mobile phones, MP3 players, and other portable electronic devices; the discovery of child pornography on such devices was rare. The large majority of child pornography possession cases involved offenders using computers at home and mainstream Internet technologies such as chat, newsgroups, and peer-to-peer networks. In both waves, about one fifth of offenders tried to hide their child pornography activities, but most used password protection of their computers rather than more sophisticated methods such as file encryption or steganography.

Wolak, Finkelhor, and Mitchell (2011) observed that more offenders in Wave 2 were using peer-to-peer networks to download child pornography. Focusing on Wave 2 offenders, those who used peer-to-peer networks were more likely to be 25 years old or younger than those who used other methods (35% vs. 19%). There were no other sociodemographic differences or differences in criminal history. There were many differences in child pornography content, however, with those using peer-to-peer networks being more likely to have images of children younger than 3, sexual penetration, violence, videos, and collections of 1,000 or more images. Most were also arrested for distribution (presumably because they shared content on the peer-to-peer network; I discuss a distinction between passive and active distribution in the next section).

It is not necessarily the case that the peer-to-peer network users were more sexually deviant, as suggested by being more likely to have images of young children or images depicting sexual violence. Those who use other methods to access child pornography may be more deliberate in their searching for child pornography content and thus may have collections that correspond more closely to their sexual interests. Peer-to-peer network users, however, may cast a wider net and download a broad range of content, reviewing it later for images and videos that correspond to their interests. Wolak, Finkelhor, and Mitchell (2011) suggested that a second factor may be how cases are triaged by police. Programs used by police to investigate peer-to-peer trading of child pornography can determine the content and number of images traded by specific users (personal communication cited in Wolak, Finkelhor, & Mitchell, 2011). Because police cannot investigate all peer-to-peer users, they focus on those who have larger collections or more extreme content.

In 2009, offenders were again unlikely to have sexual offense history (10%); only 5% were registered sex offenders. Offenders were more likely than in previous waves to have any kind of prior criminal record, less likely to be employed, slightly less likely to be Caucasian, and younger. This suggests the recent trend is to capture younger offenders and to capture offenders who are more typical of general delinquent or criminal samples (i.e., young, under- or unemployed men). There were few content differences from the previous wave in having images of children 6 to 12, depictions of penetration, or depictions of adult–child sex. Wave 3 offenders were more likely to have images of very young children, more likely to have depictions of violence, and more likely to have videos. They were also more likely to be involved in distribution, primarily through file sharing on peer-to-peer networks. Peer-to-peer offenders often have large collections, and thus it is not surprising that they were more likely to have images of very young children, depictions of violence, and video (the study coding did not capture amount of content).

POLICING

The following case helps put current anti-child-pornography policing efforts in context. The first FBI investigation into Internet child pornography was in 1993, when Doris Gardner (a special agent who started what would later become the Innocent Images National Initiative) was assigned to a team investigating the kidnapping of a 10-year-old boy. The investigators found out that the boy and his friends spent a lot of time at the home of a 64-year-old man named James Kowalski, playing computer games and sending e-mail. The boy was never found, and Kowalski was not charged in his disappearance, but police found evidence of child pornography trading on Kowalski's computers. Further investigation discovered a dozen men using the America Online (AOL) portal to exchange these images by e-mail. At the time, AOL had only a million customers in the United States, and users accessed the Internet using telephone dial up, a very slow way to exchange image files.

As reported by Sher (2007), Ray Smith, the United States postal inspector, estimated that a third of child exploitation cases in 1997 investigated by the Postal Inspection Service involved computers (e.g., e-mails to arrange sending a DVD or videotape by the mail and then sending the objects by mail). Just 2 years later, 81% of cases involved computers, and that percentage continues to be high. Most offenders in recent studies of child pornography offenders have used a computer to access child pornography content (e.g., Eke, Seto, & Williams, 2011).

A watershed event in online child pornography investigations involved Landslide Productions. This company was created by Thomas and Janice Reedy as a web portal acting as a broker between an international customer base and online pornography providers. It made relatively little money until some providers began offering child pornography. At its peak, Landslide Productions generated revenues of approximately $10 million (USD) from 1997 to 1999, with approximately a third of these revenues coming from child pornography content. The subsequent police investigation in 1999 identified a database of over 100,000 customers, with names, contact information, and credit card numbers. This large pool of suspects overwhelmed police forces as national investigations were rolled out in the United States (Operation Avalanche), Canada (Operation Snowball), and the United Kingdom (Operation Ore). Unfortunately, the information contained in the database was often out of date before the details about suspects was shared with other police services; some police services did not have the expertise or resources to pursue these cases, and it soon became evident that a substantial proportion of the credit card numbers in the database were being fraudulently used by others.

Ontario, my home province, had an advantage over many police services because of its long history with investigating child pornography cases through a special provincial unit originally called Project P. Investigators narrowed the list of Ontario suspects by looking at the frequency of logging onto the Landslide Productions portal, checking against criminal records, and conducting preliminary investigations to identify suspects who had children of their own or who had ready access to other children through their work or volunteer activities. Investigators also created a false website and contacted Landslide customers to see whether they got a response, in order to winnow offenders from individuals whose identities or credit card numbers had been stolen. In the end, Ontario investigators arrested 30 suspects and achieved a conviction rate of greater than 90% (Sher, 2007).

A CONTINUUM OF CULPABILITY

The title for this section comes from a phrase that was mentioned several times in written submissions to the U.S. Sentencing Commission prior to its public hearing on federal child pornography sentencing guidelines on February 15, 2012.[3] The notion captured in this phrase is that there is a range of culpable behavior within child pornography offending, ranging from possession of child pornography (receipt) to distribution to production. Legal and computer experts made a further distinction between passive and active distribution, with *passive distribution* referring to possessors allowing files to be shared (perhaps inadvertently, because they were unaware of how the software worked) in peer-to-peer file-sharing networks, the highest-volume method for distribution at this time. In contrast, *active distributors* interact with other individuals, perhaps belonging to secret sites or making contacts with other possessors in online forums and then arranging private trades of child pornography content.

Another possible legal distinction might be made between those who encourage production, secretive producers (e.g., individuals who use hidden cameras or surreptitiously take photographs of unsuspecting children), and those who record contact sexual offenses that they or their accomplices commit. It follows that sentences and other criminal justice responses should be titrated against the culpability of online offending (discussed further in Chapter 8 of this volume). Sentences should be more severe for individuals who record their sexual offenses than for those who covertly produce images, who in turn should be held more culpable than those who actively distribute, then passively distribute, and then possess images.

Most of the research described in this chapter refers to child pornography offenders who have possessed or distributed child pornography. Only a minority of child pornography offenders are producers. For example, 12% of the 541 child pornography offenders reported by Eke et al. (2011) were convicted for production. Similarly, producers represented only a small proportion of total child pornography cases analyzed in the National Juvenile Online Victimization Project. The number of such cases had doubled from 2000/2001 to 2006, in keeping with the increase in the total number of child pornography cases but as a result of greater law enforcement activity rather than an increase in the number of producers (Wolak, Finkelhor, & Mitchell, 2011).

Producers distributed the images in only about a quarter of Wolak, Finkelhor, and Mitchell's (2011) cases, suggesting that production was predominantly a private activity to create souvenirs or as part of a grooming process directed at

---

[3]Submissions and transcripts are available from ussc.gov/Legislative_and_Public_Affairs/Public_Hearings_and_Meetings/20120215-16/Agenda_15.htm

minor victims rather than directed toward creating new content to be shared with others. Investigators were not sure whether distribution occurred in some cases, however. Nonetheless, this finding is partially consistent with the idea that child pornography use drives a market for the production of new content and thus encourages production and direct exploitation and abuse (M. Collins, 2012; Oosterbaan, 2005; Oosterbaan & Ibrahim, 2009). Commercial production is not a strong effect; otherwise one would see a larger increase in actual production cases, independent of law enforcement activity, and a higher level of distribution by producers. Commercial production of child pornography is a tiny fraction of total production; guesstimates about the money involved are exaggerated (United Nations Office on Drugs and Crime, 2010). Instead, child pornography production appears to be driven by the memorialization of sexual abuse for future fantasy and masturbation and sometimes for blackmail purposes (Ribisl & Quayle, 2012; Sheehan & Sullivan, 2010).

Much of child pornography production is by persons already known to the depicted minor (Wolak et al., 2005). The nature of the relationship depends on victim age, with family members being more likely to be involved in images of prepubescent children, and peers or young adults in images of adolescents. The National Center for Missing and Exploited Children's 2012 analysis of cases with identified victims also revealed that producers were likely to be family members (parents were 22% and other family members were 10%), followed by family friends(47%; M. Collins, 2012). Similarly, a United States Sentencing Commission (2009) analysis of federal child pornography cases found that over half of producers were parents, guardians, or persons with care and control over the children who were photographed.

There was a trend toward more adolescent victims of child pornography production in 2006 compared with 2000/2001.[4] Besides relationship to perpetrator, what else distinguishes cases involving prepubescent versus adolescent victims? Pornography producers with adolescent victims were more likely to meet the victim online, engage in a romantic relationship or friendship, provide alcohol or drugs, and obtain self-produced images (images the youth created and sent by mobile phone or webcam). The production of child pornography involving young adolescents is part of online solicitation, wherein adults approach minors for sexual purposes, including sexual chat, exchange of sexually suggestive or explicit images, or making plans to meet to have sex. I discuss what we know about online solicitation offending in the next chapter.

---

[4]Given the trend toward the involvement of more adolescents in child pornography production cases, what explains the trend over time to have more images of young children and more explicit or violent images in child pornography collections? This apparent discrepancy may reflect two subpopulations of child pornography producers: those who sexually exploit or abuse young children in creating new content of interest to pedophilic or hebephilic users and those who involve adolescents to create content of interest to nonparaphilic users.

APPENDIX 2.1
ONLINE PEDOHEBEPHILIA SUBCULTURES

A legal online activity that may overlap with online sexual offending is participation in online forums for people who are sexually interested in boys or girls. In their online search, D'Ovidio, Mitman, El-Burki, and Shumar (2009) identified 64 websites they considered to be advocating adult–child sex according to the following four criteria: (a) they supported sexual relationships between adults and children and elimination of age-of-consent laws; (b) they provided information beyond user-generated content; (c) they were interactive in some way, by allowing user posts or by facilitating interaction among users or between users and administrators; and (d) they were in English or had an English language translation.[5] The majority of these sites were based in the United States, probably reflecting the constitutional protection of free speech through the First Amendment.

In the United States, these online forums are not illegal if carried out within clear limits, particularly banning sexually suggestive or explicit images. As for any other unusual interest group, the Internet has allowed social networks to form among individuals who would otherwise be isolated, particularly if they live in smaller communities. The Internet did not create these interests, but it can facilitate interactions among individuals with interests that are socially stigmatized, such as pedophilia or hebephilia (De Young, 1988). Among the best-known examples are Girlchat (http://annabelleigh. net) and Boychat (http://boychat.org); D'Ovidio et al. (2009) listed many other websites in their article. Looking only at administrator content (and therefore ignoring user-generated content), D'Ovidio et al. concluded that approximately a third of the sites denied harm would arise from adult–child sex, and approximately a third condemned the condemners by suggesting that individuals opposed to adult–child sex or discriminating against pedophiles were wrong.

In an earlier study of online pedohebephilic subcultures, Durkin and Bryant (1999) examined 93 posts by 41 self-identified pedophiles on the newsgroup alt.support-boy.lovers, to see whether they could identify themes in the posts that were consistent with what was then known about cognitive distortions[6]—that is, offense-supportive attitudes and beliefs held by

---

[5]As a caveat to this and other studies described next is that it is unknown how many actual users there are, because some individuals may have multiple accounts or nicknames, inflating user numbers. Also, some users may be undercover police officers or may be individuals trying to incite suspicion or conflict (referred to as *trolls* on message boards and other online forums).
[6]I avoid using the term *cognitive distortions* here because the word *distortion* implies the attitude or belief is untrue, which is an empirical question rather than a moral question. We know little about child sexuality, partially as a result of societal discomfort about the notion.

some individuals who are sexually interested in children (e.g., Abel et al., 1989). Durkin and Bryant considered anyone who identified themselves as boy-loving to be a pedophile. However, the ages mentioned in the posts that are quoted suggest that many of these individuals were either hebephiles (sexually attracted to pubescent rather than prepubescent, boys) or were interested in sexually maturing but underage adolescents, which would not meet the clinical or scientific definitions of pedophilia or hebephilia.

THEMES

The subculture themes Durkin and Bryant (1999) were interested in were (a) the accounts offered by site users, especially rationalizations of sexual interests in children or adult–child sex; (b) condemnation of condemners, where the focus is on those who condemn pedophilia or adult–child sex, including police, clinicians, and society more broadly; (c) denial of injury; (d) claim of benefits; (e) appeals to children's rights with regard to their sexuality; (f) "basking in the reflected glow," by discussing famous individuals who were also purported or known to be pedophiles or hebephiles; and (g) polythematic accounts that included more than one condemnation of condemners, appeal to loyalties, denial of injury, or basking in the reflected glow. These themes are well known in the pedophilia literature, including attitudes or beliefs about how adult–child sex can be beneficial (or, at least, not harmful); that adult–child sex is common cross-culturally and/or historically; that pedophilia, or at least sexual attraction to children, is common in men; and that any negative consequences of adult–child sex are due to parental overreaction and stigma rather than the acts themselves (e.g., O'Carroll, 1980).[7]

Jenkins (2001) also identified themes in the posts he read for his study of an online pedophilia and child pornography forum, which can be compared with the themes identified by other researchers: (a) a libertarian ideology about the Internet that emphasizes individual rights and freedoms over societal norms, laws, or morality; (b) a discourse emphasizing children's rights to make their own decisions and to have sexual expression; (c) support for a "view evil, do no evil" position—that is, that viewing child pornography was defensible if it prevented contact sexual offenses from being committed; (d) and positive views about adult–child sex. These themes are similar to those identified by other researchers, except for the unique theme regarding the Internet's sociocultural values.

---

[7]It is worth mentioning that these kinds of attitudes and beliefs are not unique to sexual offenders; they are common to any minority group that feels a need to defend itself, and in fact rationalization and justification appear to be psychological universals (e.g., Maruna & Mann, 2006).

Malesky and Ennis (2004) examined 1 week of posts on *Boychat,* the public forum I mentioned earlier for individuals who are sexually attracted to boys. Their focus was also on offense-supportive attitudes and beliefs about children and sex. Slightly more than half of the posts (53%) examined by Malesky and Ennis were legal pictures, drawings, poetry, and so forth about children, reflecting the fact that attraction to children is not exclusively sexual. Some users described romantic feelings about children, paralleling in many ways how non-pedophilic adults speak about their adult paramours (cf. Wilson and Cox's 1983 study of self-identified pedophiles). One fifth of the posts (21%) were categorized by Malesky and Ennis as having to do with seeking validation of pedophilic or hebephilic interests. Only a small proportion of posts (4%) were explicitly about sexual offending, in terms of discussing grooming tactics (i.e., how to meet a child and develop a sexual relationship; see Appendix 3.2).

The Durkin and Bryant (1999) study was recently replicated by O'Halloran and Quayle (2010). Because of a much higher frequency of postings, O'Halloran and Quayle examined only 1 month of postings, rather than 4 months, as did Durkin and Bryant. O'Halloran and Quayle categorized 127 posts (by 23 unique nicknames) using the same themes as were previously examined, except for polythematic accounts (most posters used more than one theme); they also added the theme of denial of victim, defined as statements that children initiate sexual behavior or are capable of making their own decisions regarding sex. O'Halloran and Quayle found that two thirds (65%) of the posters offered at least one form of justification, with most using more than one form. The most common combinations identified by O'Halloran and Quayle were condemnation of condemners plus claim of benefit, condemnation of condemners and denial of victim, and denial of injury plus claim of benefits.

Holt, Blevins, and Burkert (2010) examined the online pedophile subcultures by conducting a qualitative analysis of 705 threads posted on five different web forums. These forums were selected on the basis of having a range of membership sizes, high traffic and therefore more activity to analyze, and being publicly accessible so novices can find the forums relatively easily. The authors concluded that pedophile subcultures generally support and encourage emotional and, in some cases, sexual relationships with boys and girls. Almost all forum users described having sexual interests in children. Holt et al. also noted, as have others before them, that the online forums had a special jargon and other signifiers of the subcultures, including the practice of referring to someone as a *girl-lover* or *boy-lover* rather than as a pedophile (or hebephile) and referring to those who oppose adult–child sex and/or demonize pedophilia as *antis* (see also Jenkins, 2001).

Other themes identified by Holt et al. (2010) included social marginalization, adult–child sexuality, the law, and computer security. There was little opposition across forums to the belief that a sexual interest in children was normal, widespread, and misunderstood. In fact, individuals usually agreed with one another and offered a great deal of support, reinforcement, and encouragement to each other (Jenkins, 2001; Quayle & Taylor, 2002). The forums consequently became an important community for pedophiles to share aspects of themselves that they could not share offline.

Another theme identified by Holt et al. (2010) was how legal content could be emotionally or sexually satisfying. In my sporadic observations of Girlchat and Boychat, users regularly posted links to mainstream websites featuring pictures or videos of children engaged in everyday activities such as playing sports or singing. Though the images and videos contained no sexual content, the accompanying text suggested that users might still find them gratifying. I mentioned earlier that Lanning (2001) and others have referred to this kind of legal, child-oriented content as *indicative material*. Real-life encounters with children in a nonsexual context were a source of joy and were referred to as a *girl moment* or *boy moment*.

In many ways, the online pedohebephilia subculture is similar to other online communities of stigmatized or ostracized individuals: There is a bond among individuals who might otherwise not know anyone who shares their interests or dilemmas, information and support can be shared, and there is status for longevity and contributions to the group.

EFFECTS

What are the effects of these online subcultures? The social networks they provide could potentially have both positive and negative effects. The effects could be positive if individuals feel less isolated and feel supported in their determination not to act on their sexual interests in children. An example of a potentially positive interaction is described in Holt et al. (2010) by a forum contributor: "BoyLove is a natural thing, like being born gay or even straight. It's something you can't control or choose. Only thing you can control is your actions" (p. 10). But the online subcultures could also have negative effects if they (tacitly) condone criminal sexual behavior by suggesting and reinforcing views that children are not harmed, that society unjustly represses child sexuality, and that any harm that results from adult–child sex is due to parental and societal reactions rather than the experience itself. Online subcultures could also have a negative effect by directly inciting others to engage in criminal sexual behavior (see Gallagher, 2007).

Mutual reinforcement of offense-supportive attitudes and beliefs (e.g., child pornography use is victimless or is a suitable substitute for contact offending) may increase the likelihood of criminal behavior. Research on criminogenic risk factors has consistently identified the association between offense-supportive attitudes and beliefs and recidivism among identified offenders, both among sex offenders (Hanson, Harris, Scott, & Helmus, 2007; Helmus, Hanson, Babchishin, & Mann, 2012) and other offenders (Andrews & Bonta, 2010). There is little research on the online social networks of sexual offenders, but an older study of real world connections found that sexual offenders against children may indeed seek similar-minded peers: Hanson and Scott (1996) found that sexual offenders against children were more likely to know other sex offenders against children than were nonsexual offenders or rapists. One explanation for this finding is that sex offenders against children know more offenders against children because they are grouped together institutionally—for example, as participants in treatment programs. Another explanation is that some offenders against children have preexisting links with each other, as in cases where offenders trade child pornography or even share child victims. The third is that sexual offenders against children, like any other group, will prefer to socialize with like-minded individuals.

Online interactions can indeed spur criminal behavior. Jenkins (2001) observed that there is social prestige in sharing new or rare child pornography content, being technologically expert on security measures, and being active online in a forum for a long time, describing "the wise ones" on the forum he observed. A recent, notorious case in my home province of Ontario involved the arrest of a man interacting with an undercover officer who took live webcam images of sexual abuse he committed against a young girl in his home (bit.ly/ixCvJB).

I will make one final comment here on the seemingly dominant Internet culture—beyond the pedophilia subculture—which values open communication, anonymity, and privacy over regulation, security, and individual safety. Jenkins (2001) made the astute observation that someone who would never steal from a store may think nothing of downloading pirated music, movies, and software. It is highly controversial whether this dominant culture can change—or should change, in light of the freedoms it has provided, particularly in repressive regimes—but libertarian Internet culture is perhaps inextricably tied to pedohebephile subcultures. Hard-liners for Internet libertarianism have defended child pornography, not because they condone it but because the principles are judged to be more important than their moral distaste (http://techliberation.com/2009/08/12/cyber-libertarianism-the-case-for-real-Internet-freedom). To illustrate, the Tech Liberation website describes principles of cyberlibertarianism and suggests that in the case of the tension between government censorship versus online child safety, the solution should come from parent empowerment and industry self-regulation rather than from the law. At this time, known pedohebephile forums are highly likely to be monitored by law enforcement. Freedom of speech provisions would likely prevent legal efforts to ban these forums. The final sentence of Jenkins (2001) seems apropos: "We have to find a means of killing or crippling the subculture without destroying the Internet, with which so much good can be accomplished" (p. 224).

APPENDIX 2.2
VIRTUAL CHILD PORNOGRAPHY

There is a legal distinction in the United States between virtual child pornography and depictions of real, identifiable children, following the United States Supreme Court decision on *Ashcroft v. Free Speech Coalition* (2002). This legal distinction does not exist in Canada or the United Kingdom, where visual or nonvisual depictions of children who are not real people can still be criminalized. Is there a moral distinction between virtual and real child pornography? There seems to be a strong societal consensus that sexually explicit depictions involving real children should be criminalized, given the potential for exploitation or harm to the depicted children. In contrast, virtual content involves no real children. Though the idea is morally repugnant to many members of the public, could virtual child pornography be permissible if it provided a relatively safe sexual outlet for pedohebephiles? Malamuth and Huppin (2007) addressed this contentious issue of virtual child pornography in a recent law review. They suggested that laws prohibiting virtual child pornography only for convicted sex offenders would pass constitutional challenge and would also be consistent with research suggesting minimal negative effects (though not catharsis) for pedohebephiles who have not committed contact offenses.

Malamuth and Huppin's (2007) idea is not fantastical given advances in computer-generated imagery (CGI) technologies. For example, for ethical and professional reasons the Not Real People (NRP) stimulus set was digitally created as a substitute for stimulus sets that use images of real children (http://pacific-psych.com/products/nrp-not-real-people-visual-stimuli-set). Though the NRP figures are not yet photorealistic, they do elicit differential sexual responding in the studies that have used this stimulus set (Banse, Schmidt, & Clarbour, 2010; Imhoff et al., 2010). Their realism will only improve as digital imaging technology improves. One can compare the impressive CGI effects in the 2010 blockbuster film, *Avatar*, for example, with the initial efforts in films from the 1990s. If Moore's Law about the exponential increase in the power of computing and concomitant decrease in relative price continues to hold, it is easy to predict that movie-quality CGI effects will become available to the home hobbyist, as professional-quality photo manipulation software like Photoshop has. Patrice Renaud and his colleagues have been trying to develop virtual reality stimuli to assess paraphilic sexual interests (e.g., Renaud et al., 2011). These technologies could someday be available to amateurs.

It is an empirical question whether virtual content will ever be as sexually arousing and gratifying as real content. Another empirical question, beyond the moral and legal debates, is whether having access to realistic virtual depictions of child pornography would be beneficial or harmful or, if it is harmful, whether the harm is tolerable, as with legal access to tobacco products and to alcohol. I take this issue up in more detail in Chapter 6.

APPENDIX 2.3
ONLINE PARAPHILIC PORNOGRAPHY

Online pornography research has mostly focused on the availability and effects of mainstream adult pornography, particularly its increasingly explicit and impersonal sensibilities (no kissing, no foreplay, minimal nonsexual interaction, cheap digital video production). More recently, there has been research on child pornography. There are many other forms of paraphilic pornography content online, some of which is also illegal under various existing obscenity laws, which differ from country to country. This can include content depicting rape, sadism, masochism, exhibitionism, voyeurism, bestiality, and fetishism. It is probably not an exaggeration to suggest that any sexual variation, no matter how obscure or implausible, is represented somewhere on the Internet (*kaiju*, or monster pornography, being just one unusual example; http://io9.com/kaiju-porn). It is not necessarily the case, however, that someone who occasionally views images or videos depicting sadomasochistic themes sexually prefers this content or would qualify for a formal diagnosis of sexual sadism or masochism.

I am not particularly concerned about most paraphilias, even if they do meet local obscenity laws (which might include consensual depictions of explicit heterosexual or homosexual sex in some jurisdictions). I am concerned, however, about paraphilias that, if acted on, would result in illegal behavior because they involve nonconsenting persons; these include *biastophilia* (a paraphilic interest in coercive sex), nonconsensual sexual *sadism* (interest in inflicting physical pain and suffering on someone who is not consenting), *pedophilia* and *hebephilia* (sexual attraction to prepubescent and pubescent children, respectively), *frotteurism* (rubbing oneself against an unsuspecting stranger in a public place), *exhibitionism* (exposing one's genitals to an unsuspecting stranger), and *voyeurism* (viewing an unsuspecting stranger undressing or engaging in other normally private activity).

Online technologies can facilitate some forms of paraphilic behavior. For example, exposing oneself to an unsuspecting stranger on a web chat site such as chatroulette.com may be connected to exhibitionism. Similarly, an interest in voyeurism might increase demand for voyeuristic pornography (e.g., the "upskirt" or "downblouse" pornography genres), which violates the privacy of the unsuspecting victims, even if they never become aware images had been taken. This includes the phenomenon of *creep shots*, the surreptitious photographing of girls and the posting of those images online. A recent example involved the real-life identification of an individual who encouraged and facilitated the posting of images of girls that would probably not meet definitions of child pornography but clearly reflected a sexual interest in adolescents (http://gawker.com/5950981/unmasking-reddits-violentacrezthe-biggest-troll-on-the-web). Though paraphilias—such as biastophilia or nonconsensual sexual sadism—that require contact with a victim cannot be enacted online, paraphilic interest in fantasy and masturbation material can result in more demand for these kinds of content, and online technologies can facilitate offline sexual offending if it is used to meet potential victims, as when online dating or match services are used.

APPENDIX 2.4
SEXTING AMONG ADOLESCENTS

In an analysis of national American data, about 10% of child pornography cases between 1997 and 2000 involved juvenile accused (Finkelhor & Ormrod, 2004). This proportion is far below the level of involvement of juveniles in contact sexual offenses (Finkelhor, Ormrod, & Chaffin, 2009). The proportion of juvenile accused might change, however, with greater legal attention to *sexting* cases, which is defined here as the use of mobile phones or other communication technologies to transmit sexual images that would meet legal definitions of child pornography (e.g., a sexual image of oneself, a peer, or lover who is under the age of 18). This definition of sexting is consistent with the definition used by Lounsbury, Mitchell, and Finkelhor (2011), who noted the different and sometimes broader definitions used in other research on sexting in their critique of studies that have been conducted to date. Some studies have used definitions that include sexual texts that do not involve images (not illegal under current American federal law), distribution of adult pornography using mobile phones or other portable devices, and depictions of minors that would probably not meet legal definitions of child pornography (e.g., a girl in her bra and panties or a bikini).

The first large-scale sexting survey was conducted by the National Campaign to Prevent Teen and Unplanned Pregnancy and by CosmoGirl.com. This "Sex and Tech" survey of teens and young adults explored online activity, particularly sending and receiving sexually suggestive texts and images. The survey included 653 teenagers (ages 13 to 19) and 627 young adults (ages 20 to 26) in late 2008 (more details are available at http://thenational campaign.org/sextech). The respondents were stratified according to the U.S. Census and weighted to reflect the demographic composition of teenagers and young adults. The most frequently mentioned finding from this survey is that one in five teenagers had sent or posted nude or semi-nude pictures or videos of themselves. There are several limitations to acknowledge about the Sex and Tech survey, however, as noted by Lounsbury et al. (2011). First, the sample was not representative, making it difficult to extrapolate its results to provide an estimate of the national prevalence of sexting. Second, the sample included 18 and 19 year olds, who can legally transmit sexual pictures of themselves or other adults; the Sex and Tech survey found that one third of the young adult sample had sexted. Though this behavior might still be labeled as sexting, it would not be directly relevant to current policies and laws regarding child pornography. Third, the definition of sexting included the sending of semi-nude pictures, including those of individuals in a swimsuit or underwear, which would usually not meet legal definitions of child pornography. Despite these limitations, it is relevant that the survey found that 11% of girls between the ages of 13 and 16 sexted, and 15% of teens who sexted did so with someone they only knew online.

Nonetheless, there are some interesting findings regarding the circumstances and context of sexting and whether it would meet legal definitions of child pornography. First, more than 40% of teens and young adults (42% total: 47% teens, 38% young adults) responded that "pressure from guys" was a reason girls and women send and post sexually suggestive messages and images. Also, 36% of teen girls and 39% of teen boys reported that it was common for nude or semi-nude photos to be shared with people other than the intended recipient. Finally, 25% of teen girls and 33% of teen boys said they had nude or semi-nude images shared with them that were originally meant for someone else. The most notable finding to take from these results is that a private image is often shared with others.

Other more recent surveys have addressed these study limitations and produced much lower prevalence rates. I have the most confidence in the results from the Youth Internet Safety Survey, conducted by the Crimes Against Children Research Center, given their track record of methodologically sound research, nationally representative sample of youths, and precise definition of the behaviors of interest. Mitchell, Jones, Finkelhor, and Wolak (2011) and Wolak, Finkelhor, and Mitchell (2012) suggested that the prevalence of sexting among adolescents is 1%. Mitchell et al. (2011) found that 2.5% of the youths, ages 10 to 17, who completed the Youth Internet Safety Survey reported they had either appeared in or created sexually suggestive or explicit images, and 1% admitted appearing in sexually explicit (showing breasts, genitals or buttocks) images.

The Pew Internet Survey, which used more precise methodology, came up with a 4% prevalence rate for sexting (Lenhart, Ling, Campbell, & Purcell, 2010). In other words, sexting is much rarer than is commonly believed. It is still a social concern, however, because the images might be distributed widely (private images often do not remain private) and therefore become irretrievable. Also, even a 1% prevalence rate still implies many adolescents are involved, given the absolute number of this demographic segment. The 2005 American Community Survey (part of the Census data set from http://factfinder2.census.gov/faces/nav/jsf/pages/wc_acs.xhtml) reported there were 141,274,964 females in the United States; 7.8% were girls between the ages of 10 and 14, resulting in an estimated 10.7 million girls in this age category. A 1% prevalence rate implies that over 100,000 girls in the United States have been involved in sexting, as have a similar number of boys.

The most plausible explanations for sexting are adolescent risk taking and experimentation, not pedophilia or hebephilia, given the ages of the persons who are depicted and given the social–developmental context for this behavior. Wolak and Finkelhor (2011) presented a descriptive typology based

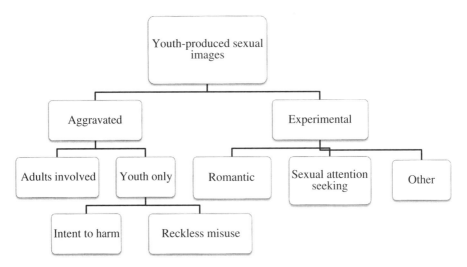

Figure 2.1. Sexting typology. From *Sexting: A Typology* (p. 1), by J. Wolak and D. Finkelhor, 2011, Durham, NH: Crimes Against Children Research Center. Copyright 2011 by Crimes Against Children Research Center. Reprinted with permission.

on 550 sexting cases reported to police in 2008 or 2009 (see Figure 2.1). They suggested a distinction between *experimental* and *aggravated* sexting. The former category involved cases in which romantic partners sent each other images or the use of images by adolescents to flirt or seek attention from others. The latter category involved cases in which sexts were used with an intent to harm—for example, to embarrass or harm the reputation of someone else, as part of an adult solicitation effort, or when the person depicted did not give consent to having the image taken (e.g., surreptitious recording). There has not been large sample research investigating the prevalence of experimental or aggravated sexting cases or examining the characteristics of the individuals involved. It is likely that these kinds of cases are overrepresented in this sample, because the cases that did not involve aggravated sexting might not be reported to police.

Wolak, Finkelhor, and Mitchell (2012) reported analyses from 675 sexting cases—weighted to represent an estimated 3,477 cases—reported to police in the United States in 2008 or 2009 (this is not a large number of cases and is similar to the number of homicides involving juveniles during the same year). Over 80% of simple production or possession cases did not result in arrest. This was true even for many of those cases involving aggravating factors (e.g., those with an intent to harm) if only juveniles were involved. Adult involvement increased the likelihood of an arrest, with two thirds of cases involving adults resulting in an arrest, as did involvement of other criminal behavior (e.g., blackmail). However, there was variability in the law enforcement response, and some teens were arrested in cases where a warning and parental involvement would probably have sufficed.

It is encouraging in this context that New Jersey and many other states are considering changes to law and policy so that adolescent sexting is not treated the same as child pornography production or distribution by adults (http://newjerseynewsroom.com/state/nj-law-makes-juvenile-sexting-an-educational-issue-not-a-crime). This would be in keeping with the common law principle that juveniles should not be subject to the same criminal penalties as adults. Leary (2010) made a cogent argument for a rational protocol that could guide prosecutors in making decisions about how to proceed in cases of self-produced child pornography (what she called *structured prosecutorial discretion*, which is not the same thing as decriminalization). She suggested that considerations might include the age of the youths, their criminal histories, the context in which the images were created, whether the image was self-produced, whether the images were distributed, and whether other sexual behavior was involved.

Though 84% of sext images were distributed, much of this involved mobile phones (Wolak, Finkelhor, & Mitchell, 2011). Only mobile phones were involved in two thirds of distribution; this content did not appear online. Though this does not preclude online distribution of sexts as child pornography, because mobile phones can be hacked, it is more complicated technically and thus less likely to result in distribution (though newer smartphones and applications make sending pictures easier).

3

SOLICITATION

As I have mentioned, most of the research on online sexual offending has focused on child pornography offenders. Yet a comparable, if not greater, concern for many parents, educators, and policymakers is the risk posed by adults who use Internet technologies—social networking sites, chat rooms, instant messaging, e-mail—to approach children and youths and solicit them to engage in activities such as sexual chat, exchange of sexually explicit images, or to meet in person so that a contact sexual offense can be committed (Mitchell, Finkelhor, Jones, & Wolak, 2010; Whittle, Hamilton-Giachritsis, Beech, & Collings, 2012; Ybarra & Mitchell, 2008). As a result, new laws designed to prevent individuals from using the Internet to sexually solicit children have been implemented (these are intended to thwart what I call *online solicitation offenders,* also referred to as *luring* or *traveler* offenders; e.g., Alexy, Burgess, & Baker, 2005; see Table 1.1). This is a new type of offense; sexual interactions with a minor that involve no physical contact

http://dx.doi.org/10.1037/14191-004
Internet Sex Offenders, by M. C. Seto

can be illegal, even if the minor is in fact an adult police officer in an under-cover role (Mitchell, Finkelhor, Wolak, & Jones, 2010).

I focus on online solicitation in this chapter, though some of the research I review also includes individuals who first initiated contact in the real world and then used Internet technologies to maintain their contact with minors. There is some overlap between online child pornography and solicitation offending, as I discuss later in this chapter. I also examine later what we know about statutory sexual offending, because the research evidence I summarize here suggests there are many parallels between online solicitation and statutory sexual offenses involving adults and legal minors who engage in "consenting" sexual activity.

I use the term *online solicitation* in this book because luring implies deceit, yet as I discuss later in this chapter, some adult perpetrators are quite frank about what they want, and many offenses do not involve travel, such as engaging in sexual chat, online exhibitionism, or distributing child pornography. As in child pornography offending, the medium is relatively new, but the nature of the criminal behavior—sexually approaching minors—is not new. What is different is the extent to which Internet technologies have amplified the pace and reach of individuals who are interested in sexually interacting with minors. Moreover, online solicitation research has focused on minors. Almost nothing is known scientifically about how Internet technologies have facilitated sexual assaults of adults, such as those by offenders who use Craigslist or dating sites to meet someone whom they intend to sexually assault (see Appendix 3.1).

EXAMPLES OF ONLINE SOLICITATION OFFENSES

Vivid and sensational examples of online grooming have been depicted on the *Dateline NBC* television show "To Catch a Predator," which collaborated with a grassroots organization called Perverted Justice to set up sting operations that are secretly recorded and then broadcast. Examples of other solicitation arrests are provided at the Perverted Justice's website (http://perverted-justice.com). A seemingly typical case was posted on May 14, 2010, when a 25-year-old man was arrested and charged after two sexual encounters with a teenage girl he met on Myspace. Sensational and highly unusual stories are included as well, however, as on May 17, 2010, in the case of a 34-year-old man charged with the murder of a 12-year-old boy after pretending to be a girl and luring the boy out of his home by sending him texts from a mobile phone (Appendix 3.2).

Leander, Christianson, and Granhag (2008) studied an unusual case by examining the chat logs and police interviews of 68 females, ranging in age from 11 to 19 (mean age = 15) who were fooled by a 29-year-old Swedish man who pretended to be an adult woman running a modeling and escort service. Some of the victims met him (posing as a putative client) for sex in real life, and many sent him (in his persona as the woman running the service) personal information, including contact information and sexually suggestive or explicit images. Notably, only three of the victims disclosed these interactions to police, and a majority did not act until police contacted them after examining the digital evidence. The victims acknowledged real-life interactions but minimized the online behavior, even though they were aware of the digital evidence. Leander et al. suggested that the victims were embarrassed about the fact that they had been tricked.

Concerns about online solicitations have led to much attention to online privacy and security for minors, including age restrictions on joining social networks such as Facebook, and investments in educational resources for schools, parents, and children. But what do we know scientifically about this danger from "online predators"? Reading popular media accounts, one would expect that children and adolescents are at risk from much older strangers who use online information (e.g., from social networking profiles) to identify potential victims and earn their trust. These online acquaintances then trick youths to meet them in real life, where they might be abducted or sexually assaulted. How real is this danger? I address the myths and empirical realities later in this chapter.

INCIDENCE AND PREVALENCE OF ONLINE SOLICITATION

Incidence

The odds are that most minors will ignore sexual solicitations. But even if only one in 100 (and the survey data discussed in this chapter suggest a higher response rate than 1%) do respond, the adult has had more success in soliciting minors online, probably at less legal risk, than if he approached minors he knew in real life. The risk is even lower for individuals who successfully hide their identities and restrict their interactions to sexual chat, masturbating or exposing themselves via webcam, and exchanging pornographic images. This distinction between online-only interactions and contact-driven solicitation is discussed later in this chapter in the section on offender typology.

A common theme across forms of online offending is that the threshold for initiating antisocial behavior is lower online than in real life for a variety of reasons. Our social psychology is built for interactions with real people in real time. Online interactions are different because they are mediated by words and images, without nonverbal cues and the awareness that one is dealing with a person. A common example is the tendency for *flame wars* (hostile disagreements that devolve into ad hominem attacks and aggressive behavior) to break out on message boards or e-mail distribution lists, because people state things in text online that they would not say in real life if facing the recipient. Suler (2004) described this as an *online disinhibition effect,* which he attributed to perceived anonymity, physical invisibility, asynchronicity of communication, and minimization of authority online. Another potential contributor is the *Proteus effect,* which refers to the effects of virtual persona characteristics on social behavior, both online and in the real world (Yee & Bailenson, 2007; Yee, Bailenson, & Ducheneaut, 2009). Yee and his colleagues (2009) demonstrated, for example, that people who were randomly assigned to have tall avatars (virtual representations) were more confident in their interactions with others than those who were assigned to have shorter avatars. Online participants do not choose their user names and avatars of their persona randomly, but it is interesting to speculate that, once chosen, these virtual representations might reciprocally influence behavior. It is also the case that our social behavior can be influenced by how others perceive us online; not only are users with tall avatars affected by this manipulation, but the people they interact with are also influenced. One could speculate that online offenders behave the way they do in part because of how they are perceived. For example, online solicitors may be more sexually aggressive than they might otherwise be because the young teens they contact expect them to be, as adult strangers who have initiated contact with the teens online.

Prevalence

In this section, I review the emerging data available on the prevalence among minors of being sexually solicited online. It is worthwhile to note that this is not the same as the prevalence of online solicitation, which would be expected to have a lower incidence because it is likely that adults engaging in solicitation will each contact multiple minors. Evidence from two Youth Internet Safety Surveys suggests that online solicitation is sufficiently common to be of concern. Approximately one in seven youths reported experiencing a sexual solicitation in the past year, with 38% of these solicitations apparently coming from adults (Mitchell, Wolak, & Finkelhor, 2007).[1] In other words, approximately 5% of youths report having been sexually solicited by an adult while online over a 1-year period. The 1-year incidence rate

---

[1] An as yet unstudied phenomenon is peer-on-peer sexual solicitation. Perhaps much of this contact is akin to flirting and other solicitations in real life, but some of this behavior is likely to be unwanted and experienced as distressing and/or aggressive.

of unwanted sexual solicitations, adult or not, decreased from 19% in the first survey to 13% in the second Youth Internet Safety Survey. Many solicitations were noncriminal (e.g., sexually suggestive comments), but some were aggressive, and some clearly involved criminal sexual behavior, such as genital exposures via webcam or transmitting child pornography.

In the Pew Internet and American Life Project's Teen and Parent Survey, conducted in fall 2006, almost one third of the 886 teenagers (ages 12–17) who reported using the Internet indicated that they had been contacted by a stranger online. This is not necessarily the same as sexual solicitation because strangers could include peers and the solicitation was not necessarily sexual; nonetheless, 7% of the youths felt scared or uncomfortable as a result of the online solicitation (Smith, 2007). A higher proportion of those who had social networking profiles or posted photos online had been contacted by strangers and felt scared or uncomfortable as a result. This survey did not specifically ask questions about sexual context, but it did illustrate that online solicitations could cause distress.

The Growing Up With Media Survey is a longitudinal study of 1,588 youths between the ages of 10 and 15, assessed over a 3-year period. The initial survey was completed from August to September 2006. Of the youths who participated in the survey, 15% reported experiencing a solicitation at this initial survey, which is quite similar to the Youth Internet Safety Survey incidence estimate (Ybarra, Espelage, & Mitchell, 2007). Three percent of the youths reported being solicited at least monthly at the initial survey, which indicates that solicitation can be an ongoing phenomenon. Looking at stability of solicitation over two assessments, 6% of youths reported experiencing solicitation during the past year at both time periods, 8% reported solicitation at the initial survey only, and 7% reported solicitation at the follow-up survey only. The observation that some youths experience multiple solicitations suggests that certain youths may be more vulnerable to solicitations because of their profiles or online activities. I discuss this idea further in Appendix 3.3. (Another more parsimonious possibility is that a small number of youths are unlucky.)

In a convenience survey of students, Dowdell, Burgess, and Flores (2011) found that 15% of middle school students (59 of 400 students with valid data) reported that they had communicated with a stranger whom they initially met online, and a slight majority (54%—32 of 59 students) of this subset met with the stranger. The majority of middle school students reported that their parents were aware they had communicated with an online stranger. In almost all cases, however, the online stranger was a minor as well, though perhaps an older minor—for example, if a 17-year-old boy solicited a 14-year-old girl. Boys tended to meet with girls, whereas girls met equally with girls or boys. Criminal acts were rare: Two boys and one girl reported being inappropriately touched or sexually assaulted as a result of their offline meeting.

In the same Dowdell et al. (2011) study, with a larger survey of high school students, the majority of the 1,151 girls and 926 boys had been asked by a stranger they met online (65% of girls and 53% of boys) to meet in person. Approximately one third of both boys and girls then met the online stranger (not necessarily an adult) with boys being more likely to have some kind of sexual interaction with the person they met (23% vs. 13%). Meeting an adult online stranger was correlated with other risky online behavior (e.g., being sexted, having a webcam), and risky online behavior in turn was predicted by delinquency factors for both boys and girls. The number of online strangers who were adults was not specified. The correlation between risky Internet behavior and delinquency suggests online and offline risk taking share commonalities.

INTERNATIONAL SCOPE

Online solicitation is an international concern, reflecting an increasing online presence of children and youths in industrialized nations. Webwise (2006) conducted the Survey of Children's Use of the Internet in Ireland with 848 Irish students between the ages of 9 and 16. The average age of initial Internet use was 8 in 2006, compared with ages 9 to 10 in 2003. The authors identified safety concerns regarding a shift toward having computers in bedrooms rather than public spaces in the house, generally low levels of adult supervision, and increasing access to the Internet using portable devices such as smartphones. Children were unlikely to talk to parents about their Internet use. Seventeen percent of the boys had viewed pornography online. Girls were more likely to post pictures of themselves online; at the same time, only a minority of respondents had posted personally identifying information publicly.

Seven percent of the students in the Webwise (2006) survey met an online stranger in real life, an increase from 4% in 2003. The majority of respondents went to the meeting with a friend, but one quarter of those who met an online stranger went alone. The majority enjoyed the experience, but some (11% of those who met an online stranger, or 0.8% of the total sample) said the stranger tried to physically hurt them. About a quarter of the online strangers who had presented themselves as a peer turned out be an adult. Only adult strangers were represented in the abusive meetings; all the meetings with other minors were either neutral or positive.

The results of the Webwise (2006) survey suggest that almost 1% of minors who are online have met an adult stranger who tried to physically harm them in some way. In the context of the other youth surveys described earlier in this section, these data suggest that some youths experience sexual solicitations, and most do not respond, but nonetheless, a significant number of minors do meet adult strangers, and some are harmed as a result. Given the number of minors in the population in contrast to the number of solicitation cases being identified by police, it is safe to infer that most real-world meetings are not reported.

OFFLINE AND ONLINE SOLICITATIONS

We do not know the extent of overlap between online and offline sexual solicitations. Are children or teens who are vulnerable to online solicitations also more vulnerable to offline sexual solicitations? Ybarra, Espelage, and Mitchell (2007) reported similar absolute frequencies of online and offline solicitations, but they did not report the extent of the overlap. There is reason to expect some overlap, given that youths who report being cyberbullied are also more likely to report bullying at school in real life (Juvonen & Gross, 2008). A May 2011 analysis of data from the 2007 School Crime Supplement of the National Crime Victimization Study data set suggested that cyberbullying is relatively uncommon, with 32% of respondents reporting ever being bullied at school, whereas 4% reported being cyberbullied (U.S. Department of Education, 2011).

In general, surveys of youth risk online need to be interpreted cautiously because the questions about sexual solicitations are often not specific to adults and thus encompass unwanted solicitations from peers (the Webwise, 2006, results suggest youths are more at risk from adults than from their peers if they do meet in the real world). This could still be of concern, given the prevalence of sexual harassment and sexual aggression between teens (McMaster, Connolly, Pepler, & Craig, 2002; Silverman, Raj, Mucci, & Hathaway, 2001), but it is not the focus of current legal and social responses to online solicitations. Official crime statistics for online sexual solicitation do not correspond to the prevalence estimates obtained in these self-report victimization surveys, suggesting that many cases go unreported, just as many contact sexual offenses are unreported.

The most comprehensive data on solicitation offenders, summarized by Wolak, Finkelhor, Mitchell, and Ybarra (2008), are based on cases involving solicitations of real youths (not undercover police officers) that were then reported to police. Solicitations that resulted in meetings are probably more likely to be reported to police because parents find out or because the youth becomes upset and discloses once the adult perpetrator ends or attempts to end the sexual relationship. Many youths ignore or at least do not report solicitations that are restricted to online interactions and that do not result in face-to-face meetings (Mitchell, Finkelhor, & Wolak, 2001). Having said that, once reported, I would expect high conviction rates—as with child pornography prosecutions—because of the digital evidence of chats and other online communications, which would be similar to the high conviction rates obtained in child pornography prosecutions.

GROOMING

Sex offenders vary in the tactics they use to commit their crimes. Some use physical force, and others use threats or other coercive methods (e.g., blackmail, exerting their position of authority), whereas others give children attention and gifts to build trust and affection (Kaufman et al., 1998). The use of noncoercive but manipulative tactics has been described as *grooming* in the sex offender literature (see Appendix 3.2). The term is also often used, however, to describe behaviors that are not intentionally manipulative. For example, Webster et al. (2012), in their research on online grooming, noted that perpetrators usually did not fake their interests (in music, sports, etc.) to gain the trust and interest of youths; instead, they sought youths who shared those interests. The fact they connected with youths because of common interests is not intentionally manipulative, though the connection might then be manipulatively used for sexual purposes. Many self-identified pedophiles report feelings of love and affection for children and prefer their company; this is reflected in psychological measures of emotional congruence or identification with children (Bernard, 1985; Des Sables, 1976, 1977; Wilson & Cox, 1983). Thus, grooming can be consciously manipulative, aimed toward victim access and compliance, or can reflect relational processes akin to those in romantic relationships with peers.

Grooming can be amplified by Internet technologies in online solicitation. Before the Internet, grooming was more dependent on already having some contact with children—for example, through family, friends, work, or volunteer activities—though there could still be chance encounters between strangers. Social networking and similar sites, however, allow strangers to contact many minors, at relatively low cost. An adult man can contact hundreds of minors quickly in only a few hours through instant messaging, for example, with little chance of being detected unless he has the bad luck of encountering an undercover police officer. This risk of detection by police can be mitigated by preferring webcam interactions and refraining from the initiation of sexual chat, which might provide an entrapment defense at any subsequent court proceeding. It does not mean there are no consequences, however, because social networking and similar sites may suspend user accounts because of behavior that violates their terms of service (the agreements that users acknowledge when joining the site).

Is pornography more commonly part of online than offline solicitations? Langevin and Curnoe (2004) studied offline offenders and found that pornography was used in only a minority (17%) of cases, though this was more common for offenders against children, where about a third of offenders with any boy victims used pornography. Hill, Briken, and Berner (2006) found that approximately a third of their sample of offenders who had committed sex crimes against children had used child pornography prior to their sexual offenses. Kaufman et al. (1998) found that pornography was more likely to be used by offenders against related versus unrelated victims and by adolescent versus adult offenders. Giving gifts or other benefits and desensitizing to touch (through play and other activities) were more common grooming tactics in Kaufman et al.'s research. In the National Juvenile Online Victimization (NJOV) Project, approximately one in five perpetrators sent sexually suggestive images of themselves, took such images of minors, or convinced minors to take images of themselves or their friends (see Wolak, Finkelhor, Mitchell, & Ybarra, 2008).

EARLY DESCRIPTIVE STUDIES

In this section, I review early accounts of online solicitation, when the Internet was first becoming widely available to the public. Lamb (1998) conducted one of the first studies of adult solicitations of minors online. Pretending to be a bisexual teenager in a chat room for gay youths, he spent 10 hours in these rooms and engaged in interactions with 1,000 screen names.[2]

Lamb reported experiencing approximately three contacts per minute, suggesting a high rate of interaction for a purported teenager in this forum. Lamb suggested the individuals with whom he interacted fell into three categories that he labeled *browsers, cruisers,* and *pornographers*. Browsers were the smallest group and seemed to be visiting the chat room to meet people. Most browsers claimed to have had a sexual relationship with a younger person and offered advice to young gay or bisexual youths. They shared stories but refrained from any direct sexual advances to teens. Cruisers were the largest group and appeared to be seeking sexual gratification through fantasy and masturbation while online. Some cruisers talked about their own experiences, whereas others described fantasies involving Lamb's persona. The pornographers focused on trading child or adult pornography and minimized

_____

[2]A thousand screen names does not necessarily mean a thousand individuals, because the same user might have multiple accounts on the forum.

their online identities and interactions. None of the persons that Lamb interacted with suggested meeting in real life.

O'Connell (2003) logged a total of 50 hours over a 5-year period, pretending to be an 8-, 10-, or 12-year-old child, usually a girl, in chat venues intended for child or teen users. Her fictitious personal history was that she had recently moved, her parents fought and did not get along, and that she had not made friends yet at her new school. In other words, O'Connell portrayed herself as a socially isolated child, consistent with research on vulnerability factors in real-world sexual offending (see also Appendix 3.3). O'Connell identified several stages in the solicitation process. Initially, an online friendship was cultivated, typically followed by the offender assessing the likelihood of detection by others. The idea of trust was then introduced. In the final stage, sexual content was introduced into conversations, such as asking whether the child had ever been kissed or had participated in sexual activities. If the child indicated she was uncomfortable with the conversation, the offender would apologize and ask for forgiveness in an attempt to reestablish trust. However, other examples given by O'Connell (2003) described more overtly coercive online interactions involving descriptions of specific sexual scenarios. O'Connell found that offenders would fluctuate between inviting and blackmailing the child to engage in cybersex. The following is an example that she gave:

> *Adult:* Tell me how you would touch my c**k [sic].
>
> *Child:* I feel uncomfortable.
>
> *Adult:* Just do it, come on just do it, what are you waiting for?
>
> *Child:* I don't want to.
>
> *Adult:* Don't let me down, come on now, I am touching you making you feel really good, I love you, come on you will like this, don't you want to make me happy? (p. 12)

Other adults made sexually aggressive statements, such as "Do as I f**king say right now, bitch, or you will be in big f**king trouble" (O'Connell, 2003, p. 9). O'Connell suggested these persons may have sought a relationship in real life rather than be satisfied with online sexual chat. The noncoercive examples of interactions that were provided are similar to the grooming process for some sex offenders with child victims.

There are a couple of caveats in interpreting O'Connell's (2003) study. She did not know the identities of those who posed as adults, and there were no requests to meet in real life. It is possible that some of the chat participants were minors pretending to be adults; also, it is not known how much of the online activity described by Lamb (1998) and O'Connell (2003) constituted cybersexual fantasy about prohibited behavior that would not have been initiated even if there was opportunity to do so in real life (cf. Briggs, Simon, & Simonsen, 2011).

In a more recent study, K. Young (2005) interviewed 22 men arrested for online sexual offenses. These cases differed from the field observations described earlier because the online interactions were with police officers and resulted in arrest. None of the men had any prior criminal record, and none had any known history of sexual offenses against children. All were arrested after communicating with an undercover police officer in a pedophilia-themed chat room. Three men possessed child pornography, and 19% purportedly had a history of sexual addiction. K. Young suggested there was evidence of sexual addiction in some of the other cases, with sexual fantasies used as a means of escaping from problems such as loneliness, relationship difficulties, or dysphoria. Half (47%) of the men reported experiencing depression or anxiety at the time of their arrest (suggesting the mood problems were not simply a result of being arrested), and 39% had a history of alcohol or drug dependence. Both mood problems and substance use are often found to be comorbid with sexual behavior problems, which is discussed further in the next chapter as one of the potential explanations for online sexual offending (e.g., Kafka & Hennen, 2003). All of the offenders seen by K. Young (2005) claimed that they discovered pedophilia-themed chat rooms (e.g., daddy4daughter) by accident and that this discovery piqued their curiosity. What K. Young did not explain is why their curiosity was piqued by pedophilia or incest themes rather than by more mainstream sexual topics. She also did not report data on interrater reliability or address the potential selection, report, or confirmatory biases of individuals seen at her Center for Online Addiction.

Krone (2005) described undercover police stings in which officers posed as children in online chat rooms. He found the interactions were faster and shorter than those described by O'Connell (2003), but he provided fewer details than she did. Krone did not find the same stages of offending suggested by O'Connell, but he did distinguish three types of conversations: (a) overtly sexual exchanges, (b) verification of the child's identity and personal circumstances, and (c) trust-building—for example, showing an interest in the child's opinions. Overtly sexual conversations included discussing sex, sending pornography, exhibitionistic masturbation, and suggesting meeting offline to have sex. Krone concluded that the majority of offenders sought quick sexual gratification from girls they met online, such as masturbating while sexually chatting and then ending the conversation upon orgasm. In contrast, there were no sexual advances when police posed as boys.

Grosskopf (2009) reviewed chat logs from 15 online solicitation cases, with additional information provided by 10 undercover police officers involved in these cases. Though the number of cases was small, the chat logs were a rich source of information about the interactions and so are discussed in some length later in the section. Also, most online solicitation cases involve adult men contacting girls, and less is known about solicitations of boys. There may well be differences; for example, girls typically spend more time than boys in chat rooms or social networking sites, whereas boys are more involved in online gaming networks provided by platforms such as Xbox or Wii and thus might be more likely to be contacted in these online forums. Last, among the cases involving boys examined by Wolak, Finkelhor, Mitchell, and Ybarra (2008), uncertainty about sexual identity or a nonheterosexual orientation were risk factors for online solicitation.

In Grosskopf's (2009) sample of 15 cases, only three of the investigations resulted in arrest. All except one of the cases involved a police officer posing as a male youth; the exception involved a referral to police after an adolescent's family discovered their teenage boy had been solicited online. The police then assumed the online identity of the victim in what is sometimes described as a *take-over investigation*. In the police stings, officers created a persona of a minor between 11 and 15 years old, with the majority pretending to be 13 or 14 years old. Officers reported that the suspects tended to present themselves as an older friend (five cases) or as a peer (five cases). Interactions revolved around asking about the boy's appearance, introducing sexual topics, asking about sexual experiences, and fantasy or role-playing. Interactions were more likely to be sexual in the gay-oriented chat rooms or if the officer pretended to be a curious gay youth. Only one respondent encountered conversations that did not progress to a sexual level.

Unlike the other descriptive studies that have been reviewed so far, timeline data were available for 11 cases involving sexual conversation; 10 suspects introduced a sexual question or statement into the conversation within 17 minutes of initial contact (Grosskopf, 2009). Over two thirds of encounters were once only, for a period lasting from 2 minutes to 3 hours. Three cases occurred over two, three, and five sessions, respectively; two other cases involved protracted contacts. Eleven cases involved suspects establishing the boy's sexuality at some stage during the interaction. This was often carried out by asking questions such as "r u gay bi or str8? [Are you gay, bisexual, or straight?]." Six suspects asked the boy to switch to a more private chat channel or wanted to talk by telephone. The officers thought requests for phone contacts were common and were a way for men to confirm they were communicating with a youth rather than a police officer. For some suspects, going to a more private chat channel might also have been a prelude to proposing a real-life meeting.

Unlike O'Connell's (2003) study, only one of the suspects in Grosskopf's (2009) study used coercive or intimidating language, threatening that he would post the boy's messages on a school bulletin board. Five types of sexual behavior were engaged in by 14 suspects, with many suspects engaged in more than one kind of sexual activity: (a) describing a sex act or sexual activity with the child, (b) engaging in other sexualized conversation, (c) sending child or adult pornography to the youth, (d) exposing himself to the youth via webcam, and (e) directly soliciting the child to meet or make contact offline. Four respondents had received requests to meet in person. One respondent believed this was a result of being in a bisexual/gay chat room where sexually explicit conversations occurred and it was common to try to arrange meetings. The three others involved requests to meet after prolonged conversations or after an online friendship had evolved. The high level of sexual conversations noted by Grosskopf (2009) are inconsistent with Krone's (2005) study in which police reported no sexual solicitations. Grosskopf suggested that Krone's study was conducted prior to police getting more proactively involved in sexually oriented chat rooms and learning to manipulate the sexual orientations of the boys they portrayed.

DeLong, Durkin, and Hundersmarck (2010) examined the cognitions of 18 online solicitation offenders on the basis of their recorded police interrogations. All were arrested as a result of proactive police investigations, some from the "To Catch a Predator" series mentioned earlier. Seventeen of the 18 individuals were seen as engaging in minimization, rationalization, or refutation of their behavior (see Kennedy & Grubin, 1992; S. Young, 1997), but it is not clear how these judgments were made. For instance, "I am stupid and made a mistake" is given as an example of rationalization, yet this may indeed be an accurate statement of the person's perceptions, given the negative consequences they had just experienced. All but one of the men showed up for a real-life meeting, so statements that they were only interested in chat, not sex, are dubious. It is interesting to compare and contrast DeLong et al.'s findings with the explanations given during police interviews by child pornography offenders studied by Seto, Reeves, and Jung (2010). In both studies, offenders tended to minimize or rationalize their online behavior, but many of the child pornography offenders in Seto et al. (2010) acknowledged that they were sexually motivated.

Finally, Martellozzo (2010) described one of the first undercover operations by the London Metropolitan Police's High Technological Crime Unit. The unit created a fictitious online profile of a girl. More than 1,300 users visited the profile; of these, 450 users with adult male profiles initiated contact, and 80 became online friends. The majority had sexual intent, either for sexual chat, transmitting pornography, exposing themselves, or meeting in real life.

Given the many differences in methodology, sampling, and research questions, it is a challenge to synthesize these descriptive studies of online solicitation. However, several common themes emerge: (a) Online solicitations can occur quickly and at high frequency, especially in forums where sexual conversations are expected (e.g., in a gay youth chat room) or where there is perceived anonymity; (b) a substantial proportion, perhaps a majority, of online interactions appear to be fantasy driven, where sexual interactions online are the foci, rather than real-life meeting; (c) cases that result in arrest are more likely to involve attempts to meet in person; and (d) once arrested, individuals are likely to minimize or rationalize their intentions or behaviors. There are many research questions that need to be addressed, including how solicitations of adults and older adolescents compare with those involving younger adolescents, whether there are differences in solicitations of boys versus girls, and how solicitations by men differ from those by women.

TYPES OF SOLICITATION OFFENDERS

The descriptive studies described in the previous section demonstrate there is heterogeneity among solicitation offenders. Lamb (1998) distinguished between browsers, cruisers, and pornographers. K. Young (2005) made a speculative distinction between solicitation offenders as situational, fantasy driven, or sexually compulsive, distinguishing them from pedophilic offenders who seek sexual contacts with young children. K. Young suggested that the sexually compulsive online offenders she worked with were more likely to be honest about their age, appearance, and identity, whereas she thought pedohebephilic offenders were more likely to pretend to be children or be purposefully deceitful and manipulative. Mitchell, Wolak, and Finkelhor (2005) compared two groups of online solicitation offenders: 124 individuals identified by undercover police in proactive investigations ("stings") and 129 individuals identified through complaints involving actual minors as victims. The minor victims were older than the minors depicted by undercover police officers, and the offenders involved in minor victim cases were less likely to be involved in sexually oriented chat rooms and spent more time online than the offenders involved in proactive investigations.

FANTASY VERSUS CONTACT-DRIVEN SOLICITATION

An interesting distinction is between those who restrict their sexual interactions with minors to online behavior (sexual chat, webcam exposure, sending pornography) and those who attempt to meet in real life. Briggs et al. (2011) examined a small sample of solicitation offenders and made this distinction between 21 fantasy-driven and 30 contact-driven solicitation offenders. Like K. Young (2005), but unlike Mitchell et al. (2005), most (90%) of the solicitation offenders were caught as a result of undercover police work. Two were take-over investigations arising after minors were approached, contacted police, and police officers took over the interactions with the suspects. The small number of remaining offenders solicited real-life minors, resulting in sexual contacts, sometimes on multiple occasions (consistent with Wolak, Finkelhor, Mitchell, & Ybarra, 2008). Approximately three quarters of the minors were presented as 14 years old and most were presented as girls. All of the offenders were male. Approximately half had been married at some point, and a third (35%) had children of their own. There was a median of 3 days of communication before an arrest or an attempt to meet in person.

For the fantasy-driven offenders, the emphasis of their online activities was cybersex, including sexually explicit chat, masturbation in front of a webcam, and other behavior akin to exhibitionism. These incidents ended when the perpetrator climaxed. All of these participants engaged in sexually explicit chat, two thirds (68%) sent nude photos of themselves, 41% masturbated during their online communications, and 29% attempted to teach the minor how to masturbate. A few of the fantasy-driven offenders did try to meet minors, but the evidence suggested that they wanted to meet to give gifts (e.g., a new webcam) to facilitate cybersex rather than to have sexual contact. The contact-driven offenders had briefer interactions directed toward meeting in real life. Comparing the two groups, contact-driven offenders were younger, less likely to have ever been married, less likely to be diagnosed with a paraphilia, and less likely to be diagnosed with narcissistic personality disorder.

Axis I psychopathology, as represented in the *Diagnostic and Statistical Manual of Mental Disorders* (4th ed., text rev.; *DSM–IV–TR*; American Psychiatric Association, 2000) classification scheme, was common in Briggs et al.'s (2011) sample. Three quarters of the 51 solicitation offenders were diagnosed with a major mental disorder (most commonly depression), adjustment disorder, or substance abuse disorder. However, this observation is confounded because it is easy to imagine how these clinical problems could be a consequence of online offending, rather than an antecedent and potential cause. Half of the sample was diagnosed with personality disorders under the *DSM* nosology; these are unlikely to be consequences of online offending, because they are based on lifetime functioning, but might still be confounded if the online offending contributed to the diagnosis. The most common personality disorder diagnoses were avoidant and narcissistic personality disorder; antisocial personality disorder was rare, reflecting a typical lack of antisocial or criminal history among online offenders (e.g., Burgess, Carretta, & Burgess, 2012). Most of the offenders had no prior felony history.

Sexually, only 10% of the sample was diagnosed with a paraphilia and none with pedophilia or hebephilia. Recall that many of the minors were depicted as 14 years old, which would fall outside of the typical age range for pedophilia and would be at the upper limit for hebephilia (Blanchard, 2010a, 2010c). Most 14-year-old girls would be showing some signs of pubertal development, on the basis of pediatric data (e.g., Herman-Giddens et al., 1997). Looking at the clinical assessment data, few of the solicitation offenders showed deviant sexual arousal when assessed using phallometric measures (Blanchard, Klassen, Dickey, Kuban, & Blak, 2001; G. T. Harris & Rice, 1996; Seto, 2001). Only two offenders possessed child pornography when arrested, and in one of these cases the offender had nude photographs of a teen he had sex with.

In contrast to the paraphilia data, a substantial number of the solicitation offenders engaged in other kinds of problematic or risky sexual behavior. They reported masturbating five times a week on average (which is not unusual in itself, but the range extended to 21 times per week), half had sexually solicited adults online as well, half had had one-night stands with an adult they met online, and 20% had paid for sex with a prostitute.

Briggs et al. (2011) suggested that the behavior of solicitation offenders might be explained as a result of social isolation and dysphoric mood, leading to a variety of online sexual behaviors. Issues for future research include examining the extent to which social isolation and dysphoric mood might be causal factors rather than correlates of personality traits, and looking at other individual differences of those who are predisposed to engage in online solicitations. A popular idea about sexual offending that has not received a lot of empirical attention is that low mood leads to sexual acting out as a form of coping (Cortoni & Marshall, 2001).

The distinction between fantasy-driven and contact-driven solicitation is intuitively appealing, but the prevalence of these types is unclear and likely to be greatly affected by how the sample is identified. For example, it may be the case that the majority of solicitation offenders are fantasy-driven, but contact-driven offenders are more likely to be reported and arrested by police and thus are more highly represented in clinical or correctional samples. If the Briggs et al. (2011) distinction is supported in further work, issues for future research include the developmental paths to fantasy-driven and contact-driven offenders, their risk to reoffend, and intervention needs.

Another interesting question is the extent to which solicitation offenders are similar to, or different from, child pornography offenders. Merdian, Curtis, Thakker, Wilson, and Boer (2011) made a distinction between fantasy-driven and contact-driven child pornography offending: Fantasy-driven offenders seek out child pornography to fuel their sexual fantasies and masturbation, whereas contact-driven offenders are involved with child pornography as part of their contact offending, either as a souvenir of offenses they have committed or to use for grooming of potential victims (I discussed the topic of grooming in an earlier section). I review this limited research literature later in this chapter.

Do fantasy-driven solicitation offenders differ from contact-driven offenders in risk to reoffend? Fantasy-driven offenders might pose a higher risk of future solicitations—for example, to the extent that their behavior is driven by sexual compulsivity—whereas contact-driven offenders might be at higher risk of future contact offending to the extent that their behavior is driven by motivation to have sex with minors. If this hypothesis is correct, then contact-driven offenders would be a higher priority for law enforcement, whereas fantasy-driven offenders might be more responsive to situational crime prevention efforts that seek to harden the online environment and decrease the likelihood of opportunistic criminal behavior (Smallbone, Marshall, & Wortley, 2008; Wortley & Smallbone, 2006). An example of situational crime prevention in this context would be to require identity authentication for social networking sites. This would prevent adults from pretending to be minors in the social network and would allow the service provider to monitor interactions between known adults and known minors on its network (if permitted under the terms of service). The same requirement writ more widely would also have an impact on child pornography offending. Whether this solution would be palatable speaks to the tension between Internet and sociocultural values of freedom, privacy, and anonymity and those of security and safety (see Morozov, 2011).

This is not to suggest that fantasy-driven behavior might not be distressing or obnoxious to the minors who are contacted, but I argue it is a necessarily lower priority than attempted or completed sexual contacts with minors. It is notable that an increasing proportion of online offenses involve proactive investigations by police (Wolak, 2011). Is this truly proactive in the sense of identifying and arresting offenders before real victimizations or escalation occurs, or is it an example of finding crime when you look for it? And for many of the naive or foolish offenders, are investigators picking low-hanging fruit?

COMPARING CHILD PORNOGRAPHY AND SOLICITATION OFFENDERS

Comparing child pornography and solicitation offenders to see how similar or different they are, and in which domains, would add to our knowledge about etiology, risk assessment, and intervention. If child pornography and solicitation offenders are quite similar in important domains, a single model might suffice. But if they are quite different—for example, if child pornography offenders are much more likely to be pedophilic or hebephilic than solicitation offenders, and the latter group is more likely to engage in a range of antisocial and criminal behavior—then their clinical and risk management needs would differ in these regards.

In what appears to be the first peer-reviewed comparison study of online offender types, Alexy et al. (2005) coded data from publicly available news stories to compare 133 *traders* (child pornography offenders) with 49 *travelers* (solicitation offenders) and 43 dual (both child pornography and solicitation) offenders. The only variables this team examined were gender, age, occupation, and geographic region. Though this is not a particularly informative study, I include it to illustrate how recent much of the research in this area is. Of more interest psychologically, Krueger, Kaplan, and First (2009) compared 22 solicitation offenders and 38 child pornography only offenders on the prevalence of psychiatric diagnoses. The two groups were relatively small, so it is not surprising that there were no significant differences in the prevalence of paraphilia diagnoses, anxiety or mood disorder diagnoses, or substance abuse disorders. Krueger and Kaplan were particularly interested in the diagnostic relevance of *hypersexuality*, which they defined as excessive sexual preoccupation and/or drive. As one might expect given the nature of their offenses, solicitation offenders were more likely to be identified as having a hypersexuality disorder involving cybersex dependence, whereas child pornography only offenders were more likely to be identified as having a hypersexuality disorder involving pornography dependence.[3]

In a recent comparison study, we compared 70 solicitation offenders with 38 child pornography offenders and 38 contact sexual offenders on demographic characteristics, self-reported and clinician-rated sexual deviance, putative dynamic risk factors as assessed by the Stable–2007 (Hanson, Harris, Scott, & Helmus, 2007), and long-term risk to reoffend (as established for contact offenders) using the Static–99 (A. J. R. Harris, Phenix, Hanson, & Thornton, 2003; Seto, Wood, Babchishin, & Flynn, 2012). Though the Stable–2007 and Static–99 have not yet been validated as risk measures among online offenders, there is some initial research to suggest that these risk factors will also have predictive validity for online offenders (see Chapter 7 for elaboration).

The Stable–2007 consists of 13 dynamic risk items rated on a 3-point scale, with 0 indicating no problem, 1 indicating some concern, and 2 indicating a definite problem. There was sufficient information to rate the following domains: sex drive/preoccupation, deviant sexual preferences, cooperation

---

[3]Hypersexuality is not recognized as a paraphilia disorder in *DSM–IV–TR* (American Psychiatric Association, 2000), but it is being considered for *DSM–5*; one of the authors of this study of online offenders, Richard Krueger, is on the *DSM–5* paraphilias working group (dsm5.org).

with supervision, capacity for relationship stability, and emotional identification with children. Each of these domains has been found to predict sexual recidivism among contact sex offenders (Hanson et al., 2007). The Static–99 is an actuarial measure of long-term risk to violently or sexually reoffend (A. J. R. Harris et al., 2003). It consists of 10 mostly historical variables capturing criminal history and victim selection. Because according to our study-selection criteria, child pornography offenders could not have any contact victims, we created a modified version of this measure by omitting the three victim-related items. The solicitation offenders could still be compared with the contact offenders on the full set of Static–99 items because the scoring manual indicates these items can be rated according to the intended victim of a solicitation offense, even if the putative minor was actually an undercover police officer.

Focusing on the two online offender groups, solicitation offenders appeared to be similar or lower on the dynamic and long-term risk measures than child pornography offenders, with fewer solicitation offenders disclosing undetected contact offenses when interviewed during a polygraph examination and fewer admitting pedophilia or hebephilia. This group also had lower scores on the Stable–2007 items pertaining to sex drive/preoccupation or deviant sexual preferences. Solicitation offenders did not differ from child pornography offenders in prior nonsexual criminal history, dynamic risk factors pertaining to antisociality (e.g., poor cooperation with supervision, substance use problems), or the modified Static–99. Child pornography offenders were more likely to be sexually deviant than were solicitation offenders.

Babchishin, Hanson, and Montgomery (2012, as cited in Babchishin, 2012) conducted a meta-analysis of a small set of studies that compared online child pornography and solicitation offenders, including the study I just described. Across studies, solicitation offenders were younger, less likely to have ever been married, less likely to be unemployed, and less likely to have substance use problems. Solicitation offenders were less likely to be paraphilic but more likely to have sexual self-regulation problems. There was no group difference in overall criminal history, but solicitation offenders were more likely to have prior sexual offenses. It was notable that solicitation offenders tended to have fewer violent offenses. In sum, solicitation offenders tended to be lower on dynamic and long-term risk factors than child pornography offenders in our study. The relevance of these putative risk factors—particularly antisociality and sexual deviance—is discussed later, including their relevance for explanatory models (Chapter 4), understanding the overlap between online and offline offending (Chapter 6), assessment of risk of recidivism (Chapter 7), and intervention (Chapter 8).

OVERLAP WITH CHILD PORNOGRAPHY OFFENDING

In the Seto et al. (2012) study, we purposefully selected online offenders with no overlap in criminal sexual behavior; that is, we selected child pornography offenders who had no known contact sexual offenses and contact offenders who had no known child pornography charges. The reality, of course, is that there is overlap across groups that are defined by criminal behavior. Some individuals will have committed child pornography and solicitation offenses, as well as real-world offenses (potentially both contact offenses and noncontact offenses such as exhibitionism or voyeurism) or some combinations thereof. Moreover, these prior offenses may be officially undetected, and the individuals may deny them when interviewed clinically. An important conceptual issue is the extent to which these different groups of offenders actually represent different populations. A related and important empirical issue is the extent to which these different forms of criminal behavior overlap.

As I discuss again in Chapter 6, a recent meta-analysis found that approximately one in eight online offenders (most of them in trouble for child pornography) has an official criminal record for contact sexual offending at the time of their conviction (Seto, Hanson, & Babchishin, 2011). What is the extent of overlap between online child pornography and solicitation offending? Some solicitation offenders possess child pornography and send it to minors they are in sexual communication with, and others produce child pornography by taking photographs or videos of minors they had sexual contact with or encourage production by asking minors to send sexually explicit images of themselves.

There is some empirical evidence on the overlap in different forms of online offending. Malesky (2007) surveyed 101 men convicted of sexual Internet crimes, most for child pornography offenses. Approximately a third of these men (35) communicated with a minor whom they met online in the hope of establishing a sexual relationship. Eighteen men attempted to set up a face-to-face meeting. Krueger et al. (2009) reported that 20 of their 22 solicitation offenders (out of a total sample of 60 online offenders identified in a retrospective chart review of cases seen between 2000 and 2004) also possessed child pornography. In the first NJOV Survey, almost 40% of offenders arrested for solicitation also possessed child pornography; this proportion went down to 21% in the second NJOV Survey (Wolak, Finkelhor, & Mitchell, 2009). As I discussed in Chapter 2, this change from the first to second waves is likely due to more proactive police investigations capturing possession-only child pornography offenders. Indeed, one of the biggest differences between the first and second wave was the role of proactive investigations: There was only a small increase in solicitation cases involving real minors but over a tripling of cases involving undercover police officers.

It is important to recognize here that the overlap that has been reported in different studies is not necessarily representative of the "true" overlap between child pornography, solicitation, and contact offending. Many different factors can influence the proportions that are identified. For example, studies of criminal justice samples would be affected by police policies to prioritize cases that involve online solicitation or contact offending, resulting in a higher proportion than if police randomly pursued cases. As another example, studies of contact offenders conducted in the past decade have tended not to report whether the contact offenders had also committed online offenses, possibly because the contact offenses are seen as the central issue in criminal justice and clinical decisions. Though sentence lengths for child pornography and contact sexual offending are comparable at the federal level in the United States (Wollert, Waggoner, & Smith, 2012), contact offenders still receive more severe sentences than online-only offenders at the state level. This is definitely the case in Canada, where most child pornography offenders receive sentences of less than 2 years, relegating them to provincial correctional systems, whereas many contact offenders receive sentences of 2 or more years, which relegates them to the federal correctional system (see Jung & Stein, 2012).

Returning to Wolak et al. (2009), approximately equal percentages of those who approached real minors and those who approached undercover police officers had contact offense histories. One might expect that fantasy-driven offenders would be less likely to have contact offending histories than contact-driven offenders. Briggs et al. (2011) did not find a significant difference between these two groups, but their base rate for prior conviction was low, and thus they had low power to detect any such difference, given their small overall sample size.

SUMMARY

There is some overlap between online child pornography and online solicitation offending, but online offenders are not generalists. Some individuals restrict their online offending to child pornography crimes; others restrict it to sexual interactions such as sexual chat or exchange of pornographic images with minors online, and others attempt to meet minors in real life using online communication tools. These different groups appear to differ in their motivations for offending and on other characteristics as well, according to the comparative data reported so far (Krueger et al., 2009; Seto et al., 2012; Wolak et al., 2009). Only some of these individuals have committed contact sexual offenses (see Chapter 6).

Of particular salience for explanations of online offending are the motivations for online offending. Neither child pornography nor solicitation offenders have much criminal history or other evidence of antisocial tendencies such as unstable education and employment histories, substance misuse, or early conduct problems at home or at school (see Chapter 5). Though child pornography and solicitation laws refer to minors under the age of 18, the majority of detected child pornography offenders tend to be involved with images of prepubescent or pubescent children, suggestive of pedophilia or hebephilia, whereas solicitation offenders tend to focus on young adolescents between the ages of 13 and 15; Wolak, Finkelhor, Mitchell, and Ybarra (2008) identified no solicitation cases involving attempted or actual contacts with real children under age 12. This does not mean solicitation offenders do not contact children under the age of 12, but any such contacts that do take place do not lead to identification and arrest.

There are two caveats in interpreting the existing research. Both have to do with possible selection biases in the samples that have been studied. First, child pornography users who are not pedophilic or hebephilic but instead are interested in depictions of sexually maturing or mature adolescents under age 18 are less likely to end up in clinical or forensic samples because they are less likely to be successfully prosecuted, given the difficulties in accurately estimating age among older teens (e.g., Stathopulu, Huse, & Canning, 2003). An illustration is the case of Traci Lords, who first (illegally) appeared in pornographic films when she was 16 years old, using fake government identification. Film producers and viewers were not aware she was a legal minor until her true age was revealed 20 months later (en.wikipedia.org/wiki/Traci_Lords).

It is not always easy to determine if someone is a minor. It is this ambiguity that may drive some of the popularity of the "barely legal" genre in mainstream pornography, where young, petite actresses can convincingly appear to be minors, especially when dressed in school or cheerleader uniforms. It is unambiguous, however, when someone possesses sexual images of prepubescent or pubescent children, and this contributes to the high conviction rates that are obtained for child pornography prosecutions (Motivans & Kyckelhahn, 2007).

The second caveat is that some individuals might well be interested in soliciting children younger than adolescents between the ages of 12 and 15 but are unable to do so because few younger children are online and unsupervised by an adult. Parents may be more likely to intervene when there is suspicious online activity involving their younger children; teens, however, may successfully hide their online interactions from their parents, just as they hide some of their real-world friendships and experiences. Younger children are also less able or willing to participate in sexual chat and are unlikely to be in the position to meet in the real world, making them less appealing to those who are using online technologies to solicit children. This appears to be changing over time, however. In a recent survey of research conducted in the United Kingdom, the Council on Child Internet Safety found data indicating a quarter of 8- to 11-year-olds were using social networking sites such as Facebook, despite age restrictions in the terms of service (Spielhofer, 2010). (Facebook requires its members to be 13 or older, but it is easy to circumvent this restriction by lying, because there is no objective age verification.)

It is therefore conceivable that there is a smaller difference in the sexual motivations found among child pornography and solicitation offenders than has been observed in studies so far. The apparent group difference might be partially a result of selection (child pornography users who are primarily sexually interested in adolescents are less likely to be prosecuted) and access (solicitation offenders who are primarily sexually interested in prepubescent children have fewer opportunities). Consistent with this idea, Mitchell et al. (2005) found a difference in the distributions of ages for actual minors involved in solicitation cases compared with the depicted ages of minors in undercover police stings (e.g., posing as a parent offering sexual access to a 9-year-old). My opinion is that—despite all these caveats and limitations—there are still meaningful differences between child pornography and solicitation offenders overall.

MYTHS AND REALITIES

In a prominent *American Psychologist* review, Wolak, Finkelhor, Mitchell, and Ybarra (2008) summarized their research program on online solicitation offenders, drawing from multiple waves of the NJOV Study and the Youth Internet Safety Survey. They illustrated their empirical findings by contrasting them to myths (unfounded assumptions) about online "predators" that seem to be driving laws and policies about this social problem. Wolak, Finkelhor, Mitchell, and Ybarra (2008) identified the following major assumptions: (a) Young children or naive minors are at great risk of harm from "online predators," (b) children and youths are naive about revealing their personal information and thereby protecting their online privacy and security from these predatory adults, (c) men are pretending to be similar-aged peers when they approach unknown children online, (d) adult perpetrators are lying to youths about their sexual intentions and intentionally engaging in grooming tactics, and (e) children who reveal personal information or go to see a stranger they met online are at risk of sexual assault or abduction.

But what does the research evidence indicate? The following sections draw heavily from Wolak, Finkelhor, Mitchell, and Ybarra (2008) because the Crimes Against Children Research Center has the most comprehensive

American data on solicitation offending. Wolak, Finkelhor, Mitchell, and Ybarra's (2008) data set is distinguished from the other studies cited in this section because they focused on cases where real-life meetings with real minors did take place, as opposed to cases where adults interacted with undercover police officers or pursued online-only interactions.

Stranger Danger

Wolak, Finkelhor, Mitchell, and Ybarra (2008) reported that their surveys suggested approximately one in seven youths has been sexually solicited online. However, most solicitations were from peers and likely involved someone the youth already knew (e.g., someone from the same school or the friend of a friend). This is not to suggest peer-to-peer solicitations cannot be coercive or aggressive, but they are less likely to be threatening than solicitations from adult strangers. A small proportion of youths have been sexually solicited by an adult, and in some of those cases the solicitation was from an adult the adolescent already knew in real life. It is the case, though, from the descriptive studies reviewed earlier in this chapter, that most solicitations by adults involve strangers met online (e.g., Grosskopf, 2009; Lamb, 1998; Martellozzo, 2010).

Lying About Age

Of the identified cases involving adult offenders, only 5% of those charged with solicitation offenses pretended to be a teenager themselves; a minority did pretend to be younger than they actually were, but they still admitted being an adult (Wolak, Finkelhor, Mitchell, & Ybarra, 2008). Though the descriptive studies do not specifically mention any deception, the impression is that the researchers, posing as minors, were aware they were being contacted by adult personas.

Grooming

In general, the offenders did not lie about their sexual intentions, though they might have exaggerated or lied about their interest in long-term romance or lied about their physical appearance or social or relationship status (as is true as well for other online interactions). Youths who agreed to real-life meetings knew they were meeting to engage in sexual activity, and the majority of youths who met the adults (73%) had repeat encounters. Consistent with this idea that the sexual intent of the adults is not hidden are the observations reported by Lamb (1998) and others that the interactions were obviously sexual at an early stage. An opposing view was presented by O'Connell (2003), who suggested that grooming took place over time. Wolak, Finkelhor, Mitchell, and Ybarra's (2008) finding that most adults did not lie about their sexual intentions does not mean that there was no manipulation, because adolescents could be misled about romantic intentions.

Risk of Assault or Abduction

Wolak, Finkelhor, Mitchell, and Ybarra (2008) found that solicitation cases rarely involved violence: 5% of solicitation cases identified in their research involved use of threats or force. Abduction was rare, though one quarter of the solicitation cases started as missing-person reports because the youth ran away with the offender or lied to parents about his or her whereabouts (Wolak, Finkelhor, Mitchell, and Ybarra, 2008). I expect that cases involving threat, force, or abduction are more likely to be reported to police, so there is less selection bias for these kinds of cases. This would not be the case for online-only interactions that may annoy or distress minors; most are unreported to police, as is evident from the gap between the number of youths who have been sexually solicited by an adult online and the number of reports made to police or tip lines.

Young or Naive Children

In the solicitation cases involving real minors examined by Wolak, Finkelhor, Mitchell, and Ybarra (2008), no minor was younger than 12, half were 13 or 14 years old, and the modal age of the minors was 15. This is not consistent with suggestions that solicitation offenders are pedophiles or hebephiles who sexually prefer physically immature children and seek them out online. Some of the young adolescents may have been prepubescent or pubescent in appearance, but most of the minors were sexually developing or developed. My hunch would be that the typical adolescent involved in solicitation cases appeared older than their chronological age, on the speculation that physically precocious adolescents are more likely to be responsive and/or targeted for adult solicitations online. This is in keeping with much research showing that adolescents who begin puberty earlier are more likely to engage in a wide range of risky sexual behaviors (e.g., Deardorff, Gonzales, Christopher, Roosa, & Millsap, 2005).

Youths may not be as naive as some adults would think (or would prefer to think). They are savvy about online contacts from unknown individuals (Mitchell, Finkelhor, & Wolak, 2007) and take precautions regarding their privacy (Hinduja & Patchin, 2008). At the same time, age restrictions for online networking sites are easy to circumvent (Hinduja & Patchin, 2008), and youths who are careful about their privacy can still inadvertently reveal sensitive information (Mishna, McLuckie, & Saini 2009). As reported in Appendix 3.3, multiple Internet safety surveys suggest that most youths are careful about revealing personal information online. Youths do engage in risky online behaviors, but only a small minority would be considered at risk of sexual solicitation by engaging in multiple such behaviors.

STATUTORY SEXUAL OFFENDING

The research I have described so far has suggested that online solicitation cases involving attempts or contacts with real minors have more in common with prototypical statutory sexual crimes than they do with prototypical contact sexual offenses involving children or younger adolescents.[4] Statutory sexual crimes involve cases when an adult has sex with a willing minor below the legally defined age of consent, currently 16 in Canada and ranging from 14 to 18 in the United States (modal age = 16). Statutory sexual crimes accounted for approximately a quarter of all sexual crimes involving minors in the United States in 2000 (Troup-Leasure & Snyder, 2005). Wolak, Finkelhor, Mitchell, and Ybarra (2008) estimated that online solicitation cases account for approximately 7% of statutory sexual crimes reported to law enforcement, according to data obtained in 2000. The proportion may have grown since then, in parallel with increased Internet availability and online activity. In the rest of this chapter, I discuss the literature on statutory sexual offending because I believe it can inform our understanding of online sexual solicitation.

Many of these sexual relationships are not reported to law enforcement, in part because many minors do not see themselves as crime victims, though they may be aware that their sexual relationship with an adult was illegal. This is an important selection effect in the study by Wolak, Finkelhor, Mitchell, and Ybarra (2008) because cases that were not detected by parents or other responsible adults would probably not be reported to police unless the adolescent was unhappy about his or her involvement. Solicitation cases that are reported to authorities typically involve young adolescents and much older adults, after discovery by a parent or other responsible adult. Consistent with this idea, in the Crimes Against Children Research Center research (Wolak, Finkelhor, & Mitchell, 2004), solicitation offenders were typically 10 or more years older than the minors they approached.

As mentioned earlier, the self-reported prevalence of online solicitations relative to the number of law enforcement cases clearly illustrates that

---

[4]This is not my original idea, as this resemblance of online solicitation of real minors and statutory sexual offending was suggested by Wolak, Finkelhor, Mitchell, and Ybarra (2008).

many online solicitation cases involving adult contacts with real minors go unreported. Many sexual solicitations are either ignored by minors, or if there is legal involvement, the minor does not see himself or herself as the victim of a crime. This highlights the reality that legal responses to online solicitation, though necessary, will not be a sufficient response to this phenomenon. Even with greater reporting of incidents to police, many cases will remain undetected. Given these facts, public education and prevention efforts are more likely to pay off in terms of reducing the risk of sexual exploitation of minors.

The same is likely true for statutory sexual offenses. Only those cases where the adolescent sees himself or herself as a victim of crime, or a parent or another responsible adult becomes aware of the sexual contacts and acts accordingly, will be reported to police. Estimates of the prevalence of statutory sexual offending (see the next section) far exceed official investigation numbers. As life in general, and sexual behavior in particular, involves more online technology, I expect the incidence and prevalence of online sexual solicitations of minors to approach the rates of adult–minor interactions that fall under the rubric of statutory sexual offending.

PREVALENCE OF STATUTORY SEXUAL OFFENSES

This leads to the next question: What is the prevalence of statutory sexual offenses? Hines and Finkelhor (2007) reviewed the statutory sexual offending literature. The Vermont Youth Risk Behavior Survey found that 1% of girls ages 11 and 12 and 4% of girls ages 13 to 15 reported voluntarily having sex with a male who was 5 or more years older (Leitenberg & Saltzman, 2000). A national study found that a little over 1% of girl respondents had sex for the first time before the age of 14 with someone who was 6 or more years older (Abma, Martinez, Mosher, & Dawson, 2004). Manlove, Moore, Liechty, Ikramullah, and Cottingham (2005), in the National Survey of Family Growth in 2002, found that 13% of adolescent girls had a sexual experience with an adult male who was 3 or more years older. The typical age difference was 3 or 4 years. Eighty percent of the sexual experiences were described as voluntary, which suggests that the remaining 20% were experienced as coerced in some way.

In an analysis of data from the National Incident-Based Reporting System (NIBRS), drawn from 21 states between 1996 and 2000, Troup-Leasure and Snyder (2005) found there was one statutory rape (the legal term for statutory sexual offenses) for every three forcible rapes reported to police in 2000. Extrapolating from these NIBRS data, Troup-Leasure and Snyder estimated there were approximately 15,700 statutory rape cases reported to law enforcement agencies in the United States in 2000. To repeat this point, the number of reported cases is clearly smaller than the number of cases reported by minors in self-report surveys.

The 2005 American Community Survey (part of the U.S. Census data set from http://factfinder2.census.gov/faces/nav/jsf/pages/wc_acs.xhtml) estimated that there are 141,274,964 females in the United States. Approximately 8% were girls between the ages of 10 and 14, resulting in an estimated 11 million girls in this age category. Extrapolating from the estimate of the Youth Risk Behavior Survey that 1% of girls are aged 11 to 12, approximately 110,000 girls (and 4% of older girls, which would be more in line with the age ranges of girls in the NJOV Study's solicitation cases) would have had sexual experience with a man, a number that is clearly smaller than the NIBRS estimate of reported cases in 2000. In other words, this suggests that approximately 15% of statutory sexual contacts are reported to police. Offline encounters are less visible than online encounters, because there is no digital record of antecedent contacts. It is not unreasonable, then, to extrapolate that a large majority of online solicitations leading to sexual interactions are not reported to police. The number of statutory offenses may increase because the average age of onset of puberty has steadily declined over the past century, over the same time period that the legal age of consent has gone up (from 14 to 16 in Canada in 2008). This increases the window when an adolescent is physically mature enough to be sexually attractive to nonparaphilic adult men yet is below the legally mandated age of consent.

CHARACTERISTICS OF STATUTORY INCIDENTS

In their analysis, Troup-Leasure and Snyder (2005) found that 95% of the statutory incidents they examined involved female minors, and almost all of these incidents involved older males as perpetrators. The perpetrators were adults in the majority (82%) of cases. The majority of female adolescents were 14 or 15 years old, and the median age difference was 6 years, so the male was typically a young adult. The younger the girl, the more likely it was that the male was also a minor. It was rare for statutory sexual offenses to involve strangers: 29% of offenders were considered boyfriends or girlfriends of the minors, and another 62% were considered friends or acquaintances. Arrests occurred in less than half (42%) of the incidents, though this arrest rate was slightly higher than for forcible rape (35%). Arrests were less likely if the older person was the minor's boyfriend or girlfriend.

Research indicates that female youth predictors of entering a statutory sexual relationship include general risk taking, juvenile delinquency, and a history of sexual abuse (Darroch, Landry, & Oslak, 1999; Elo, King, & Furstenberg, 1999; Flanigan, 2003; Manlove et al., 2005). Early intercourse experience with a much older sexual partner seems to be part of a troubled developmental trajectory, with psychosocial problems both preceding and following the sexual involvement (Bingham & Crockett, 1996).

The NIBRS data also indicated that male adolescents were involved in 5% of cases; in these cases, 94% of the older persons were female, suggesting that most statutory offenses, whether the youth was male or female, involved heterosexual participants. The median age difference for male adolescents was 9 years, which is larger than the median age difference for female adolescents. Retrospective surveys have also found that 5% of men report having a voluntary sexual relationship with an adult woman when he was an adolescent (Condy, Templer, Brown, & Veaco, 1987; Fromuth & Burkhart, 1987; Manlove et al., 2005). The majority of these relationships were viewed as casual, involved multiple sexual contacts, and were described as wanted by the males, at least at the time. Youth risk factors were similar to those for adolescent girls, including being younger and coming from disadvantaged family backgrounds.

SAME-SEX STATUTORY RELATIONSHIPS

Little is known about same-sex statutory relationships; as described in the previous section, most cases involve opposite-sex dyads. Van Naerssen (1991) described different types of relationships between boys and adult men. The least studied are relationships involving adolescent girls and adult women. Kilpatrick (1986) surveyed a stratified female sample and found that approximately 1% had a masturbation experience before the age of 15 with an unrelated woman. Voluntary and nonvoluntary experiences were not distinguished.

WHAT ARE THE EFFECTS

What are the effects of these statutorily prohibited sexual relationships? The minors often view interactions as wanted and voluntary and do not report ill effects afterward. However, there may be cognitive dissonance, recall bias, and selection effects that influence who reports past experiences and what they report in surveys. Statutory sexual relationships are of social concern even if the youth does not object, because of the risk of youth exploitation (especially if they are already vulnerable) and the personal and social costs of unwanted teenage pregnancies, sexually transmitted diseases, and subsequent sexual exploitation. Wolak, Finkelhor, Mitchell, and Ybarra (2008) also noted that sexual relationships between young adolescents and much older persons place them at risk of exploitation, and young adolescents who engage in early sexual activity are at higher risk of teenage pregnancy, sexual coercion, and other problematic outcomes. Longitudinal and prospective follow-up studies of youths involved in sexual relationships with adults are needed to better understand the effects of statutory sexual offenses.

Independent of harm, is the prohibition of sexual relationships involving adults and youths below a legally determined age justified? One can apply the analogy of age prohibitions regarding use of alcohol. Some youths may indeed be able to consume alcohol safely before they reach the legally defined age, but it is impractical to have a test-based law for access to alcohol, compared with a blanket prohibition against youths below the legal drinking age being able to purchase alcohol. Similarly, though it is a controversial idea, some youths may be able to meaningfully consent to a sexual relationship with an older partner and might even benefit from such contact. This is an empirical question, obscured in a moral and socio-cultural fog. But whatever the answer to this question, it is impractical to have a test-based law for age of consent for sex, and thus there is logic to blanket prohibitions of statutory sexual relationships. Adolescents are less experienced than the adults and are still in the flux of their cognitive and emotional development and therefore are less able to make informed decisions about sex.

CONCLUSION

It is a conundrum why solicitation offenders continue to set up meetings and seek real-world contacts when there has been so much media attention about this phenomenon and the negative consequences involved. Though the individual risk is low—as the ratio of number of solicitations to number of arrests suggest—the consequences are severe if one is detected. (The same question could be asked of child pornography offenders.) A third of the 51 solicitation offenders in Briggs et al. (2011) wondered if the minor they were interacting with was actually an undercover police officer, indicating they were aware of the risks involved, yet they still attempted to meet after receiving some reassurance from the officer. Is part of the allure of solicitation the riskiness itself, as seems to be true for other risky sexual behavior such as *bare-backing* (having sex without using a condom), participating in online casual sex sites, and purposefully seeking sex with someone who is HIV positive? Are these solicitation offenders naive, like child pornography offenders who take no technical precautions to protect their identity and security, never believing they might get caught? Or is the compulsion to engage in this online sexual activity strong enough to overcome one's caution?

Some offenders do attempt to protect themselves while online—for example, by speaking on the phone to try and verify that they are speaking to a real minor (Grosskopf, 2009) or by pursuing webcam exchanges where they can see the person with whom they are interacting online. One of the reasons some solicitation offenders may so urgently press for the minor to send them a photograph or to initiate sexual chat may be to get evidence that they are interacting with a minor. Though an adult could easily send a photograph of a minor as a ruse or engage in realistic sexual chat using teen jargon, solicitation offenders may believe that such acts would support an entrapment defense if they were to be prosecuted. A wily solicitation offender would avoid any incriminating communications until receiving sufficient reassurance, suggesting that police efforts are more likely to catch those who are less apt.

The available evidence on solicitation offenders suggests that the Internet has facilitated sexual offending that previously occurred without technological involvement: meeting and grooming young adolescents for sexual contact, as in statutory and contact-driven solicitation offenses. But Internet technologies may also have created a new type of offender, in the form of fantasy-driven solicitation offenders (see Seto & Hanson, 2011). Some of these individuals might have engaged in obscene telephone calling before the Internet age, hoping they might happen upon a minor, but the odds of a successful search were low both in terms of speaking with an actual minor and engaging them for more than a few moments of talk before the minor hung up (see Appendix 3.4). With call tracing, there was also the risk of detection, unless the caller was using a telephone that could not be traced back to him. I suspect that most fantasy-driven offenders would never approach an actual youth to engage in sexually explicit chat in real life, given the potential consequences.

FUTURE DIRECTIONS

There is undoubtedly a selection bias in solicitation research because only cases known to police are studied and only some cases are reported to police. Therefore, cases are likely to involve undercover police stings, with the rest involving cases where minors (or parents) reported to police (Mitchell et al., 2005; see Appendix 3.5). One can assume that reports are more likely when the minor is young and the parents are thus upset by the discovery that their child is involved with a much older adult, when real-world contacts take place, or when the relationship goes badly and the minor becomes upset (e.g., after a breakup). We know little about solicitations that are not reported to police, whether restricted to online behavior only or involving real-life contacts that end amicably. An important avenue for further research is the role of Internet technologies in solicitations of adults for meetings that result in sexual coercion or assaults. It would also be worthwhile to study the phenomenon of fantasy-driven solicitations of adults that annoy or upset the recipients and the phenomenon of exhibitionistic behavior in a nonconsenting forum (i.e., excluding online solicitations or cybersex that is mutually consenting).

APPENDIX 3.1
ONLINE CONTACTS LEADING TO SEXUAL
OFFENSES AGAINST ADULTS

I have mentioned already that I am not aware of any empirical research on the roles that the Internet and related communication technologies have played in sexual offenses involving adult victims. The focus, so far, of legal and public policy discussions has been on sexual offenses involving minors. There have been media stories, however, about cases of sexual assaults that began from contacts initiated on Craigslist or other services, including classified ads, social networking sites, and dating sites. The following links to media stories were all active as this book goes to press. I have included brief descriptions of how the Internet played a role in these cases of sexual assault, rape, and sexual homicide. The details are sometimes bizarre, in keeping with the media tendency to focus on sensational cases.

- This story describes a homicide suspect who used Craigslist to target women advertising erotic massages. He allegedly attempted to rob one masseuse, and when she fought back, he struck her and then shot her through the heart: http://msnbc.msn.com/id/30314735
- A man arranged the rape of his ex-girlfriend by posting an online classified ad with her photograph, claiming she had rape fantasies and providing sufficient details so she could be found. A week later, a man responded to the ad, breaking into her home, tying her up, and raping her at knife-point under the purported belief he was fulfilling her sexual fantasies: articles.latimes.com/2010/jan/11/nation/la-na-rape-craigslist11-2010jan11
- This story describes a man convicted of multiple incidents of rapes of women advertising "erotic services" online. As a result of this case and other cases involving prostitutes, Craigslist stopped posting erotic service classified ads: msnbc.msn.com/id/30875839/
- In this case, a man was arrested after sexually assaulting his unconscious girlfriend and then posting a live video of it online: transworldnews.com/NewsStory.aspx?id=91849&cat=14

There are an unknown but large number of other online sexual crime victims, in particular victims of *voyeurism* (using surreptitious photographs or videos taken in public places or videos from webcams in bathrooms or bedrooms), whose images are then posted online. There are many amateur sites carrying voyeuristic images (*upskirt* and *peeping* are typical keywords for this content), in addition to professional sites that have produced seemingly "real" voyeuristic content. Putting aside commercially produced voyeuristic pornography, the women and teenage girls who are featured in voyeur images have little recourse. They can get a cease-and-desist order to have the images removed from a particular website, but that does not eliminate the copies that may have been made, and it comes at the cost of identifying oneself in legal documents.

Because of the dearth of research on online sexual offending against adults, we have no idea of prevalence or characteristics of the offenders, victims, or crimes. At the time this section was first drafted (December 2011), there were news items about a potential serial killer operating on Long Island, targeting commercial sex workers who were advertising online. How many sex workers are advertising online? How many have been sexually assaulted by customers who contacted them online, and does this differ from the base rate for sex workers operating in more traditional venues such as brothels or on the street?

Online advertising services have had to respond to the problem of sexual offending. Craigslist no longer carries erotic service classifieds, and Backpage.com is taking increasing criticism for carrying these kinds of advertisements. In April 2011, an online dating service (Match.com) began screening users against sex offender registries following the case of a woman who was sexually assaulted after meeting a man who had contacted her on the site. Subsequent investigation determined that he was a registered sex offender.

It is clear even from this brief list of anecdotes that the Internet is now part of the overall sexual offending landscape for finding victims, blackmailing victims to gain compliance or silence (e.g., using sexually explicit or compromising photographs that were sent as part of online interactions), or as evidence in prosecuting cases (digital traces of e-mails, texts, and instant messages can be used to corroborate suspect and victim statements).

The legality is unclear to me, but there are also examples of virtual rapes and virtual child molestation in online communities such as Second Life. These incidents may also reflect fantasy-driven behavior (cf. Briggs, Simon, & Simonsen, 2011). Online fantasies are of concern, tied to the availability of online pornography depicting sexual violence and paraphilic content. To what extent is this "harmless" sexual fantasy and to what extent is it influencing attitudes, beliefs, and norms about acting out fantasies and influencing the likelihood such acts will be committed in real life? The following is a link to a story about virtual rape in Second Life: wired.com/culture/lifestyle/commentary/sexdrive/2007/05/sexdrive_0504

In one final sexual offense story, this time involving youths rather than adults, a youth was convicted of tricking male classmates into sending him nude photographs of themselves by posing as a girl on Facebook. He then used the photographs to blackmail the classmates into meeting him (pur-portedly as a friend of the girl they had communicated with online). He then performed fellatio on them and took further photographs using his mobile phone: wired.com/threatlevel/2010/02/teen-gets-15-years-for-sex-extortion/?intcid=inform_relatedContent

APPENDIX 3.2
GROOMING TACTICS

Many online solicitation interactions can be viewed as examples of grooming, wherein adults contact minors and attempt to engage them in sexual interactions online and/or to arrange meetings where sexual activities will take place. Thus, what we know about grooming in real life may shed some light on the processes of online solicitation. Grooming can be defined as the tactics an individual uses to earn the trust of children they approach as potential sexual crime victims. Such tactics are clearly different from overtly coercive or aggressive tactics such as using threat or physical force to gain compliance. Real-world tactics can include positive attention, offering gifts or money, and slowly introducing physical touch—for example, in the context of tickling or play wrestling. An important aspect of grooming, whether offline or online, is that certain children are more likely to be approached: Extra attention is more likely to be an effective tactic with lonely or socially isolated children, for example, and gifts or money are more likely to be effective with children who are living in impoverished circumstances.

Some research on grooming exists, though not as much as one might expect, given the prominent role that grooming plays in discussions of prevention strategies and sex offender treatment. The following review borrows heavily from my previous book because there is little new material on grooming (Seto, 2008; see also Craven, Brown, & Gilchrist, 2006). Lang and Frenzel (1988) studied offenders against girls aged 14 or younger and found that those who offended against related girls differed from those who offended against unrelated girls in several ways: Incest offenders were more likely to commit their sexual offenses in the context of cuddling, playing games, or sneaking into the child's bedroom. This finding—that many sexual offenses against children occur in ordinary day-to-day activities—has been supported in subsequent studies (Wortley & Smallbone, 2006).

Conte, Wolfe, and Smith (1989) interviewed 20 adult male sexual offenders about their crimes. These men reported that they were able to identify vulnerable children and then target these vulnerabilities when committing their crimes. This included children who were particularly friendly and open or, conversely, needy, unhappy, or sad; children living in single-parent homes; and children who had previously been victimized in some way. The majority of these offenders said they had befriended children and established a relationship with them before initiating any sexual contact. Similarly, half of 33 adult male sexual offenders interviewed by Budin and Johnson (1989) reported that they victimized their own children or sought "passive, quiet, troubled, lonely children" (p. 79) from single-parent homes. These offenders thought that child sexual abuse prevention programs could be effective if the programs taught children how to disclose being sexually abused, saying no to adults, learning about acceptable touching, avoiding strangers, and running away if approached by someone they did not know.

In one of the larger and more systematic studies, Kaufman et al. (1998) examined the tactics of 114 adolescent sex offenders and 114 adult sex offenders; half of each group offended against related children, and the other half had offended against unrelated children. Overall, sexual offenders were more likely to use nonviolent tactics than to use threat or force. Adolescents were more likely than their adult counterparts to use pornography or to use threat or force in committing their offenses. Offenders against related children were more likely to use pornography or give gifts, whereas offenders against unrelated children were more likely to provide alcohol or drugs to the child before or during sexual contacts. Other research on the modus operandi of sex offenders also informs our understanding of what might make some children and youths more vulnerable to sexual offenses (Kaufman, Hilliker, & Daleiden, 1996; Kaufman, Hilliker, Lathrop, Daleiden, & Rudy, 1996; Leclerc, Beauregard, & Proulx, 2008; Leclerc, Proulx, Lussier, & Allair, 2009).

There is less research on online grooming. Malesky (2007) gave examples of tactics online solicitation offenders used that were quite similar to those used by contact offenders, including looking for signs of neediness and any hints that the child might be receptive to sexual topics. For example, one of his participants reported, "Neediness is very apparent when a child will do anything to keep talking to you" (p. 27). O'Connell (2003) described how online adults would engage her fictitious child persona in ways to build trust and would back off and apologize if she indicated she was uncomfortable with the introduction of sex, and in this way they attempted to rebuild trust. She also described, however, interactions that were clearly coercive or aggressive.

APPENDIX 3.3
VULNERABLE YOUTHS

Adolescents vary in their susceptibility or responsiveness to online sexual solicitations. Many might ignore or be only amused or bemused by sexual solicitations online, but some will become distressed as a result of messages or other communications from strangers, and a small number may respond by engaging in sexual chat, exchanging sexually suggestive or explicit images or videos, or arranging to meet in the real world. What distinguishes vulnerable youths who will receive or respond to online solicitations from those who will not?[5]

J. Peter and Valkenburg (2006) surveyed 412 teens and found that those who talked to strangers online were younger, had longer chats, and went online to meet people, for entertainment, or because they lacked social skills. Prentky et al. (2010) found that high school students they surveyed who met adults offline were more likely to report engaging in risky online behaviors such as visiting sexual sites, receiving sexual images from someone online, having someone chat with them about sexual topics when they did not want to, and having been sexted (see also Dowdell, Burgess, & Flores, 2011; Lee, Li, Lamade, Schuler, & Prentky, 2012). Using sexually suggestive nicknames and posting sexually suggestive images (e.g., posing in a small bikini or bra and panties) increased the likelihood of sexual solicitations. For example, the offenders interviewed by Malesky (2007) talked about how they preferred any profiles with sexually suggestive content. Girls are more vulnerable than boys, except perhaps boys who are gay or questioning their sexual identities (Wolak, Finkelhor, Mitchell, & Ybarra, 2008). Youths who have a history of sexual abuse are more at risk of becoming involved in sexual interactions with adults online, just as they appear to be for other risky sexual behavior as well (see Koenig, Doll, O'Leary, & Pequegnat, 2004). In fact, the similarities between online and offline vulnerability factors is quite striking, suggesting that youths at risk for real-world sexual solicitations are the same youths who may be more at risk online as well.

Data from the Youth Internet Safety Survey are particularly relevant (Ybarra, Espelage, & Mitchell, 2007). Risky online behaviors identified in this multiple-wave survey, in order of prevalence, included: posting personal information online (56%), interacting with strangers online (43%), having strangers on a buddy or friend list (35%), using the Internet to make rude

---

[5]This question is not intended to be construed as victim blaming. The adults are legally and morally responsible for their actions; nonetheless, it would be naive and empirically untrue to suggest that all youths are equally at risk or that youth behavior is completely unrelated to online interactions, sexual or otherwise. My interest in asking the question is to determine what is known about at-risk youths to better inform education and prevention efforts.

or nasty comments about someone (28%), sending personal information to strangers who were met online (26%), downloading images from file-sharing programs (15%), visiting X-rated sites on purpose (13%), using the Internet to harass people the youth is mad at (9%), and talking online to strangers about sex (5%). Wolak, Finkelhor, and Mitchell (2008) suggested that the least prevalent factors may be the most effective at identifying youths who are at risk for meeting an online stranger in real life. Among Internet users ages 10 to 17, 15% were considered to be high-risk users who communicated online with unknown strangers and who met at least four of the other items on Ybarra et al.'s (2007) risky online behavior checklist. An important next study to undertake is longitudinal research to see whether scores on this youth risk checklist can predict future online solicitations.

Another relevant study on potentially risky online behavior is the Teen Internet Survey by Cox Communication (2007). In a large, geographically representative sample of American teens between the ages of 13 and 17, a majority (71%) of respondents had online profiles, with half of these profiles being fully viewable by the public. Half or more of the teens had posted photos and information about where they attended school. Moreover, these teens said they were not concerned about posting personal information online. At the same time, the teens were increasingly more careful about responding to stranger contacts, with only a third (31%) responding to these kinds of contacts. Forty-one percent said their parents had discussed Internet safety "a lot" with them. Teens whose parents had talked with them were more careful with personal information and were less likely to respond to stranger contacts. Parent knowledge and supervision about online technologies usually lags that of their children nowadays, making it more difficult for parents to monitor and supervise online activity. This may become less of a concern as the current Internet generation grows older and has children of their own, though they may well be baffled by some of the future technologies that will be adopted by those children. Information on safety behavior is critical for education and prevention efforts. The focus so far has been on the frequency of solicitation and risky online behaviors. More research is also needed to address the related questions of how youths respond to sexual solicitations and when or where they might meet the previously unknown adult.

Hinduja and Patchin (2008) examined a random selection of Myspace profiles and found that 28% of the youths listed their school and 57% included a personal picture; however, few youths provided their full name (9%) or telephone number (0.3%). These results suggest that the problem of personal information disclosure on sites such as Myspace is less common than many have assumed and that a large majority of adolescents take some precautions when using the Internet. Anxiety about youths and insufficient online privacy may be overblown, yet there are some reasons to be concerned. In the

Sophos IT technology study, investigators created a fake Facebook profile and sent out 200 friend requests to strangers (http://www.sophos.com/en-us/press-office/press-releases/2007/08/facebook.aspx). Many of the Facebook users responded, inadvertently or purposefully revealing aspects of their profiles such as date of birth, e-mail address or instant messaging nicknames, and school or workplace locations.

Finally, Mitchell, Finkelhor, and Wolak (2007) found that 4% of Internet-using youths who participated in the second Youth Internet Safety Survey had received an online request to send a sexual picture of themselves. One of these 65 youths complied. Receipt of a request for a sexual picture was correlated with being female and African American, engaging in online sexual behavior, having a history of physical or sexual abuse, being in the presence of friends, communicating with an adult, communicating with someone who they met online, and interacting with someone who had attempted to meet them in the real world.

APPENDIX 3.4
PARALLELS BETWEEN ONLINE AND OFFLINE PARAPHILIC BEHAVIOR

ONLINE AND OFFLINE EXHIBITIONISM

Though I have suggested that fantasy-driven solicitation offenders may represent a new type of sexual offending, there are still some commonalities between fantasy-driven solicitation and existing forms of criminal sexual behavior. Fantasy-driven offenders who are sexually gratified by exposing themselves via webcam or by sending sexual pictures of themselves to unsuspecting minors may share some psychological similarities with exhibitionists who expose themselves to minors in real life. Like exhibitionists, fantasy-driven offenders can realize their sexual fantasies without seeking physical contact with someone.

Exhibitionistic behavior is uncommon in the general population. In a population-representative sample of 2,450 Swedish respondents between the ages of 18 and 60, we found that 3% of the respondents (two-thirds male, one-third female) reported they had ever exposed their genitals to a stranger in their lifetime (Långström & Seto, 2006). This exhibitionistic behavior would not necessarily meet diagnostic criteria because the survey we examined did not include questions about motivation, frequency, persistence, or intensity. Nonetheless, engaging in exhibitionistic behavior was significantly and positively associated with being male, having greater self-reported psychopathology, reporting greater substance use, and having overall greater sexual interest and activity, including number of sexual partners, frequency of masturbation, and frequency of pornography use. Online solicitation offenders who engage in exhibitionistic activity online may share some of these characteristics (see Chapter 5).

The question then is why men who expose themselves seek minors (mostly adolescents). One possibility is that they are exposing themselves to both minors and adults because the activity rather than the target is sexually gratifying, but adults are less likely to report it or to have another person (e.g., parent, guardian) who would report it if they found out about the exposure. I am not aware of systematic data on the incidence or prevalence of unsuspecting and unwanted exposure by adult Internet users. Another possibility is that the taboo element or stronger reactions from exposing to a young adolescent is part of the sexual gratification. Police may not detect exhibitionistic women (a third of the exhibitionistic participants in Långström & Seto, 2006, were women) because their behavior mostly goes unreported, as do many other sexual offenses committed by women.

Some exhibitionists are simultaneously sexually interested in children or young adolescents and may be purposefully targeting these minors. MacDonald (1973) reported that 20% of exhibitionists in their sample exposed to victims between the ages of 5 and 13. Finkelhor, Ormrod, Turner, and Hamby (2005) found that three per 1,000 youths had been exposed to by an adult in the past year, compared with seven in 1,000 who had been exposed to by a peer. Mohr, Turner, and Jerry (1964) found that, of 55 exhibitionists, the 23 who exposed to children were more likely to reoffend than those who exposed to adults.

Should we be concerned about online exhibitionists? There is evidence that real-world exhibitionists have a high rate of recidivism, usually for exposing themselves again (e.g., Langevin et al., 2004). However, there is also some risk that they will escalate to contact sexual offending, particularly those who have another atypical sexual interest such as pedophilia. Firestone, Kingston, Wexler, and Bradford (2006) conducted a follow-up study of exhibitionists and found that those who showed more sexual arousal to children when assessed phallometrically were more likely to subsequently commit a violent offense in the future, including a contact sexual offense. Of the exhibitionists, 32% were convicted for a violent offense after an average follow-up period of 13 years; 24% committed a new sexual offense, which could include convictions for new episodes of exhibitionism. However, in a sample of 202 incidents perpetrated by 106 identified offenders, Bader, Schoeneman-Morris, Scalora, and Casady (2008) did not find that exposing to child victims was associated with the occurrence of more criminal sexual behavior.

TELEPHONE SCATOLOGIA AND ONLINE SEXUAL CHAT

The sexual chat aspects of online solicitation share some features with *telephone scatologia* (obscene telephone calling), a now old-fashioned paraphilic activity wherein individuals obtained sexual gratification by calling an unsuspecting stranger and making sexual statements to them, masturbating while talking to the victim or when thinking about the interaction afterward (see Pakhomou, 2006). Telephone scatologia is an older technology-facilitated sexual offense. Someone who would never have the nerve to make sexual comments to a stranger they encounter on the street might be willing to engage in this behavior behind the perceived anonymity of a telephone call. Obscene telephone calls were predominantly committed by heterosexual men against women and predominantly against strangers. Calls to strangers are more likely to be paraphilic in motivation than calls to coworkers, acquaintances, ex-girlfriends, and other women who are already known in some way, because the latter categories can represent sexual harassment.

I am not aware of data on the frequency of obscene telephone calls—it is possible that records are retained by telephone companies, but they are not in the public domain—but I assume the frequency of obscene telephone calling has gone down over time as countertechnologies such as caller ID, call blocking, and call tracing reduced the anonymity of obscene telephone calls and increased the risk of negative sanctions as a result of the behavior. Another major force influencing the frequency of obscene telephone calls is the wider reach (and greater perceived anonymity) of the Internet.

Some men have a specific sexual interest in obscene telephone calling, but some nonparaphilic men have engaged in this behavior as well. For example, Freund, Watson, and Rienzo (1988) found that 6% of male students and 14% of male volunteers recruited at a job placement center admitted having made obscene telephone calls. Surveys have indicated that a majority of women have received obscene telephone calls, although many do not report them to the telephone company or police (see Price, Gutheil, Commons, Kafka, & Dodd-Kimmey, 2001). Because obscene telephone calls are seen as a "low harm" or "low risk" crime, it is often treated as a misdemeanor when it is prosecuted at all. Nonetheless, some victims report anxiety or fear as a result of receiving such calls (Sheffield, 1989). There is limited research on the effects of receiving online sexual solicitations. Similar effects—anxiety or fear—have been reported by some solicitation recipients.

Someone who wants to "talk dirty" can do so with a willing partner (cf. the novel *Vox*, by Baker, 1992) or can pay someone to speak with them on commercial telephone sex lines. However, some initiators may be unwilling or unable to pay to call commercial phone sex lines, and others may be excited by the fact the interaction is intrusive and unwanted. Similarly, some online solicitation offenders may be sexually aroused by sending sexual messages to unsuspecting strangers because it is unwanted and intrusive, rather than in spite of these aspects. As with other potentially paraphilic behavior, it is necessary to carefully evaluate the individual's motivations.

Some clinicians and researchers have suggested that real-life exhibitionism and obscene telephone calling are variants of each other, on the basis of the high likelihood that they co-occur (e.g., Abel, Becker, Cunningham-Rathner, Mittelman, & Rouleau, 1988; Price et al., 2001). Freund (1990) suggested that both exhibitionism and obscene telephone calling were *courtship disorders*, which he described as distortions of the normal phases of courtship, specifically the pretactile phase when a potential sexual partner is approached. Some fantasy-driven solicitation offending may fall in this category, if a meaningful distinction can be made between online only interactions that are intended to be unwanted and intrusive and those that are intended to be fantasy only among adults or with a "consenting" minor.

APPENDIX 3.5
POLICE ENTRAPMENT

Many solicitation offenders are identified through proactive police investigations in which undercover police officers take on a youthful persona and engage in online interactions to identify individuals who will sexually solicit them (Briggs, Simon, & Simonsen, 2011; Mitchell, Wolak, & Finkelhor, 2005; Wolak, 2011). Does this kind of police effort represent entrapment? Fulda (2002) was one of the first to raise this concern after reviewing newspaper stories about 74 Internet solicitation cases, with 20 involving police stings. A majority of offenders showed no evidence that they were a risk to children, because they had no criminal history, no complaints or allegations to police or child protection agencies about sexual behavior involving children, and no known child victims. The offenders did engage in criminal behavior by soliciting a minor online, which led to their arrest, but they did not appear to have been predisposed to commit the crime, or similar crimes, in the absence of police investigation efforts. Moore, Lee, and Hunt (2007) provided a legal perspective on the entrapment defense in online police stings. The authors concluded that the success of this defense depends on whether there is evidence the police officer tried to convince the suspect to engage in a particular behavior, how long the interaction lasted, and whether the suspect showed evidence of reluctance to engage in the criminal act(s). In a subsequent paper, Fulda (2007) suggested that proactive online investigations amount to preventive detention of individuals, some of whom may commit sexual offenses in the future, with many false positives (individuals who pose no risk, but who are identified as at risk) and likely many false negatives (individuals who do pose a risk to children but do not respond to police efforts) as well.

In contrast to Fulda's (2002, 2007) argument against proactive police investigations, Mitchell et al. (2005) noted that in their sample of 124 solicitation offenders identified through proactive police investigations, some of these offenders were clearly of concern to criminal justice authorities. Thirteen percent had committed contact sexual offenses with real minors, 41% possessed child pornography, and these offenders went to meetings—often bringing sex-related items—so it appeared they intended to meet a minor for sexual purposes. Mitchell et al. (2005) concluded that proactive investigations of online solicitation offenders can be good policy because these investigations can identify some individuals before contact offenses occur, identify some individuals who were already committing contact offenses, deter others, and identify individuals who possess child pornography. Their data did not address opportunity costs from investing in online solicitation investigations versus other kinds of investigations, and their data did not address the issues of false positives or false negatives.

One difficult issue that has not been discussed in any depth is the possibility that police are engaging in more proactive investigations of online sexual offenders because of the increase in resources—particularly the number and training of investigators, including specialized Internet Crimes Against Children task forces and specialized units or officers in local and state agencies—that have become available as a result of public concerns about online offending. There has simultaneously been a reduction in demand for investigations of child sexual abuse cases, driven by a large decline in these cases over the past decade (Finkelhor & Jones, 2006; Mishra & Lalumiere, 2009). More police officers are therefore available to pursue online cases, particularly those that are "low-hanging fruit" and lead to high conviction rates (over 90%, according to Motivans and Kyckelhahn, 2007; see also Wolak, Finkelhor, & Mitchell, 2008). Compared with child sexual abuse cases, which can be difficult to prosecute because they mostly rely on witness testimony and circumstantial evidence, online investigators have digital evidence of chat logs, images, and online sessions.

An important policy question is how to make the use of law enforcement resources more efficient and effective. Can police efforts be triaged by priority, where priority is determined in large part by the risk that suspects may pose of committing contact sexual offenses? I raised this issue at the United States Attorney General's summit on child exploitation in October 2011 (http://www.justice.gov/iso/opa/ag/speeches/2011/ag-speech-1110141.html). This risk or likelihood of contact sexual offending can be divided into three parts: (a) the past, where intervention might identify previously unknown victims; (b) the present, where intervention could stop ongoing abuse; and (c) the future, where intervention can reduce the likelihood of new victims. How could police focus on those who pose the greatest risk, given the number of possible cases far exceed existing and even realistically possible resources?

4

ETIOLOGY

This chapter describes different ways of thinking about the use of the Internet to facilitate sexual offending and examines how well the existing data on offender and offense characteristics fit with conventional (contact) sex offender models, particularly those that are currently being adapted for the assessment and treatment of online offenders. In this chapter, I describe a set of models that are being created or adapted to explain online sexual offending. In the following chapter, I present the evidence pertaining to particular factors that have been identified as important.

The evidence suggests different etiological models are needed to explain online child pornography and solicitation of minors. Elliott and Beech (2009) reviewed existing models of online offending. Broadly speaking, the different models fall into four approaches: (a) Online offending is another manifestation of the same factors that explain contact sexual offending but in a different context; this approach involves modifying existing models of sexual offending; (b) online offending is the result of offense-specific factors

http://dx.doi.org/10.1037/14191-005
Internet Sex Offenders, by M. C. Seto
Copyright © 2013 by the American Psychological Association. All rights reserved.

associated with problematic Internet use; (c) online offending is the result of offense-specific factors associated with sexual addiction or compulsivity; and (d) online offending is a new form of offending that requires the development of new explanatory models. I briefly review each of these approaches in the following sections.[1]

ADAPTED MODELS OF INTERNET SEXUAL OFFENDING

Middleton, Elliott, Mandeville-Norden, and Beech (2006) examined the applicability of Ward and Siegert's (2002) pathways model to explain contact sexual offending in a sample of 72 Internet offenders. The main premise of the pathways model is that offenders typically follow one of several common pathways to sexual offending, with pathway-typical deficits, precursors, and behaviors. The hypothetical pathways are summarized in Table 4.1. Middleton and his colleagues found some support for the emotional dysregulation and interpersonal deficits pathways in online offending, but half of the online offenders could not be assigned to one of these five pathways, which raises concerns about the utility of this model. A majority of offenders in the Middleton et al. sample (60%) produced elevated scores on one or more of the psychometric measures selected to distinguish the different pathways, including offense-supportive attitudes and beliefs (such as a view that children can benefit from sex with an adult), emotional congruence (identification) with children, loneliness, and emotional dysregulation. The remaining 29 offenders did not produce elevated scores on any of the measures. Of those who had elevated scores, 33 offenders could be easily assigned to one of the five pathways. Ten men had elevated scores on measures reflecting two or three of the theoretical pathways but did not meet the criteria for being included in the multiple dysfunctions pathway.

All 15 offenders in the intimacy deficits (35%) pathway reported high levels of loneliness, and most reported experiencing low self-esteem. None reported serious difficulty in controlling their negative emotions, and none espoused high levels of offense-supportive attitudes and beliefs about children or sex. This pathway could also be characterized as a social inadequacy pathway. A third of the classifiable offenders (33%) were assigned to the emotional dysregulation pathway; all of these men reported difficulty dealing with their negative emotions, and 10 also showed deficits in empathy for victims of sexual abuse. Only two offenders (15%) were assigned to the distorted sexual scripts pathway. Both had high levels of emotional congruence

---

[1]There have also been some suggestions that child pornography offending may have some factors in common with pathological collecting behavior (see Appendix 4.1).

TABLE 4.1
Pathways Model of Contact Sexual Offending

Pathway	Description
Intimacy deficits	Distal factors are insecure attachment and difficulties forming relationships with adults. Offenders are characterized by loneliness, poor social skills, and low self-esteem. Offenders in this pathway sexually prefer adults but may turn to children as substitutes.
Distorted sexual scripts	Distal factors are early sexualization and possibly sexual abuse. Offenders are characterized by deficits in offense-supportive attitudes and beliefs, misreading of sexual cues, sensitivity to rejection, and low self-esteem. Offenders have distorted sexual scripts, equate sex with intimacy, and may turn to children when feeling rejected or blocked.
Emotional dysregulation	Distal factors are use of sex as a coping strategy and linking sex with emotional well-being. Offenders are characterized by problems with controlling anger, identifying emotions, impulsivity, and personal distress. They experience sexual arousal in strong emotional states, and this drives opportunistic offending.
Antisocial cognitions	Distal factors are antisocial attitudes and beliefs and feelings of superiority over children. Offenders are characterized by offense-supportive attitudes and beliefs, patriarchal beliefs, impulsivity, and poor delay of gratification. Offenses can occur when offenders are sexually needy and when the opportunity arises, because the offender disregards social norms about sex with children.
Multiple dysfunctions	Distal factors are early sexualization, impaired attachment styles, and antisocial cognitions. Offenders are characterized by entrenched offense-supportive attitudes and beliefs and sexual preference for children, resulting in approach behaviors.

Note. Descriptions adapted from Ward and Siegert (2002).

with children. Only one offender was assigned to the antisocial cognitions pathway. He endorsed high levels of offense-supportive attitudes and beliefs but had no other elevated scores. Last, only one offender was assigned to the multiple dysfunctions pathway, with elevated scores on all measures.

The Middleton et al. (2006) study was constrained by its small sample size, with some pathways having only a few assigned offenders. It was also constrained by its reliance on self-report measures; offenders might have truly espoused offense-supportive attitudes and beliefs, for example, but might not have been willing to admit to them on a questionnaire, even though pertinent evidence might have been available from past interviews or other sources. The study could have benefitted from including additional measures, given that many offenders could not be classified on the basis of the small set of self-report measures that were used.

To further test the applicability of the pathways model, Middleton (2009) collected data on a larger sample of 213 Internet offenders and compared them with a sample of 191 contact sexual offenders against children. There were a number of similarities between the online and contact offender groups, with the largest memberships for both Internet and contact offenders in the intimacy deficits and emotional dysregulation pathways. More Internet offenders, however, scored in the dysfunctional range on all psychological measures. It was again the case, though, that many online offenders could not be assigned to one of the five pathways.

These results can be compared with a recent comprehensive assessment using multiple sources of information about 275 incarcerated male sex offenders (Kingston, Yates, & Firestone, 2012). Using a wide range of questionnaire and file data to test the self-regulation model, Kingston et al. (2012) were able to distinguish these contact offenders according to the Ward and Siegert (2002) pathway and showed that the various groups of offenders differed in their treatment needs and risk to reoffend, according to actuarial risk scale scores (see Chapter 7).

Gannon, Terriere, and Leader (2012) also tested the pathways model using a different analytic strategy with data from 10 psychometric measures from 97 sex offenders with child victims, to see if they could empirically derive different groups that corresponded to the proposed pathways. The results were mixed: Three of the groups resembled Ward and Siegert's (2002) proposed pathways (antisocial, intimacy deficits, and multiple problems), but two other groups were quite different. One was labeled *impulsive* and included antisocial features, whereas the second was labeled *boy predator* and bore some resemblance to the concept of sexual deviance. Gannon et al. may have found support for more pathways if they had a suitable set of measures. To illustrate, it would be impossible to replicate a sexual deviance pathway if one did not have reliable and valid measures of deviant sexual interests. I also think it is important to include data that do not rely solely on self-report.

PROBLEMATIC INTERNET USE

In this approach, online offending is viewed as an extreme example of problematic Internet use, which represents a spectrum of problematic behavior, from spending too much time or money online, to Internet "addiction," to criminal conduct (Carnes, Delmonico, Griffin, & Moriarty, 2007; Quayle & Taylor, 2003). Of particular relevance is problematic online sexual behavior, including excessive use of mainstream pornography, adult sexual chat, and casual sex. The "triple A engine" of accessibility, affordability, and (perceived) anonymity could interact with individual vulnerability factors and contribute to other forms of problematic online sexual behavior (A. Cooper, Delmonico, Griffin-Shelley, & Mathy, 2004).

Davis (2001) proposed a cognitive behavioral model of problematic Internet use that distinguished between specific problems (online pornography use, online gambling) and generalized problems (excessive or purposeless use). Davis suggested that existing psychopathology such as depression or social anxiety was a necessary diathesis that interacted with a ruminative cognitive style, low self-efficacy, and negative self-appraisal. Similarly, I. A. Brown (1997) described a hedonic management model that suggests online offending is used to manage negative mood states. This model can be compared with notions that sexual offenders use sex as way of coping with negative mood, just as substance abusers turn to particular substances to do so (Cortoni & Marshall, 2001; Lewis, 2011; Neidigh & Tomiko, 1991).

Quayle and Taylor (2003) extended Davis's model to understand problematic Internet use in the form of child pornography crime, drawing on a qualitative study of 23 child pornography offenders. In Quayle and Taylor's model, setting events are antecedents, labeled as either *distal* (e.g., sexualized childhood experiences) or *proximal* (sexual interest in children). Predisposed individuals then engage with the Internet using their computer skills and knowledge of online technologies and justify their increasingly problematic use with cognitions that rationalize or minimize responsibility for their actions. Problematic Internet use is influenced by and influences psychological and social factors, including sexual fantasy, risk taking (in the context of the perceived anonymity of the Internet), and increased real-world social isolation.

Taylor and Quayle (2003) examined the roles that the Internet can play in our lives outside of the sexual domain: again, providing anonymity (Chou & Hsiao, 2000); as a way of coping with negative mood (Morahan-Martin & Schumacher, 2000); as a means of facilitating group cohesion and self-presentations (Lamb, 1998); and in developing new ways of thinking (Granic & Lamey, 2000). For example, a socially isolated and awkward man can present himself online as confident and popular and can accrue online status by being knowledgeable about technical topics and active in particular subcultures. Indeed, that same man can present himself online as a youth or as a woman, as he wishes.

There is little research on problematic Internet use among online sexual offenders. Laulik, Allam, and Sheridan (2007) studied 30 child pornography offenders who spent an average of 12 hours a week seeking child pornography online. This time did not include time spent online for other purposes. The standard deviation was 7 hours, however, meaning that some of the offenders might spend 20 or more hours a week seeking child pornography. Moreover, time spent viewing child pornography was inversely related to clinical and personality functioning, as assessed using a broad psychopathology measure. This link might not be causal, because it could be the case that those individuals with more difficulties spent more time online, as opposed to more time online causing their difficulties. Another possibility is that a common predisposition or set of predispositions leads to both child pornography viewing and psychopathology.

Krueger, Kaplan, and First (2009) reported that 30% of their sample of 60 online offenders tried to limit their computer use and thereby control their online sexual behavior, suggesting this subgroup had concerns about their online behavior in terms of compulsivity or ability to control it. Prentky et al. (2010) found that general Internet preoccupation was uncorrelated with contact offending among Internet offenders, but did distinguish those who had committed child pornography-only offenses from other offenders.

RELATIONSHIP EFFECTS

Problematic Internet use does not take place in a vacuum. Stack, Wasserman, and Kern (2004) analyzed data from the General Social Survey in 2000 and found that happily married couples were much less likely to use Internet pornography than respondents who did not report being happily married. In a sample of over 1,000 respondents, Whitty (2003) found that both men and women perceived online sexual activity as infidelity and that pornography use alone was still viewed as emotional infidelity. Schneider (2000) surveyed 94 partners of "cybersex addicts" and found that a decrease in sexual intimacy coincided with the onset of online sexual behavior, which suggests relationship problems are not a consequence of chronic Internet use. This does not mean relationship problems are a cause, however, as another factor could lead to both relationship problems and problematic online behavior (e.g., mismatched levels of sex drive and preoccupation). Or there can be a negative feedback loop between relationship intimacy and online problems, both feeding the other.

There is other evidence of relationship problems playing a role in problematic online behavior. Schneider (2000) reported results from a convenience sample of 94 partners of treatment clients who had engaged in problematic online sexual behavior and who were identified by contacting therapists. Ninety of the 94 partners were women who were involved with male clients. The partners were aware of the online problem for an average of more than 2 years but suspected it had been going on for much longer.

Seven of the clients were using child pornography, and one had sex with an underage person. Though only a minority of the clients had engaged in sexual behavior involving minors, the prevalence (8%) was higher than found in the general population (readers can compare this rate with prevalence estimates for sexual behavior involving minors in Chapter 3).

All of the clients viewed online pornography and masturbated to that pornography; other online activities included sexual chat, interacting with others sexually via webcam, setting up real-life meetings, and phone sex or real-life meetings with persons who they met online. In half the cases, the partners said the problematic user was not interested or was only slightly interested in sex with them; they thought online sexual activity had displaced their sex lives. This is not proof that online activities cause a lack of sexual interest in partners, of course, because a lack of interest in partners could have driven online sexual activity. For clients who were no longer interested in sex, recurrent themes identified by Schneider (2000) were (a) the partner felt hurt, angry, sexually rejected, inadequate, or unable to compete with online sexual partners; (b) the client made excuses to avoid sex with the partner (e.g., not being in the mood, too tired); (c) when they did have sex, the client appeared distant, emotionally detached, and interested only in his or her own pleasure; (d) the partner ended up doing most or all of the sexual initiation, sometimes in an attempt to get the client to decrease online activities; (e) the client blamed the partner for their sexual problems; or (f) the client wanted the partner to participate in sexual activities which she found objectionable.

A. Cooper, Galbreath, and Becker (2004) conducted a survey of 384 male participants regarding their online sexual behavior. A. Cooper et al. distinguished between those who went online for education, to meet someone, or to socialize, and those who engaged in online sexual behavior to deal with stress or other problems. The latter group was larger, more likely to have relationship problems, more likely to have others express concern about their online activity, and more likely to masturbate. This suggests a distinction between online offenders who prefer children and who may seek intimacy and an ongoing relationship, and those who are seeking impersonal sexual opportunities (see also Galbreath, Berlin, & Sawyer, 2002).

SEXUAL ADDICTION OR COMPULSIVITY

In the sexual addiction or compulsivity view, an explanation that is offered by a substantial minority of child pornography offenders (Seto, Reeves, & Jung, 2010), sexual addiction or compulsivity can be fed by the easy access of pornography and other sexual opportunities online, including sexual chat, commercial sex, and casual sex encounters (Carnes et al., 2007). It is interesting to note here that we found that child pornography offenders seen in a clinical setting were more likely to offer this explanation than those interviewed by police (Seto et al., 2010). Though the police and clinical samples were different in a variety of ways, it is tempting to speculate that some child pornography offenders decided that sexual addiction or compulsivity was a more palatable explanation to give when being evaluated for treatment than when first investigated by police.[2]

Shaffer (1994) distinguished between a sexual addiction versus an obsessive–compulsive model for syndromes such as excessive pornography use (see also Gordon, 2002). He argued that the core of psychological addiction is the influence of something—drugs in particular but potentially also activities such as gambling or sexual behavior—on cognition and mood. This includes craving to use the addictive substance or engage in the addictive activity to feel normal or good. Failing to satisfy this craving can cause anxiety, depression, agitation, and irritability. Many individuals can become physically tolerant of substances such as cocaine, but only a subset will become addicted. What distinguishes those at risk of addiction? One mechanism mentioned by Schwartz and Masters (1994) is the belief that the addictive substance or activity makes everything else all right and the reliance on the addiction to cope with distress and discomfort instead of having a broader range of coping responses (see my friend Marc Lewis's 2011 book on the neuroscience of craving and addiction).

In contrast, others have espoused a compulsivity model to explain excessive online sexual behavior, as exemplified by research on the Compulsive Sexual Behavior Inventory (Miner, Coleman, Center, Ross, & Rosser, 2007). The common phenomenology across addiction and compulsivity models is that the individual feels compelled to engage in the problematic sexual behaviors. What is the difference? Shaffer (1994) suggested that addiction is *ego-syntonic*: engaging in the behavior feels good, and so the person is tempted and must actively resist the urge to engage. Nonetheless, many might experience shame or guilt after doing so. In contrast, an obsessive–compulsive behavior is *ego-dystonic*: the person does not want to engage in the behavior at all but feels compelled. In an ideal world, the addict could engage in the desired activity without experiencing the negative effects; in that same ideal world, the compulsive individual would not engage in the activity.

---

[2]Lundy (1994) described the history of sexual addiction as a concept. Carnes (1983) made the concept of sexual addiction or compulsivity more widely known and popular through his book, *Out of the Shadows,* which examined the possible association of sexual addiction and sexual offending. Earlier terms to describe a similar sexual behavior syndrome includes *nymphomania, satyriasis,* and *Don Juanism.*

A distinction can be made in assessment by determining the extent to which the behavior made the person feel good and was wanted, especially at the beginning (before the negative effects started adding up). But Shaffer (1994) suggested that treatments would be highly similar whether conceptualized as an addiction or obsessive–compulsive behavior. Whether the addiction or compulsivity model is correct is important because it should influence case conceptualization and how one proceeds with interventions.

Researchers have examined sexual compulsivity in other risk-related domains, particularly risky sexual behavior for the transmission of AIDS or other sexually transmitted diseases (e.g., seeking many casual sexual partners, having unprotected intercourse). Kafka and Hennen (2003) suggested sexual compulsivity and hypersexuality played a role in what they described as *paraphilia-related disorders*, problematic sexual behaviors that share some topological features of paraphilias such as pedophilia or exhibitionism but that do not meet diagnostic criteria. An example of a paraphilia-related disorder is one in which a person compulsively uses online mainstream pornography, despite its negative impacts on his finances, employment, and relationships. Winters, Christoff, and Gorzalka (2010) conducted a large Internet survey of individuals concerned about their sexual behavior and found that what they described as *dysregulated sexuality* was strongly correlated with high sexual desire, suggesting sexual compulsivity and hypersexuality might be manifestations of the same underlying psychology. Winters et al. wondered if there were meaningful distinctions between sexual addiction, sexual compulsivity, and impulsive sexual behavior.

SEX AS COPING

Another model that is related to both problematic Internet use and sexual addiction and compulsivity models views sex as a means of coping with negative affect such as loneliness, sadness, anger, and stress (see Serran & Marshall, 2006). Masturbating and fantasizing to online pornography is distracting and can temporarily make the person feel better. Cortoni and Marshall (2001) found that child molesters were more likely to use sex as a way of coping with negative affect than rapists or other kinds of offenders.

There is other research to support the idea that sexual behavior may be used as a means of coping with negative affect. Pithers, Marques, Gibat, and Marlatt (1983) examined the antecedents of sexual offenses as part of the foundational research on the translation of the relapse prevention model to sex offender treatment and found that offenders retrospectively reported that negative affect preceded three quarters of their offenses. Hanson and

Harris (2000) found that acute changes in negative affect were associated with acute fluctuations in likelihood to reoffend, such that noticeable increases in negative affect were associated with greater risk. This association may be mediated by deviant sexual fantasy; Proulx, McKibben, and Lusignan (1996) found that the experience of negative affect was associated with having more deviant sexual fantasies, which in turn could lead to more deviant sexual behavior. A series of studies has suggested that contact sex offenders with child victims cope less effectively than other offenders, indicating that coping through sex may be distinctive of this offender type (Marshall, Cripps, Anderson, & Cortoni, 1999; Marshall, Serran, & Cortoni, 2000).

More work is needed to understand the mechanisms by which sexual fantasy and behavior are associated with (maladaptive) coping among predisposed individuals. One view is that deviant sexual fantasy is a means of coping with negative affect; another is that deviant sexual fantasy is more likely when the person's resolve to abstain is weakened by negative mood and any associated feelings of hopelessness or helplessness. Also, the conceptualizations and research have focused on sex as a way of coping with negative affect. It is also possible that sex can be used as a way of enhancing positive affect, with different mechanisms at play depending on affect and depending on individual differences such as personality traits. For example, extraversion may play a more important role in a link between positive affect and using sex to cope, whereas neuroticism may play a more important role in a link between negative affect and using sex to cope.

SEXUAL COMPULSIVITY AND ONLINE OFFENDING

Consistent with the idea of sexual addiction or compulsivity playing a role in online sexual offending, Krueger et al. (2009) thought a third of their sample of 60 online offenders had a hypersexuality disorder, characterized by pornography dependence for child pornography offenders and cybersex dependence for solicitation offenders. Anecdotally, many of the online offenders reported an interest in atypical pornography of myriad kinds, seeking taboo-breaking, and therefore more thrilling, content.

MOTIVATION–FACILITATION MODEL OF SEXUAL OFFENDING

I first described a motivation–facilitation model of sexual offending against children in Seto and Barbaree (1997) and then again in Seto (2008), though I did not name the model at the time. In the motivation–facilitation model of sexual offending, individuals with a paraphilic motivation to com-

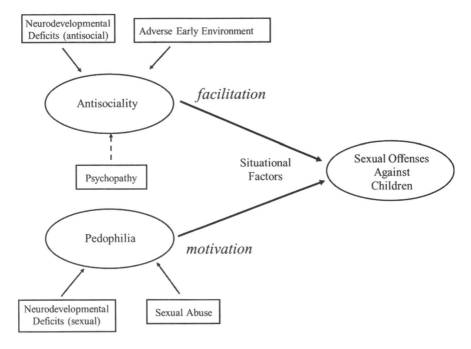

Figure 4.1. Motivation–facilitation model of sexual offending against children. Adapted from *Pedophilia and Sexual Offending Against Children: Theory, Assessment, and Intervention* (p. 95), by M. C. Seto, 2008, Washington, DC: American Psychological Association. Copyright 2008 by the American Psychological Association.

mit a sexual crime, high sexual preoccupation or drive, or an absence of other viable sexual outlets, are more motivated to seek out opportunities to sexu-ally offend and do so when circumstances permit than do individuals with-out these sexual motivations (see Figure 4.1). For sexual offending against children, the age and gender of children who are at risk varies according to the motivation: Pedophiles prefer prepubescent children, and those who are driven by nonpedohebephilic motivations prefer older youths, usually ado-lescent girls. The motivations are explicitly sexual though not necessarily paraphilic in this model; the model is not consistent with the idea that sexual offenders are primarily motivated by nonsexual motivations based on power, control, traumatic reenactment, or other psychological needs (though there may be exceptions and these secondary motivations may play a role). The offender might feel more powerful or more in control when sexually offending, but this is usually a byproduct of the offending—for example, as a result of having physical or psychological control over the victim or the positive affect that comes from sexual gratification—rather than a cause of offending.

Antisocial tendencies facilitate acting on these sexual motivations, because these tendencies can overcome psychological and situational inhibitions against sex with children. Inhibitions include anxiety and fear about negative consequences, morals, social norms, and legal prohibitions. Individuals who are high in risk taking, impulsivity, or callousness are more likely to act on their sexual motivations because they are less sensitive to or concerned about the risks involved, do not reflect upon the potential consequences of their actions, or are indifferent to the harm they might cause. Individuals with an antisocial orientation are less likely to espouse moral positions against adult–child sex or to respect laws prohibiting this conduct.

Individuals who are low on these facilitating factors are unlikely to act on their sexual motivations because inhibitions are usually present and sufficiently strong. If this model were applied to sexual offending against children, it could explain why some pedophiles act freely on their sexual interests and commit sexual offenses against children when there are opportunities, why some pedophiles do not attempt sexual contacts but do indulge their sexual interests by seeking child pornography and masturbating while viewing this content, and why some unknown number of pedophiles may not act at all on their pedophilia, living a celibate life. Similarly, some individuals with high sex drive or preoccupation may freely engage in sexual contacts with pubescent or postpubescent minors; some do not engage in such activities but may seek out and masturbate to a variety of pornography, including "child" pornography (depicting adolescents); and some do not act on their sexual desires.

Last, the motivation–facilitation model posits that sexual offending can be facilitated by situational factors as well as the individual differences described previously. Situational factors include (a) access to potential victims, (b) life events that elicit negative affect (as mentioned earlier in this chapter) and (c) the acute effects of alcohol or drug use (see Seto & Barbaree, 1995). Situational crime prevention strategies (see Chapter 8) are aimed at addressing these situational risk factors, just as primary and secondary prevention efforts might address sexual motivations and facilitators that reduce the incidence of sexual offenses.

For online sexual offending, the motivation–facilitation model can explain and integrate a range of observations that I discuss in further detail in the next three chapters: (a) Why excessive sexual preoccupation or sexual deviance is characteristic of many online offenders, yet their sexual recidivism rates are low (Seto, Cantor, & Blanchard, 2006; Seto, Hanson, & Babchishin, 2011); (b) why online offenders tend to score lower, as a group, on measures of antisocial tendencies than contact offenders (this difference would be even larger if the comparison is restricted to online offenders with no known history of contact offending; Babchishin, Hanson, & Hermann, 2011); (c) why antisociality measures predict recidivism among online offenders, as it does for other offender populations (Eke & Seto, 2012; Seto & Eke, 2005); and (d) why solicitation offenders score higher than child pornography offenders on measures of antisocial tendencies (Seto, Wood, Babchishin, & Flynn, 2012).

The motivation–facilitation model also produces new, testable hypotheses about online offending: (a) There should be an interaction between sexual deviance and antisociality in the prediction of new sexual offenses, as has been found in studies of contact offenders (e.g., Seto, Harris, Rice, & Barbaree, 2004); (b) contact-driven solicitation offenders should score higher than fantasy-driven solicitation offenders on sexuality and antisociality risk factors and that child pornography offenders with any solicitation or contact offending history should score higher than child pornography only offenders; (c) online sexual offenders should score higher on sexual deviance and sexual preoccupation than other individuals engaging in problematic online behavior that is nonsexual in nature (e.g., excessive gaming, online gambling); and (d) online sexual offenders should score lower on perceived sexual opportunities in real life, though they might not differ in actual sexual opportunities (reflected in their attractiveness, contact with potential sexual partners, and social skills). It is the perception that matters: Lalumière and Quinsey (1996) found that self-admitted sexually aggressive men actually had more sexual partners than nonaggressive men, for example, but still differed from nonaggressive men by being less satisfied with their sexual lives.

FINAL COMMENTS

Studies are accumulating on online offender characteristics (Babchishin et al., 2011) and the offending behaviors and trajectories of online offenders (Seto et al., 2011). Group comparison studies are of particular value for understanding the psychology of online sexual offending, as I discuss in the next chapter. More data are needed on solicitation offenders and more comparisons of online offender types are needed, such as comparisons of fantasy-driven and contact-driven solicitation offenders and comparisons of dual offenders to online-only or contact-only offenders.

A number of different models have been proposed to explain online offending. Broadly speaking, online offending can be paraphilic, hypersexual, compulsive or addictive, or specifically pathological in response to Internet-specific properties (as posited in models of problematic Internet use). Another psychopathology that might be relevant involves collecting psychology (see Appendix 4.1). In the review offered here, it is clear these models share some features in common, including the notions that (a) mood and online sexual behavior can influence each other; (b) there can be positive reinforcement of online sexual behavior through sexual arousal, masturbation, and fantasy, as well as through positive social interactions with like-minded individuals; (c) attitudes and beliefs can be influenced by online interactions and vice versa; (d) habituation can lead to increased and more intense use of pornography or other online sexual outlets; and (e) for at least some individuals, boredom with fantasy or active encouragement of others can promote contact sexual offending. There is almost a complete absence of literature on the development of online sexual offending, which will become an increasingly important topic as younger people—who are growing up with the Internet—become involved (Appendix 4.2).

Explanatory models should influence directions taken in assessment and intervention. For example, the motivation–facilitation model suggests that sexual motivations are central and thus need to be assessed and managed effectively to reduce recidivism. This could include teaching self-regulation skills using cognitive behavioral techniques, redirecting the individual to more prosocial sexual outlets when possible (e.g., through relationship skills training, if that is a deficit), and sex-drive reducing medications for high-risk offenders. Addressing trait and state (situational) facilitators through increasing self-management capacities would also reduce sexual (and nonsexual) offending.

For reasons that are unclear to me, explanatory models of sexual offending tend to be complicated and focused on process (e.g., problematic Internet use or compulsive online pornography use) rather than on the causes of behavior. Online offenders (and sex offenders more generally) are not a different species; the same psychological processes we all share are involved but with different inputs (for pedophiles, children rather than adults are sexually and romantically attractive) and thresholds for action (excessive sexual preoccupation or high sex drive lead to lower thresholds for initiating sexual behavior than typical levels of sexual preoccupation or drive). Similarly, I have argued that "cognitive distortions" is a misnomer for offense-supportive attitudes and beliefs, which are examples of rationalizations in which we all sometimes engage when trying to explain behavior that does not fit with our sense of selves.

It is likely that online child pornography is attracting individuals who are sexually interested in children but who would have not taken the risk before the advent of the Internet to order child pornography from a mail-order business or attempt to contact individuals to trade with. Compared with their pre-Internet counterparts, such individuals are, ceteris paribus, expected to be lower in impulsivity, risk taking, and other personality traits associated with the likelihood of engaging in even more serious illegal behavior such as having sexual contacts with children. It is impossible to go back in time and conduct this research, but I would speculate that a (retrospective) comparison of pre-Internet and current online child pornography offenders would reveal systematic differences on measures of antisocial tendencies. Because the Internet has lowered the threshold for access to child pornography, it might also be the case that pre-Internet child pornography offenders would score higher on measures of sexual deviance or sexual preoccupation. Even those who are only curious about child pornography can access it now, whereas the same curious individuals would probably not have invested the effort and incurred the risk of obtaining child pornography before the advent of the public Internet.

APPENDIX 4.1
COLLECTING PATHOLOGY

Lanning (2001) was one of the first writers to suggest that child pornography users access child pornography to fuel their sexual fantasies, just as many adult men use adult pornography to provide stimulation for masturbation and fantasy. Lanning also suggested that collecting child pornography could be a rewarding goal in itself, beyond the sexual arousal and gratification of the content that was depicted. Taylor and Quayle (2003) subsequently suggested, "Material is often collected even when it has no arousing properties for the individual but because it is part of completing a series or is new" (p. 94).

Some child pornography offenders may collect an image series because it can tell a story that enhances their sexual arousal. Another motivation may be to obtain hard-to-get content that can be traded online: For example, someone may collect the complete image series of a young prepubescent boy, even though he is only sexually interested in girls, because the boy images have a high value that can be used to trade for more of his desired content. Anecdotally, individuals with rare images or with complete sets of well-known image series have high status online (Jenkins, 2001; Taylor & Quayle, 2003). As a consequence of tactical trading, my suggestion in Chapter 2 that child pornography collections are an objective window into someone's sexual preferences is tempered by the fact that some content may not be indicative but may instead be saved for trading purposes. This tendency would attenuate any relationships we might expect between child pornography content and outcomes; for example, the expectation that a preference for images of boys rather than girls might be more strongly related to new sexual offenses involving boys. Similarly, peer-to-peer trading of child pornography and cheap memory storage means pornography collections may be "contaminated" by undesired content that is simply ignored and not deleted. One hypothesis is that highly active traders will tend to have more organized collections, which facilitates identifying material to exchange with others.

Though each individual image may not have much value in terms of potential sexual gratification, given that the offender may already have most of a set depicting similar content, obtaining those final few images may become a goal in itself. There are anecdotal reports of individuals who are highly motivated to find the final few images to complete a child pornography series, even though they may already have hundreds of images of a particular girl or boy and thousands of other images for fantasy and masturbation purposes. Carey (2008) described collecting psychology more generally. The literature on collecting psychology for memorabilia and other collectibles is relatively sparse, but it would be interesting to examine the conceptual and empirical similarities and differences.

APPENDIX 4.2
DEVELOPMENT OF ONLINE SEXUAL OFFENDING

There is almost no published research on adolescent online offenders. There are some case reports of adolescents involved in child pornography and some survey data from the Crimes Against Children Research Center confirming that some adolescents are charged with child pornography offenses or for approaching younger adolescents online (Wolak, Finkelhor, & Mitchell, 2012; Wolak, Finkelhor, Mitchell, & Ybarra, 2008). Studies of adolescent offenders are needed to understand the development of online offending, especially for a generation that grew up with an ever-available Internet, compared with the offenders in their 30s or 40s who comprise a substantial proportion of clinical and correctional samples that have been described in the literature.

Studies of adolescent online offenders are needed to understand if the same explanatory models apply. Adolescents who are charged with child pornography offenses for possessing images of similar-aged partners or acquaintances are unlikely to have the same sexual motivations as much older adult offenders. In particular, experimentation and risk taking may play a more prominent role in adolescent online offending, especially with regard to offenses involving minors who are similar in age (e.g., sexting or solicitation of similar-aged peers). This does not mean, of course, that some adolescents are not motivated by a sexual interest in young children or are not beginning to exhibit through their online sexual behavior signs of excessive sexual preoccupation or sex drive.

Moultrie (2006) reported a case study of seven adolescents detected for downloading child pornography. Two of the adolescents were known to have sexually offended in addition to their index possession offense: One youth was arrested for taking pornographic photographs of local children, and the other had sexually abused his younger sister and another young girl, which he admitted after being arrested for the child pornography offenses. Only one adolescent had been arrested for a nonsexual crime, involving the fraudulent use of a credit card to access a commercial child pornography site. There was evidence to suggest sexual deviance was relevant for some adolescents because two of the adolescents had written detailed sexual fantasies about the abduction and rape (and murder, in one case) of young children. These stories were exchanged with others via e-mail. Two adolescents transmitted images of themselves masturbating via webcam. However, all of the adolescents denied being sexually aroused by younger children prior to their involvement with child pornography, though some admitted they were sexually aroused by children at the time they were involved in treatment.

Consistent with adult online offender research, all of the boys were regarded as average or above average in intelligence, and all were doing reasonably well academically. Only one adolescent had any concerns about behavioral problems (attention-deficit/hyperactivity disorder was mentioned). The boys varied in their interpersonal functioning: All had adequate social skills, but two reported extreme social isolation, two had difficulties in their peer relationships, and the majority thought they did not fit in with their peer group.

Consistent with some of the explanations given by adult offenders involved with child pornography, approximately half of the adolescents claimed that they began using adult pornography online and gradually turned to depictions of younger persons over time. Forensic computer analyses revealed that all of the adolescents asked others online for child pornography images, specifying preferred ages, gender, and sexual acts in some cases. At the same time, the adolescents had smaller collections than typically found with adult offenders, and none had engaged in extensive cataloguing or other evidence of collecting behavior.

Seto et al. (2013) examined correlates of child pornography viewing in a young adult population sample, reanalyzing the Swedish data reported by Seto et al. (2010). Child pornography viewing was defined by an item regarding depictions of adult–child sex (a more conservative definition because child pornography can depict children alone or children having sexual contacts with other children). We found significant associations of child pornography viewing with self-reported antisocial behavior and with some sexual history variables. The most interesting correlates were (a) viewing other atypical pornography, particularly pornography depicting violence; (b) having permissive subjective norms about adult–minor sex; and (c) having friends who had viewed child pornography and condoned having sex with a child. The influence of peers is relevant to the previous chapter's discussion about online pedohebephilic subcultures (see Appendix 2.4). Adolescents who discover they are sexually attracted to children or interested in child pornography may understandably turn to such sites in the absence of real-life supports and resources, especially in light of the severe stigma associated with pedophilia and hebephilia.

The Sex and Tech Survey (see Chapter 2, this volume) showed that sexting is more common among young adults than adolescents (http://thenationalcampaign.org/sextech/PDF/SexTech_Summary.pdf). Such behavior, however imprudent, is not illegal if it involves only adults. Given the more prominent role of experimentation and risk-taking in adolescent offending and the broader developmental expectation of adolescence-limited offending (Moffitt, 1993), one would expect that most adolescents involved in online offending would desist as they enter adulthood. In many cases, then, criminalization of adolescent online offending may lead to unintended consequences, in terms of the iatrogenic effects of incarceration (time away from family and from school and work opportunities), stigma (sex offender registration is required in some states, even for juveniles), and greater association with delinquent peers in custodial or treatment facilities, which is known to be a criminogenic influence in itself (Dishion, McCord, & Poulin, 1999).

5

ONLINE OFFENDER CHARACTERISTICS

Before further reviewing the research on online offender characteristics, it is necessary to discuss selection effects that may have influenced the results of these studies. Most of the research described in this book has been conducted on identified offenders, who are expected to differ in meaningful ways from those who remain undetected. For example, identified offenders are probably more careless or impulsive and therefore less likely to take effective precautions to avoid being caught than those who remain undetected. Identified offenders may be more sexually compulsive, because those who are better able to control their sexual urges may engage in less online offending and thereby reduce their risk of detection. Jenkins (2001) suggested that naive or technologically unsophisticated users are more likely to be caught.

I previously discussed how police and prosecution decisions may influence what we know about identified child pornography offenders; individuals who only have images of underage adolescent girls or boys are less likely to be arrested or prosecuted than those who have images of prepubescent

http://dx.doi.org/10.1037/14191-006
Internet Sex Offenders, by M. C. Seto
Copyright © 2013 by the American Psychological Association. All rights reserved.

or pubescent children. Opportunity may influence what we know about solicitation offenders, because those who are interested in young children are unlikely to act or be detected because fewer young children are online (though this is changing as connected devices become more readily available in our daily lives). Given the number of detected offenders relative to child pornography users on peer-to-peer networks and the prevalence rates of online solicitations from self-report studies compared with law enforcement data, detected online offenders clearly represent only the visible tip of the iceberg in an ocean of online criminality.

Those who are careful can still be caught, of course, but they are at less risk than those who are careless. Cautious offenders are expected to be more security-conscious and may avoid interacting with others online, given that undercover police officers may be active in any publicly accessible forums. Instead, they may focus on using peer-to-peer file-sharing systems and avoid any interactions with others; all that is required is a high-speed connection and knowledge of the "right" search keywords. In this context, it is worth noting that studies of peer-to-peer networks have consistently shown that many Internet protocol addresses (which are proxies for the number of users) are involved in child pornography trafficking (Canwest News Service, 2009; Prichard, Watters, & Spiranovic, 2011; Steel, 2009; United States Department of Justice, 2010).

Nielssen et al. (2011) showed there are differences between offenders detected by proactive police work and those who are detected by other means (e.g., when a witness comes forward to report child pornography content to police). They obtained data from 52 offenders detected by undercover police and 53 by other means. Those who were detected by police had more child pornography images but were less likely to meet diagnostic criteria for a major mental disorder, less likely to use substances, and less likely to report childhood sexual abuse. A caveat regarding this study is that some of those who were detected by other means were not criminally charged, so some of the group difference might be due to criminal status, in addition to detection method. Excluding those who were not criminally charged, the two groups still differed in total amount of images and history of childhood sexual abuse. The result regarding amount of images is sensible, because someone who is more actively involved in accessing child pornography statistically increases the likelihood he will cross paths with a police officer online. Sexual abuse history is a correlate of later antisocial behavior, sexual offending, or clinical psychopathology (Salter et al., 2003; Widom & Ames, 1994).

The complications of selection and other biases in research on clinical or correctional samples of online offenders make self-report research valuable because relatively little is known about undetected online offenders. Anonymous online surveys are a good way to reach these individuals, even though these studies are themselves subject to the methodological concerns of socially desirable responding, lack of objective verification of self-reported information, and lack of longitudinal data. Riegel (2004) was able to survey a large sample of self-identified boy-attracted pedophiles, many of whom admitted to using child pornography on at least an occasional basis. Ray, Kimonis, and Donoghue (2010) described some of the challenges of using online surveys, in particular the need to guarantee anonymity in light of understandable anxiety and fear about electronic tracking and potential access to records by law enforcement. Ray, Kimonis, and Seto (in press) described an online survey of problematic mainstream pornography users that was able to identify a subset of individuals who admitted to using child pornography (see earlier description of this study in Chapter 2).

With these methodological caveats in mind, in this chapter I review the research literature on characteristics of online offenders. I focus first on sociodemographic characteristics, then criminal history, and then psychological factors that are potentially relevant to etiological models of online offending (Chapter 4), risk to reoffend (Chapter 7), or intervention (Chapter 8). I am also interested in the degree to which knowledge of the characteristics of online offenders fits with different offender typologies that have been proposed. These typologies are also reviewed in this chapter because different types or subgroups of offenders may have different origins and may pose different risks and needs.

This chapter draws heavily from the findings of a recent meta-analysis by Babchishin, Hanson, and Hermann (2011), who did a comprehensive review of the literature on online sexual offenders. This team identified studies representing 27 independent samples of Internet offenders; nine of these studies directly compared Internet offenders and contact sexual offenders. They conducted statistical comparisons when there were three or more samples available for analysis, with the majority of the samples from the United States, United Kingdom, or Canada; about half of the studies were drawn from peer-reviewed journal articles or book chapters. Reflecting how new online offending research is, the median study year was 2009, and the range was from 2000 to 2009. All samples included child pornography offenders; about half also included online solicitation offenders, but the proportions of types of online offenders were not always clear from individual study descriptions. It is safe to assume, on the basis of criminal justice statistics, that the majority of offenders represented in this meta-analysis had committed child pornography offenses. Babchishin et al. (2011) assumed that newer studies of child pornography offenders involved the Internet, because most recent cases do involve the Internet (e.g., Faust, Renaud, & Bickart, 2009; Seto & Eke, 2005, found that most of their offenders used the Internet to obtain child pornography, but approximately one fifth still had nondigital content).

GROUP SPECIFICITY DESIGNS

Group specificity designs shine light on potential causal candidates by identifying variables that distinguish a group of interest—such as online sex offenders—from a relevant comparison group—such as contact sex offenders (Garber & Hollon, 1991; see Table 5.1). Finding few group differences supports the idea that online offenders and contact offenders are drawn from the same population but perhaps are detected at different times or at different stages in their offending trajectories or are subject to different selection biases. For example, it may be that online offenders are detected before they have progressed to contact sexual offending, because it is easier to express one's sexual interest in children by accessing child pornography than finding opportunities with children in real life. Finding many group differences, however, would suggest that online and contact offenders are drawn from different populations and thereby potentially pose different risks, needs, and intervention requirements. A mixed pattern of differences would suggest a mixture of these two opposing positions (e.g., see Seto & Lalumière, 2010). Variables that distinguish online offenders from contact offenders could then be pursued in longitudinal research to examine trajectories and outcomes and in experimental research to determine whether randomized interventions that target these variables can reduce the likelihood of onset or maintenance of offending. Factors that do not distinguish between the two groups cannot be a sufficient cause of online sexual offending, though they might play a more complex causal role in explaining online sexual offending, for example, in interactions with other factors.

Babchishin et al. (2011) concluded that online offenders (which often included both online-only and dual offenders) are less antisocial, on average, than contact offenders, with less criminal history and lower scores on psychopathy measures; however, they were more likely to be sexually deviant in terms of phallometrically assessed sexual arousal to children, self-reported sexual fantasies, and clinician ratings. Focusing on a few of the individual studies to illustrate this conclusion, Bates and Metcalf (2007) found that their sample of 39 child pornography offenders scored higher in emotional loneliness, lower in emotional identification with children, lower in empathy deficits for children, and lower in offense-supportive attitudes and beliefs than did their sample of 39 mixed contact offenders. Webb, Craissati, and Keen (2007) reported that their sample of 90 child pornography offenders had fewer previous sexual convictions but were more likely to have problems with sexual self-regulation than did their sample of 120 child sexual abuse offenders. Child pornography offenders were less likely to express offense-supportive attitudes about children and sex and less likely to be involved in an intimate relationship. They also scored lower on a measure of psychopathy. Finally, Elliott,

TABLE 5.1
Summary of Specificity Design Studies Comparing Online and Contact
Sexual Offenders, Including Nine Comparison Studies Reported
by Babchishin, Hanson, and Hermann (2011)

Study	Online	Contact	Summary of findings
Bates & Metcalf (2007)	39	39	Online offenders scored higher in emotional loneliness but lower in emotional identification with children, child empathy deficits, and offense-supportive attitudes and beliefs.
Elliott, Beech, Mandeville-Norden, & Hayes (2009)	505	526	Online offenders were lower in offense-supportive cognitions, victim empathy deficits, and impulsivity but higher in perspective-taking deficits and fantasy.
Matsuzawa (2009)	26	26	Minnesota Multiphasic Personality Inventory (MMPI) scale scores tended to be in normal range, but noncontact offenders did score higher in social introversion and negative mood than contact offenders.
Middleton (2009), Table 12.1	213	191	Largest memberships for both Internet and contact offenders in the intimacy deficits and emotional dysregulation pathways. More Internet offenders scored in the dysfunctional range on all four psychological domains, suggesting a more heterogeneous group. Almost half of the sample, however, could not be assigned to any of the five pathways outlined by Ward and Siegert (2002).
Neutze, Seto, Schaefer, Mundt, & Beier (2011)[a]	42	45[c]	No differences on measures of offense-supportive cognitions, victim empathy, affective problems (loneliness, depression, or neuroticism), conscientiousness, sex drive, and self-efficacy.
Reijnen, Bulten, & Nijman (2009)[b]	22	112	No difference on MMPI scales.
Seto, Cantor, & Blanchard (2006)[a]	100	178	Online offenders showed relatively greater sexual arousal to children than to adults (see Figure 5.1).

(*continues*)

TABLE 5.1
TABLE 5.1
Summary of Specificity Design Studies Comparing Online and Contact Sexual Offenders, Including Nine Comparison Studies Reported by Babchishin, Hanson, and Hermann (2011) *(Continued)*

Study	Online	Contact	Summary of findings
Seto, Wood, Babchishin, & Flynn (2012)[d]	118	38	The three groups of offenders were compared on criminal history (age at conviction, number of prior non-sexual arrests), risk measures (VASOR and Static–99), dynamic risk (Stable–2007), and admissions of unknown contact offenses or pedo-hebephilic interests. Child pornography offenders were more likely to admit pedohebephilic sexual interests than the other two groups. In addition, child pornography offenders had more problems than the other two groups with sexual self-regulation and deviant sexual interests as rated on the Stable–2007.
Sheldon & Howitt (2008)[a]	26	25	Online offenders were lower on offense-supportive cognitions, except for beliefs about children as sexual beings.
Tomak, Weschler, Ghahramanlou-Holloway, Virden, & Nademin (2009)	48	104	Online offenders had significantly lower scores on the Pd and Sc scales and also on L and F of the MMPI (2nd ed., Hathaway et al., 1989).
Webb, Craissati, & Keen (2007)	90	120	Online offenders had more sexual self-regulation problems but were lower on psychopathy and offense-supportive attitudes and beliefs and less likely to be in an intimate relationship.

Note. Most offline offenders were contact offenders, but not in every case (e.g., Neutze et al., 2011, included offenders who did not have physical contact with their victims but masturbated in front of a child and a few who engaged in sexually explicit talk or showed pornography).
[a]Neutze et al. (2011), Seto et al. (2006), and Sheldon and Howitt (2008) also included dual offenders, that is, individuals with both online and contact offenses. [b]Reijnen et al. (2009) examined sociodemographic characteristics as well and found that online child pornography offenders were significantly younger on average, were single and lived alone in most cases, and more often had no children of their own. [c]Like the other studies, Neutze et al. (2011) were able to compare by lifetime history as well as activity in the previous 6 months; on the basis of their offending activity in the past 6 months, participants were classified into one of three groups: recently inactive participants (*n* = 40), recent child pornography only offenders (*n* = 64), and recent child sexual abuse offenders (*n* = 51). There were very few differences between these recent activity groups as well. [d]Seto, Wood et al. (2012) included 38 child pornography and 70 solicitation offenders. All of the online offenders denied contact sexual offenses in their clinical interview, but 51% of the child pornography offenders disclosed an undetected contact offense during the polygraph examination, compared with 29% of the luring offenders and 50% of the contact offenders.

Beech, Mandeville-Norden, and Hayes (2009) reported group differences on seven of their 15 self-report measures, with 526 contact sex offenders scoring higher than 505 online offenders on offense-supportive cognitions and victim empathy deficits but lower on perspective-taking deficits, lower in fantasy, higher in cognitive impulsivity, and as more external in their perceived locus of control.

ONLINE OFFENDER HETEROGENEITY AND UNDETECTED OFFENDING

In addition to the selection issues raised at the beginning of this chapter, the combination of child pornography and solicitation offenders in the online offender samples examined by Babchishin et al. (2011) may obscure differences with contact offenders, to the extent that these two online offender groups differ in meaningful ways. I have already reviewed evidence to suggest that these two types of online offenders differ in their sexual interests: The majority of child pornography offenders are likely to be pedophiles or hebephiles, according to their sexual arousal patterns and self-report (Seto, Cantor, & Blanchard, 2006; Seto, Reeves, & Jung, 2010), whereas most solicitation offenders (at least those who actually meet or attempt to meet with minors) are unlikely to be pedophiles because they focus on adolescents between the ages of 13 and 15 (Wolak, Finkelhor, Mitchell, & Ybarra, 2008). Some online solicitation offenders—those preferentially targeting 12 or 13 year olds—may be hebephilic. Consistent with this idea, we recently reported that solicitation offenders scored lower on measures of sexual deviance than did child pornography offenders (Seto et al., 2012). Fewer solicitation offenders admitted sexual interests in prepubescent or pubescent children or disclosed undetected sexual offenses, and solicitation offenders received lower clinician ratings on the sexual deviance items of the Stable–2007 (Hanson, Harris, Scott, & Helmus, 2007) when compared with the online child pornography offenders.

Another important methodological consideration in conducting and interpreting comparison studies is the influence of undetected offenses on group comparisons. Comparing online offenders who have committed undetected contact offenses with contact offenders who have committed undetected online offenses would attenuate any differences that might be found. Studies vary greatly on how thoroughly they verify the sexual offending histories of offender groups; most have relied on official criminal records. Studies of online offenders have paid more systematic attention to contact offending history because that is the greatest concern; they have varied, however, on how thoroughly they distinguish online offenders according to contact offending history. The purest possible comparison for detecting group differences would involve online-only and contact-only offender samples, verified by both official records and self-report.

It would be particularly helpful if self-report was honest, because offenders were assessed as part of their participation in treatment, after trust had been established, as part of polygraph interviews, or after reassurance of anonymity or confidentiality (e.g., in research using a certificate of confidentiality in the United States; Abel et al., 1987; Ahlmeyer, Heil, McKee, & English, 2000). The trade-off of these self-report comparisons is that individuals who had participated in treatment may provide different responses (e.g., regarding offense-supportive attitudes and beliefs) than they would have prior to treatment participation.

SOCIODEMOGRAPHIC CHARACTERISTICS

In this and the following sections, I consider all studies that have described samples of online offenders. I emphasize the findings reported by Babchishin et al. (2011) but sometimes refer to individual studies and newer group specificity studies that have appeared since Babchishin et al.'s meta-analysis was conducted.

Gender

The strongest sociodemographic correlate of online offending is gender. Online offenders are extremely likely to be male, even when compared with contact sexual offenders, who themselves are significantly more likely to be male than the general offender population (which in turn is male-biased compared with the general population's ratio). Many studies have found only a few female online offenders; for example, in our research studies and studies by the Crimes Against Children Research Center, 99% of offenders are male (Eke, Seto, & Williams, 2011; Wolak, Finkelhor, & Mitchell, 2005). Only seven of 199 child pornography offenders in Fortin and Roy (2007) were women, and only one of these women offended on her own.

There are several plausible explanations for this large gender difference that are also useful in thinking about the origins of (online) sexual offending. First, males are more likely to take risks and engage in antisocial behavior than are females, on average, as reflected in the large gender differences in both official and self-reported criminal behavior (Quinsey, Skilling, Lalumière, & Craig, 2004). There is an even larger gender difference in sexual offending, though the difference is larger for offenses involving adults than for offenses involving children (Atkinson, 1996; Greenfield, 1997; Motiuk & Vuong, 2002).

Second, most identified pedophiles are male, with only some case reports of women who meet the clinical definitions of pedophilia (e.g., Chow & Choy, 2002; A. J. Cooper, Swaminath, Baxter, & Poulin, 1990). Hebephilia is less studied, but men should be disproportionately represented in samples of hebephiles as well because there is a large gender difference in the prevalence of all paraphilias that have been studied (with the exception of masochism) and because hebephilia and pedophilia are topographically linked (Blanchard et al., 2012).

Third, there is a moderate gender difference in interest in pornography and casual sex (Petersen & Hyde, 2010), which could help explain males' greater involvement in online pornography (including illegal pornography) and sexual solicitation of strangers online. The fact that contact sex offenders are more likely to be male than offenders in general indicates the gender difference is greater than the gender differences in criminal behavior, antisocial personality, and risk taking. The fact that online offenders are even more likely to be male than contact offenders suggests something specific about being online is involved as well.

Anonymous survey data has suggested that some women view child pornography (Seigfried, Lovely, & Rogers, 2008), and I mentioned earlier in this book the possibility that women may engage in sexual solicitation of minors and remain undetected because the minors are not distressed or worried about the solicitations.[1] Observations that some women in roles of authority (e.g., schoolteachers) commit sexual offenses involving young adolescents suggests some women do contact adolescents online for sexual purposes.

Age

Babchishin et al. (2011) found that online offenders are younger, on average, than contact sexual offenders in the six studies that compared the two groups. Online offenders are also younger in comparison with the general male population. This sociodemographic observation can be parsimoniously explained as a by-product of younger age being correlated with greater Internet involvement. If Internet adoption explains the age finding, then one would expect smaller and eventually no age differences between online offenders and other sexual offenders as Internet users grow up and Internet use becomes ubiquitous in developed countries.

---

[1]I have indicated my reservation about this survey study by Seigfried et al. (2008) earlier. The potential discrepancy between officially detected and self-reported online offending requires further research.

Education

Babchishin et al. (2011) found that online offenders are better educated, on average, than contact sexual offenders in four comparison studies. A difference in education was also found in McWhaw's (2011) unpublished thesis comparing 53 online-only and 53 contact-only offenders. Again, this observation may reflect the fact that Internet use is positively correlated with education level at this time, with more highly educated individuals being more active online. If this is correct, one would expect smaller differences in education as Internet access becomes more intuitive, user friendly, and ubiquitous. For example, future developments in voice- and touch-activated interfaces can facilitate Internet activity for individuals who might otherwise be discouraged by the technicalities of accessing peer-to-peer networks.

Intelligence

Blanchard et al. (2007) found a similar group difference in intelligence. Child pornography offenders scored higher in intelligence than contact sexual offenders, with an average IQ score close to the population average of 100, whereas contact sexual offenders are typically 10 points below the population average, consistent with research showing that offenders generally score lower on intelligence tests than the general population (e.g., White, Moffitt, & Silva, 1989). This is again likely to be the result of a selection effect, whereby Internet offenders are using computers to commit their crimes, and less intelligent individuals would be expected to be less proficient with these technologies. Interfaces that make Internet use easier should reduce this difference.

The observed difference in intelligence between online and contact offenders is in the opposite direction expected: A meta-analysis found that pedophilic sex offenders (contact offenders with child victims below the age of 12) scored lower in intelligence than nonpedophilic sex offenders or other kinds of offenders (Cantor, Blanchard, Robichaud, & Christensen, 2005). Child pornography offenders are more likely to be pedophilic than contact offenders with child victims (Seto et al., 2006); thus, if the pedophilia and intelligence association held across offending behaviors, one would expect child pornography offenders to score lower, rather than higher, than contact sex offenders on measures of intelligence.

Ethnicity

Babchishin et al. (2011) found in three comparison studies that Internet offenders are significantly more likely to be Caucasian than are contact sexual offenders. The proportion of Caucasians among online offenders is greater than the proportion among general offenders or the general population. What explains this disproportionality, and is it relevant to our understanding of etiology, risk, or intervention?

The discrepancy in ethnicity could be a function of ethnic differences in Internet use. However, data from surveys completed for the Pew Internet and American Life Project indicated that Blacks access the Internet less than do Whites, which fits with the observed distribution. Yet, Hispanics were on par or even a little ahead of Whites as of 2009, and Asians have the highest Internet usage, even after statistically controlling for age, gender, income, and education level (Jacobs & Albert, 2008). The National Telecommunications and Information Administration in the United States has data showing that Whites were ahead of non-Whites in Internet use up to the mid-2000s. Should we thus expect to see more non-White Internet offenders in coming years?

Marital Status

There were not enough comparison studies for statistical analysis by Babchishin et al. (2011), but online offenders (nine samples) were less likely to have ever been married than the general population, on the basis of normative data. This difference in marital status compared with the general population may be related to differences found in some studies on measures of interpersonal and affective functioning, including social skills, loneliness, and self-esteem (Middleton, Elliott, Mandeville-Norden, & Beech, 2006; Webb et al., 2007). It may also reflect the prominent role of pedophilia and hebephilia in child pornography offending: Individuals who are sexually attracted to prepubescent or pubescent aged children are less likely to enter adult relationships.

PSYCHOLOGICAL FACTORS

Mann, Hanson, and Thornton (2010) suggested that a major advance in our understanding of sexual offending and the assessment of risk of recidivism will come from identifying psychologically meaningful risk factors, which they defined as plausible causes of sexual offending that can predict recidivism and that can help drive interventions. For example, demonstrating that pedophilia is a psychologically meaningful risk factor for sexual offending against children—which is supported by many converging lines of evidence—suggests that addressing pedophilic thoughts, fantasies, urges, and sexual arousal is a critical component of interventions aimed at reducing such offenses (see Seto, 2008).

This section again draws on the meta-analysis by Babchishin et al. (2011) but includes individual studies as well if (a) comparison studies were not included in the meta-analysis because they appeared after the analysis was conducted, (b) studies are relevant but did not involve comparisons of online and contact offenders, or (c) there are specific details about individual studies that I want to highlight. Many of these psychological factors have been identified in explanatory models of sexual offending (discussed in more detail in Chapter 4) and in dynamic risk research on contact sex offenders (Chapter 7).

Group comparisons suggest areas in which online offenders are similar to or different from contact offenders in the factors that might help explain their offending or that might predict reoffending in the future. Sociodemographic factors play a role, as demonstrated in the previous section. A challenge in the psychological domain is the lack of a sufficient number of studies to reliably detect differences. More research is needed, but in the meantime, the current evidence suggests the following.

Offense-Supportive Attitudes and Beliefs

Offense-supportive attitudes and beliefs are central to many contemporary models of contact sexual offending (see Ward, Polaschek, & Beech, 2006). The common hypothesis is that sex offenders are more likely to endorse attitudes and beliefs that justify or rationalize criminal sexual behavior. Some men, for example, may believe that children are not harmed by sexual contacts with adults, making it more likely that they are willing to engage in such behavior. Because contact offenders have directly offended against children whereas only some online offenders have done so, one would predict that contact offenders would score higher on measures of offense-supportive attitudes and beliefs. Babchishin et al. (2011) found no group difference in the four studies that examined offense-supportive attitudes and beliefs, however.

Though they are central to theoretical and clinical accounts of sexual offending, it is not obvious that offense-supportive attitudes and beliefs should matter. First, measures of these attitudes and beliefs are often transparent, and thus the "correct" response is relatively easy to determine. Individuals who are trying to present themselves in the best possible light, as they might during an evaluation to inform sentencing, treatment, or supervision decisions, may understandably lie about their attitudes and beliefs. Second, these attitudes and beliefs may actually be a result rather than a cause of sexual offending, in line with the large, established literature on cognitive dissonance (Festinger, 1957). In this unorthodox view, an individual commits an offense, such as downloading child pornography or soliciting a child for sexual purposes, that is inconsistent with his view of himself as an otherwise "good" and "moral" person. One way to reconcile cognitive dissonance is to unconsciously shift one's attitudes and beliefs. For example, if the individual believes children are not harmed by being depicted in child pornography or being sexually solicited online, the offender can still view himself as a good and moral person. The other option, changing one's behavior, is impossible for the past and potentially difficult for the future.

Third, offense-supportive attitudes and beliefs may be examples of a tendency to engage in rationalization that is common among offenders and among humans in general (Harmon-Jones & Mills, 1999). Other offenders, not only sex offenders, also espouse attitudes and beliefs that rationalize their criminal behavior. Individuals who steal may believe there is no victim because property losses can be covered by insurance, or individuals who commit physical assaults may believe the victim deserved it because of their "provocative" behavior. In contrast to this "universalist" perspective on human psychology and the psychology of offending, it is also possible that the attitudes and beliefs that are supportive of online offending may differ from those that are supportive of contact offending. Research examining the offense-related attitudes and beliefs of online offenders is needed to determine whether specific measures are required. For example, the belief that viewing child pornography is an acceptable substitute for sexual contact with children is likely to be more salient for online child pornography offenders than it is for contact offenders.

Emotional Identification (Congruence) With Children

Emotional identification or congruence with children has been cited by many theorists as an important explanation for sexual offending against children (e.g., Finkelhor, 1984). In this view, individuals who feel more affinity with children than to adults are more likely to fill their emotional and other relational needs with children, especially if other risk factors are also present, such as impulsivity, tolerance for the risk of getting caught, or lack of suitable opportunities with adults.

Emotional identification can be viewed as a correlate of pedophilia, wherein someone who is sexually attracted to children also finds himself drawn to children emotionally and psychologically (see Seto, 2008). Because child pornography offenders are more likely to be pedophilic or hebephilic than contact offenders, on average, one would expect online offenders to also score higher on measures of emotional identification with children (Seto et al., 2006). However, one could speculate that individuals who are high in emotional identification with children are more likely to commit contact sexual offenses because they would seek out more opportunities to be with children. There was no difference in emotional identification with children in four studies reviewed by Babchishin et al. (2011), suggesting any role of emotional identification is complicated, perhaps involving subgroups who are low or high on this dimension. In a recent meta-analysis, McPhail (2010) found that contact offenders with child victims did not report significantly more emotional congruence with children than non-sex offenders; subgroup analysis revealed that the exceptions were extrafamilial offenders with boy victims.

Loneliness

Marshall and others (e.g., Cortoni & Marshall, 2001; Marshall, Serran, & Cortoni, 2000) have suggested that loneliness and other negative states can contribute to sexual offending because individuals who are lonely may be more likely to seek sex as a way of coping. If consensual sex is not available, then at-risk individuals may resort to the use of coercive tactics against adults or seek out inappropriate targets such as children (where coercion may also be used). Moreover, individuals may be lonely because they are socially isolated or lack skills to develop healthy relationships and thereby may be at greater risk of sexual offending (Dreznick, 2003). This factor could be more salient for online offenders because online offenders spend more time online and therefore have less time for real-life interactions. Some online offenders may go online in part because of loneliness, social isolation, or social anxiety (Taylor & Quayle, 2003). Again, however, there was no group difference in loneliness for the four studies reviewed by Babchishin et al. (2011). In a study that was not included in the meta-analysis, Wall, Pearce, and McGuire (2011) found no differences on measures of emotional avoidance between 15 online offenders, 18 contact offenders with child victims, 25 nonsexual offenders, and 25 nonoffending controls.

Lack of Empathy

Lack of empathy has also been included in explanations of sexual offending because individuals who are more callous are presumably more willing to act in ways that might harm others. Following this logic, one would expect contact offenders to score lower on measures of empathy than would online offenders. This prediction was supported by the results of three comparison studies reviewed by Babchishin et al. (2011), which found that contact offenders scored lower on measures of victim empathy than online offenders. It would be interesting to see whether the same group difference was found using general measures of empathy.

SEXUAL DEVIANCE

One psychologically meaningful domain where online and contact offenders clearly differ is in sexual deviance, even though only three studies totaling 435 offenders were available for Babchishin et al.'s (2011) meta-analysis. In one of these studies, my colleagues and I examined the sexual arousal patterns of 100 child pornography offenders and compared them with the arousal patterns of 178 sex offenders with child victims, 216 sex offenders with adult victims, and 191 general sexology patients presenting with concerns about noncriminal sexual behavior such as fetishism or sexual compulsivity (Seto et al., 2006). None of the men in the latter three groups had any known history of child pornography possession.

As a group, the 100 child pornography offenders showed significantly greater sexual arousal to children, relative to adults, than the other groups (see Figure 5.1). Of the 100 child pornography offenders, 53 had a prior history of sexual offenses directly involving children, and 47 had no history; these two groups did not significantly differ in their relative sexual arousal to children. In contrast, McCarthy (2010) compared 56 child pornography only offenders with 51 dual offenders (child pornography plus contact offenses). The dual offenders were more likely to be diagnosed with pedophilia and were more likely to have committed prior sexual offenses.

Overall, the majority (61%) of child pornography offenders in Seto et al. (2006) showed a preference for depictions of children over depictions of adults. We concluded that child pornography offending might be a stronger diagnostic indicator of pedophilia than sexually offending against a child (Seto et al., 2006). Our explanation was that some nonpedophilic men opportunistically offend against children; this would include antisocial men who seek sexual gratification from adolescents who show some signs of sexual development but are below the legally defined age of consent (see Graupner, 2000). These results were subsequently replicated in the same laboratory using a new sample of child pornography offenders (Blanchard et al., 2007).

People can freely choose the kind of pornography they want to see. Legal and freely available adult pornography is abundant on the Internet; thus, few nonpedophilic men would choose illegal child pornography unless there was a personal significance to the child pornography content. Some Internet users might look at child pornography out of curiosity, but they would be unlikely to save the content on their computers or repeatedly view it. As a result, an undifferentiated group of offenders with child victims would show less sexual arousal to children, on average, than a group of child pornography offenders.

I am not aware of similar studies involving a group of online solicitation offenders, other than our recent three-group comparison study (Seto, Wood, Babchishin, & Flynn, 2012). I would expect to see smaller or no difference

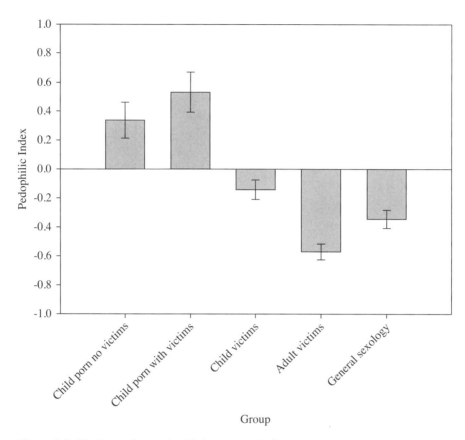

Figure 5.1. Phallometric results. Higher scores indicate greater response to children relative to adults. Groups are child pornography offenders with no known child victims, dual offenders (both child pornography and known child victims), offenders with child victims only, a comparison group of nonpedophilic sex offenders, and general sexology patients. From "Child Pornography Offenses Are a Valid Diagnostic Indicator of Pedophilia," by M. C. Seto, J. M. Cantor, and R. Blanchard, 2006, *Journal of Abnormal Psychology, 115,* p. 610–615. Copyright 2006 by the American Psychological Association.

between solicitation and contact offenders or a difference in the opposite direction (some contact offenders will be pedophiles or hebephiles, whereas most solicitation offenders are not expected to be paraphilic).

Legal scholars have frequently criticized this research when it is used in court proceedings to justify arguments for longer sentences (presumably on the logic that pedophilic child pornography offenders necessarily pose a high risk of harm to children). For example, Hamilton (2012) raised concerns about the selection of our (Seto et al., 2006) sample from a specialty sexual behavior clinic (which we acknowledged); the fact that 20% of the original sample was excluded for different reasons, including no laboratory responding, and the fact that stimuli included pubescent children and therefore included hebephilia and not just pedophilia. These limitations would have weakened our conclusions if they had differentially affected the groups. For example, excluding nonresponders is only a serious problem if more child pornography offenders or more contact offenders were excluded for this reason.

Another potential limitation of the study by Seto et al. (2006) that Hamilton (2012) did not raise is that we might have detected conditioned responding to visual sexual stimuli in the phallometric lab, given that child pornography offenders had viewed a lot of this kind of content, almost by definition (Quayle, 2008). If this conditioning explanation is correct, then child pornography offenders may not be more likely to have pedophilia than contact offenders but may be more likely to respond pedophilically because they are more responsive under laboratory conditions. A counterargument is that desensitization might also play a role in sexual response to children, such that photographs of nude children shown in the lab are less arousing than the sexually explicit images and videos the child pornography offenders have previously seen.[2]

Babchishin et al. (2011) also examined two other group comparison studies. The first was reported by Sheldon and Howitt (2008), who compared 16 Internet offenders, 25 contact offenders, and 10 dual offenders (both online and contact offenses) on the sexual fantasies they acknowledged on the Wilson Sexual Fantasy Questionnaire. Online and dual offenders were more likely to report sexual fantasies about girls under age 15 than contact offenders. Contact offenders, in contrast, were more likely to report sexual fantasies that involved some form of confrontation and nonconsent (e.g., making obscene telephone calls, exhibitionism) with another person than did online offenders.

The second study examined clinician ratings of sexual deviance on the Stable–2007, a dynamic risk measure for contact sex offenders (Wood, Seto, Flynn, Wilson-Cotton, & Dedmon, 2009). Online offenders scored higher in sex drive/preoccupation and sexual deviance than contact offenders. In a subsequent analysis with more participants and additional data collection, we were also able to examine information about self-reported sexual interests and behavior that were not included in the Babchishin et al. (2011) meta-analysis (Seto et al., 2012). As I described in Chapter 3, we again found that online offenders scored higher on sexual drive and sexual deviance than contact offenders on the Stable–2007. They were also more likely to self-report sexual

---

[2]If desensitization or habituation occurs, even more child pornography offenders would have been identified as pedophilic in the laboratory if our stimuli were sufficiently intense. These ideas can be tested by further studies using audio-only stimuli—because most (detected) child pornography is visual in nature—and by including explicit sexual stories describing penetration and other sexual acts.

interests in prepubescent or pubescent children. Solicitation offenders scored lower than child pornography offenders on these variables, again supporting the potential value of distinguishing these two types of online offenders.

Overall, the results of these comparison studies suggest that pedophilia is likely among child pornography offenders but unlikely among solicitation offenders. This initial conclusion is consistent with other research that supports a link between pedophilia and child pornography offending, including an early qualitative study by Quayle and Taylor (2002), who interviewed 13 men who were convicted of downloading online child pornography. Many, but not all, of the men acknowledged that the content they downloaded was sexually arousing and corresponded to their sexual fantasies. They also claimed, however, that they downloaded child pornography because it was novel or because it completed series they were collecting (see my previous comments about collecting psychology in Appendix 4.1). Jenkins (2001), in his observations of posts to an online forum for "child lovers," noted a strong overlap of group membership with child pornography use. In contrast to the findings reported by Babchishin et al. (2011), McWhaw (2011) found that his sample of 50 online-only offenders were less, rather than more, likely to be identified as having pedophilic sexual arousal than 51 contact-only offenders (58% vs. 82%). It is not clear why McWhaw found discrepant results in his unpublished study.

Riegel (2004) found that most of the 290 respondents to his anonymous online survey reported they were sexually attracted to boys. Ninety-five percent of the respondents also reported viewing child pornography online, with a majority viewing it "frequently" (59%) and two thirds admitting that they masturbated while viewing child pornography. Assuming deception is not a concern, this again shows there is a meaningful association between pedophilia and child pornography use, consistent with Seto et al.'s (2006) findings. Approximately one in five (18%) respondents indicated they had also viewed nondigital content (which turns out to be a predictor of recidivism among identified child pornography offenders; see Faust et al., 2009, discussed further in Chapter 7). Only 5% of the sample had never viewed child pornography. A majority of the respondents thought that viewing child pornography reduced their urges to engage in sexual contact with boys. Unfortunately, the veracity of this claim was not examined, for example, by comparing users and nonusers of child pornography in their sexual contacts with boys. Riegel did not ask about sexual contacts, ostensibly to avoid any threat of incrimination for survey respondents.

Buschman and his colleagues interviewed 38 child pornography offenders, first in a standard clinical assessment and then as part of a polygraph examination (Buschman, Wilcox, Krapohl, Oelrich, & Hackett, 2010; see also Buschman & Bogaerts, 2009). Forty-five percent of the offenders admitted masturbating to child pornography, but all denied masturbating to images depicting sexual violence, and all denied having any sexual contacts with children. The offenders claimed that they were more likely to masturbate to depictions of adolescents than to children aged 13 or younger. In contrast to the clinical interview, all of the offenders admitted masturbating to child pornography during the polygraph interview, and they admitted that they were more likely to masturbate to images of young children (age 6 and under) than children between the ages of 7 and 13 or adolescents. Forty-five percent admitted sexual contact with a child, for a total of 37 victims. Only three cases had been reported to police, and none resulted in criminal prosecution. All were first-time offenders, according to official records. These results show the discrepancy between what offenders are willing to admit in a clinical context versus what they might be willing to disclose under the threat of deception detection (putting aside the controversy about the validity of polygraph disclosures).

Analyzing data from the German Dunkelfeld Prevention Project, which I discuss again in Chapter 8, Kuhle, Konrad, and Beier (2011) reported that hebephilic participants used more child pornography (of young adolescents, presumably) than pedophilic participants. The greatest use of child pornography was reported by nonexclusive pedophiles or hebephiles, probably because their sexual interests are broader than those of an exclusive pedophile or an exclusive hebephile, and thus more child pornography is interesting to them. The participants also reported other paraphilic interests, especially voyeurism, sexual sadism, and fetishism.

Examining the same data set, Neutze, Seto, Schaefer, Mundt, and Beier (2011) reported that 45% of their sample of 257 pedophiles and hebephiles (with the majority preferring boys) had one additional paraphilic interest, rating masturbatory fantasies about this additional content as quite or very sexually arousing. Sixty-one percent reported engaging in other paraphilic behavior. Similar paraphilic overlap was reported by Frei, Erenay, Dittmann, and Graf (2005) in their small sample of Swiss child pornography offenders and in our study of child pornography offenders in Canada (Seto, 2009). Neutze et al. also reported the results of a comparison of 57 child pornography only offenders with 56 contact only offenders and 144 mixed offenders, classified on the basis of their self-reported sexual offending. Mixed offenders were more likely to report other paraphilic interests and reported higher sexual preoccupation than the other two groups.

OTHER MOTIVATIONS

As I noted in the previous chapter, sexually deviant fantasies and interests are not the sole motivation for online offending. Many child pornography offenders, and a minority of solicitation offenders, may engage in criminal online behavior because of pedophilia or hebephilia, but other motivations include addictive or compulsive behavior involving pornography or sex more broadly, progressive habituation of sexual response due to high levels of pornography or online sexual activity, commercial gain, and curiosity. I do not include individuals who access child pornography accidentally or unknowingly here because these individuals are not motivated to access this content (e.g., when child pornography files are included in a large compressed file purporting to contain adult pornography or when they are downloaded as a result of malware or hacking).[3] Some of these motivations are nonsexual—for commercial gain or curiosity, for example—and thus fall outside the motivation–facilitation model of sexual offending I described in the previous chapter.

There are some data on nonparaphilic motivations for online offending. Because there are usually no objective means of assessing these other motivations, this research has relied on self-report and thus is subject to reporting and other biases. It is understandable that offenders might claim sexual addiction, for example, if they are arrested and charged with child pornography or solicitation, because this is a more palatable explanation to oneself, one's family, and to judges or juries than pedophilia or hebephilia. Given these caveats, Seto, Reeves, and Jung (2010) found that 43% of the combined 84 child pornography offenders in their study acknowledged that they were sexually interested in children or child pornography. The offenders also claimed other explanations, particularly curiosity and accidental access, though a majority of offenders admitted they deliberately accessed child pornography. Explanations could change over time—for example, an offender might claim curiosity or accidental access when first questioned by police but subsequently acknowledge deliberate access and a sexual motivation after being challenged with the digital evidence and with persistent questioning. Relatively few offenders claimed Internet addiction, child pornography as a substitute for contact offending, or indiscriminate sexual interests. Our total sample consisted of 50 individuals who were interviewed by police and subsequently convicted of child pornography offenses and 34 postconviction child pornography offenders who were assessed by clinicians. The only significant group difference in explanations was in sexual addiction: The clinical sample was more likely to claim this motivation.

Surjadi, Bullens, van Horn, and Bogaerts (2010) looked at the self-reported motivations of 43 Internet offenders, after excluding seven

---

[3]It is hard to imagine how online solicitation offenders might accidentally engage in sexual interactions with minors, unless they were under the genuinely mistaken belief they were actually interacting with an adult who was playing a minor in fantasy role playing.

offenders with prior contact offenses (thus, 14% of the initial sample had a contact offense history; this study was not included in the Seto, Hanson, & Babchishin, 2011, meta-analysis). The offenders completed an Internet function questionnaire, with the highest average rating for an avoidant function (avoiding real life problems), followed by sexual motivations (pedophilic or other). Approximately a third of the offenders (32%) claimed they never masturbated to child pornography, whereas the others acknowledged they did masturbate to this content. Twenty-seven percent of the sample admitted masturbating the first time they encountered child pornography, whereas 40% claimed they started masturbating later (most commonly, within 2 months of their first encounter with child pornography). Those who acknowledged masturbating to child pornography were more likely to report being sexually aroused by children or being sexually aroused by another paraphilic interest; they also scored higher on the avoidant function. It is odd that this difference was found for those who masturbated the first time they viewed child pornography, but not for those who masturbated later. These data are consistent with explanations offered by some child pornography offenders that they were not initially sexually interested in children but developed a stronger or more specific sexual response on repeat viewing. A skeptic might wonder, however, whether this might be rationalization.

One of the distinctive aspects of online offending is that there is objective evidence to infer motivation, through forensic analysis of computer drives and other storage media; it is possible to obtain details about child and other pornography content. For example, having pornography depicting paraphilic sexual activities or objects, especially if there is a lot of it and it represents a sizeable proportion of total pornography, suggests the person is sexually interested in that type of content. Recency and frequency of access and other evidence of interest (e.g., organizing content by themes into separate folders) would also be informative. So too would the ratios of different kinds of pornography content; someone with similar amounts of pornography depicting adults, children, sadomasochism, and fetishism might be hypersexual, whereas someone with a pornography collection that mostly includes child pornography would have a harder time making this argument. In addition to pornography, a thorough forensic analysis could also examine e-mails, chat logs, and other text that might reveal more information about motivations (Glasgow, 2012; Stabenow, 2011). Unfortunately, these data are not usually accessible to clinicians because the focus of police investigations and prosecutions is criminal online behavior. The fact that someone has a large amount of mainstream adult pornography, for example, might not be recorded systematically because this content is not illegal.

PSYCHIATRIC SYMPTOMS

There has been relatively little research on psychiatric comorbidity among online or contact offenders. There is some reason to expect mood problems among sexual offenders, given models that suggest emotional dysregulation plays a role in sexual offending (Finkelhor, 1984; Hall & Hirschman, 1991; Ward et al., 2006) and some studies suggesting a link between disturbed mood and compulsive or excessive sexual behavior (Kafka, 1997). Krueger, Kaplan, and First (2009) found no differences in psychiatric diagnoses between their groups of 22 solicitation offenders and 38 child pornography only offenders; however, they did not have a comparison group of contact offenders.

ANTISOCIALITY

Criminal history is an established risk factor for recidivism among every offender population that has ever been studied and thus is highly likely to be relevant for online offenders as well. Criminal history is also important because it is an indicator of *antisociality* (antisocial tendencies), a broad constellation of predispositions including antisocial personality traits such as risk taking, impulsivity, callousness, offense-supportive attitudes and beliefs, substance misuse, and associations with criminal peers. Our conceptualization of antisociality (Lalumière, Harris, Quinsey, & Rice, 2005; Seto, 2008) is similar to Donovan and Jessor's (1985) notion of a general deviance syndrome (see also Farrington, Piquero, & Jennings, in press; McGee & Newcomb, 1992; Moffitt, 1993). Antisociality plays an important role in etiological models of general and sexual offending, including sexual offending against children (Andrews & Bonta, 2010; Lalumière et al., 2005; Seto, 2008). Prior contact sexual offending is particularly important because online offenders with such a history can be scored using existing sex offender risk measures, whereas the validity of these measures for online offenders with no prior contact offending is less clear (see Chapter 7).

Several studies have found that online offenders are less likely to have a prior criminal history, and they score lower on measures of antisocial tendencies than contact offenders. Motivans and Kyckelhahn (2007) looked at federal prosecutions of child exploitation cases in the United States over a wide span of years and found that child pornography offenders were less likely to have a prior felony conviction than contact offenders. In a United Kingdom sample, Webb et al. (2007) compared 120 contact offenders with child victims and 90 Internet child pornography offenders on criminal history and scores on the screening version of the Psychopathy Checklist, a well-validated measure of psychopathic personality traits. Child pornography offenders had less extensive criminal histories and lower scores on psychopathy. Child pornography offenders also scored lower on offense-supportive attitudes and beliefs and negative peers, as assessed using the Stable–2007 sex offender risk measure (discussed in more detail in Chapter 7). McWhaw (2011) compared 53 online-only offenders and 53 contact-only offenders and found that contact-only offenders had more extensive sexual and nonsexual criminal histories and were more likely to have had conditional release violations than online-only offenders. As I noted earlier in this chapter, Babchishin et al. (2011) found that online offenders scored higher on measures of victim empathy than did contact offenders.

Across studies, Babchishin et al. (2011) found that online offenders were unlikely to have a prior criminal history involving nonsexual offenses; in their meta-analysis, 12% (136 of 1,150) of the online offenders had one or more prior nonsexual offenses. We did not find a significant difference in nonsexual arrest history in a comparison of child pornography, solicitation, and contact offenders (Seto et al., 2012), but this was not an ideal comparison for examining criminal history because the contact offenders were selected to be lower risk because of the way the cases were identified for evaluation and data analysis: Offenders had to undergo a polygraph examination to be part of the study sample, and only contact offenders with less extensive criminal histories were referred for these examinations. In a study that was published after the Babchishin et al. meta-analysis was conducted, Jung, Ennis, Stein, Choy, and Hook (in press) also found that a group of 50 child pornography offenders had a less extensive criminal history than a group of 101 contact offenders. It is notable that the same difference was found when comparing child pornography offenders with 45 noncontact sex offenders, most of whom had engaged in exhibitionistic acts. There were more similarities than differences across these three sex offender groups; when there were significant differences, child pornography offenders tended to have fewer problems (e.g., substance use, childhood behavior problems, school or work problems).

In another recent study of federally incarcerated offenders, Magaletta, Faust, Bickart, and McLearen (2012) compared 26 contact sex offenders with child victims and 35 child pornography offenders on a broad-band measure of clinical and personal functioning, the Personality Assessment Inventory. There were a number of differences between these two groups. Notably, child pornography offenders were similar to male norms but significantly lower than contact offenders on scales tapping into antisociality, including dominance, aggression, antisocial features, alcohol use problems, and drug use problems. Both groups of sex offenders were higher in anxiety and depression than the male normative sample.

SEXUAL OR PHYSICAL ABUSE HISTORY

There is converging evidence that sexual abuse history is a distinguishing feature for contact sexual offending, among both adolescents and adults. Two meta-analyses have found that both adolescent and adult sex offenders are significantly more likely to have histories of sexual abuse than their non-sexually offending counterparts (Jespersen, Lalumière, & Seto, 2009; Seto & Lalumière, 2010). Most, but not all, of the sex offenders in these meta-analyses had committed contact sexual offenses. The difference between sexual offenders and their nonsexually offending counterparts was smaller or statistically nonsignificant for physical abuse history, suggesting a specific association between sexual abuse and sexual offending; the results for physical abuse history also contradict the idea that sex offenders might simply report more maltreatment. There is longitudinal evidence that abuse and other forms of maltreatment predict later delinquency, including sexual offending (Maxfield & Widom, 1996). Further longitudinal evidence was reported by Salter et al. (2003), who found that approximately 10% of children who had been sexually abused were later detected for sexual offending. Taken together, these different lines of evidence support the notion that sexual offenders are more likely to have been sexually abused themselves (this is often referred to as the *abused–abuser or cycle of abuse hypothesis*).

It does not appear that the abuse–perpetration link exists solely because sex offenders are more likely to claim sexual abuse histories, because the relatively small number of studies that examined other sources of data (e.g., parent or teacher reports, official child protection records) also showed a group difference in the same direction (Seto & Lalumière, 2010). Maxfield and Widom (1996) followed a cohort of children who were deemed not through self-report but by child protection workers to have been maltreated. In addition, the sexual-abuse–sexual-perpetration link has been found in community samples in anonymous surveys; for example, we found that sexual coercion history predicted perpetration of sexual coercion in a population-representative sample of young Swedish and Norwegian men (Seto, Kjellgren, et al., 2010). The strength of the association was attenuated but remained statistically significant even after we controlled for antisocial and sexual behavior correlates, further lending support to the specificity of this link.

Experiencing sexual abuse does not play a role in the persistence of sexual offending because sexual abuse history does not predict new offenses among identified adult sexual offenders (Hanson & Bussière, 1998; Hanson & Morton-Bourgon, 2004, 2005). There may be something about experiencing sexual abuse that increases the risk of onset of sexual offending, though more research is needed to rule out a third variable explanation, such as a predisposition toward risk taking that increases the likelihood of being sexually abused and also increases the likelihood of sexually offending for the first time.

One causal possibility is that sexual abuse influences psychosexual development. The critical element may be exposure to sexual violence and/or age-inappropriate exposure to sex; Seto and Lalumière (2010) found that adolescent sex offenders were also more likely to have been exposed to sexual violence in the family and to have an early exposure to sex or pornography than other adolescent offenders. Burton (2000) reported that the offending behaviors of adolescent sexual offenders were correlated with the behaviors they experienced themselves as sexual abuse victims. Factors that may influence an effect of sexual abuse include the age, gender, and relationship of the perpetrator to the victim; the duration and intrusiveness of the sexual behaviors; and whether the child experienced any sexual arousal as a result of the contact. Rind, Tromovitch, and Bauserman (1998) showed that being threatened or forced into sexual activity as a child was associated with negative mental health and other outcomes. Koenig, Doll, O'Leary, & Pequegnat (2004) reviewed the literature on the associations of childhood sexual abuse and later general sexual adjustment. These included studies demonstrating a link between childhood sexual abuse and risky sexual behavior such as unprotected intercourse, more casual sexual partners, unwanted pregnancy, infection with sexually transmitted diseases, and adult sexual victimization.

The parallel research on potential mediators of the sexual abuse–perpetration link has not been quantitatively reviewed in the adult sex offender literature, except in the case of pornography use: These studies find that adult sex offenders do not differ from adult nonoffenders in their age of first exposure to pornography or frequency of use (Allen, D'Alessio, & Emmers-Sommer, 2000). It is not clear how much sex offenders differ in their psychosexual development from non-sex offenders. Sexual offenders against children have a less extensive adult sexual partner history, whereas sexual offenders against adults may be similar or even higher on these same variables than non-sex offenders. A few studies suggest that adult sex offenders were more likely than other men to report engaging in some form of sexual behavior—masturbation, consensual intercourse, or sexual offending—after viewing pornography.

Babchishin et al. (2011) examined abuse history and found that online and contact offenders were similar to each other and significantly more likely to have a history of sexual abuse than men in the general population. There was a trend for online offenders to be less likely to have physical abuse histories compared with contact offenders, consistent with Maxfield and Widom's (1996) finding that physical abuse predicts delinquency and criminality (i.e., contact offenders are more likely to have prior criminal histories than Internet offenders).

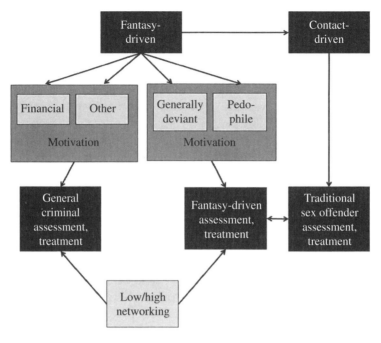

Figure 5.2. Proposed child pornography offender typology. From "The Three Dimensions of Online Child Pornography Offending," by H. L. Merdian, C. Curtis, J. Thakker, N. Wilson, and D. P. Boer, 2011, *Journal of Sexual Aggression, 19,* 130. doi:10.1080/13552600.2011.611898. Copyright 2011 by Taylor & Francis. Adapted with permission.

ONLINE OFFENDER TYPOLOGIES

The evidence described in the previous three chapters suggests there are meaningful differences between online child pornography and solicitation offenders and that there may be types of offenders within these populations. Online offenders include sexual solicitation offenders who target adults and those who use Internet technologies to commercially exploit children or women for sexual purposes. Among those who solicit adults, a distinction can be made between those who approach potential victims of sexual assault and those who engage in intrusive sexual interactions that do not require physical contact, akin perhaps to obscene telephone calling in an earlier technological era. Some types are described in Figure 5.2.

Different online offender typologies have been proposed to make sense of the heterogeneity that has been observed, first anecdotally by law enforcement and clinical professionals and then more systematically in recent studies. These typologies are summarized in Table 5.2. Most of these typologies have not been tested in large, representative samples of Internet offenders,

TABLE 5.2
Online Offender Typologies

Source	Typology
Elliott & Beech (2009)	Reviewed offender typologies proposed by Krone (2004) and Sullivan and Beech (2003), integrating them with a contact offender typology developed by Lanning (2001): *periodically prurient* (who access child pornography sporadically, impulsively, and/or opportunistically), *fantasy-only* (who are sexually interested in children but have no known history of contact offending), *direct victimization* (who use online technologies as part of a broader involvement with offending, including viewing child pornography and soliciting minors), and *commercial exploitation* (who use the Internet to make money, e.g., selling child pornography or facilitating prostitution involving minors).
Fortin & Roy (2007)	Translated from French. Labels were assigned by me rather than by the authors because they do not label every proposed type. Examined data from sample of 199 child pornography cases prosecuted in Quebec. Distinguished between *explorers* (who are young, with little or no criminal history), *solo purchasers* (who purchased or sold commercial content), *communal traders* (who trade with others and who are involved in online communities), *high-risk offenders* (a small group of only eight members but who had more extensive criminal history, including child pornography and/or contact offending), *collectors* (the largest group, who had no interactions with others online and did not use commercial sources), *groomers* (who used child pornography instrumentally, attempting to meet or engage in cybersex with minors).
Hartman, Burgess, & Lanning (1984)	Offline child pornography offender typology: *Closet collectors* secretively obtain child pornography without contact sexual offending or communication with others, *pedophile collectors* sexually prefer children and are likely to have committed contact offenses as well, *cottage collectors* engage with other offenders, and *commercial collectors* are motivated by financial gains rather than sexual interests.
Henry, Mandeville-Norden, Hayes, & Egan (2010)	Using a self-report test battery, the authors distinguished three distinct groups of Internet offenders (all but one had committed child pornography offenses) in a sample of 422 men. The three groups were labeled *apparently normal* (near or within the normal range on all tests), *inadequate* (significant social–affective problems such as loneliness and under assertiveness, without serious problems with offense-supportive attitudes and beliefs, callousness, or emotional identification with children), and *deviant* (characterized by social–affective deficits as well as very poor victim empathy and endorsement of offense-supportive attitudes and beliefs).

(continues)

TABLE 5.2
Online Offender Typologies   *(Continued)*

Source	Typology
Krone (2004)	Distinguished between the following types of online child pornography offenders: *browsers* (who encountered child pornography accidentally but decided to save it), *private fantasy offenders* (who fantasize about children and may seek out corresponding text or images), *trawlers* (who are involved in a variety of pornography and who engage in curious or experimental viewing of child pornography), *nonsecure collectors* (who download, trade, or purchase child pornography through open sources), *secure collectors* (who collect child pornography and use security countermeasures to avoid detection), *groomers* (who focus on soliciting minors for cybersex or real-life meetings but who use child pornography as part of online interactions), *physical abusers* (who have committed contact offenses and for whom child pornography is supplemental, e.g., for fantasies or as record of offending), *producers* (who record child pornography images or videos and distribute them to others), *distributors* (who possess child pornography for the purpose of selling or distributing with no imputation about sexual motives).
	Methodology or evidence used is not described, so it appears to be a rational formulation. Some of the distinctions do not easily fit (e.g., private fantasy) and some of the distinctions are fine and unlikely to be related to important psychological characteristics. For example, whether collectors use secure or nonsecure methods to obtain child pornography may shed light on their technical expertise but does not indicate anything about the likelihood they are sexually interested in children or the likelihood they would seek sexual contacts with children.
Lamb (1998)	Categorized persons frequenting youth gay chat rooms as *cruisers* (who misrepresented themselves online and were primarily interested in cybersex), *browsers* (who were genuinely curious and interested in meeting people), or *pornographers* (who gathered and traded pornography).
McLaughlin (2000)	Distinguished between child pornography collectors, travelers (solicitation offenders), and producers.
O'Connell (2003)	Describes proposed typology of online interactions rather than online offenders.
O'Connor (2005)	Examined 76 police briefs for child pornography possession between 1997–2003 and categorized offenders as *accidental* (those who had accidental access, e.g., downloading large blocks of pornography and not realizing some of the files depicted child pornography), *curious* (those who viewed child pornography because it can be found and they are curious, typically having small collections), *morally indiscriminate* (those who have a wide range of pornography, including paraphilic or extreme content), *entrepreneurial* (those who collect child pornography, possibly for financial gain and may have committed contact offenses), *addicted/problem-aware* (those who are aware of their addiction to child pornography or sexual attraction to children but who are unable to control their sexual fantasies). O'Connor suggested the addicted/problem-aware offenders might pose the greatest threat of contact offending.

TABLE 5.2
Online Offender Typologies   *(Continued)*

Source	Typology
Sullivan & Beech (2003)	Distinguished between three types of offenders. *Type 1:* Offenders collect child pornography as part of a broader pattern of sexual offending, including sexual contacts with children. *Type 2:* Offenders collect child pornography to fuel their sexual interest in children. *Type 3:* Offenders collect child pornography out of curiosity.

but it is nonetheless interesting to observe the similarities across the proposed models.

I propose an integrative typology that focuses on criminal behavior and primary motivations for online sexual offending. First, there is a meaningful distinction between those who are involved in child pornography and solicitation of minors. Among those who are involved in child pornography, there are individuals who are accidentally involved through downloading large sets of files, as O'Connor (2005) suggested, or whose computers are hacked or infected by viruses (*accidental*); individuals who seek child pornography because they are curious or interested in testing the boundaries of online behavior (*curious*); individuals who are indiscriminately involved in a variety of transgressive online sexual behavior, including accessing illegal content such as child pornography or violent pornography, solicitation of minors and adults, and seeking prostitutes (*indiscriminate*). Indiscriminate offenders are sexually motivated, unlike curious or accidental offenders. Indiscriminate offenders might have pedophilia or hebephilia as well as other paraphilic interests, or they may be characterized by high sex drive, sexual preoccupation, and sexual compulsivity.

Some individuals collect large amounts of child pornography that is sexually interesting to them, but the collection itself is also psychologically gratifying (*collectors*). Collectors are likely to be pedohebephilic but, ceteris paribus, are unlikely to have committed contact offenses. Collectors are more likely to be involved in online communities as well, because of the amount of time they spend online and because of the opportunities to trade with others and gain status by sharing rare images. All of the previous groups may only download content or may trade with others as well. The last group is those who produce and distribute child pornography (*producers*), either for commercial reasons or to gain status by providing new child pornography content that can be traded with others.

Among those who engage in solicitation of minors, there may be a meaningful distinction between those who engage in interactions with minors to fuel sexual fantasies and attain sexual gratification while online (what Briggs, Simon, & Simonsen, 2011, called *fantasy-driven offenders*) and those who engage in online interactions with the goal of meeting for sex in real life (*contact-driven offenders*). Some solicitation offenders may be pedohebephilic, but it appears the majority is not. Note that the fantasy-driven offenders do not necessarily prefer minors; some may be curious, experimenting, or are sexually indiscriminate, soliciting both minors and adults.

FINAL COMMENTS

More empirical work is needed, but there is support for the propositions of the motivation–facilitation model, emphasizing sexual deviance or sexual preoccupation as primary sexual motivations for many cases of online sexual offending. Typologically, there is some support for different motivations underlying child pornography offending, but the research on online solicitation offending is lagging the work on child pornography offenders. Antisociality factors are important: Online offenders are sexually motivated to engage in online criminal behavior but are less likely to commit sexual offenses offline, presumably because they are relatively low in antisociality, as reflected in their lower criminal involvement, higher scores on victim empathy, and lower scores on psychopathy (Babchishin et al., 2011; Webb et al., 2007). If the motivation–facilitation model is correct, then we would expect online offenders to score lower on measures of specific antisocial traits such as risk taking and impulsivity.

Our knowledge of the characteristics of online offenders is accumulating rapidly. Research evidence suggests that online offenders differ from conventional contact offenders in a number of potentially meaningful ways for the purposes of etiological modeling, risk assessment, and intervention. First, there is a group difference in intelligence and education level that is likely a result of how online sexual offenders are identified; by definition, online offenders use computer technologies to commit their crimes, and computer users are likely to be more intelligent and more highly educated, on average, than nonusers. This has implications for how online offenders are likely to perform in treatment, where both intelligence and education will probably be correlated with understanding the treatment content, completing any reading and writing assignments, and overall compliance with treatment and supervision conditions. It also is likely to influence risk of recidivism, including further online offenses, given that online offenders are likely to have more cognitive and material resources to help them desist (discussed in Chapter 6). Second, online offenders are lower, on average, on major criminological risk factors such as criminal history, antisocial personality traits, and substance use problems. Though they score higher on sexual deviance than contact offenders, their risk of recidivism appears to be lower (see Chapter 7), further supporting the importance of facilitation factors in explaining sexual offending. Online offenders appear to be higher in self-control than contact offenders, on average (see Seto & Hanson, 2011).

The number of comparison studies is small, but online offenders are lower or not different, on average, from contact offenders on psychologically meaningful risk factors that have been examined. This includes offense-supportive attitudes and beliefs, emotional identification with children, loneliness (poor interpersonal functioning), and poor empathy. This suggests that treatment programs for contact offenders could be modified for online offenders, given that they share some criminogenic needs (Hanson, Harris, Scott, & Helmus, 2007; Seto & Fernandez, 2011).

Various typologies of online offenders have been proposed, but most have not been formally tested. Some distinctions fit with the empirical data we have so far, such as a distinction between those who are sexually attracted to prepubescent or pubescent children and those who may engage in online offending for other reasons, but the prevalence of proposed types, distinctions between them, and potential differences in risk of recidivism and intervention needs have not been explored. An exception is the typology proposed by Henry, Mandeville-Norden, Hayes, and Egan (2010), who used a standardized test battery to distinguish between what they described as apparently normal, inadequate, and deviant offenders. However, the authors did not include specific measures of deviant sexual interests or antisocial tendencies, both of which are likely to be important dimensions of risk and intervention need among online offenders. Also, Henry, Mandeville-Norden, Hayes, and Egan (2010) relied on self-report measures, which are influenced by socially desirable responding and may tend to reflect current functioning rather than functioning preceding the index offense (the offense that led to the identification of an individual for clinical service and research).

The evidence leads me to believe that contact offenders, online pornography offenders and online solicitation offenders represent three different, albeit overlapping, populations. This is on the basis of comparison studies suggesting differences in offender characteristics and motivations, differences in the topography of the criminal sexual behavior, distinctions between fantasy-driven and contact-driven solicitations, and as we see in subsequent chapters, evidence of differences in offense history and risk of recidivism. This idea— that online offenders are composed of different overlapping populations—has many implications for prevention and other interventions.

6

THE CONNECTION BETWEEN ONLINE AND CONTACT OFFENDING

Jenkins (2001) wrote that "view evil, do no evil" was reportedly the motto of Adrian Thompson, a British man convicted in 2000 for child pornography crimes in the United Kingdom. This motto was intended to capture the idea that child pornography could be a substitute for contact sexual offending among individuals who were sexually attracted to children. Is this idea correct? Is the use of child pornography cathartic and thus potentially the lesser evil? In a similar vein, are fantasy-driven solicitation offenders—those who currently restrict their sexual interactions with minors to sexual chat, pornography, requests for suggestive or explicit photos, and exhibitionism via webcam—less likely to seek sexual contacts with minors?

The idea that viewing child pornography could be cathartic—serving as an outlet for sexual desire for children through masturbation and thereby reducing the likelihood of seeking sexual contacts with children—is obviously controversial. A majority of Riegel's (2004) online sample of self-identified boy-attracted pedophiles claimed that viewing child pornography reduced

http://dx.doi.org/10.1037/14191-007
Internet Sex Offenders, by M. C. Seto

their urges for sexual contact with children. There are serious problems with interpreting this result, however, including potential selection bias (who chose to respond to the survey?), a social desirability bias (the desirable response is to claim a reduced rather than increased urge), and the absence of questions about sexual contacts with children; all these factors may have influenced whether child pornography use was indeed inversely related to contact offending, as the respondents believed it to be. (Riegel did not ask questions about sexual contact, claiming he wanted to avoid putting respondents at risk of self-incrimination, but he did ask questions about urges or desires to have sexual contact with children.) Perhaps the most fundamental problem is that people are not good at identifying the causes of their own behavior, making self-report data about potential causes difficult to interpret.

Strong evidence of a cathartic effect of access to child pornography would come from experimental research where individuals are randomly assigned to child pornography exposure or a control condition and then followed over time to determine outcomes. This is obviously ethically challenging research and would be almost impossible to conduct. In the absence of experimental research on child pornography, we must rely on weaker inferences provided by correlational research conducted at the group or individual level (discussed later), either in the form of cross-sectional surveys examining child pornography use and sexual contact with children or longitudinal research looking at prediction of contact offending from knowledge of child pornography use.

Drawing on population-level studies, some researchers have suggested that pornography use may have a cathartic effect on sexual offending, with increasing pornography availability usually correlated with declining rates of sexual offenses in different jurisdictions and time periods (e.g., Diamond, Jozifkova, & Weiss, 2011; Diamond & Uchiyama, 1999; Kutchinsky, 1973, 1991). For example, Diamond et al. (2011) examined sexual offense rates in Czechoslovakia before and after the fall of the Communist regime in November 1989, after which pornography became much more readily available. The official sex crime numbers went down after 1989, despite an increase in population. Diamond et al. also reported that child pornography became more available, both online and offline, in Czechoslovakia as a result of regime change, yet the number of child sexual abuse crimes went down after this increased availability. Finkelhor and Jones (2006) documented a marked decline in child sexual abuse cases in the past 20 years in the United States, over the same time period that the Internet has become more available and, as a result, online child pornography and solicitation opportunities have become more available as well.

In my opinion, these aggregate-level data are not convincing evidence that individuals who have more access to pornography are less likely to commit sexual offenses. Aggregate-level studies are different from individual-level studies that look at the correlations between pornography use and sexual offending across individuals, which I review in the next section. A major limitation of using aggregate-level analyses to infer effects on individual behavior is that many third variables could explain the aggregate-level correlations that are observed. This is also true for individual-level correlational studies, which I review in the next section, but individual-level studies can control for individual differences in propensity to sexually offend, whereas aggregate-level analyses cannot control for these individual differences (though they can control for sociological factors that might be relevant, e.g., law enforcement capacity). For example, the association between mainstream pornography availability and declining sexual offending rates might be hypothetically explained by a shift toward more progressive social values, which would tolerate more pornography being available, in support of greater freedom of expression, but would be intolerant of offense-supportive attitudes and beliefs about women and children, which would lead to fewer sexual offenses to the extent that such beliefs are associated with offending.

To me, a big challenge for conclusions drawn from aggregate-level data that greater pornography availability has led to a decline in sexual offending is that there has been an overall decline over the past 20 years in any offending in Canada, the United States, and Western Europe (Zimring, 2006). The crime decline in turn is associated with an even broader trend toward less risk taking in health, driving, and noncriminal sexual behavior (Mishra & Lalumière, 2009). This suggests that the decline in sexual offending is part of a broader and puzzling shift in behavior. It is more parsimonious to try to identify the factors that have led to this broad shift in risk taking and antisocial and criminal behavior than to develop unique explanations for each behavioral domain. No one has identified plausible explanations for why increasing pornography use might also explain declines in motor vehicle accidents, school dropouts, and other negative social or health outcomes.[1]

Zimring (2006) examined different explanations for the broad decline in both self-reported and officially recorded crime in the United States (which was also observed elsewhere, including Canada and Western Europe) in the 1990s and early 2000s and found that explanations that were suggested from aggregate-level data were not supported when individual-level data were analyzed. For example, unemployment is positively correlated with crime at the individual level, such that those who are unemployed are more likely to commit crimes. Yet both Canada and the United States showed

---

[1]Pornography use could be related to the decline in risky sexual behaviors, for example, if anxiety about HIV/AIDS infection has led to less partnered sexual activity and concomitantly more solo sexual activity involving masturbation to pornography.

similar declines in crime rates through the 1990s, even though Canada had higher unemployment in the 1990s than in the 1980s, whereas the United States experienced economic growth and lower unemployment during the same time period.

Malamuth and Pitpitan (2007) discussed methodological issues of aggregate-level analyses, as did Kingston and Malamuth (2011). Individual differences clearly play an important role in sexual offending (Lalumière, Harris, Quinsey, & Rice, 2005; Seto, 2008). Responding to the Diamond et al. (2011) study—and the study authors' conclusion that the results support a "displacement function" of pornography on potential sex offenders—Kingston and Malamuth (2011) pointed out that the effects of pornography interact with individual differences, such that individuals who are already at risk of sexual offending show the strongest negative effects of exposure to pornography, a point that has been made by others (e.g., Seto, Maric, & Barbaree, 2001). In the rest of this chapter, I further address this question by reviewing experimental and correlational research on the effects of mainstream pornography (no studies have been conducted on child pornography), examining the contact offending histories of online offenders, and comparing online offenders with and without contact offending histories.

UNDERSTANDING THE EFFECTS OF PORNOGRAPHY ON SEXUAL OFFENDING

There continues to be a vigorous debate about the effects of pornography on sexual offending. Does pornography use increase the risk of sexual offending, does it have a cathartic effect, or are the two phenomena unrelated? For this book, given the focus on internet-facilitated sexual offending, the primary question is whether exposure to child pornography increases the risk of sexually offending against children.[2] Some writers have argued that there is a detrimental effect of pornography on sexual offending, with experimental studies showing that pornography exposure in the laboratory at least temporarily increases the endorsement of offense-supportive attitudes and beliefs and also increases physical aggressiveness, both of which are seen as underlying factors for sexual offending against peers or adults (Kingston, Malamuth, Fedoroff, & Marshall, 2009; Malamuth, Addison, & Koss, 2000; Vega & Malamuth, 2007). At the same time, the results of population-level studies

---

[2]The effects of violent pornography on rape and sexual assault would also be relevant because violent pornography is prohibited under obscenity legislation in some jurisdictions. Similarly, the availability of exhibitionistic and voyeuristic pornography online might influence the rates of these real-world sexual offenses.

have mostly shown an inverse association between pornography availability and sex crime rates (e.g., Diamond et al., 2011).

Bhuller, Havnes, Leuven, and Mogstad (2011) drew a different conclusion about the effects of pornography from a natural quasi-experiment in Norway that controlled for some third-factor explanations in aggregate-level studies. In the Bhuller et al. study, the authors examined sexual crime rates across regions of Norway as broadband access became available. They found that approximately 3% of sexual crimes could be attributed to the introduction of higher speed Internet access, which greatly facilitates access to pornography compared with the slow dial-up access that previously existed. The results from this study suggest a small positive effect of pornography on sexual crime rates, which is inconsistent with Diamond et al. (2011) and other aggregate-level studies.

In the next section, I briefly review findings from the individual-level correlational and experimental studies. This literature has been reviewed extensively and recently, and thus there is little reason to retrace all the steps. Each study design has its strengths and limitations, so convergence of findings would increase our confidence in the conclusions that can be drawn about the effects of pornography.

CORRELATIONAL STUDIES

Individual-level correlational studies fall broadly into two approaches. The first category consists of cross-sectional studies that compare known groups on pornography use to see whether pornography use is a distinguishing and therefore potentially causal factor. Allen, D'Alessio, and Emmers-Sommer (2000) reviewed the relatively small set of studies that compared pornography use between sex offenders and other groups of men. The hypothesis that sex offenders would use pornography more often or earlier than other men was not supported. Across seven studies that asked questions about sexual behavior after pornography use, however, sex offenders reported they were more likely to fantasize, masturbate, or engage in sexual intercourse after viewing pornography.

The second approach involves studies that examine the associations between pornography use and sexual offending either retrospectively (in cross-sectional studies) or prospectively (in longitudinal studies). Examples of cross-sectional studies include Boeringer (1994) and Crossman (1995); both studies found correlations between pornography use and self-reported sexual aggression in samples of male college students. Hunt and Kraus (2009) reported data supporting the idea that early exposure to pornography (between the ages of 6 and 12) was correlated with online pornography use, whereas both childhood sexual abuse and early exposure to pornography were correlated with sexual aggression as a young adult. These same factors were identified as relevant to adolescent sexual offending in our meta-analysis (Seto & Lalumière, 2010), again suggesting early exposure to pornography can disrupt normal sexual development. This is an important matter that requires more research because an emerging societal issue is that age at first exposure to pornography is decreasing. Ybarra and Mitchell (2005) found that 8% of youths between the ages of 10 and 13 have deliberately sought pornography online.

LONGITUDINAL STUDIES

Malamuth, Linz, Heavey, Barnes, and Acker (1995) looked at pornography use and prediction of sexual aggression in a representative sample of almost 3,000 men. Pornography use predicted sexual aggression over a 10-year period (all data were based on self-report). The results of Malamuth and his colleagues were replicated by Vega and Malamuth (2007) with additional measures of psychopathy, as a further test of Malamuth's confluence model of sexual aggression against women, which proposes that male sexual aggression against women could be explained by the interaction of hostile masculinity (negative, stereotypical views about women and sex) and an impersonal orientation to sex. Vega and Malamuth found that high pornography use added to general antisociality factors in the prediction of sexual aggression in a sample of 102 male college students. In fact, high pornography use accounted for more variance than the general antisociality factors, probably because college students had a limited range of antisociality compared with the general population or especially offenders. It should be noted that Vega and Malamuth (2007) found low reported rates of sexual aggression overall and, though the association was significant, their figure suggests only a small difference between the high-pornography risk group and lowest risk group.

Kingston, Fedoroff, Firestone, Curry, and Bradford (2008) examined self-reported prior pornography consumption and recidivism among 341 sex offenders with child victims; the offenders were at risk for an average of 8.4 years in the community, with a maximum of 15 years at risk. The overall sexual recidivism rate was 11%, and the violent recidivism rate (which included contact sexual offending) was 21%. Even after controlling for other risk factors such as criminal history, pornography use predicted violent (including sexual) recidivism, interacting with estimated risk using a validated, actuarial risk measure (see Chapter 7). Both overall frequency of pornography use and use of child or violent pornography predicted violent recidivism but only among higher-risk offenders. Unfortunately, this study did not include data specifically on the frequency of child or violent pornography use.

Ybarra, Mitchell, Hamburger, Diener-West, and Leaf (2011) analyzed longitudinal data and found that exposure to violent pornography predicted sexually aggressive behavior. Data on over 1,100 adolescents between the ages of 10 and 15 were collected in three waves over a 3-year period. The youths were asked questions about exposure to violent and nonviolent pornography and perpetration of sexually aggressive behavior (which was broadly defined to include physical sexual coercion, sexual harassment, and unwanted technology-assisted sexual solicitation). Over the three waves, an average of 23% of the youths intentionally used pornography, and 5% of youths had been sexually aggressive. Only 4% of the youths, however, were exposed to violent pornography; intentional use of violent pornography was associated with a six-fold increase in perpetration of sexually aggressive behavior, whereas there was no significant increase in odds of perpetration for exposure to nonviolent pornography. Similar odds ratios were observed for boys and for girls. One methodological issue in this research is that Ybarra et al. used a broad measure of sexual aggression to obtain a sufficient base rate for data analysis; the base rate for physical sexual coercion alone was too small. This broad definition may explain the similar sexual aggression rates found for boys and girls. I would expect a large gender difference if the definition was narrower and restricted to more forceful behavior. Similarly, there is little or no gender difference in studies looking at physical aggression when it is broadly defined, but there is a large gender difference when one focuses on physical aggression resulting in physical injuries.

EXPERIMENTAL STUDIES

Allen and his colleagues conducted two meta-analyses in the 1990s of experimental studies of pornography effects. The first review showed that exposure to mainstream adult pornography had a significant, medium-sized effect on negative attitudes about women (offense-supportive attitudes and beliefs), and the second review showed that exposure to pornography had effects on physical aggression in laboratory analog tasks (Allen, D'Alessio, & Brezgel, 1995; Allen, Emmers, Gebhardt, & Giery, 1995). Similar effects were also shown for adult pornography depicting violence, consistent with an even larger experimental literature showing that exposure to violent media content (television, film, video games) has an effect on subsequent aggression (C. A. Anderson & Bushman, 2002; C. A. Anderson et al., 2003). An example of an experimental study is one conducted by Zillman and Bryant (1998), who experimentally administered pornographic or nonpornographic films for an hour a week for 6 weeks. On the seventh week, both male and female participants who had viewed pornography were less satisfied with their partner in areas such as affection, physical appearance, sexual curiosity, and sexual performance. They also rated sex without emotional involvement more positively.

Possible mechanisms for pornography's experimentally demonstrated effects include social learning, excitation transfer, and habituation (desensitization). In *social learning*, one's attitudes, beliefs, and perceptions of social norms are influenced by environmental inputs. Seeing female actors who are highly sexually receptive and who respond enthusiastically to male overtures (even those that are coercive or impersonal) may influence some men to believe that women in real life act in similar ways. Also, seeing male actors engage in sexually violent acts without negative consequences may suggest that such behavior is more acceptable or tolerated. In *excitation transfer*, the physical and sexual arousal elicited by exposure to pornography can be expressed in aggression if the person is then provoked. Finally, in *habituation*, repeated exposure to similar content produces smaller and smaller sexual responses, causing the person to need more intense, real-life experiences to achieve the same level of excitement or gratification.

In the specific context of child pornography, social learning may play a role to the extent that viewers believe that adult–child sex does not harm children (because the children do not appear to be harmed) or because they view adult–child sex as more common than believed (see Jung, Ennis, & Malesky, 2012). Excitation transfer would operate in a similar fashion as for adult pornography: Someone who viewed child pornography and became aroused as a result might be temporarily more likely to act on an opportunity with a child than if that person had not been first exposed to child pornography (Hill, Briken, & Berner, 2006; Langevin & Curnoe, 2004; Wheeler, 1997). Hill et al. (2006), for example, reported that of the sex offenders they assessed who had had child victims, approximately a third had used child pornography to sexually excite themselves prior to an offense. One potentially critical difference between experimental research on exposure to pornography, such as the study by Zillman and Bryant (1998), and exposure to pornography in the real world is that users in the real world presumably masturbate to orgasm during the exposure, which might elicit the same excitation transfer.

In terms of habituation, an individual who initially viewed "barely legal" and teen-focused content might find himself searching for younger and younger children, and increasingly explicit depictions, after chronic exposure. The habituation explanation fits with the self-reports of some online child pornography offenders who claimed that they became bored with less explicit images or images of older children and sought more intense images as a result (Taylor & Quayle, 2003; Seto, Reeves, & Jung, 2010). In keeping with this explanation,

Laulik, Allam, and Sheridan (2007) reported that online child pornography offenders spent an average of 12 hours a week seeking and viewing child pornography; this would result in many exposures over a long period of time.

INDIVIDUAL DIFFERENCES

I have already mentioned that a major finding from research on the effects of pornography is that individual differences play a big role. The effects of pornography depend a great deal on preexisting attitudes and beliefs, sexual history, and antisociality (Malamuth et al., 2000). What are the potentially important individual differences for child pornography? Being inclined toward pedophilia or hebephilia is one important difference, as discussed in Chapter 2. Of particular interest is the study by Bogaert (2001), who looked at predictors of pornography choice among 160 male undergraduate students. As he expected, individual differences were predictive of pornography choice, with men who were higher in antisocial tendencies having a stronger preference for violent or child pornography content than those who were lower on these traits. Up to half the variance in preference for violent content could be explained by a combination of individual differences and self-reported arousal to violent content. Similarly, self-reported arousal to child pornography and antisociality significantly predicted interest in pornography with child sex titles.

Bogaert's (2001) results are consistent with the confluence and motivation–facilitation models, both of which suggest that antisocial tendencies such as impulsivity, hostility, callousness, and egocentrism are important facilitators. Individuals high on these tendencies are less likely to reflect on the consequences of their actions and are less concerned about the potential impacts of their behavior on others. Malamuth et al. (1995) showed that men in the community who were sexually motivated and also high in antisocial tendencies were more likely to commit sexual aggression when followed longitudinally. These same antisocial tendencies play a prominent role in the sex offender risk assessment literature (reviewed in the next chapter), suggesting they are also important in explaining persistence of sexual offending, whether it is committed against children, teens, or adults.

SUMMARY

Experimental studies have suggested there is a moderate effect of pornography on the proximal factors of offense-supportive attitudes and beliefs and physical aggression in the laboratory (Allen, D'Alessio, et al., 1995;

Allen, Emmers, et al., 1995).[3] Other experimental research has suggested that repeated exposure to pornography can lead to habituation under certain contexts; this may lead to a search for novel or more intense stimuli and is consistent with some explanations given by self-identified pornography "addicts." There is also research to suggest that exposure to pornography can lead to greater relationship and partner dissatisfaction, which could then lead to the pursuit of casual, impersonal sex and more opportunities for sexual aggression to take place (see Lalumière et al., 2005). Individual differences play an important role, both in choosing to expose oneself to pornography and in interacting with the effects of pornography exposure. Experimental results are consistent with individual-level correlational studies but not with population-level correlational studies. The large and contentious literature on the effects of pornography is reviewed in detail elsewhere (e.g., Malamuth et al., 2000).

CATHARSIS

A cathartic effect of exposure to child pornography would not be consistent with individual-level correlational, longitudinal, and experimental research on the effects of mainstream pornography. Because it is illegal to possess child pornography for any reason in the United States, experimental research on the effects of exposure to child pornography cannot be conducted under current American law. Correlational and longitudinal research is possible, by relying on self-report or file information about child pornography use, but we can only infer causality from such studies.

My opinion, drawing from the experimental adult pornography research, is that exposure to child pornography interacts with individual differences (such as pedophilia or hebephilia and antisociality) to result in more permissive attitudes and beliefs about children and sex, a greater willingness to have sex with a child if there were no negative consequences, and a greater dissatisfaction with one's current sexual life. Men who are not already predisposed to commit sexual offenses against children would be unlikely to show any effects of brief exposures to child pornography. For men who are not at risk, even prolonged exposure to child pornography is unlikely to have any notable impact on likelihood of engaging in sexual offenses involving children. After all, police investigators and forensic analysts who have been exposed to child pornography for long periods of time as a result of their work can

---

[3]No experimental work has shown an effect of pornography on sexual aggression directly. It is unlikely such an effect could ever be shown, given the role of individual differences, the likely small effects of the limited exposure possible in a laboratory setting, and the challenges of finding a suitable analog for sexual aggression in the laboratory.

be distressed or adversely affected by this exposure, but there is not even anecdotal evidence to suggest that they have become more likely to sexually offend against children. Nonoffending volunteers who have participated in past phallometric studies and who have been exposed to sexual child stimuli have not contacted the research team or institutional review board about adverse effects. If there is any effect, it is presumably weak and transient. Men who are predisposed, however, are more likely to seek out child pornography and more likely to experience sexual arousal and desire that might translate to sexual behavior directed toward children if facilitating factors are present.

The effects of pornography may depend on the timing of exposure. A study of adult sex offenders by Mancini, Reckdenwald, and Beauregard (2012) looked at pornography exposure as an adolescent versus as an adult, as well as pornography use just before committing a sexual offense, to determine the effects of these factors on the subsequent amount of physical injury and humiliation of the victim. Use of pornography as an adolescent was associated with greater physical injury, whereas use of pornography as an adult had no significant association. Use of pornography just before sexual offense commission was associated with less rather than more physical injury. These results could be evidence of longer-term learning or habituation effects from adolescent pornography exposure. (Alternatively, pornography use may be explained by a third variable such as an interest in casual, impersonal sex or high sexual preoccupation.)

AN ENDLESS DEBATE

There continues to be heated debate about the effects of mainstream pornography after decades of research on this subject. The experimental research is conclusive in showing that exposure to pornography has moderately negative effects on relevant attitudes and aggressive behavior in the laboratory. Individual-level correlational studies suggest pornography use is associated with sexual aggression. Aggregate-level correlational data, however, suggest that increasing pornography availability is associated with declining sexual crime rates (see Appendix 6.1).

The debate about the effects of pornography is reminiscent of the seemingly interminable debate about the effects of exposure to violent media (e.g. television, films, video games) on physical aggression. Though policymakers and public opinion remain divided on this question, the empirical evidence on the effects of violent media is persuasive, with meta-analytic reviews showing that there is a small to moderate effect of violent media on aggression across study designs, in that exposure to violent media increases aggression (see C. A. Anderson & Bushman, 2002; C. A. Anderson et al., 2003).

Is the opposition to the idea of media effects driven more by consideration of the science or by concerns about censorship of pornography and violent media? It seems to me that the debate about media violence is fueled by media stories that question the scientific evidence, often offering a lone dissenting view against the accumulated research. There is the possibility of self-interest in media outlets that question the idea that the violent content they show may have negative effects on individuals and on society. It is ironic that media commentators and journalists might hold this position, because the media would not exist if its representatives did not believe content influenced society (e.g., in news and advertising).

Though suggestive, the evidence on violent media and on the effects of mainstream pornography does not directly address questions about the effects of child pornography. One advantage of online offending research is that forensic computer analysis can provide digital evidence about pornography use, such as the amount and types of pornography that were viewed, recency of viewing or access, and how often files were viewed again. My colleague Angela Eke and I are currently completing a follow-up study in which our team coded information from digital evidence to see whether parameters of child pornography can predict recidivism (discussed further in the next chapter; Eke & Seto, 2012). Examples of research questions that could be addressed by digital content analysis include the following: Are contact offenders using more pornography online than comparison groups of other offenders? Is there a correspondence between the kinds of pornography contact offenders view and their actions (e.g., child pornography and child sexual abuse, violent pornography and rape, exhibitionistic pornography and exhibitionism)?

SEXUAL OFFENDING HISTORY

From a clinical and policy perspective, it is important to consider the extent to which online offenders have already committed contact sexual offenses and the timing of these online and contact offenses. We recently conducted a meta-analysis examining contact sexual offending history (Seto, Hanson, & Babchishin, 2011), identifying 21 studies, with a combined sample size of 4,464 offenders, which had usable data on contact sexual offense histories. Approximately one in eight (12%) of the online (mostly child pornography) offenders had an official record for contact sexual offending, whereas in the subset of six studies using self-report data (total of 523 online offenders), approximately one in two (55%) had committed a contact sexual offense. Studies usually did not distinguish contact offenses involving children and contact offenses involving older adolescents or adults. The self-report result is more tentative because of the smaller number of studies and smaller sample size and because some of those who denied undetected offenses could have lied.

There are two main findings to highlight in the Seto et al. (2011) meta-analysis: (a) The difference between official known and self-reported offending illustrates again the gap in reporting (or adjudication) of sexual crimes and (b) though some of the offenders who denied committing contact sexual offenses may have lied, not all online offenders have already committed contact sexual offenses. (Unless one assumes that all individuals who denied any contact offenses lied, which would defeat the point of collecting self-report data at all.)

The so-called Butner Study Redux by Bourke and Hernandez (2009) was a statistical outlier in our meta-analysis of sexual offense history studies. Bourke and Hernandez found that approximately a quarter (24%) of their sample of 155 child pornography offenders had an official record of contact sexual offending, but most (85%) of their sample acknowledged having a history of contact offending after participating in treatment and, in about half of the cases, undergoing polygraph examinations. This particular study has been the subject of controversy since it was first presented at conferences in 2000 and then delayed in the publication process for several years, for reasons that remain unclear. Hamilton (2012) speculated that it was a result of the authors being unwilling to change their text to be more cautious about the generalizability and limitations of their research.

The high-contact sexual offending history prevalence reported by Bourke and Hernandez (2009) has been cited in criminal proceedings to support requests for longer sentences or more restrictive treatment or supervision conditions (Gelber, 2009; Hansen, 2009). The logic seems to be as follows: Evidence that someone is likely to have committed contact offenses in the past, and therefore is at greater risk of offending in a similar fashion in the future, should affect sentencing. At the same time, the Bourke and Hernandez study has been criticized because it was thought that they had provided strong incentives for the participants to admit to sexual contacts, even if this was not true, as a sign of treatment progress (Hamilton, 2012; *Johnson v. United States*, 2008; see also *United States v. Comstock*, 2009). Another criticism of the Bourke and Hernandez study is that the Butner treatment program was the only one of its kind at the time in the federal correctional system, and thus the treatment participants might have been a highly selected sample. Other criticisms are that offenders were expected to disclose undetected victims and faced expulsion or other consequences if they did not do this, given that acceptance of responsibility was one of the program rules. Because they were on a special unit for sex offenders and would be transferred back to a unit within the general inmate population, this could have been a strong incentive to falsely report contact sexual victims.

Hamilton (2012) cited a training video by Andres Hernandez, in which he acknowledged that there was peer pressure to disclose, as well as the potential demand characteristics arising from the fact that the clinicians also conducted the research (PublicResourceOrg, 2009, June 6, June 7). Hamilton also noted that the definition of contact sexual offending used in the Butner Study Redux research was sufficiently broad that it could include sexual contacts with another adolescent that occurred when the offender was himself an adolescent, as well as statutory sexual offenses involving noncoercive sexual contacts with someone under the legal age of consent. Yet another issue is that only half of the treatment participants were polygraphed, and it might be that those who denied any additional victims were more likely to be referred for this kind examination. Such interviews can be stressful and, if repeated for those who continued to deny any undetected offenses, the prospect of ending the polygraph examinations might be another incentive to report additional victims.

In response to these criticisms, Michael Bourke, the lead author of the study, stated in an e-mail to me that no incentives were provided for disclosures: Most offenders were ineligible for parole or time off for good behavior, offenders who disclosed were more rather than less likely to be expelled from treatment, and there were no rewards for disclosure within the treatment program (M. Bourke, personal communication, June 8, 2011). Bourke further explained that he was not allowed to rebut criticisms of the study while working as a U.S. Federal Bureau of Prisons employee; however, he is now employed by the United States Marshall Service. Whatever the explanation(s) for the high rate reported by Bourke and Hernandez (2009), it is not controversial to conclude that some child pornography offenders have committed contact sexual offenses that were not reported to police, as is true for many other kinds of criminals and crimes.

The Butner Study Redux is frequently cited in federal courts because it is the only peer-reviewed publication about the offense histories of federally sentenced child pornography offenders. There is another study, however, that is being published as a book chapter and has therefore not been subject to the same level of peer review as a journal article (Wollert, Waggoner, & Smith, 2012). In the 72 child pornography offender cases collated by this team, 14% of offenders had previously been convicted of contact sexual offenses and 21% of having any prior contact or noncontact sexual convictions. Of the 108 child pornography offenders collated by Probation Officer Andres (representing all child pornography offenders supervised in his federal district since 1999) for Justice Jack Weinstein of the Eastern District of New York, approximately 20% disclosed sexual contact with a minor, which again could include legal contacts as an adolescent and statutory sexual contacts (also described in Wollert et al., 2012). Though not entirely clear from the second-hand description of these data by Wollert and his colleagues (2012), this seems to be the figure for new disclosures and is much lower than the rate reported by Bourke and Hernandez's (2009) sample. It is also in the lower range compared with the other self-report studies in our meta-analysis (Seto et al., 2011).

We do not know how many online solicitation offenders have committed contact sexual offenses in the past. Most of the offenders represented by the studies in the Seto et al. (2011) meta-analysis had committed child pornography offenses. The results were surprisingly consistent across three recent studies of solicitation offenders: Four percent of the solicitation offenders who approached undercover police officers in 2006 in the study by Wolak, Finkelhor, and Mitchell (2009), 4% of the solicitation offenders in Briggs Simon, and Simonsen (2011), and 5% of the solicitation offenders in Seto, Wood, Babchishin, and Flynn (2012) had prior sexual offense convictions. Reflecting the same trend as shown in Seto et al.'s (2011) meta-analysis, in the one study that had self-reported offending history information, 29% of the solicitation offenders in Seto et al. (2012) disclosed undetected prior sexual offenses.

UNDETECTED ONLINE OFFENDERS

Jenkins (2001) observed that the number of detected child pornography offenders identified in clinical or correctional samples does not tell us how many individuals are using child pornography, because many users are undetected. The number of users greatly exceeds the number of detected offenders, according to prevalence estimates from population studies (Seto, Kjellgren, et al., 2010) and analyses of unique Internet protocol (IP) addresses accessing known child pornography files on peer-to-peer networks, where the number of IP addresses far exceeds the number of detected offenders (Canwest News Service, 2009; Steel, 2009; United States Department of Justice, 2010).

Detection is not random, so studies of only identified offenders are unlikely to be representative of all online offenders. For example, if only 10% of child pornography users had ever offended against children but contact offending greatly increased the risk of detection by police–for example, the victim reports the contact offending and then child pornography is discovered–then many detected child pornography offenders might have a contact offending history. As mentioned in Chapter 2, the National Juvenile Online Victimization Project found that approximately one in five child pornography offenders used one or more methods to hide their activity (Wolak,

Finkelhor, & Mitchell, 2011). Logically, a higher proportion of undetected child pornography offenders would be successfully using these methods, to the extent that these methods can reduce detection. Surveys of undetected child pornography users allow us to identify factors that may be associated with detection (Ray, Kimonis, & Seto, in press; Riegel, 2004; Seigfried, Lovely, & Rogers, 2008). There have not yet been peer-reviewed surveys of adult solicitation offenders, as far as can be discerned from searches of major publication databases such as PubMed, PsycINFO, and Google Scholar.

Knowing whether a child pornography offender has a history of contact sexual offending does not directly address the question of risk to commit future offenses. Almost all of the sexual offenders followed in the recidivism studies reviewed by Hanson and his colleagues (Hanson & Bussière, 1998; Hanson & Morton-Bourgon, 2005) had committed contact sexual offenses, yet the composite rate of detected sexual recidivism was 13% after an average of 5 to 6 years' follow-up. Longer term follow-ups have suggested a third of sexual offenders with child victims will be detected for new sexual offenses after 20 to 30 years (Hanson, Steffy, & Gauthier, 1993; Prentky, Knight, & Lee, 1997). Some offenders may commit offenses that are not officially detected, but these data are not consistent with the idea that previously committing a sexual offense means that the offender will almost certainly reoffend (e.g., Levenson, Brannon, Fortney, & Baker, 2007). Offenders vary a great deal in the risk they pose of future offending. I address the research on future offending and predictors of recidivism in the next chapter.

COMPARING ONLINE OFFENDERS WITH AND WITHOUT CONTACT HISTORIES

Comparing online offenders with and without contact offense histories sheds light on factors that distinguish those who go beyond viewing child pornography or engaging in sexual interactions online from those who do not. The etiological models described in Chapter 5 and the risk factors for contact offending identified in Chapter 7 suggest sexual deviance and antisociality factors are important. Dual offenders (online plus contact offending) may differ from online-only and contact-only offenders in meaningful ways as well.

There are some relevant studies. Seto, Cantor, and Blanchard (2006) compared 53 child pornography only (based on both official records and self-report) offenders with 47 dual offenders. These two groups did not significantly differ in their phallometrically assessed sexual arousal to children, which is surprising because one would expect the likelihood of being a pedophile (or strength of sexual response to children when assessed phallometrically) would distinguish those who act on their sexual interests by having contact with a child from those who do not.

McCarthy (2010) compared 56 child pornography offenders who had no known sexual contact with children and 51 dual offenders on a range of demographic, criminological, and sexological variables (most based on self-report). Dual offenders were more likely to report using illicit drugs, more likely to have a prior sexual offense (but not a prior nonsexual offense), and more likely to be diagnosed with pedophilia. Even so, only a minority of dual offenders had any prior sexual offense history or had been diagnosed with pedophilia. Dual offenders were more likely to report masturbating to child pornography, more likely to view child modeling sites, and more likely to read sexual stories involving minors, which suggests they were more likely to be pedophiles or to have stronger sexual preoccupations.

McCarthy (2010) also found that dual offenders were more likely to contact minors, send child or adult pornography to minors, and attempt to meet minors online. They were also more likely to network on pro-pedophilia forums with others who were sexually interested in children. There was no significant difference in adult pornography use. Dual offenders were also more likely to engage in adult cybersex, consistent with the idea that dual offenders are higher in sexual preoccupations. Combined with the group difference in prior sexual offense history and pedophilia diagnosis, McCarthy's results suggest dual offenders were more sexually deviant, engaged in a wider variety of online criminal sexual behavior, and posed a greater risk to reoffend than online-only offenders.

Another recent comparison study found that dual offenders differed from online-only offenders by scoring higher on a measure of antisocial and criminal behavior. Prentky et al. (2010) had data on 113 online-only offenders, 176 contact sex offenders with child victims, 60 dual offenders, and three small comparison groups of 35 rapists, 27 other sex offenders, and 55 nonsex offenders. This research team was interested in the question of what distinguished Internet-only from contact offenders, focusing on two scales created from their questionnaires: 11 items on preoccupation with the Internet (they expected online-only offenders to score higher than the other groups on this scale) and 13 items on lifetime antisocial behavior (they predicted contact offenders to be higher on this scale). Both dual and contact offenders had significantly more antisocial behavior than Internet-only offenders, whereas the Internet-only and dual offenders had significantly higher scores on Internet preoccupation, partially supporting the authors' predictions (see Lee, Li, Lamade, Schuler, & Prentky, 2012).

Lee et al. (2012) found that a one-point increase on their antisocial behavior scale was associated with a 33% increase in the probability of being a contact offender. A person with the highest possible score of 13 on the antisocial behavior scale was very likely to be a contact offender (84% probability); the probability was near certain (99%) if the same person had the lowest possible score on Internet preoccupation. In contrast, scores on an Internet preoccupation scale were not significantly predictive of group membership. Antisocial behavior also differentiated online-only from dual offenders.

Prentky et al. (2010) reported that all three groups were similar in their self-reported exposure to soft-core and hard-core pornography. As in previous studies, there was also no group difference in age at first exposure to soft-core or hard-core pornography. However, Internet offenders were more likely to report viewing pornography involving animals, urine or feces, bondage or sadism, or rape, compared with contact offenders or male college students.

Given how the groups were identified in the Prentky et al. (2010) study, it is not surprising that online offenders were more likely to have viewed child pornography at a young age. The most prevalent self-reported content category was depictions of adolescents in their late teens, which I suspect reflects a response bias because it is not in line with objective analyses of child pornography content from police databases or case files (see Chapter 2). Nonetheless, 10% to 13% of Internet offenders reported their first exposure to child pornography was before the age of 12, compared with 3% of the contact offenders. This finding does not distinguish correlation from causation, of course. It is highly plausible, in keeping with my views on pedophilia, that some individuals who were sexually interested in children began expressing that interest by looking for child pornography around puberty and then continued to express it by viewing child pornography through adolescence and/or adulthood (Seto, 2008, 2012). An alternative possibility is that online offenders were exposed to child pornography by others and that this early exposure had a causal effect on psychosexual development (Seto & Lalumière, 2010).

Neutze, Seto, Schaefer, Mundt, and Beier (2011) had a unique sample of 155 self-identified male pedophiles or hebephiles who sought help from an outpatient treatment clinic following a mass media campaign in Germany to recruit persons concerned about their sexual interest in children. Of the 137 men with complete lifetime history information, 42 (31%) had viewed child pornography only, 45 (33%) had committed contact sexual offenses against children only, and 50 (36%) were dual offenders (excluding the most recent 6 months). There were no differences across these lifetime history groups on the self-report measures of emotional or intimacy deficits, offense-supportive cognitions, sexual self-regulation problems, conscientiousness, or socially desirable responding.

On the basis of their criminal sexual activity in the previous 6 months, 40 (26%) of the 155 participants had been inactive, 64 (41%) had viewed child pornography, and 51 (33%) had sexually offended against a child. Of the 51 men who sexually offended against a child, the majority (39 of 51, 76%) had direct contact with the child, seven exposed themselves or masturbated in front of a child, and the remaining five took pornographic photographs, showed pornography, or had sexual conversations with the child. In total, one fifth of the sample viewed child pornography monthly or less often, and a third viewed child pornography daily or weekly. The only significant difference across these groups was in awareness of their risk to sexually offend, with child pornography offenders scoring lower than those who had sexually offended against a child. This last result is probably due to the fact that the salience of risky situations and triggers was greater for those who had recently sexually offended against a child.

The self-reported histories and activity of the Neutze et al. (2011) sample have both pessimistic and optimistic implications. From a pessimistic standpoint, almost all of the participants had committed a sexual offense of some kind in their lifetime, either by accessing child pornography or having sexual contacts with minors. On the optimistic side, a quarter had been inactive in the previous 6 months, suggesting there is an opportunity for intervention to support continued desistance among mostly undetected offenders. Moreover, those who had viewed child pornography or who had sexual contact with a child were willing to identify themselves as treatment candidates, suggesting a genuine motivation to seek help to change their behavior.

Overall, these comparison studies of Internet offenders with or without contact offending histories have suggested that, again, those who commit contact offenses are higher in antisocial tendencies (McCarthy, 2010; Prentky et al., 2010), sexual deviance (McCarthy, 2010; Prentky et al., 2010; but not Seto et al., 2006), and sexual preoccupation (McCarthy, 2010). Online-only and dual offenders do not differ in psychological factors such as loneliness, empathy, emotional identification with children, and offense-supportive attitudes and beliefs (Neutze et al., 2011).[4]

IS CHILD PORNOGRAPHY OFFENDING A GATEWAY CRIME

There are surprisingly few data pertinent to the question of the timing of child pornography and contact offending among dual offenders. In a study by Webb, Craissati, and Keen (2007), the large majority of offenders claimed they had committed contact offenses before they were first exposed to child pornography. In McCarthy's (2010) study, 84% of the dual offenders claimed

---

[4]This does not mean these are not dynamic risk factors in the prediction of future sexual offending. Groups defined on lifetime or recent (6 months previous) behavior might not differ on these variables, yet changes on these variables could still predict recidivism in the future, as they do among conventional sex offenders.

their contact sexual offenses preceded their child pornography offense. This is not consistent with the idea that child pornography is a major gateway crime that leads to contact sexual offending. Instead, contact offending opportunities arise in adolescence or early adulthood, and some already at-risk individuals take these opportunities. At-risk individuals who are sexually attracted to prepubescent or pubescent children may also seek child pornography, whereas less antisocial (or, put another way, more prosocial) individuals may seek child pornography only, refraining from contact sexual offending. The most prosocial may abstain from any sexual offending.

This temporal ordering may change over time, however, because high-speed access to the Internet has only become widespread over the past decade. Prentky et al. (2010) found that 13% of online-only offenders and 10% of dual offenders reported their first exposure to child pornography at the age of 11 or younger, compared with 3% of the contact offenders. I would expect these percentages to go up as studies are conducted in the next decade with offenders who have grown up with the Internet and who most likely had their first exposure to pornography of any kind (including child pornography) online.

Given that the average offenders in these studies were in their 30s, contact opportunities would have been more readily available than access to child pornography online when they were adolescents or young adults. The reverse situation is true for youths today, who will likely be exposed to child pornography early in adolescence (just as they are exposed to hard-core pornography at an increasingly younger age) and thus may view child pornography before ever committing contact sexual offenses. This still would not mean that viewing child pornography is a gateway crime. The motivation–facilitation and confluence models described in Chapter 4 suggest that individual differences are going to matter more than simple exposure to child pornography. Individuals who are not sexually interested in children are unlikely to show an effect of child pornography exposure beyond surprise, shock, or disgust.

Even child pornography production is not always a gateway to contact offending, though the link is more obvious because the production offender is usually already in close proximity to the child. Wolak, Finkelhor, Mitchell, and Jones (2011) found that one third of production arrests in 2001 and 2006 did not involve any charges for contact sexual offenses, suggesting that offenders took photographs only.

CRITICAL ASSUMPTIONS IN ONLINE OFFENDER POLICIES

Hamilton (2012) suggested that legal policy and practices have been driven by three key assumptions, expanding the historical focus of law enforcement on harm to children to potential harm to children: (a) Child pornography offenders are undetected contact offenders, (b) child pornography offenders are pedophiles, and (c) contact offenders are pedophiles. The subsequent assumption she discusses but does not list is (d) pedophiles are very likely or certain to commit further sexual offenses. The evidence reviewed so far in this book does not fully support any of these assumptions. Up to half of child pornography offenders, but not all, have committed undetected contact sexual offenses (Seto et al., 2011); a majority, but not all, of child pornography offenders are pedophiles (Seto et al., 2006); perhaps half, but again not all, of contact sex offenders are pedophiles (Seto, 2008); and pedophiles are at greater risk of sexually offending compared with non-pedophiles, ceteris paribus, but their absolute risk is low in the absence of antisociality and situational factors acting as facilitators (e.g., Seto, Harris, Rice, & Barbaree, 2004).

APPENDIX 6.1
MORE ON EXPLANATIONS FOR THE PORNOGRAPHY
AND SEXUAL OFFENDING LINK

Malamuth, Addison, and Koss (2000) discussed in much more detail the potentially reciprocal effects between pornography and sexual offending, whereby higher-risk individuals are more likely to seek out pornography, particularly violent pornography, and also show greater effects of exposure to (violent) pornography. I discussed some of these ideas in the main text of this chapter, but I expand on them here for those who are interested, because of the centrality of understanding the pornography and sexual offending link for online sexual offending. Individuals who seek out sexual content in one form often seek it out in other forms; there is no a priori reason to expect that someone who accesses pornography online differs in meaningful ways from someone who accesses the same kinds of pornography through DVDs, magazines, or other physical media (J. Peter & Valkenburg, 2006). The one big difference is that the accessibility and affordability of online pornography is much greater than offline pornography, and greater perceived anonymity may increase engagement with online pornography.

It is possible that the associations between online pornography and sexual offending are stronger because sexual interests are less constrained, given the greater availability of online content versus going to a local pornography retailer. However, seeking child or violent pornography in nondigital format, as in a magazine or video, may indicate a stronger enthusiasm for the content than merely stumbling across it while searching for mainstream pornography. Detailed comparisons of types and sources of pornography use are needed to test these ideas.

Individuals at higher risk for making sexual contact with children are more likely to seek out child pornography and may be more likely to show effects of their exposure to child pornography, such as becoming sexually preoccupied or fantasizing more often about contact with a real child. If similar psychological processes are involved in the effects of child pornography, one would predict that child pornography users would have more permissive attitudes about sex with children, greater dissatisfaction with their current sexual life (in terms of wanting more sexual contact with children than they currently might have), and a greater willingness to act upon their sexual interests than nonusers.[5] These effects are expected to interact with other

---

[5]Babchishin, Hanson, and Hermann (2011) found that online offenders did not differ from contact offenders on measures of offense-supportive attitudes and beliefs, but this does not mean that online child pornography offenders would not differ from nonusers (who are similar in other respects) or from the general population.

predisposing risk factors, such that small effects are expected among pedophiles who otherwise do not engage in antisocial behavior, and large effects are expected among pedophiles who have already had sexual contact with children or have engaged in other illegal behavior.

Malamuth et al. (2000) emphasized that individual differences are important in estimating the effects of pornography. Probably the biggest individual difference is being male: Allen et al. (2007) conducted meta-analysis of 19 studies and found that men experience greater sexual arousal and more positive affect in response to written or visual depictions of sex than do women (see also Petersen & Hyde, 2010). For violent pornography, already having hostile attitudes about women interacts with pornography exposure to increase the risk of sexual aggression. Accordingly, having permissive attitudes about sex with children may interact with child pornography exposure. Exposure to this material can strengthen and build on existing cognitive schemata, and child pornography content can subsequently serve as a trigger for particular thoughts and emotions about children and sexuality. For example, Paul and Linz (2008) showed "barely legal" or ordinary adult pornography content to both men and women and found that both genders who were subsequently shown neutral depictions of girls were faster at recognizing sexual words than those who were originally shown ordinary adult pornography.

Another way pornography can influence behavior is in the effect of arousal states on information processing, a sex-induced myopia akin to the cognitive myopia that can occur as a result of anxiety or alcohol intoxication (Abbey, Zawacki, & McAuslan, 2000; Seto, 1992; Steele & Joseph, 1990). For example, viewing pornography and becoming sexually aroused may cause someone to focus on sexual cues that are present but not on cues of nonconsent, fear, or distress. This may explain phallometric study findings on the effects of preexposure to explicit sexual content and may also explain the findings on the arousal responses of nonoffending men to stories about rape once they have been primed by watching a pornography clip (see Barbaree & Marshall, 1991). In these studies, preexposure to mainstream pornography increased subsequent sexual responding to depictions of rape, suggesting increased sexual arousal can reduce inhibitions or facilitate response to socially sanctioned content.

Even early exposure to nonexplicit sexual depictions may have an effect. J. D. Brown et al. (2006)[6] and R. L. Collins et al. (2004) reported the results of longitudinal studies showing that early exposure to sexual content (not necessarily pornography; they also examined depictions of sexuality on television or in movies that were not explicit) predicted adolescent sexual behavior, such

---

[6]An interesting finding in the study by J. D. Brown et al. (2006) is that the relationship was found for Caucasian teens but not African American teens. Is this related to the consistent finding that child pornography offenders are disproportionately Caucasian?

that adolescents who were exposed early in life to sexual content were more sexually active later. Again, one cannot rule out third-variable explanations: Those who seek out sexual content may have different sexual trajectories. I discussed in a previous section the challenges of interpreting correlational data, whether cross-sectional or longitudinal and whether at the individual- or aggregate-level, as evidence of causation.

The increasingly early exposure of youths to hardcore pornography online, in all its many variants, is arguably one of the largest unregulated quasi-experiments in history. What are the potential effects of this exposure on psychosexual development? Though it is likely that predisposed children and youths would seek out more extreme or potentially paraphilic content in the first place, some may be initially motivated by curiosity (rather than an existing sexual interest), and even those who already have existing predispositions might require certain environmental inputs for negative outcomes to occur.

Within a single generation, many youths are being exposed to pornography and sexual solicitations to a much greater extent than was ever possible before the advent of the Internet. We do not know what impact so much ready exposure to hardcore pornography, including paraphilic content, will have on these youths, now and when they are adults (see C. Anderson, 2012; Becker & Stein, 1991). Sabina, Wolak, and Finkelhor (2008) reported on an online survey of 563 college students. Ninety-three percent of the young men had been exposed to online pornography as an adolescent. Fifteen percent had been exposed to child pornography, but this exposure was infrequent. Few of the students reported strong effects on emotions or attitudes, but the survey items were not specifically about exposure to child pornography or depictions of sexual violence. Also, theories on the effects of pornography suggest interactions with individual differences, and thus only some students would be expected to show observable effects of exposure to child pornography or sexual violence.

7

RISK ASSESSMENT

The central issue driving political and practical concerns about Internet-facilitated sexual offending is the likelihood that online offenders will commit new sexual offenses. This was certainly the subject of the bulk of the questions I was asked during my presentation at the United States Attorney General's summit on child exploitation in October 2011 and during my testimony to the United States Sentencing Commission in February 2012 (ussc.gov/Legislative_and_Public_Affairs/Public_Hearings_and_Meetings/20120215-16/Agenda_15.htm). There are two ways of approaching this issue, the first looking backward and the second looking forward: (a) What is the likelihood that an online offender has a history of contact sexual offending? (b) What is the likelihood that an online offender will go on to commit a contact sexual offense in the future?

http://dx.doi.org/10.1037/14191-008
Internet Sex Offenders, by M. C. Seto

The sexual offending history question was touched on in the previous chapter. Looking forward, the emerging research on recidivism[1] has focused on child pornography offenders, who are much larger in number than solicitation offenders and have been identified long enough ago (solicitation laws are newer than child pornography laws) that there are several years of follow-up data after their release from custody. In the second meta-analysis reported by Seto, Hanson, and Babchishin (2011), we identified nine samples of mostly child pornography offenders (total sample size of 2,630 online offenders) followed for an average of 3.4 years. Across studies, the recidivism rates for child pornography, violent (including contact sexual) and sexual offenses were relatively low compared with the average recidivism rates obtained for typical samples of sexual offenders (e.g., Hanson & Morton-Bourgon, 2005), even taking into account the shorter average follow-up times in the online offender studies. Approximately 5% of the child pornography offenders were caught for a new sexual offense of some kind: 3.4% for a new child pornography offense and 2.1% for a new contact sexual offense. Several online offender studies had no sexual recidivists.

Sexual recidivism is defined here as new criminal offenses that involve sexual conduct. It may involve physical contact (sexual assault, sexual contact with a child or someone else not able to legally consent) or sexual activity that does not involve contact but takes place without the other person's consent (e.g., exhibitionistic or voyeuristic behavior, new child pornography offenses). Some researchers have argued that violent recidivism is a more important factor to examine in recidivism studies of sex offenders, first because the public is concerned about violence itself and second because some ostensibly nonsexual offenses (assault, abduction, attempted or completed homicide) may actually be sexually motivated (Rice, Harris, Lang, & Cormier, 2006).

Recent follow-up results that were not included in our meta-analysis have also suggested a low sexual recidivism rate. In a sample of 180 federally sentenced child pornography offenders obtained by combining Wollert, Waggoner, and Smith's (2012) sample and a probationer sample from the Eastern District of New York, two individuals had committed a new child pornography offense, one had committed a noncontact sexual offense (unspecified), and one had committed a new contact sexual offense (von Dornum, 2012; Wollert, 2012). In a recent study by Jung, Ennis, Stein, Choy, and

---

[1]Recidivism studies predict new offenses that are officially detected through arrest and prosecution. These offenses are a subset of all new offenses that are committed by individuals who are part of follow-up studies. An important practical question is whether officially detected offenses are a biased sampling of all new offenses (e.g., if more violent or egregious offenses are more likely to be reported to authorities), and what effect any bias might have.

Hook (in press) conducted in Canada, 7% of the child pornography offenders had a new sexual offense during the short follow-up period (averaging less than 2 years), compared with 5% for noncontact or contact offenders. Jung et al. also reported that any new sexual offenses matched the group classification (i.e., child pornography offenders committed new child pornography offenses, etc.).

These observed recidivism rates will increase with longer follow-up periods, and not all new offenses are detected by authorities. Nevertheless, these rates are substantially lower than typically found for contact sexual offenders, suggesting that online offenders, particularly online-only offenders, are a relatively low-risk group. Nonetheless, online offenders are not homogeneous with regard to risk; some online offenders do pose a relatively greater risk of sexual recidivism.

In this chapter, I briefly review what we know about contact sex offender risk assessment and then summarize the emerging research on risk factors for recidivism among online offenders. I discuss risk assessment at length because it is central to the risk, need, and responsivity principles of offender rehabilitation that I discuss later when reviewing treatment and other interventions. I end the chapter with recommendations on how to best assess online offender risk to reoffend.

CONTACT SEX OFFENDER RISK ASSESSMENT

For a more detailed review of contact sex offender risk assessment, please see Chapter 7 in Seto (2008) or one of the recent books, book chapters, and review articles in this highly active area (e.g., Otto & Douglas, 2009; Quinsey, Harris, Rice, & Cormier, 2006). There are a number of major findings to highlight before discussing the application of sex offender risk assessment models and evidence to online offenders: (a) pessimism about forecasting future behavior being no longer warranted, (b) advances in knowledge about risk factors, (c) advantages of structured or actuarial assessment approaches, (d) static versus dynamic risk. I discuss each of these major risk topics briefly next.

Pessimism About Predicting Recidivism

Pessimism about the ability to predict recidivism among identified sex offenders is no longer warranted, given the research developments since Monahan's (1981) discouraging synopsis on risk assessment. We can predict recidivism with moderately good accuracy using one of a number of validated risk measures that have been developed for contact sex offenders in the past

2 decades. Some studies suggest the best risk appraisal measures are hitting a predictive ceiling (Quinsey et al., 2006), given the complex, nonlinear, and dynamic influences on human behavior; the fact that offenders are motivated to hide their intentions and to hide evidence of any new crimes they commit; and the attempt to predict behavior over the long term (years).

Major Dimensions of Risk

The development of valid sex offender risk measures was built on steady scientific advances in our knowledge of recidivism risk factors. A number of highly robust predictors of criminal recidivism have been identified across diverse samples of offenders: younger age at first contact with the criminal justice system, prior criminal history, substance abuse, and antisocial personality traits, particularly psychopathy. These risk factors—which reflect *antisociality*—are robust across types of crimes or offenders, including mentally disordered offenders, female offenders, and contact sexual offenders (Bonta, Law, & Hanson, 1998; Bonta, Pang, & Wallace-Capretta, 1995; Hanson & Morton-Bourgon, 2005). At the same time, sex offender specific factors reflecting *sexual deviance*—paraphilia, sexual arousal to children or sexual violence, sexual victim characteristics, and so forth—further contribute to the prediction of sexual recidivism. Quantitative reviews of the sex offender follow-up research have confirmed that many risk factors for sexual recidivism fall into one of the two major risk dimensions of antisociality and sexual deviance (Doren, 2004; Hanson & Bussière, 1998; Hanson & Morton-Bourgon, 2005; Quinsey et al., 2006).

Karl Hanson, one of the world's authorities on sex offender risk assessment, suggested there is also a third dimension—*poor interpersonal competence*—that contributes to sex offender recidivism risk (Hanson & Morton-Bourgon, 2004, 2005). This third dimension includes disrupted attachment, failure at adult relationships, and emotional congruence with children, which describes feeling more comfortable and preferring the company of children. These interpersonal indicators might also be alternatively conceptualized as correlates of sexual interest in children. Pedophilic individuals might be less comfortable with adults than with children, less likely to have adult sexual partners or long-term adult romantic relationships, and to be more likely to prefer the company of children, just as teleiophilic individuals are (often) less comfortable with children (especially if they do not have children of their own) than with adults, do not usually have sexual or romantic relationships with children, and are more comfortable with adults.

In their recent review of the literature on sex offender risk factors, Mann, Hanson, and Thornton (2010) discussed what risk variables mean or signify, on the assumption that the psychological meaning of risk factors can guide intervention. For instance, interpersonal difficulties due to problems with social skills or other interpersonal competencies require different interventions (e.g., social skills training) than do interpersonal difficulties that reflect a lack of interest in adult relationships (e.g., as a result of exclusive pedophilia or hebephilia). The same risk factor has different meanings for two individuals, and treatment needs to be tailored accordingly.

Superiority of Actuarial or Structured Assessment Approaches

There are different approaches for combining risk-related information. Unstructured judgment involves the subjective appraisal and weighing of putative risk factors, followed by a global statement about risk to reoffend (e.g., stating that the offender is low, moderate, or high in risk to reoffend). Prior to the development of structured assessment guides, this was the traditional approach to clinical risk assessment: a person was interviewed, file information was reviewed, and then a subjective opinion about risk was given (Doren, 2002). Validation research showed that unstructured judgments often fared no better than chance, leading to the pessimism expressed by Monahan (1981) and others about the ability to predict future offending.

In contrast to unstructured judgments, structured judgments involve using a checklist or other guide to focus one's attention on a specific set of putative risk factors. I call them *putative risk factors* here because the factors might not be empirically related to recidivism or might even be negatively related to the outcome of interest so that predictive accuracy is impaired. For example, a structured checklist might consider more serious victim injury in the most recent violent offense to be indicative of greater risk of future violence, when it is actually negatively associated with violent recidivism (Quinsey et al., 2006). Another issue with structured guides is that empirically supported risk factors might be so highly correlated with each other that they provide redundant information about future offending.

Actuarial measures differ from structured guides because they involve a set of empirically identified risk factors that are weighted and combined using explicit rules to provide probabilistic estimates of the outcome. Each risk factor uniquely contributes to the prediction of future offending, and thus it is not redundant even if it is correlated with other risk factors included in the actuarial measure. Some authors refer to any measure that contains a list of empirically identified risk factors and an objective scoring procedure as being actuarial in nature, but a key feature of actuarial measures (in my opinion) is that probabilistic statements can be made. Probabilistic estimates of outcome indicate the proportion of people with the same score (or who score within a range of scores) who are expected to reoffend within a specified period of opportunity.

A widely used and well-known example of an actuarial sex offender risk measure is the Static–99. The Static–99 is designed to estimate the probability of sexual or violent recidivism among adult men who have committed a contact or attempted contact sexual offense, whether against a child or an adult (http://static99.org; Hanson & Thornton, 2000). The Static–99 has good predictive accuracy compared with other risk scales and is currently the most cross-validated sexual offender risk assessment measure for adult sex offenders, with over 60 studies examining its predictive validity (Hanson & Morton-Bourgon, 2009). The Static–99 items include offender age at release or anticipated onset of risk to reoffend in the community, having lived with a lover for at least 2 years, any nonsexually violent index conviction, any prior nonsexually violent conviction, number of prior charges or convictions for sexual offenses, prior sentencing dates, any convictions for noncontact sexual offenses, any unrelated sexual victims, any stranger sexual victims, and any male sexual victims. These Static–99 items are similar to items that appear on other risk measures that draw from the same risk literature.[2] Scores on different measures positively correlate with each other (e.g., Barbaree, Seto, Langton, & Peacock, 2001; Langton et al., 2007).

The actuarial approach is well established in other contexts, such as determining insurance premiums or in estimating cancer survival times. (The dictionary definition of an *actuary* is someone who specializes in the statistics of risk, especially as it relates to insurance calculations.) In a similar way, the Screening Scale for Pedophilic Interests is an actuarial measure for determining the likelihood that a sex offender with child victims will show a sexual preference for children over adults when assessed phallometrically (Seto, Harris, Rice, & Barbaree, 2004; Seto & Lalumière, 2001). Each additional point on the scale is associated with a greater probability of showing a pedophilic sexual arousal pattern. One can easily imagine actuarial measures in other areas of clinical practice, such as the development of a scale to predict the likelihood, in a specified follow-up period, that someone who has experienced a depressive episode will relapse and experience another depressive episode or that someone with schizophrenia will relapse and experience another psychotic episode.

On average, actuarial or structured measures produce more accurate predictions than unstructured clinical judgments, for reasons that include better reliability and validity—with an explicit set of variables, operational definitions, and coding rules versus idiosyncratically identified risk factors combined subjectively—and an avoidance of cognitive biases that reduce accuracy (Hanson, Bourgon, Helmus, & Hodgson 2009; Hanson, Harris,

---

[2]This fact may explain why there appears to be little gain in predictive accuracy from combining different risk measures in intuitive or mathematical ways (Seto, 2005).

Scott, & Helmus, 2007). These universal biases include heuristics such as the primacy and recency effects, representative heuristics, and availability heuristics that are helpful in some domains, but not in the behavioral prediction domain (Gigerenzer, Todd, & the ABC Group, 1999; Kahneman, 2011). Other challenges for unstructured clinical judgments of risk to reoffend include determining how to optimally select and weigh the most relevant risk factors and how to subjectively combine highly correlated factors such as criminal history and antisocial personality traits. Individuals with more extensive criminal histories score higher on antisocial personality traits, and individuals who are higher on measures of antisocial personality traits are more likely to engage in criminal behavior.

In the context of online sexual offending, the fact that child pornography offenders are likely to be pedophiles may cause evaluators to assume they are at high risk of contact sexual offenses involving children in the future, because pedophilia is a strong predictor of sexual recidivism among identified sex offenders (Hanson & Morton-Bourgon, 2005). The motivation–facilitation model of sexual offending against children suggests, however, that only those child pornography offenders who have poor self-control of their pedophilic or hebephilic interests would act on them. Poor inhibitory control is revealed in relatively high scores on measures of risk taking, impulsivity, or similar antisociality traits, or it occurs situationally because of alcohol or drug intoxication, high levels of stress, or depressed (or hypomanic) mood. Similarly, the fact that some online solicitation offenders have attempted to meet a minor in real life, where sexual contact might have taken place, would suggest such individuals are at high risk of doing so again. But only a minority of contact sexual offenders, all of whom have committed contact sexual offenses at least once, will go on to sexually reoffend in this way, even after decades of opportunity (Hanson, Steffy, & Gauthier, 1993; Prentky, Knight, & Lee, 1997). Antisociality factors play the critical facilitation role (Lee, Li, Lamade, Schuler, & Prentky, 2012).

Structured or actuarial measures are increasingly used in sex offender risk assessments, especially when the stakes are high, as in postincarceration, indeterminate civil commitment proceedings in the United States, or Dangerous Offender hearings in Canada that can result in indeterminate prison sentences (Jackson & Hess, 2007; see Appendix 7.1). Structured or actuarial risk assessments are recommended in best practice guidelines produced by the Association for the Treatment of Sexual Abusers (ATSA), the largest international organization representing professionals working with sex offenders (ATSA, 2011).

Static Versus Dynamic Risk

Most sex offender risk research has focused on risk to reoffend over the long term, considered in terms of years or even decades. Long-term risk is best predicted by static factors that are historical in nature, such as prior criminal history, or by factors that are highly unlikely to change given our current abilities, such as having pedophilia or being a psychopath. In contrast to these static risk factors, dynamic risk factors can change over time and may therefore be more effective in assessing shorter term fluctuations in risk to reoffend, such as changes over periods of days, weeks or perhaps months. Ideally, dynamic risk factors are also more amenable to intervention, thereby identifying important treatment and supervision targets.

Alcohol use problems can illustrate the distinction between static and dynamic risk. A history of alcohol misuse is an established static risk factor for long-term risk to reoffend among both sexual and nonsexual offenders (Hanson & Morton-Bourgon, 2005). Starting to using alcohol again or becoming intoxicated are dynamic risk factors that can be monitored and targeted in treatment and supervision. A second germane example is pedophilia, also an established static risk factor, whereas increasing difficulty regulating sexual thoughts, fantasies or urges about prepubescent children is a dynamic risk factor. Someone with pedophilia can experience variation in the strength of their sexual attraction to children, and even someone without pedophilia can experience some sexual response to prepubescent children, as evidenced by the community survey results reported in Chapter 1.

Though static risk factors are better understood than dynamic risk factors, the empirical literature has advanced quickly in the past 10 to 15 years with the development of dynamic risk measures. The most prominent sex offender measure is the Stable–2000, which assesses 16 factors that can change over time (months or years) and that are related to the probability of officially detected recidivism (Hanson et al., 2007). Each of these 16 factors is rated on a three-point scale, with 0 indicating no problem, 1 indicating some concern, and 2 indicating that the problem is present. The 16 Stable–2000 risk factors can be rationally organized into six domains, each of which can be monitored and targeted by interventions: The *significant social influences* domain represents the balance of positive and negative influences in a person's social world, particularly including family and friends; the *intimacy deficits* domain represents the stability of intimate relationships, including loneliness or social rejection, a lack of concern for others, emotional identification with children, or hostility toward women; the *sexual self-regulation* domain represents problems in regulating sexual behavior, including high sex drive or sexual preoccupation, maladaptive use of sex as a way of coping with negative mood or other concerns, and deviant sexual interests; the *attitudes supportive of sexual assault* domain represents offense-supportive attitudes and beliefs, including sexual entitlement, attitudes tolerant of rape, and attitudes tolerant of adult–child sex; the *cooperation with supervision* domain represents compliance and cooperation with supervision requirements; and the *general self-regulation* domain represents problems with general regulation of behavior, including impulsivity, poor cognitive problem-solving skills, and negative emotionality or hostility. After scoring the items, the highest score in each domain is counted, resulting in total scores that can range from 0 to 12.

Seto and Fernandez (2011) recently demonstrated that a typical sample of adult male sex offenders can be categorized into four dynamic risk groups on the basis of their relative scores on the Stable–2000: (a) a low-needs group that scores below the overall mean on all items; (b) a typical group with intermediate scores; (c) a sexually deviant group that scores relatively high on deviant sexual interests, sexual preoccupation, emotional identification with children, and offense-supportive attitudes and beliefs about sex with children; and (d) a pervasive high-needs group who scores high on many items. The Stable–2000 measure can add to the prediction offered by actuarial risk measures, suggesting that a comprehensive sex offender assessment would include both static risk and dynamic risk assessment (Allan, Grace, Rutherford, & Hudson, 2007; Hanson et al., 2007; Olver, Wong, Nicholaichuk, & Gordon, 2007).

Other sex offender risk measures include dynamic risk items; these measures include the Minnesota Sex Offender Screening Tool–3 (Duwe & Freske, 2012) and the sex offender version of the Violence Risk Scale (Duwe & Freske, 2012; Olver et al., 2007). More studies are needed that use truly dynamic study designs, however, because many studies purporting to examine dynamic risk have assessed it at one time only to predict subsequent sexual offenses, which essentially treats the dynamic risk scores as static risk factors. In contrast, a truly dynamic risk design assesses dynamic risk factors multiple times and examines the ability of changes in scores to predict recidivism (S. L. Brown, St. Amand, & Zamble, 2009; Chagigiorgis, Michel, Laprade, Ahmed, & Seto, 2011; Hanson et al., 2007; Quinsey, Coleman, Jones, & Altrows, 1997).

The Stable–2007 is an updated version of the Stable–2000, with a number of changes in the items, including revisions of the scoring criteria for two items ("lovers/intimate partners" became "capacity for relationship stability," and deviant sexual interests include an explicit scoring of victim history) and deletion of the three attitude items (sexual entitlement, attitudes tolerant of rape, attitudes tolerant of adult–child sex) because they were not related to sexual recidivism, possibly because of training or coding problems in the implementation of the Stable–2000. The overall Stable–2007 score is determined on the basis of a simple addition of items. The Stable–2000 has been validated multiple times, however, whereas the Stable–2007 has been validated in only a relatively small number of studies so far (Hanson et al., 2007).

IMPLICATIONS FOR ONLINE OFFENDERS

Knitting these threads of risk assessment research together, we can hypothesize that structured or actuarial risk measures emphasizing static risk factors will do better than unstructured judgments of risk in predicting long-term recidivism among online offenders. Existing follow-up studies only extend approximately 6 years. We can also predict that the same two major dimensions of risk factors—antisociality and sexual deviance—will be important in identifying online offenders who are more likely to reoffend. As discussed in Chapters 2 and 3, there is good reason to believe that many child pornography offenders will be likely to have pedophilia or hebephilia, so they are expected to score higher on deviant sexual interests. Sexual deviance is less important for solicitation offenders, only a few of whom might meet diagnostic criteria for pedophilia or hebephilia; some solicitation offenders, however, may score relatively high on measures of sexual preoccupation and sex drive (as might some child pornography offenders, if their explanations for their crimes are credible; Seto, Reeves, & Jung, 2010).

Among either group of online offenders, we would expect individuals who show more signs of antisociality to be at greater risk of sexually offending in the future, whether online or offline. Classic antisociality indicators include offender age at first contact with the criminal justice system, extent of prior criminal history, failure on conditional release (reflecting an unwillingness or inability to abide by rules even with the force of law and potential re-imprisonment behind it), antisocial personality traits (particularly psychopathy), substance use problems, and lifestyle instability (e.g., sporadic employment despite being able to work; Seto & Eke, 2005; Wakeling, Howard, & Barnett, 2011). There is some evidence (see Developing a New Risk Measure later in the chapter) that offending-specific variables—specifically, the ratio of boy to girl child pornography content and having nondigital child pornography—predict child pornography and any sexual recidivism, respectively (Seto, 2009). Other Internet-specific variables (total amount of child pornography, time spent online) have been proposed to be related to risk but have not yet been empirically demonstrated to be predictive (Eke & Seto, 2012).

The developers of the Static–99 have suggested that solicitation offenders who have attempted to meet a minor in real life (even if they actually met an undercover police officer) can be scored using this measure, though users are cautioned in the Static–99 guidelines that there were few such offenders in the development samples, and it is unclear whether the probabilistic estimates would apply (A. J. R. Harris, Phenix, Hanson, & Thornton, 2003). Any dual offender can be confidently scored using the Static–99 or another established actuarial risk measure because they already have a contact sexual offense in their history, and such offenders comprised most of the development samples.

The Static–99 includes a "noncontact offense history" item that would apply to online offenders and individuals who have committed exhibitionism or voyeurism offenses. This is similar to the Risk Matrix 2000 (Thornton et al., 2003), a risk measure widely used in the United Kingdom and discussed in more detail in Applying Established Risk Measures later in this chapter. It is not yet clear how to proceed in the risk assessment of pornography offenders with no history of contact or attempted contact offending, or in the assessment of fantasy-driven solicitation offenders.

Static Risk Factors

My colleague Angela Eke and I published the first peer-reviewed study on child pornography offender recidivism (Seto & Eke, 2005). Because we only had access to law enforcement registry data, we were limited in the risk factors we could examine; we did not have clinical assessment data or other potentially rich sources of risk-related information. We could look at criminal history closely, however, because we had access to national police records of new charges and convictions. We found that child pornography offenders with any kind of prior criminal history—including nonsexual offenses such as theft, possession of narcotics, or assault—were at significantly greater risk of sexual recidivism during the average follow-up period of approximately 30 months. Slightly over half (56%) of the sample had any prior criminal record, a quarter (24%) had prior contact sexual offenses, and 15% had prior child pornography offenses. It is not surprising that having a history of contact sexual offending was a strong predictor of sexual recidivism. Four percent of the sample committed a new contact sexual offense in the relatively short follow-up period.

In an extended follow-up of the Seto and Eke (2005) sample, which included adding the child pornography offenders who had been registered in Ontario during the interim, we found that a third of the total sample of 541 adult male child pornography offenders (34%) committed any kind of new offense during the follow-up period: 4% of offenders committed new contact sex offenses, an additional 2% of offenders were charged with historical contact sex offenses (i.e., previously undetected offending that came to light following the index child pornography conviction, or what we called *pseudo-recidivism*), and 7% of offenders committed a new child pornography offense (Eke, Seto, & Williams, 2011). As in the previous study by Seto and Eke, we found that criminal history variables predicted recidivism. We also found that younger age at first criminal charge predicted sexual recidivism. These findings establish that child pornography offending is orderly, because young offender age and criminal history are two of the best-established risk factors in criminology and forensic psychology.

Offender age at the time of release was not a significant predictor of recidivism in Eke et al. (2011). This is consistent with other research showing that age at first contact with the criminal justice system is a better predictor of recidivism than age at time of release, suggesting that aging is less important than some authors have argued (G. T. Harris & Rice, 2007; for contrary opinions, see Barbaree, Langton, Blanchard, & Cantor, 2009; Wollert, Cramer, Waggoner, Skelton, & Vess, 2010). Child pornography offenders who already had a history of contact sexual offending had higher sexual recidivism rates than the expected base rates for typical sexual offenders reported by A. J. R. Harris and Hanson (2004). Those who had no history of contact offending almost never committed such offenses during the follow-up period, despite the fact that a majority were likely to be sexually interested in children (Seto, Cantor, & Blanchard, 2006).

In an unpublished study presented at an annual conference of the ATSA, Faust, Renaud, and Bickart (2009) examined the predictors of recidivism in a large federal sample of 870 male child pornography offenders assessed by the United States Federal Bureau of Prisons between 2002 and 2005. The average length of follow-up was almost 4 years, with a sexual re-arrest rate of 5.7%. Of the 30 predictors that were available to these researchers, five were significant predictors of sexual re-arrest. Sexual re-arrest was associated with lower education, being single, having non-Internet child pornography, prior sexual offender treatment, and not having depictions of adolescent minors. Lower education and single status are also classic criminological variables. Having non-Internet child pornography may reflect a greater, deeper, or longer standing interest in child pornography, given that most child pornography is now readily accessed online. Prior sexual offender treatment may have acted as a proxy variable for prior sexual offending history or greater clinical needs, rather than as an indication of an iatrogenic effect of treatment (though an undesired effect cannot be ruled out). Not having any depictions of adolescent minors suggests the recidivists were more likely to be pedophiles or hebephiles and therefore attuned to images of younger youths.

Conditional Release Failure

In the follow-up study by Eke et al. (2011), we also examined failures on conditional release because of the criminal justice interest in (a) whether individuals accused of child pornography offenses should be released on bail while awaiting trial and (b) how convicted individuals might fare if they are released on probation or parole. Working with the Ontario Provincial Police, my coauthors understood that police investigators and threat analysts were interested in these issues because these officers were often called to testify regarding bail eligibility. A quarter (24%) of our sample had one or more charges for failure on conditional release—on bail, probation, or parole—during the follow-up period, which is comparable with the conditional failure rates observed among contact sexual offenders with child victims (e.g., Barbaree, Seto, & Maric, 1997; Motiuk & Brown, 1993). The circumstances of failures were known for 114 of the 130 offenders who failed their conditional release in our study. Of these known violations, a little over half were for being with children alone, using computers or the Internet to contact children or access (child) pornography again, or committing another sexual offense. The remaining offenders violated conditions for not registering with police as required by provincial sex offender registration law, using alcohol when prohibited as a condition of their community release, or committing nonsexual, nonviolent offenses, such as theft or possession of narcotics. Failure on conditional release was predicted by younger offender age at the time of their first criminal charge (i.e., age of first entry into the criminal justice system). (See Appendix 7.2.)

The recidivism rate observed by Eke et al. (2011) was not a statistical outlier in the recidivism meta-analysis reported by Seto et al. (2011), but it was at the upper end of the observed range. It is a puzzle why there was such a difference between Eke et al. and other follow-up studies that have detected zero contact sexual recidivism, such as Endrass et al. (2009), even though the latter study had a longer follow-up time. One explanation is that Eke et al. used new criminal charges as the criterion for recidivism, whereas Endrass et al. used new convictions, a more conservative outcome; two of the child pornography offenders in Endrass et al. were being investigated for contact sexual offenses at the time of their follow-up analysis.

Second, the samples seem to be different in static risk level, because those in the Endrass et al. sample were less likely to have a prior criminal history: Only 5% (11 offenders) had a prior conviction for a violent (including sexual) offense, and only two offenders had a prior contact sexual offense, whereas a quarter of the Eke et al. sample had a prior contact sexual offense. This difference might be explained by the fact that the Swiss offenders studied by Endrass et al. were identified because they were Landslide Production customers (see Chapter 2) and thus were predominantly low-risk possession-only offenders. Ninety-five percent confessed to the allegations in court, even though only 55% were convicted because there was only physical evidence in their computers' temporary caches, which was not deemed to justify a conviction. In contrast, the offenders studied by Eke et al. included all child pornography offenders on the provincial sex offender registry, and these criteria offences included not only accessing, possessing, or distributing but also producing child pornography. Some of the offenders in our sample might have been identified for contact sexual offenses first, and then child pornography convictions were obtained when illegal content was found in a search of their computers.

At various conferences over the past several years, we have reported on the preliminary results of another child pornography offender follow-up study. This study is following a sample of 301 Ontario child pornography offenders identified through their police case files. As one might expect, this sample overlaps extensively with the provincial registry sample reported by Eke et al. (2011), because we collected data in the same province over a similar time period. The important distinction, however, is that we had access to the police case files, which not only contained information about offender age and criminal history but also investigator notes from interviews of the suspect (possibly including interviews with spouses or girlfriends, family members, or coworkers), information about the child pornography content seized by police, information about how and where child pornography was accessed according to forensic computer analysis, information on mental health history, and any clinical assessments that were completed as part of subsequent trial proceedings (e.g., a psychological or psychiatric evaluation at the request of the defense lawyer). We included only cases that resulted in one or more child pornography offense convictions and were either not appealed or were not successfully appealed. The case files were open until the case went to court and resulted in either a stay of proceedings, acquittal, or conviction; all cases we examined had resulted in conviction.

Police Case File Study

In this police case file study, we confirmed that offender age and criminal history (coded in different ways) predicted violent (including contact sexual) recidivism as well as child pornography recidivism. In addition, we found that self-reported interest in pubescent children and substance misuse were significant predictors of contact sexual offending, whereas the ratio of boy to girl content in the child pornography was predictive of child pornography recidivism. In our initial presentations of preliminary results in 2009 and 2010, we identified several interesting variables that showed promise as predictors. These variables included sharing a residence with children, living alone, having disorganized child pornography content, and having contact information such as an e-mail address or instant messaging nickname for children where there was no justifiable reason in the eyes of the research assistants. The first two variables necessarily referred to different subgroups of offenders because one could not live with children and live alone at the same time. In regard to that last variable, having contact information was considered to be justifiable if the offender was related to the child or had contact information as a result of his work or volunteer activities (e.g., having the addresses and phone numbers for children in a class or sports team). We are currently updating the results with the latest outcomes and therefore a longer average follow-up time.

Pseudo-Recidivism

A methodological consideration in all sex offender follow-up research—whether it is research to validate a risk assessment measure or to evaluate the impact of treatment or other interventions—is *pseudo-recidivism*, which we and others have defined as previously undetected contact offenses in an individual's history that come to the attention of law enforcement after an index conviction for child pornography or another sexual offense (Eke et al., 2011). In other words, pseudo-recidivism represents new criminal charges and convictions that occur when a prior victim comes forward following the publicity surrounding an index offense or after a thorough police investigation. An unexpected finding from the study by Eke et al. (2011) was the substantial number of pseudo-recidivists that were found—representing approximately a third of new criminal charges or convictions that were recorded—which was possible only because we had sufficient information about the offenses underlying new charges or convictions from reviewing the specific police occurrence reports instead of relying on "rap sheets" that record only charges and convictions.

Pseudo-recidivism has implications not only for interpreting the specific study by Eke et al. (2011) but also for thinking about other sexual offender prediction results. The outcome of most concern, from a public safety perspective, is new offenses committed by offenders after they are released from custody and again pose a potential risk to the community. The public safety concern is about future behavior resulting in victimizations; judges need to make decisions about sentences, and parole board officials and evaluators need to make decisions about eligibility for release to the community. Public safety is not (directly) protected by prosecutions for criminal behavior that was committed in the past. Historical sexual offenses still ought to be addressed, for the sake of justice principles and in respect of victims' rights, but the distinction between pseudo-recidivism and "true" recidivism is meaningful for both policy and practice questions. Some sex offender follow-up studies have made this distinction (e.g., Langton, 2003) but other recidivism studies have not (e.g., Barbaree et al., 2001).

APPLYING ESTABLISHED RISK MEASURES

I am not aware of studies that have prospectively examined the predictive validity of existing risk measures in a large sample of online offenders followed for a longer period of time, such as 5 or more years of opportunity.

In offender populations that have been studied, including contact offenders, most new offenses tend to take place within the first 5 years after release. However, several studies suggest that such measures will continue to be useful in assessing the risk of recidivism posed by online child pornography offenders. I am not aware of any studies that have followed solicitation offenders, who would be expected to differ from child pornography offenders in recidivism because they are expected to differ on risk-related factors (e.g., presence of pedophilia or hebephilia, prior criminal history).

First, Webb, Craissati, and Keen (2007) found that the Stable–2000, a well-established dynamic risk measure for contact sex offenders, significantly predicted probation failure and "risky sexual behavior" after a follow-up period of 18 months. Risky sexual behavior included behaviors such as accessing adult pornography on a daily basis but did not include new sexual offenses because none were observed in this study during this time frame. This study did not show that Stable–2000 scores predicted sexual recidivism, but it did suggest that scores could predict proximate behavior; probation failure could include suspicious behaviors such as being around a child unsupervised by a responsible adult, and accessing online pornography could put one at greater risk of involvement with child pornography (whether by accident or on purpose).

Barnett, Wakeling, and Howard (2010) examined the ability of an actuarial risk measure widely used in the United Kingdom but less well known in North America, the Risk Matrix 2000, to predict recidivism among 513 child pornography offenders. The Risk Matrix 2000 incorporates the following items: offender age, sexual sentencing history, any additional sentencing history, ever having a live-in relationship, ever having a noncontact sexual offense, and whether any sexual victims were male or strangers. The measure was modified to reflect the online offending sample by excluding the male, stranger, and noncontact items. The modified Risk Matrix 2000 significantly predicted contact sexual recidivism after 2 years, even though the base rate of new offenses was low, at 1.4%. The association was driven by the fact that offenders in the very high risk category (which could only be possible if they had an extensive criminal history) were much more likely to commit contact sexual offenses than offenders in the other three categories (there were only 26 offenders in the very high category).

Wakeling et al. (2011) extended this follow-up research by examining how the modified Risk Matrix 2000 and another risk scale for general recidivism used in the United Kingdom, the Offender Group Reconviction Scale 3 (OGRS3; Howard, Francis, Soothill, & Humphreys, 2009), predicted recidivism in a large sample of 1,344 child pornography offenders after 1-year (1,326 offenders) or 2-year (994 offenders) follow-ups. Though the new conviction rates were again quite low at 2.1% and 3.1%, respectively, both measures significantly predicted sexual recidivism, with areas under the (receiver operating characteristic) curve (AUC) comparable to those found for actuarial risk scales such as the Static–99 and Risk Matrix 2000 in contact sex offender samples. Wakeling et al. noted that the online offenders had significantly lower scores on the OGRS3 compared with contact sex offenders. The OGRS3 is a measure of risk of general recidivism and can be thought of as a proxy measure of general criminal risk factors. This finding is again consistent with the notion that online offenders, on average, are less antisocial than contact sex offenders (see Chapter 5).

Nonetheless, the (offense-specific) Risk Matrix 2000 and (general) OGRS3 produced similar predictions of sexual recidivism in the Wakeling et al. (2011) study, whereas the OGRS3 was better for predicting recidivism of any kind. This is consistent with contact sex offender research that has shown that both sex offender specific and general criminal risk factors can predict sexual recidivism (Hanson & Morton-Bourgon, 2005). Further analysis suggested that adding OGRS3 to Risk Matrix 2000 scores improved the prediction of violent (including sexual) recidivism, again consistent with past findings that individuals who are high both in sex offense specific factors and in general criminological factors are at the greatest risk of sexual recidivism (Hanson & Bussière, 1998; Hanson & Morton-Bourgon, 2005). Wakeling et al. suggested that this latter result may be due to the OGRS3 being designed to predict recidivism after 1 or 2 years, whereas the Risk Matrix 2000 is designed to predict longer-term recidivism. However, many new offenses occur in the first few years of opportunity. Another possible explanation is that the OGRS3 has more items, potentially capturing more variance in recidivism risk among offenders, and is thus a "purer" measure of antisocial and criminal tendencies.

Three quarters of the sexual recidivism identified by Wakeling et al. (2011) was Internet related. This was especially so for Internet "specialists," that is, those individuals who had no history of any other type of offending and thus tended to have low scores on the risk measures compared with the rest of the sample. Neither the Risk Matrix 2000 nor the OGRS3 significantly predicted recidivism among Internet-only offenders, due to the low base rate of recidivism observed for this subgroup (there were few new offenses to predict and thus much less statistical power to detect any real association). This is consistent with the findings reported by Seto et al. (2011) and Eke et al. (2011). Wakeling et al. (2011) wondered whether clinical judgment might fare better than the scales because of this low base rate issue. Our knowledge about risk assessment approaches, reviewed at the beginning of this chapter, suggests that clinical judgment would not fare well; the most accurate approach would be to predict no sexual recidivism in this very-low-risk group. Any type of recidivism was also uncommon in the Wakeling et al. study, at

8% after 1 year and 11% after 2 years. These results are consistent with the idea that online offenders are low risk, as a group, and suggests further that online offenders are more likely to commit further online offenses than they are to commit contact sexual offenses, consistent with a specialist rather than generalist view of their criminal behavior.

Overall, these prediction studies fit with theories of sexual offending that emphasize the major risk dimensions of antisociality and sexual deviance (Hanson & Morton-Bourgon, 2005; Lalumière, Harris, Quinsey, & Rice, 2005; Seto, 2008; Ward, Polaschek, & Beech, 2006). All of these theories suggest that in a group of individuals likely to be characterized by sexual deviance by dint of their accessing of child pornography, antisociality factors will discriminate recidivists from nonrecidivists. Research showing that actuarial risk measures are robust across contact offender type also supports the idea that existing measures, with some modifications, would have predictive validity for online offenders (e.g., Bartosh, Garby, Lewis, & Gray, 2003).

DEVELOPING A NEW RISK MEASURE

The early research evidence reviewed in the previous section suggests that modifications of existing risk measures are likely to yield good predictive accuracy in follow-ups of online sexual offenders. More research is needed using existing risk measures for larger samples and/or longer follow-up periods. But if these initial findings are replicated and extended in subsequent research, then it is likely that existing risk measures will suffice—after some adaptation—for the important purpose of evaluating online offender risk of recidivism. It is unlikely that a brand-new risk assessment tool, developed specifically for online offenders, would produce a large increase in predictive accuracy.

Another issue that needs to be addressed in large-scale follow-up research is the extent to which probabilistic estimates of recidivism apply to online offenders. Recent research shows that these estimates vary across time and across jurisdiction, which requires regular updating of scale norms (Helmus, 2009; Helmus, Hanson, Thornton, Babchishin, & Harris, 2012). Only Wakeling et al. (2011) have provided probabilistic estimates of sexual recidivism across risk categories. Their results suggest the association between risk scores and sexual recidivism is driven by those in the very high risk category of the Risk Matrix 2000, who almost by definition, already had a history of contact sexual offending. Though the recidivism rates across risk scores or risk categories may vary, the rank ordering of offenders by risk measures should be robust across time and jurisdiction.

Seto (2009) and Witt (2010) have suggested that existing risk measures should be able to at least rank order offenders, which is useful for many risk-related decisions, such as institutional placement, treatment intensity allocation, and supervision assignment. Witt (2010) also nicely summarized other potential risk factors from dynamic risk research and models of sexual offending.

The low base rate of sexual recidivism among online-only offenders suggests that there is little variance in risk in this subgroup to predict. The most accurate risk statement is to assume that an online-only offender with no prior criminal history of any kind is not going to sexually reoffend. Because existing risk measures are already applicable to online offenders who have also committed contact sexual offenses, the follow-up research to date has suggested that an online-offender-only risk measure is unlikely to be successful. Having said that, with a sufficiently large sample and follow-up time, it may be possible to identify some significant offense-specific correlates of sexual recidivism that might add to the prediction provided by established risk factors, and thereby increase predictive accuracy for the online offender population.

It is also possible that for risk evaluations focusing specifically on new online offenses, offense-specific risk factors may come into play, justifying a special-purpose tool. For example, in our police case file study, we found that the ratio of child pornography emphasizing boys relative to the content emphasizing girls was predictive of child pornography recidivism (Seto, 2009). Faust et al. (2009) reported that having nondigital child pornography content and having child pornography only depicting prepubescent children were predictors of sexual re-arrest. Studies with large samples and longer follow-up times are needed to identify other potential offense-specific correlates. Such studies will be challenging to conduct with child pornography offenders because potentially important details about their child pornography content and collecting behavior might not be recorded in a systematic way for analysis. This was brought up several times at the United States Sentencing Commission hearing in February 2012, where several witnesses mentioned that clinically relevant information is not passed on after the basic information required for prosecution and sentencing purposes has been captured (http://ussc.gov/Legislative_and_Public_Affairs/Public_Hearings_and_Meetings/20120215-16/Agenda_15.htm). For example, the federal sentencing guidelines provide an enhancement if any child pornography content depicts sexual violence. Once that is proved, it is not necessary to report how many sexually violent child pornography images there were, what proportion of the total collection that this type of content represents, or whether other potentially paraphilic content was in the possession of the offender.

DYNAMIC RISK ASSESSMENT OF ONLINE OFFENDERS

What about dynamic risk assessment of online offenders? Webb et al. (2007) found that Stable–2000 scores predicted risky sexual behavior in the short-term, but it is not yet demonstrated whether this dynamic risk instrument would predict sexual recidivism. In their review, Elliott and Beech (2009) suggested that stable dynamic risk factors such as those encapsulated by the Stable–2000 might not apply to online offenders. Instead, they hypothesized that certain acute dynamic risk factors that fluctuate over hours or days rather than weeks or months might be more relevant for risk management. These more acute, dynamic factors might include victim access, emotional collapse, collapse of social supports, substance use, sexual preoccupation, and rejection of treatment or supervision. These same factors have been shown to be relevant for contact sexual offenders (Hanson et al., 2007). Elliott and Beech suggested additional offense-specific factors may contribute: unsupervised computer use, inappropriate online searching or other activities, and overall problematic Internet use. They suggested that going online again, coupled with other increases in acute risk such as sexual preoccupation, could presage a new online offense.

Given the similarities found so far in risk factor research for online versus contact sexual offenders, the principle of parsimony (Occam's Razor) and the expectations of the motivation–facilitation model and other models of sexual offending, it is reasonable to expect that established dynamic risk factors also play a role in online sexual offending. In particular, given the comparison research reported in Chapter 5, poor general and sexual self-regulation problems are likely to be the key targets for monitoring and intervention. My recommendations for the assessment of online offenders are provided in Resource B.

FINAL COMMENTS

Empirically based risk assessments and risk-based policies are critical if we want to maximize the efficiency and effectiveness of our responses to online sexual offending. This principle holds true across all the decision points in the clinical, social service, or criminal justice systems, from police or child protection agency investigation, to prosecution, sentencing, institutional placement, security requirements, treatment assignment, and supervision intensity. Early results suggest that modified versions of existing risk scales are likely to work well with online offenders, though the probabilistic estimates may not generalize (Wakeling et al., 2011). Research to test this issue requires follow-up research with large samples of online offenders. As

Seto (2009) and Witt (2010) have suggested, modified static risk measures should be able to rank order online offenders according to risk to reoffend, even if the probabilistic estimates are not correct. Dynamic risk measures are also likely to operate in a sensible way with this emerging offender population on the basis of emerging knowledge about how online offenders are similar to and different from conventional sexual offenders.

In the absence of conclusive research on validated and recognized risk assessment measures, current risk assessment is made on the basis of guesses about the right approach or measure to use. According to discussions I have had with clinicians across Canada and the United States while giving talks or workshops, some clinicians are returning to subjective judgment, whereas others are using or modifying existing sex offender risk scales. It is notable in this context that the United States Attorney General's *National Report on Child Exploitation* (United States Department of Justice, 2010) gets some risk factors right (e.g., prior sexual offending) on the basis of expert input, but other factors that are listed have not yet been empirically demonstrated (e.g., duration of online child pornography use). Witt, Merdian, Connell, and Boer (2010) cautiously identified candidate risk factors for assessing online child pornography offenders in the context of parental fitness evaluations, including whether there is evidence the parent communicated with other online offenders, whether there was evidence from images or chat logs of other paraphilic interests, and whether there was any evidence of interaction with children, including sexual chat or solicitations to meet in real life. All of these variables make sense to me in light of the research discussed so far, but none of these have yet been empirically demonstrated to predict recidivism among online offenders.

As an example of counterintuitive risk information, Osborn, Elliott, Middleton, and Beech (2010) reported what seemed to be an inverse relationship between estimated risk (on the basis of the Risk Matrix 2000) score and the severity of the collected images in terms of sexual intrusiveness or violence. This correlation was contrary to the sentencing principles adopted by the U.K. Sentencing Advisory Panel and by the U.S. Sentencing Commission, where the severity of child pornography images is an aggravating factor for sentencing. (The sentencing practice could still be justified on the basis of society's abhorrence for such images, but it would not stand alone on the implicit assumption that image severity reflects risk.)

A Seeming Paradox

There may appear to be a paradox in the risk and recidivism results reported in this chapter and in previous chapters. Among identified sex offenders, pedophilia is a robust and important risk factor, having one of the strongest associations with new sexual offenses in meta-analyses conducted by Karl Hanson and his colleagues (Hanson & Bussière, 1998; Hanson & Morton-Bourgon, 2005). Yet online child pornography offenders, many of who are likely to be pedophiles, have a relatively low recidivism rate, at least in the follow-up studies we were able to examine in Seto et al. (2011).

This seeming paradox is resolved when we remember that the motivation–facilitation model requires both motivation (such as pedophilia or hebephilia) as well as facilitation factors (such as antisocial personality traits) for contact sexual offenses to occur (Seto, 2008). Many online child pornography offenders may indeed be motivated to have sex with children, but many do not have the necessary facilitation factors for this to occur, given their relatively low scores on psychopathy, antisocial attitudes and beliefs, and criminal history. It is not surprising, then, that approximately 45% of child pornography offenders in the subset of six self-report studies examined by Seto et al. (2011) denied having and had no known history of sexual contacts with children. It is also not surprising that many child pornography offenders denied any history of sexual contacts in the Neutze, Seto, Schaefer, Mundt, and Beier (2011) study or that approximately a quarter of the self-identified pedophiles and hebephiles had not engaged in any criminal sexual behavior in the previous 6 months.

The overall sexual recidivism rate observed for online offenders (mostly child pornography offenders) is higher than the sexual offense rates observed among individuals released from custody for nonsexual offenses, however, though this comparison should be interpreted with caution given the different time periods (Langan, Schmitt, & Durose, 2003; Seto et al., 2011). This is another potential resolution of the seeming paradox between offender characteristics and recidivism. Online child pornography offenders are more likely to sexually offend against a child than would a randomly selected nonsexual offender or man from the general population, but they are less likely to do this than is someone who has already had sexual contact with a child. A parallel can be drawn with the complex relationships observed between schizophrenia and violence: Individuals with schizophrenia are more likely to commit violence than nonschizophrenic individuals from the general population, but they are less likely to violently reoffend than nonschizophrenic offenders (Quinsey et al., 2006). Schizophrenia can be simultaneously viewed as a risk factor for violence in the general population but as a "protective" factor in the offender population. Similarly, child pornography offending can be viewed as a risk factor for sexual offending against children in the general population but as a "protective" factor in the sexual offender population. This does not mean that child pornography use has a cathartic effect, only that it is a marker of lower risk of future offending within a sample of individuals identified for committing sexual crimes.

More research on recidivism and risk factors associated with recidivism is clearly needed, including further validations of unmodified and modified versions of existing scales. This takes time, to both accumulate a large enough sample and to follow that sample for a sufficient period of time, focusing in particular on online-only offenders. We have no data at all on how to proceed with risk assessments of female or adolescent Internet offenders or of fantasy-driven solicitation offenders. We also need validation studies to confirm that the Static–99 (or other actuarial risk measures) do predict sexual recidivism among contact-driven solicitation offenders, as expected, and that dynamic risk assessment measures will function in a sensible manner.

Undetected Offending

Research is also needed to determine the predictive or additive value of self-reported but previously undetected (contact) sexual offending. As previously discussed, the Bourke and Hernandez (2009) Butner Study Redux is regularly cited in courts during the sentencing phase, in support of the idea that most child pornography offenders have committed undetected contact sexual offenses and therefore pose a greater danger to children in the future. Though this particular result was a statistical outlier, other self-report studies have suggested a little more than half (55%) of online offenders admit contact sexual offending (Seto et al., 2011). The implication is that undetected sexual offenses would predict sexual recidivism. This may be surprising, but this has not yet been empirically demonstrated for sexual offenders. Research among general correctional samples of offenders has suggested that self-reported criminal history (which could include undetected offenses) does predict recidivism (Kroner & Loza, 2001; Walters, 2006), but confirmation is required in the sex offender population.[3]

Recapitulation

Reviewing current laws and policies regarding online offending, one gets the strong and regrettable sense that we are recapitulating some of the wrong steps taken in the 1970s and 1980s in responding to child sexual abuse. The focus of political and public attention in the 1970s and 1980s was "stranger danger," particularly the risk of abduction and even homicide from

---

[3]Another possible implication from how the Butner Study Redux findings are used in court proceedings is that the online offender should be punished for his undetected offenses, just as sentencing for a burglar might take into account the likelihood that there are multiple undetected burglaries for every detected crime resulting in a charge and conviction. The legal threshold for admissibility of such evidence is lower at sentencing than for conviction in the first place. Some lawyers have argued, however, that this view is not legally defensible (von Dornum, 2012).

schoolyards, playgrounds, or other public places, and a (mistaken) belief that groups of offenders often formed conspiracies (so-called sex abuse rings) to victimize children. Once identified, it was believed that most, if not all, sex offenders with child victims were pedophiles and that such individuals were therefore highly likely to reoffend sexually.

In reality, though strangers do commit a small proportion of sexual assaults, the majority of sexual offenses against children are committed by family members or acquaintances—that is, individuals already known to the child. In about a third of cases, the perpetrator is also a minor. Abductions and homicides do—heartbreakingly—take place, but many sexual offenses against children do not involve the use of threat or force and do not result in physical injury. Though the psychological consequences can be dire for some victims, many others do not suffer long-lasting, serious harm (Rind, Tromovitch, & Bauserman, 1998). Though some offenders do conspire with others, most offenders commit their sexual crimes alone. My best guess, drawing from diverse lines of research, is that a slight majority (perhaps 50%–60%) of sex offenders are pedophiles (Seto, 2008). And last, the majority of sex offenders are not known to have sexually reoffended 5 to 10 years after their release from custody (Hanson & Bussière, 1998; Hanson & Morton-Bourgon, 2005).

As discussed in more detail in Chapter 3, public education campaigns about online sexual offending have often focused on the danger posed by online strangers in terms of sexual solicitation, the risk of personal information being used to possibly abduct and sexually assault young children, the gateway from child pornography to contact sexual offending, and the sexually mercenary tactics of "predators." But the research belies many of these assumptions (Wolak, Finkelhor, Mitchell, & Ybarra, 2008). Some of the other claims that have been made about online sexual offending should also be examined with skepticism. There have been cases of child pornography offenders who produce new content to share with others online, but the incentives to do this are not large, given Wolak, Finkelhor, Mitchell, and Jones's (2011) finding that the number of producers has not gone up across the phases of the National Juvenile Online Victimization project (Wolak, Finkelhor, & Mitchell, 2011) and the observation that only about a quarter of producers distributed the images. In other words, approximately three quarters of producers are creating content for their own use only.

The fact that bold claims about (online) sexual offending are made, and the fact that they are often unfounded or not supported in subsequent research, should give everyone great pause. American sex offender policies, in particular, are a baffling and frustrating mix of the Draconian and/or ineffective, singling out sex offenders as a special class of offenders (see Chapter 8). Sex offenders must register in publicly accessible databases, often for the rest of their lives; they are often restricted by where they can live postrelease, and they run the risk of civil commitment to a mental health facility after serving their prison sentence.

These claims about sex offenders drive public policy and practice, and thus can lead to inefficient and ineffective responses to the problem of online sexual offending. Dollars and time spent on education campaigns warning youths about the dangers of communicating online with strangers, for example, are dollars and time that cannot be spent on education focusing on at-risk youths and on the right messages about the risks of exploitation or mistreatment by adults they interact with online. Dollars spent on incarcerating child pornography only offenders for long periods of time are not available for other criminal justice purposes. Long sentences for child pornography only and fantasy-driven solicitation offenders mean that these individuals cannot participate in the lives of their families and communities. If we, as a society, are going to make these choices, then we should strive to make them fairly and effectively in light of the scientific knowledge we have about online sexual offending. We would also want to use the information gained from risk assessment research to guide interventions, both in targeting higher risk individuals and in identifying potential targets for offender treatment or supervision.

APPENDIX 7.1
PROBABILITY VERSUS SEVERITY

Existing sex offender risk measures provide estimates of the likelihood of a new sexual or violent offense. This is helpful for subsequent decisions, in line with the risk principle of offender rehabilitation (discussed further in Chapter 8), which argues that interventions are more likely to be effective when they are titrated to the risk of recidivism posed by the offenders. However, a new violent offense might range from a simple assault (punch or kick) to homicide, and a new contact sexual offense might range from sexual touching to sexual homicide. Though there are some data to suggest that offenders with higher scores on the Violence Risk Appraisal Guide (Otto & Douglas, 2009) also tend to commit more serious violent offenses (A. J. R. Harris, Phenix, Hanson, & Thornton, 2003; Quinsey et al., 2006), existing risk measures do not provide estimates of offense severity.

A primary challenge is technical: Large and/or aggregate sample studies are needed to provide probabilistic estimates of offense severity, because one would require a sufficiently large group of recidivists to distinguish even broadly defined levels of offense severity. In other words, individuals who score higher on risk measures may tend to commit more serious offenses if they do recidivate, but we cannot yet anchor judgments about severity like we can about likelihood on the basis of probabilistic estimates that are provided. Risk assessment is usually not only concerned with probability, however, but also severity. Even a low-probability risk of recidivism is of concern to decision makers if the expected severity is high. It is for this reason that decision makers tend to be conservative with individuals who have committed homicide; even though the observed recidivism rates are quite low for this offender group, the fear is that the person might kill again. Because risk measures do not provide estimates of expected offense severity, structured or unstructured judgments are used to estimate this aspect of risk (Hart & Logan, 2011).

To illustrate, I recently testified in a court proceeding in Canada where one of the critical issues was the risk posed by the offender, particularly the potential severity of any new sexual offense he might commit. My testimony and other evidence are part of the public record, so I can describe it here. In *R. v. Matthew Byers*, a young man with no prior criminal history was stopped by police for drinking a can of beer in a public park early one morning. On searching his backpack, police officers discovered printouts of child pornography images; writings describing sexually sadistic fantasies involving the abduction, torture, and murder of a girl between the ages of 6 and 12; and other suspicious items, including duct tape, latex gloves, condoms, and girl's underwear. The writings were sexually explicit and violent. Alarmingly, the subsequent investigation determined that the girl's name was the same first name as the daughter of a friend of

Mr. Byers. The writings also included a list of items and details regarding how he would gain access to the girl's house and where the crimes would take place.

Mr. Byers was subsequently convicted of possession of child pornography, attempted murder, and sexual assault, because there was evidence that he had indeed broken into his friend's residence, where the young girl he had described in his sexual fantasies lived. He had also prepared a site at his workplace in ways that corresponded to his written descriptions. The judge accepted the prosecution's argument that Mr. Byers had been incredibly and luckily interrupted in carrying out a real plan to abduct, sexually assault, and then kill a young girl who was known to him. The judge rejected the defense argument that the writings reflected sexual fantasies that had no bearing on reality and that did not describe inchoate offense plans. On conviction, the prosecution filed an application to have Mr. Byers designated as a "dangerous offender," which would result in an indeterminate prison sentence in Canada (see http://www.publicsafety.gc.ca/prg/cor/tls/dod-eng.aspx#a02 for background).

Because Mr. Byers had been convicted of the violent offenses of attempted murder and attempted sexual assault, actuarial risk assessments could be completed by the forensic psychiatrists and psychologists involved in the dangerous offender application hearing. I was one of these experts, called by the prosecution. Mr. Byers did not score in the higher ranges of either the Sex Offender Risk Appraisal Guide (Quinsey et al., 2006) or the Static–99, unlike the typical offender referred for a dangerous offender or long-term offender designation under Canadian law (Bonta, Zinger, Harris, & Carrière, 1998; Trevethan, Crutcher, & Moore, 2002). Mr. Byers's risk in terms of likelihood of recidivism was not under much dispute during the hearing.

Instead, the three main areas of contention at the hearing were (a) the severity of any subsequent new sexual offense that might occur, given the sexually sadistic content of his writings; (b) whether he met the diagnostic criteria for sexual sadism and for antisocial personality disorder; and (c) whether his risk of recidivism, taking into account likelihood and severity, could be effectively managed in the community under a long-term supervision order, given expert testimony regarding his agreed-on diagnosis of pedophilia and contentious diagnoses of sexual sadism and antisocial personality disorder. The judge accepted the prosecution's argument that the combined risk of recidivism, taking both probability and severity into account, met the legal criteria for designation as a dangerous offender, and Justice di Tomaso did not believe Mr. Byers could be safely managed in the community under long-term supervision. As a result, Justice di Tomaso found Mr. Byers to be a dangerous offender on July 6, 2011 (http://www.torontosun.com/2011/07/16/byers-case-could-prove-key-test-for-the-courts).

APPENDIX 7.2
DIFFERENT RISK PRIORITIES

Having repeatedly mentioned the importance of risk-based decision making throughout this chapter and throughout this book, it is worth recognizing here that concern about risk to reoffend is not monolithic. Different professionals have different priorities regarding suspect/offender risk and therefore may focus on different sets of risk and protective factors.[4] Law enforcement professionals, for example, often need to prioritize cases quickly to determine who to investigate first. They are then most interested in risk factors that are readily available to them early in an investigation (e.g., suspect age, occupation, prior criminal record) and less interested in risk factors that might be important in estimating risk of recidivism but that require clinical or in-depth assessments that would not be conducted until after investigations are completed, such as the scoring of a modified actuarial risk measure. Other examples of risk factors that are less available to police might include whether someone meets the diagnostic criteria for pedophilia or sexual sadism, that person's score on a validated measure of psychopathy, or a detailed forensic computer analysis outlining many different parameters about online child pornography use or sexual solicitation.

Many police officers are concerned about identifying current or potential child victims, particularly children depicted in child pornography images (see Sher, 2007). This means police are likely to prioritize cases where someone is likely to have committed undetected contact offenses in the past, is concurrently offending directly against children, or is producing child pornography and therefore directly exploiting the children in the images. Each of these temporal viewpoints may represent different risk considerations because the factors that distinguish whether someone has committed undetected contact offenses may be different from those that distinguish whether someone has produced child pornography. Research involving the correct comparison groups (with or without officially undetected offenses, production vs. possession or distribution of child pornography) is required.

In contrast, child protection laws usually focus on the identification of children who are at risk of maltreatment, including sexual exploitation or abuse, or who are currently being maltreated.[5] Thus, child protection pro-

---

[4]*Protective factors* are those factors that neutralize or reduce the effects of risk factors that increase the likelihood of an undesired outcome. An example would be having a strong prosocial adult role model, which can offset the individual and social disadvantages of children who are at risk of juvenile delinquency and criminal behavior (Werner, 1993).

[5]Laws vary from jurisdiction to jurisdiction, but my impression from speaking with professionals in many different jurisdictions is that the focus of child protection is on children who can be identified rather than risk to children as a class of persons in general.

fessionals are particularly concerned about the risk an individual poses to identifiable children, such as children living in the same residence as a suspect or children in the suspect's workplace if they are directly involved with children on a regular basis as a teacher, coach, daycare provider, and so forth. The opinion that someone may pose a high risk to offend against children as a class of persons is relevant information, but child protection authorities cannot take direct action if no child is identified as being at risk. A coresiding child who is deemed to be at risk, however, could be removed, or the suspect could be required to move out as a condition of that child staying with the remaining parent or guardian.

In another example of different risk priorities, a risk-related question that may matter more to child protection workers than to law enforcement is whether child pornography content is indicative of which children might be at most risk of being victims of sexual offending. For example, does a man with a child pornography collection focusing on girls who appear to be between the ages of 10 and 14 pose an unacceptable risk to his 7-year-old stepdaughter or his 12-year-old son once he has served his sentence and is no longer in custody (see Heil, Ahlmeyer, & Simons, 2003)? Law enforcement is more broadly concerned about the risk this individual might pose of sexually offending against any child, irrespective of age or gender.

Child protection workers face a particularly difficult challenge because they must balance the risk of child sexual exploitation or abuse with the potential harm to children that would be caused by the breakup of the family, whether the separation is temporary or permanent. A similar delicate balance is required when assessing and making decisions about parental custody and access when allegations of online sexual offending are raised (Witt, Merdian, Connell, & Boer, 2010). Though the decision point is likely a conservative one, child protection workers do need to consider that the removal of a suspect who has never sexually abused his children and who poses minimal risk of doing so may result in financial hardship, stress, and other negative consequences for the child and for his or her family. Law enforcement, on the other hand, is most concerned about false negatives (suspects erroneously thought to be low risk to offend again and who subsequently victimize someone).

Mandatory minimum sentences (federally, in the United States, and coming in Canada with the passage of an omnibus crime bill called the Safe Streets and Communities Act), sex offender registration, and notification and residency requirements may cause even more hardship to the family and might therefore have the unintended consequence of reducing family member disclosures about online offending. Similarly, criminal penalties and the risk of family breakdown many inhibit some child incest victims who want the sexual offending to stop but do not want the perpetrator removed (Palmer, 2011).

Law enforcement and child protection agencies often work closely together. Complaints to child protection agencies may be simultaneously reported to police, and police may seek involvement of child protection if there are children in the suspect's household. Police are in a position to record details that may be helpful to child protection and clinical professionals who work with online offenders further downstream. These details might include whether children are in the household, whether the suspect works or volunteers in a capacity that brings them into regular contact with children, and what the parameters are of the child pornography content in terms of amount, age, and gender of children depicted, presence of other paraphilic pornography, and whether there was violent content.

Glasgow (2010, 2012) commented in more detail on the kinds of digital evidence that can be available to police through forensic computer analysis and that could be useful for both research and applied purposes. Though the amount of potential information is large and the forensic analysis can be time consuming, especially with the pressures of limited resources and long waiting lists, some of it can be automated, and it could represent useful clinical data (Fortrell, Debrota, & Hakes, 2012). Glasgow proposed the following list of digital evidence: (a) a record of online search terms (he specifically mentioned search engines, but searches on peer-to-peer networks might be even more helpful); (b) details about the timing and duration of use of Internet pornography (both illegal and legal); and (c) chat logs (which could be helpful in attempting to distinguish between fantasy-driven and contact-driven solicitation offenders and also the degree of active involvement in trading child pornography and pedophile subcultures).

Stabenow (2011) wrote about how, as a prosecutor, he analyzed digital evidence to make decisions. First, he reviewed the entire child pornography collection to see the scope of content. He then examined the metadata from a forensic digital analysis to identify patterns in when the files were created, accessed, or modified. Last, he would review what he described as "secondary materials," including online chat logs, e-mails, and other information that might help put the online sexual offending in context. He acknowledged that this approach was more labor and resource intensive than a simple count of image types, so it is likely only suitable for a subset of cases where the information is particularly salient.

Like Stabenow (2011), von Dornum (2012) also noted that providing such detailed analysis of computer evidence in every case would be too resource intensive to be tenable—for example, if more detailed forensic analysis results were required for sentencing guidelines. At the federal level, there are enhancements simply if there are more than 600 images,[6] there is any con-

---

[6] A 5-second video is arbitrarily assigned a value of 75 images, so a single video can meet this sentencing enhancement threshold.

tent depicting sadistic or violent images, or if there is content depicting a child under the age of 12. The sentencing guidelines should be as simple as possible, yet still capture important variation in dangerousness and culpability.

Details about child pornography collections and other pornography use are not usually available through court documents because police and prosecutors need only to prove possession, distribution, or production of child pornography to make the conviction. The prosecution might only need to show the worst 10 images to the judge and/or jury to make the conviction. Whether the images are of boys or of girls is not legally pertinent, but it does appear to be relevant to the risk of further child pornography offenses (Eke & Seto, 2012). Similarly, the police and prosecutors are not usually concerned about legal pornography or even obscene material (e.g., content depicting bestiality) that carries a less serious penalty than child pornography. However, this information can be helpful in understanding the online pornography use and sexual interests of offenders. Without details from police or court documents, clinicians may have to rely on offender self-report, which can be misleading or incomplete.

Glasgow (2010) also suggested a set of rules for discerning preferred from nonpreferred pornography. He illustrated these rules through the content analysis of a single case, comparing the offender's self-reported sexual interests in eight age–gender categories, corresponding to those used in a viewing time assessment. *Viewing time assessments* involve the presentation of a series of pictures of persons varying in age and gender while the person completes a relevant task, such as rating whether they find the depicted person sexually attractive (Abel, Huffman, Warberg, & Holland, 1998; G. T. Harris, Rice, Quinsey, & Chaplin, 1996). There were discrepancies between offender self-report and child pornography content because the offender reported more interest in adult women and less interest in juvenile males than his content suggested. Specifically, the offender claimed 85% (inferred, because the figure does not specify percentage or number) of his pornography focused on adult females, and 15% focused on juvenile males, whereas in reality, 35% of his content depicted adult females and 45% depicted juvenile males, with small percentages for other categories.

8

INTERVENTION

Once identified, many online offenders are likely to require intervention of some kind, though not all online offenders require treatment—that decision depends on their risk to reoffend, treatment needs, and other considerations. However, it is likely that treatment and supervision will be required as part of a sentence or, in jurisdictions where early release is possible, to earn credit toward parole. My recommendations for online sex offender treatment are presented in Resource C.

We know much less about online offender treatment and other interventions than we do about online offender characteristics and risk to reoffend. This seems to be the typical course in the criminology and forensic psychology literatures: Attention is paid first to understanding who the offenders are and then to understanding the risk they pose for committing further offenses, particularly offenses that might involve harm to another person. Treatments are offered on the basis of intuition and past experiences,

http://dx.doi.org/10.1037/14191-009
Internet Sex Offenders, by M. C. Seto

guided, it is hoped, by empirically supported treatments for similar offender populations and knowledge of risk factors that might be amenable to change. Treatments are then evaluated retrospectively, which means that treatment outcome data are unavailable until programs have been in operation for years. In the sex offender field, many programs adopted the relapse prevention model through the late 1980s and 1990s, and it is still the dominant treatment model (McGrath, Cumming, Burchard, Zeoli, & Ellerby, 2009). The relapse prevention approach was borrowed and modified from the addictions field, on the basis of some perceived similarities between repetitive substance use and repetitive sexual offending. The sex offender field is now undergoing a major renovation, with the good lives model (Yates, Prescott, & Ward, 2010) gaining in popularity despite an absence of methodologically rigorous evaluations (see the next section of this chapter).

Key questions have yet to be addressed regarding online offender interventions, including what the most important treatment targets are, how they should be targeted, and whether interventions can reduce recidivism. While waiting for ultimate outcome research examining recidivism, treatment evaluations can look at pre–post changes in treatment and other more proximal treatment outcomes (e.g., institutional conduct, conduct while on supervision in the community; although see Seto, 2003). Because of the many real and perceived difficulties in implementing randomized clinical trials (RCTs), few sex offender treatment outcome studies have incorporated these informative designs (see Marshall & Marshall, 2007). In fact, only a few RCTs have ever been reported for contact sex offenders (see Hanson et al., 2002; Seto et al., 2008). I am not aware of any RCTs or well-controlled nonrandomized trials underway for online sexual offenders.

Before talking specifically about treatment and other interventions for online offending, I review some key principles and findings from offender intervention more generally, particularly research on contact sex offenders. These principles and empirical findings provide a context for understanding promising directions to take in responding to online offenders.

THE RELAPSE PREVENTION APPROACH

Relapse prevention is a cognitive behavioral treatment model that assumes there is a predictable, roughly linear process by which an at-risk individual moves to committing a sexual offense, just as someone with an addiction might move to using alcohol or another substance again after a period of abstinence. To interrupt this process, the relapse prevention approach tries to teach individuals how to identify risky situations or triggers that increase the likelihood of a relapse. The relapse process is idiosyncratic, so individuals have to identify their own triggers, risky situations, and lapses. Once these awareness and identification skills are developed, individuals need to learn and practice strategies to avoid risky situations and to cope with situations that cannot be avoided. For child pornography offending, a risky situation might include participating in a pedophilia forum or viewing legal pornography online, and lapses might include having sexual fantasies about a child seen in a social networking profile or masturbating to a legal image of a child depicted in a mainstream magazine. Relapse would involve accessing child pornography again.

Programs that describe their approach as relapse prevention vary greatly in their format and content because there is no standardization or widely accepted manual (Laws, Hudson, & Ward, 2000; McGrath et al., 2009), but relapse prevention programs typically share common elements, including the identification of high-risk situations and triggers, development of avoidance and coping strategies, and the use of cognitive behavioral techniques to interrupt the relapse process. An excellent example of the relapse prevention approach is the Sex Offender Treatment Evaluation Project (SOTEP) started by Janice Marques and her colleagues in 1985 with funding from the California state legislature (Marques, Nelson, Alarcon, & Day, 2000). This is the first and, thus far, only peer-reviewed RCT of a relapse prevention program. Incarcerated adult offenders were randomly assigned to treatment or no-treatment conditions after being matched for age, criminal history, and victim age. Treatment participants attended a 2-year cognitive behavioral hospital program developed on the basis of relapse prevention principles, followed by a 1-year aftercare program in the community, whereas no-treatment volunteers stayed in prison receiving usual services. There was no ethical objection to the no-treatment condition because the number of eligible offenders exceeded the available treatment spots.

Though Marshall and Marshall (2007) suggested otherwise, this program was carefully designed and implemented. The impact of treatment was evaluated both for proximal outcomes such as pre–post treatment changes on relevant measures and for the ultimate outcome of interest, criminal recidivism. Treatment targets included accepting personal responsibility for one's sexual offenses, decreasing offense-supportive attitudes and beliefs, decreasing deviant sexual arousal, understanding relapse prevention concepts, and learning how to identify high-risk situations and triggers and how to avoid or cope with these situations and triggers. Treatment consisted of thrice weekly group sessions, individual sessions, and additional ad hoc groups that focused on topics such as sex education, relaxation training, social skills training, and stress and anger management. Group content was manualized to standardize the format and content, but individual therapy sessions were tailored to individuals, and other group programs were recommended on the basis of individual assessments of needs. For example, more than two thirds of the sample had significant substance abuse histories and were therefore also asked to participate in a group treatment focusing on substance abuse. Offenders identified as having deviant sexual arousal patterns underwent behavioral conditioning to reduce deviant arousal.

The final outcome data collection was completed in 2001, with an average follow-up time of 8 years after release from custody. Unfortunately, after all the hard work that went into funding, implementing, and delivering the SOTEP program, there was no statistically significant difference in recidivism comparing treated offenders with volunteer no-treatment controls and a third comparison group of offenders who refused treatment (Marques, Wiederanders, Day, Nelson, & van Ommeren, 2005). There was a nonsignificant trend for offenders who victimized children to be more likely to reoffend after treatment (22% treated vs. 17% volunteer controls), whereas offenders who victimized adults tended to be less likely to reoffend (20% treated vs. 29% volunteer controls). There was still no significant group difference after statistically controlling for additional risk factors beyond offender age, offense history, and victim age.

ONLINE SEX OFFENDER TREATMENT

Anecdotally, I know that existing treatment programs for online offenders have adapted the relapse prevention model, presumably because this is a model they already know well and consider to be applicable because many of the risky situations and triggers could be the same (e.g., seeing an attractive child), and many of the coping and avoidance strategies could also be similar. A major difference from conventional relapse prevention programs might be a greater focus on online behavior, including time spent surfing the Internet, time spent viewing legal adult pornography, participation in social networks, and participation in online pedophilia forums. Explanations of online offending and studies of online offender characteristics suggest that other potential treatment foci would include empathy for children depicted in child pornography (many offenders view child pornography as a "victimless" crime), problematic Internet use more generally, sexual self-regulation problems, and interpersonal deficits. Online offenders appear to be lower risk, on average, than conventional sex offenders, so programs that have created separate streams typically require fewer sessions or provide less intense service, in keeping with the risk principle. The Internet Sex Offender Treatment Programme (i-SOTP; Middleton, Mandeville-Norden, & Hayes, 2009; see later section) in the United Kingdom, for example, prescribes fewer sessions than the standard sex offender treatment program.

Because there is an empirical vacuum about online offender treatment, treatment decisions are being made on the basis of intuitions and best guesses. For example, there is ongoing debate on the Association for the Treatment of Sexual Abusers (ATSA) Listserv for professional members about the advantages or disadvantages of combining online offenders with contact sex offenders. Some programs have created separate groups or treatment streams, such as the child pornography offender–only group at Toronto's Centre for Addiction and Mental Health or the United Kingdom's national i-SOTP. Other treatment programs have combined offenders, on the principle that offenders with different offending trajectories and treatment needs can learn from each other, just as sex offenders against children and offenders against adults might learn from each other.

In the following section, I describe four specific interventions aimed at online sexual offending. I selected these because they represent a range of different options, from modifications of existing sex offender treatment programs to the creation of an online self-help website and a major prevention and outreach effort trying to reach at-risk individuals before they engage in illegal behavior. The interventions discussed are (a) the Butner sex offender treatment program, the source of data for the study by Bourke and Hernandez (2009); (b) the i-SOTP offered by probation services in the United Kingdom; (c) the self-help content of croga.org; and (d) the Dunkelfeld Prevention Project. I spend the most attention on the i-SOTP because it has some (limited) evaluation data and has been implemented on a national basis in the United Kingdom.

Butner Federal Treatment Program

Training videos on the Butner program by program staff, including psychologist Andres Hernandez, are available from the Federal Judicial Center on YouTube. The Butner Federal Correctional Institution Sex Offender Treatment Program is described in Bourke and Hernandez (2009) as an intensive sex offender specific treatment program at a medium security federal prison. According to Michael Bourke, one of the coauthors, treatment participants did not earn a chance for early release by being in the treatment program, so presumably only those who were internally motivated to change participated in the program; offenders who were only externally motivated and who would only be interested in treatment to gain early release would not apply.

Butner participants underwent a comprehensive evaluation that included psychological testing, polygraph interviewing, and phallometric testing. The treatment program was approximately 18 months in duration and used cognitive behavioral techniques in both structured and unstructured treatment activities. Treatment participants were housed together, so there was a milieu component to treatment as well. Offenders also participated in 60 weeks of psychoeducation focusing on the following topics: criminal thinking errors, management of deviant sexuality, emotional self-regulation, victim impact and empathy, social and intimacy skills, communication skills, relapse prevention, and community reentry skills. I think it is fair to say that the program is similar to the SOTEP model. This program has not been formally evaluated, as far as I know.

Internet Sex Offender Treatment Programme

The i-SOTP was developed by David Middleton et al. (2009) in the United Kingdom and is now the national program offered to offenders on probation. It draws on the pathways model of sexual offending, the good lives model, and croga.org content and is arguably the most clearly articulated treatment program at this time. The i-SOTP was developed because a third of new sex offender cases seen by the probation service were Internet-related, creating long waiting lists for the regular sex offender treatment programs (Ministry of Justice, n.d.). Also, treatment providers were concerned about combining online and contact sex offenders in the existing national sex offender treatment program. The treatment providers had questions about the applicability of some of the treatment components and targets of the conventional prison-based program for medium and high-risk offenders (Core SOTP) and probation programs.

The i-SOTP incorporates cognitive behavioral principles, elements of 12-step addiction programs, self-help (croga.org), and positive psychology (Hayes & Middleton, 2006). The i-SOTP is less intense than the standard probation program, involving fewer (20–30) sessions and more content focusing specifically on online behavior. Recall that many online offenders have no prior criminal history and, on average, pose a low risk of sexual recidivism (Seto, Hanson, & Babchishin, 2011). The 20 to 30 sessions are organized into six modules: (a) motivation to change, (b) functional analysis of online behavior, (c) attitudes and beliefs, (d) interpersonal deficits, (e) self-regulation, and (f) relapse prevention and new life goals. These modules correspond to major dynamic risk factors identified in contact sex offender research using the Stable–2000: offense-supportive attitudes and beliefs, interpersonal deficits, general self-regulation problems, and sexual self-regulation problems.

A notable feature of the i-SOTP content is a focus at the beginning of the program on motivation to change, rather than assuming participants are in the program willingly or that teaching the concepts and skills is sufficient for individuals who have no intention of refraining from online offending again. Another notable feature is the development of new, prosocial life goals as part of treatment, consistent with both positive psychology and good lives model principles (see later section). After all, what does the offender live for once online offending is no longer an option? Online offending filled certain needs in that person's life, and removing that option leaves those needs unfulfilled. How can the offender prosocially fill those needs (e.g., being online a lot because he is lonely) or shift needs that cannot be fulfilled legally (experiencing sexual gratification from images of children or sexual interactions with minors online).

I am not aware of any recidivism outcome data for the i-SOTP, which was introduced without an RCT. Using 12 psychometric measures that were part of a standard battery, Middleton et al. (2009) reported results from a pre–post treatment evaluation of 264 online offenders who had participated in i-SOTP. There were significant positive changes on 10 of the 12 measures. Unfortunately, there was no comparison group in this analysis, so it is not clear whether the changes can be attributed to the treatment program instead of to alternative explanations such as the passage of time, ongoing probation, participation in other treatment programs, or selection effects. The selection effect exists because only those who completed the program could complete the posttreatment measures. These individuals may differ in meaningful ways from those who were terminated or who dropped out during the program (see Hanson et al., 2002).

It would be helpful if there were a more rigorous evaluation of i-SOTP with either a no-treatment (e.g., waiting list) or treatment-as-usual comparison group, in order to make stronger inferences about the effects of the i-SOTP. Also, longer term follow-up research is needed to determine whether treatment-related changes on the specified targets are related to reductions in recidivism.

Croga.org

Croga.org is an online self-help website offering materials for professionals and for help-seeking individuals. Originally developed by Ethel Quayle and her colleagues at the Combating Paedophile Information Networks in Europe (COPINE) Project and now maintained by the Lucy Faithfull Foundation in the United Kingdom, the croga.org website blends concepts derived from relapse prevention, cognitive behavior therapy more generally, addiction recovery, and 12-step self-help programs. It covers a range of topics similar to those covered by the other programs described here. This content is delivered in a series of short modules that include self-report assessments. The module titles are self-explanatory: "Understanding How You Use Illegal Images," "Images ARE Children," "The Internet and Fantasy," "Dealing With Bad Feelings," "Online relationships," "Problematic Collecting," and "Relapse Prevention."

The main aim of the croga.org website is to reach individuals who are engaging in problematic online behaviors, ideally before they have committed contact offenses. Because many such individuals are undetected by authorities, self-help and outreach services are essential to any comprehensive response to the problem of online offending. This program has not been formally evaluated. Such evaluation would be difficult because it would rely on self-report (given the anonymous nature of the interface) and it would be difficult to find a suitable comparison group; however, even showing a high participation rate on entry and significant pre–post changes would be some encouragement for this approach. If empirically supported, anonymous online support is cost effective and readily scalable.

Dunkelfeld Prevention Project

The English language summary site dont-offend.org describes the German Dunkelfeld (translation: "dark field") Prevention Project, which is aimed at reaching at-risk individuals who might never come to the attention of the mental health and criminal justice systems (hence, dark field). This is an innovative clinical and research project that was able to benefit from major foundation funding, mainstream media campaigns, and government support. The Dunkelfeld Project was initiated by a team in Germany, based at the Charité hospital in Berlin and led by Klaus Beier, who recognized that undetected sex offenders are unlikely to seek help, given the severe stigma associated with self-identifying as sexually interested in children or admitting to sexual behavior involving children. The German Charité team recognized they had a perhaps unique opportunity because there is no mandatory reporting law in Germany outside of the rare circumstance when homicide or risk of homicide is involved (Beier et al., 2009).

With funding from the Volkswagen Foundation and pro bono work by media partners, the clinic was able to advertise through billboard ads and television and radio spots. Individuals who contacted the clinic were assured of their confidentiality and offered an evaluation. Many were then identified as having pedophilia or hebephilia. Most of these individuals had engaged in some form of illegal sexual behavior in their lifetimes, either by accessing child pornography or by having sexual contacts with children (Neutze, Seto, Schaefer, Mundt, & Beier, 2011). Some had not committed any offenses in the previous 6 months, however, suggesting there was room for positive change. If one takes the estimate that 1% of men have sexual thoughts, fantasies, or interest about children (not an unreasonable estimate based on the studies cited in Chapter 1), this translates to approximately 250,000 German men who are at risk according to the current population size. The impact of providing prevention-oriented services to this population is potentially huge and cost-effective (e.g., Aos, Lieb, Mayfield, Miller, & Pennucci, 2004; Aos, Phipps, Barnoski, & Lieb, 2001).

During the media campaign, a total of 1,415 individuals contacted the project between June 2005 and March 2011. Many of these individuals were under some form of legal supervision and were therefore ineligible for the program, and others could not participate in treatment in Berlin because of long traveling distances or the presence of major mental illness. Of the initial contacts, evaluations were completed on 622 men, and treatment was offered to 319 men. Outcome data are now being collected and analyzed. The Dunkelfeld Project is unusual because the self-identified pedophiles and hebephiles who responded to the mass media awareness campaign were not at risk of mandatory reporting obligations, except in the extremely unusual exception of homicide. Even so, reaching 1,415 individuals over a 5.5-year period (an average of 280 or so persons per year) demonstrates how difficult outreach is in the current climate.

The paucity of self-referred services is highlighted by the regular contact I receive as a result of my previous book and online information about my research by persons who are concerned about their sexual interest in children and their behavior in this respect. Some private practice clinicians will see these individuals, but there is the constraint of revealing one's identity and the fear that confidentiality may be breeched if the person were to admit to illegal sexual behaviors; the individuals may be constrained in their treatment by their uncertainty about the clinician's legal responsibility to report. For example, in my home province of Ontario, provincial law (the Child and Family Services Act) mandates that all residents—not only mental health professionals—are required to report to a child protection service (Children's Aid Society) if they believe an identifiable child is at risk of maltreatment, including sexual exploitation or abuse. An at-risk offender may be reluctant to talk about sexual communications with a minor online because a search warrant executed to seize and analyze their computer might identify the minor.[1] Cost might also be a concern for individuals who do not have access to private health coverage or subsidized or public health services.

OTHER INTERVENTION OPTIONS

My review of these four specific treatment approaches is not exhaustive. A variety of other treatments are being offered; in particular, many online offenders are seeking treatment for sexual addiction or compulsivity because

---

[1]This issue was recently discussed in a "Savage Love" column involving my colleague, James Cantor (Savage, 2012).

they attribute their criminal behavior to these causes rather than to pedophilia (Seto, Reeves, & Jung, 2010). Cynically, some of these individuals may be seeking a more palatable explanation for their criminal behavior than acknowledging that they are sexually interested in children or in child pornography (though many, somewhat surprisingly, do acknowledge this interest). Nonetheless, it is plausible that sexual compulsivity (given the heated debate about whether one can be addicted to sex or to online behavior) explains some online sexual offending.

The questions, then, are how to identify and intervene with this subset of online offenders. Programs for online offenders are increasing in number. For example, there is the cybersex addiction model provided by the Internet Behavior Consulting group. This program has its own workbook and a combination of relapse prevention, cognitive behavior therapy, and 12-step elements (http://www.internetbehavior.com). The specific program has not formally been evaluated; the same is true for sexual addiction and compulsivity programs more generally. The lack of rigorous evaluation across treatment approaches is frustrating, partly because clinicians and clients cannot benefit from empirically driven advances in treatment techniques and targets and partly because there is a risk that low-risk offenders might be made inadvertently worse as a result of the intervention. For example, an online offender who seeks out a sexual addiction program because it is a more palatable explanation to him for his criminal behavior might never address the pedophilia underlying his use of child pornography and thus may never learn to manage this major motivation for seeking child pornography or sexual contact with children in the future.

RISK, NEED, AND RESPONSIVITY

An encouraging feature of the i-SOTP is that it directly addresses the risk principle of correctional rehabilitation articulated by Andrews and Bonta (2010). The *risk principle* states that the intensity of services should be matched to the recidivism risk posed by offenders, with lower risk offenders receiving less intensive services and higher risk offenders receiving the most intensive services. In accordance, i-SOTP has fewer sessions and is less intense than the standard sex offender treatment program for conventional sex offenders. (In prison, the core sex offender treatment program is combined with an extended program for the higher risk offenders.)

Andrews and Bonta (2010) also articulated the need and responsivity principles of correctional rehabilitation. The *need principle* states that interventions that address criminogenic needs—that is, dynamic risk factors that can be changed and that are associated with differences in the likelihood of recidivism—are more effective than interventions that do not address these needs. If sexual self-regulation problems are a criminogenic need for online offenders, programs that address this domain will produce better results than programs that address noncriminogenic needs such as self-esteem, acceptance of responsibility, and remorse (Hanson & Bussière, 1998; Hanson & Morton-Bourgon, 2004). The research summarized in Chapter 5 is particularly germane with regard to the need principle.

In keeping with broader psychotherapy findings, the *responsivity principle* states that interventions are more effective when they are tailored to the individual's learning style and capacity. We know more about risk factors and criminogenic needs, however, than we do about the factors that affect offender responsivity to treatment. The general psychotherapy literature suggests that treatments that are skills focused, pragmatic in terms of goals, and that use classic learning techniques such as role modeling, rehearsal, and reinforcement fare better than treatments that do not have these features. We also know that therapist and relationship factors—including genuine warmth and regard, a nonconfrontational style, encouragement and rewards for treatment progress, and gentle but firm direction—explain a large part of the variance in treatment outcome (see Marshall, Marshall, Serran, & O'Brien, 2011). In fact, these nonspecific aspects often explain more outcome variance than specific aspects of different brands of therapy.

Decades of research have shown that correctional programs that meet the risk, need, and responsivity principles produce better results than programs that do not. The same appears to be true for conventional sex offender treatment: In a meta-analysis of 23 outcome studies, Hanson, Bourgon, Helmus, and Hodgson (2009) found that the magnitude of the difference in recidivism rates between treated and comparison groups of sex offenders was related to the extent to which the programs met these three principles. Programs that were judged to adhere to all three principles produced the largest differences in recidivism rates. It would follow, then, that any treatment program for online offenders would have a more positive impact to the extent that it adheres to these principles.

MOTIVATION TO CHANGE

In my opinion, one of the most plausible reasons that SOTEP did not reduce sexual recidivism as hoped is that one of the foundations of the relapse prevention approach was questionable. Relapse prevention assumes that the treatment participant is motivated to refrain from offending but lacks the skills and supports to do so. However, teaching someone how to recognize risky situations and how to cope with deviant sexual fantasies or other proximal factors that increase the likelihood of offending can only reduce reoffending if that person is motivated to apply those skills when faced with real-life opportunities. Some offenders are motivated to sexually offend and indeed would seek out new opportunities to do so if they could avoid being detected and punished for the behavior. As described earlier in this volume, some pedophilic men believe children can benefit from sexual relationships with adults (or, at least, are not harmed by the experience) and that their sexual contacts with children are part of ongoing, romantic, and mutually beneficial relationships. Some of these individuals will not use relapse prevention skills, even if they successfully learn the concepts and skills and do well in terms of pre–post treatment change on relevant measures, because they do not want to refrain from further sexual contacts with children or further involvement with child pornography.

Relapse prevention might be effective for the subset of sex offenders (online or contact) who sincerely want to refrain from future offending and can learn and apply the skills they learn. The challenge, then, is to determine how to reliably and validly assess someone's motivation to change and refrain from sexual offending. After all, some offenders will falsely claim to be motivated to change and refrain from offending for the "right" reasons; how can we distinguish those who are being truthful from those who are lying? Others may not be aware of their motivations—a state with which we are all familiar—and therefore may not know what they hope to gain from treatment and what they intend to do in the future.

Another approach is required for those who do not have a genuine motivation to refrain from sexual offending. Hudson, Ward, and McCormack (1999) and others have recognized this distinction between offenders motivated to avoid offending and those who are not motivated to do so and have suggested that there are different pathways to sexual offending. Building on this pathways idea, these authors suggested that there are four major routes to sexual offending:

- The *avoidant–passive* pathway is characterized by an intention to refrain from sexual offending accompanied by a lack of effective strategies to achieve this goal. When opportunities to offend arise, individuals may act impulsively, using passive or covert tactics to commit their sexual offenses—for example, indiscriminately downloading large amounts of "teen" pornography on a peer-to-peer network knowing that some of that content might constitute child pornography. When their efforts to refrain from offending fail, individuals in this pathway experience negative affect and cognitive dissonance as a result.
- The *avoidant–active* pathway is also characterized by an intention to avoid sexually offending but is accompanied by more

active tactics such as consuming alcohol to suppress deviant sexual thoughts. Again, opportunities arise and individuals may act impulsively. Failure is again associated with negative affect and cognitive dissonance.

- The *approach–automatic* pathway is characterized by a motivation to commit offenses, and activation of offense-supportive schemas in particular circumstances. For example, an offender may see a pretty girl in a tight T-shirt and shorts in the park, start thinking about how she is dressing "provocatively," and then sexually touch her if there is an opportunity. Planning is rudimentary, so offenses tend to occur impulsively and opportunistically. Offending is accompanied by positive rather than negative affect, because the individual has achieved his goal.
- The *approach–explicit* pathway is again characterized by the intent to commit sexual offenses but with planning and positive affect throughout the offending process, from initial desire to completion of the offense. Unlike the other three pathways, individuals in this pathway have an intact self-regulation style but with an antisocial goal.

Only offenders in the avoidant pathways might benefit from mainstream relapse prevention. The self-regulation treatment model builds on this pathways view of sexual offending (see Yates, Prescott, & Ward, 2010). Motivational enhancement, relapse prevention and other cognitive behavioral techniques are used to improve strategies among avoidant offenders and to encourage approach offenders to want to refrain from offending. Building on this self-regulation approach in turn, the good lives model adds elements from positive psychology about identifying prosocial life goals and building on personal strengths, rather than focusing only on a negative goal (refraining from offending) and addressing deficits (Good Lives Model, 2011). The central logic of the good lives model is that sexual offending previously fulfilled personal goals, whether the goal was sexual gratification, distraction from negative mood, or temporarily assuaging loneliness. Once sexual offending is no longer a viable option, what is the individual left with as life goals? If no positive life goals are systematically identified and developed, that individual may be more likely to fall back into habitual (and dysfunctional) patterns of thoughts and behavior.

Early studies on these interrelated conceptual and clinical frameworks—pathways, self-regulation, and good lives—have shown that contact sexual offenders can be reliably assigned to the theoretical pathways and differ in expected ways in terms of their biographic characteristics and clinical needs. Bickley and Beech (2002) assigned 87 sex offenders with child victims to the four pathways and found that those in the avoidant pathways were more likely to be married, to have children of their own, to have offended against related victims, and to score lower on measures of offense-supportive attitudes and beliefs and emotional identification with children than offenders in the approach pathways. Yates and Kingston (2006) found that offenders in different pathways differed in their actuarially estimated risk to sexually reoffend. Offender types distinguished by victim age, victim gender, and relationship to offender were found across all four pathways, demonstrating that offending pathway was not redundant with existing offender typologies on the basis of victim choice.

In one of the largest validation studies, Kingston, Yates, and Firestone (2012) examined the self-regulation and pathways model in a sample of 275 adult male sex offenders. Their first challenge was to determine how to assign offenders reliably to the different pathways, which was achieved with acceptable interrater reliability using a relatively simple algorithm. (Previous studies had used global judgment to assign offenders to different pathways.) Of the initial sample of 280 offenders, only five could not be assigned to a pathway. This finding can be contrasted with the results of studies by Middleton and his colleagues, in which almost half of online offenders could not be assigned to a pathway (Middleton, 2009; Middleton, Elliott, Mandeville-Norden, & Beech, 2006). Of the remaining 275 offenders in the Kingston et al. study, 54 (20%) were assigned to the avoidant–passive pathway, 45 (16%) followed an avoidant–active pathway, 75 (23%) followed an approach–automatic pathway, and 101 (37%) followed an approach–explicit pathway.

The second goal for Kingston et al. (2012) was to determine how the different pathways differed in offender characteristics, actuarially estimated risk to reoffend, and treatment needs. Offenders in the approach pathway had more prior offenses, more victims, and were more violent in their most recent offenses. Pathways were correlated with offender type on the basis of victim characteristics but were not redundant, consistent with Yates and Kingston (2006): Incest offenders were more likely to be in the avoidant–passive pathway, whereas rapists were more likely to be in an approach pathway, particularly the approach–automatic pathway. Approach offenders scored higher on actuarial measures of risk than avoidance offenders.

There were also differences across pathways in terms of the major risk dimensions of sexual deviance and antisociality. Offenders in the approach–automatic pathway tended to be low in sexual deviance and high in antisociality, whereas those in the other pathways were relatively high in sexual deviance. Offenders in the approach–explicit pathway were also higher in antisociality than those in the two avoidance pathways. These results make sense: Offenders in the approach pathways would be expected to endorse offense-supportive attitudes and beliefs about sex with children, and these attitudes and beliefs are part of existing risk assessments. Similarly, antisocial individuals who are less concerned about the rights of others would be more likely to be willing to act on their motivations to sexually offend and thus more likely to be in an approach pathway.

These results are encouraging empirical support for the pathways model. There are more questions, however. An assumption of the pathways model is that an individual follows a predictable trajectory in their offending. What about someone who vacillates between approach and avoidance orientations? What about someone who is sometimes passive and sometimes active in his offending process? One response would be to assign offenders according to the dominant pathway in their offending history, but this heterogeneity in offending behavior may be meaningful in terms of differences in risk, needs, or treatment response.

Another issue for the pathways model is that individuals are less likely to admit to undetected offenses early in treatment and may be miscategorized on the basis of only those offenses that were known at that time. More details about the offending and disclosures of unknown victims may provide much richer information for accurate classification, but this would likely come after being in treatment for some time. If offenders in different pathways require different treatment foci, how does the treatment plan change accordingly?

Another important question is whether offenders in different pathways respond differently to treatment and risk to offend. A particularly interesting question is whether information about an individual's offending pathway can add to what is already known about his risk to reoffend on the basis of existing risk measures. In other words, is the offending pathway informative about risk, first in itself and then in addition to other information?

RIGOROUS TREATMENT EVALUATION

Kingston et al. (2012) is one of the first larger scale studies examining the reliability and validity of the self-regulation model. It is striking that new treatment models such as the good lives model and the self-regulation model are already beginning to supplant relapse prevention in sex offender treatment programming (McGrath et al., 2009), despite the absence of outcome data at this point and investment in less rigorous study designs in the evaluations that are being implemented (Good Lives Model, 2011 [http://goodlives model.com/glm/Evaluations.html]). It seems as if the offender treatment field is recapitulating the mainstream adoption of relapse prevention of over 20 years ago on theoretical and clinical appeal, rather than on empirical evidence. To be fair to early adopters of relapse prevention, there was no existing theoretically founded treatment approach when it was introduced, other than behavioral conditioning of deviant sexual arousal, so it proliferated in a treatment framework vacuum. Will we find that treatment based on the self-regulation or good lives model will not lead to a reduction in sexual recidivism when offenders are eventually evaluated 10 to 15 years from now?

RCTs are the gold standard in outcome evaluation and are considered to be essential evidence for authorities such as the U.S. Centers for Disease Control and Prevention, the U.S. Food and Drug Administration, the Cochrane Collaboration for systematic reviews in health care (http://www.cochrane.org), and the Campbell Collaboration for systematic reviews in education, social welfare, and criminal justice (http://www.campbellcollaboration.org). Other study designs have methodological or analytic limitations that weaken the inferences that can be made about the effects of treatment. For example, studies that compare individuals who complete treatment with those who refuse or drop out of treatment are limited by the fact that treatment refusal or dropout in itself is related to recidivism risk (Hanson & Morton-Bourgon, 2005). Some or even all of the apparent difference in recidivism between treated and comparison groups could be attributed to this self-selection effect.

The advantages and disadvantages of RCTs compared with other study designs have been much discussed and debated, so I will not repeat them here: The conclusions are too disheartening (but see Marshall & Marshall, 2007; Seto et al., 2008). SOTEP was one of the few RCTs that have been conducted in adult sexual offending. None produced encouraging results, unfortunately, unlike the small number of RCTs that have been conducted for children with sexual behavior problems (Carpentier, Silovsky, & Chaffin, 2006) or for adolescent sex offenders (Borduin, Schaeffer, & Heiblum, 2009; Letourneau et al., 2009). I am not aware of any current RCTs in the adult sex offender field, whether for online offenders or contact offenders, and there seems to be great pessimism about conducting these important evaluations because of political (and clinical) opposition to not providing treatment to offenders who want it, even though the number of offenders can exceed the number of treatment spots that are available (see Marshall & Marshall, 2007). Such research might not be fundable when dollars for research on sex offenders are scarce.

The importance of RCTs continues to be hotly debated, which unfortunately means that the sex offender and related fields will not form a consensus that could drive funding and motivation for rigorous treatment evaluation. As SOTEP demonstrated, methodologically rigorous evaluations take time, money, and sustained effort. Such evaluations require steely professional and political resolve because they are difficult to implement and complex to conduct and evaluate. Nonetheless, there are possible solutions. My coauthors and I have suggested the following:

> Possible solutions include educating stakeholders and the general public about the importance of RCTs and the costs of providing unproven

treatments; aggregating data from multiple sites conducting small-scale RCTs; using random assignment to alternative treatments when one treatment has a known effect; and examining the particular effect of a treatment component such as social skills training by randomly assigning sex offenders to either a program that includes social skills training or a program that does not. We strongly believe that our field will not move forward if we collectively throw up our hands and give up in the face of the obstacles to RCTs. Rather than debating the value of RCTs and alternative designs, we should be debating how to tackle these challenges. (Seto et al., 2008, p. 7)

The sex offender treatment field is in a period of transition, and providing either relapse prevention or a pathways/self-regulation/good lives program is justifiable, but not in the absence of program evaluation. For those who believe the current outcome data support the efficacy of relapse prevention, drawing from less rigorous evaluation study designs (Hanson et al., 2002; Lösel & Schmucker, 2005), this kind of trial represents an evaluation of incremental utility: Does the new treatment approach improve on the outcomes that can be obtained using relapse prevention? For those (including me and some of my colleagues) who place the most weight on the SOTEP clinical trial and therefore believe that relapse prevention has no significant effect on recidivism, the alternative-treatments design represents a comparison of a new treatment approach with a neutral condition. Either way, the results of a true RCT comparing two different programs would greatly advance our knowledge about sex offender treatment. It is encouraging that the ATSA, the largest international organization of professionals working with sexual offenders, has issued position statements in support of RCTs (Association for the Treatment of Sexual Abusers, 2010), and Duwe (2012) has initiated a small RCT to evaluate an implementation of the circles of support and accountability model, which recruits community volunteers to assist and monitor sex offenders as they re-enter the community.

CRIMINAL JUSTICE SANCTIONS

Treatment is not the only intervention for online sexual offending. Offenders who are detected by the criminal justice system face serious legal penalties in terms of sentencing and supervision requirements. Ideally, the prospect of these criminal justice sanctions would act as a deterrent and reduce recidivism. Unfortunately, the evidence is clear that criminal sanctions do not reduce recidivism; in fact, harsher criminal sanctions increase the risk of recidivism, probably as a result of lost prosocial influences, such as family involvement and employment, or the exposure of individuals to even more antisocial influences from other prisoners (Andrews & Bonta, 2010; Lipsey, 1998). It is well established that punishment tends to have less of an effect on behavior than reward; moreover, punishment is effective only when it is certain and occurs soon after the offending event. None of these conditions is met through criminal justice sanctions, where many offenders are not reported to police, there is a low probability of detection per transgression, and investigations and trials can take months, if not longer, to complete.

Criminal sanctions still serve the important purposes of offering justice for victims, signaling society's moral opprobrium toward the behavior, and incapacitation for a period of time for those individuals who pose an unacceptable risk to public safety. Because of the high costs of imprisonment, long sentences are best reserved for high-risk offenders. As with treatment, the risk principle can apply in sentencing as well: Sentencing is more likely to be efficient and effective when it is titrated to offender risk of recidivism (Andrews & Bonta, 2010).

Mandatory Minimum Sentencing

For the reasons I have just stated, mandatory minimum prison sentences reduce the efficiency of criminal justice sanctioning. The increasing numbers of online offenders being prosecuted (with high conviction rates because of the digital evidence that can be brought to bear at trial) necessarily result in higher costs, potential overcrowding, and reduced availability of treatment and other resources (U.S. Sentencing Commission report, 2011). According to the most recent U.S. Sentencing Commission report, there were 1,667 child pornography offenders in the federal system in fiscal year 2010. This total number represents only a small proportion (a little over 2%) of federally sentenced offenders, but it represents 72% of all federally sentenced sex offenders, thereby posing a big demand on sex offender resources within the federal correctional system. Yet the vast majority of these offenders had no prior criminal record.

This disconnect between sentence length and offender risk has led to some federal court judges in the United States balking at imposing the mandatory minimum sentence (Hansen, 2009). There has also been major media attention to this issue, including *New York Times* coverage of cases where individuals received life sentences for possession of child pornography (Goode, 2011). Possibly reflecting judicial discontent, departure rates from federal sentencing guidelines have increased steadily from 2009 to 2011 (Specter & Hoffa, 2012).

One could imagine rippling effects of this discontent with current sentencing practices, including local decisions to prosecute at the state level rather than the federal level and shifts in law enforcement decisions toward fewer arrests and prosecutions. Wolak (2012) demonstrated that federally sentenced offenders were twice as likely to receive sentences of 5 years or longer, even after controlling for seriousness (indicated by amount of images, having sadistic or violent images, or being involved in online sexual chats). As a result, there appears to be interest in revising the federal sentencing guidelines. Evidence for this interest includes opinion surveys of federal judges; increasing departure rates; testimony to the U.S. Sentencing Commission by judges, prosecutors, and defenders; and a public hearing on February 15, 2012 (I have already cited my testimony and the testimony of other expert witnesses at that hearing). The open question is whether the lawmakers who make decisions about sentencing provisions are guided more by the easy political score of being "tough on crime" than by the science and experiences of stakeholders.

A Continuum of Culpability

Most stakeholders recognize that there is a continuum of culpability from possessor to active distributor to producer to abuser. The proportionality principle of sentencing suggests that the most severe sentences should be for those who directly harm children (abusers) or who "memorialize or broadcast the abuse" (von Dornum, 2012, p. 12) of children depicted in child pornography (producers). Active distributors who engage in interactions with others in the trade of child pornography fall somewhere in the middle because they may help create or maintain a market for this content. Possessors and passive distributors—such as those individuals who (perhaps inadvertently or unwittingly) make files available through peer-to-peer networks but who do not actively trade with others—should receive less severe sentences.

Whatever the severity of sentences ought to be, there should be meaningful variation in sentencing if this continuum of culpability is recognized. Directly contradicting this idea of proportionality and the commonsense notion that someone who has sexually abused a child should have a more severe sentence than someone who has images of that same act, sentences for federal child pornography offenders are about the same length as those received by contact offenders in the federal system; according to 2010 data from the U.S. Sentencing Commission, both groups have average sentences of approximately 10 years.

In their analysis of federal sentencing data, Wollert, Waggoner, and Smith (2012) noted that the average sentence length for first-time child pornography offenders tripled from 1994 to 2008. Moreover, an analysis reported by von Dornum (2012) showed that first-time offenders were sentenced only 10 months less, on average, than repeat offenders in fiscal year 2010. In Canada, Jung and Stein (2012) found that contact offenders have, on average, sentences that are almost three times the average sentence length of child pornography offenders. This odd state of affairs is a result of mandatory minimum sentencing and sentencing enhancements introduced with the Prosecutorial Remedies and Other Tools to End the Exploitation of Children Today (PROTECT) Act of 2003, which pushed federal sentences near the top of the statutory range, such that even first-time child pornography offenders with no prior criminal history can end up in the higher range of sentence length.

COMMUNITY MANAGEMENT

Criminal justice sentencing may also include community supervision. One of the likely conditions of supervision involves a ban or restrictions on computer use or Internet access—for example, through the use of monitoring software to track online activity, including e-mail, instant messaging, and surfing history. Restrictions may become more likely than bans as more and more of everyday life includes Internet-related technologies, including education and employment, making a full ban almost impossible.

There are limitations to restriction of online access. One is whether supervising officers have the time and technical savvy to review logs and detect suspicious activity, even with automated reports from monitoring software programs. Another is the ready availability of the Internet without ever using personal or work computers, including access through public libraries, Internet cafes, and pay-as-you-go smartphones. Technology can help with supervision of this kind, but it is not a panacea. Stabenow (2011) made the cogent point that there are finite supervision resources, and requiring long terms of supervision for low-risk offenders means probation officers cannot devote more time to contact offenders and higher risk online offenders.

Beyond technology, there may also be the conventional concerns of community supervision, including unsupervised contact with children, use of alcohol or other substances, and education or work stability, to the extent that research shows these to be dynamic risk factors. Webb, Craissati, and Keen (2007) found that online offenders, as a group, are more amenable to community supervision than contact offenders because child pornography offenders were less likely to miss a community treatment or probation supervision meeting and were less likely to drop out of treatment.

LAW ENFORCEMENT

Law enforcement is part of a comprehensive response to online offending. Because the numbers of offenders far exceed police capacities, however, even with more funding and resources, prioritization of law enforcement efforts is critical. Eke and Seto (2012) reviewed the literature on risk assessment of online offenders and made suggestions on how law enforcement can prioritize cases on the basis of readily available information. In particular, prior criminal history is readily available to police. Recently, Long and his colleagues developed the Kent Internet Risk Assessment Tool (KIRAT), which can be used by police to prioritize online offense cases that are more likely to involve contact sexual offending as well (McManus, Long, & Alison, 2011). The tool was developed in a series of small studies comparing child pornography offenders and dual offenders (i.e., individuals who have committed both child pornography and contact sexual offenses). Variables that distinguished the two groups could be useful for risk prioritization purposes. The KIRAT includes information about previous sexual offending that would be known to the police (allegations, cautions, or convictions), evidence the suspect has ready access to children (e.g., resides with children), and any evidence of production of child pornography or grooming of minors online. Long, Alison, and McManus (2012) compared 60 child pornography offenders and 60 dual offenders, with more detailed information about child pornography content and online behavior for a subset of 30 offenders in each group. The KIRAT is currently being rolled out in the United Kingdom by the Child Exploitation and Online Protection Center.

An analogy can be drawn to drug enforcement. The numbers of individuals possessing personal use amounts of illegal substances such as marijuana far exceed police capacities. Past prosecutions in the war on drugs have resulted in incarceration on a massive scale, with great personal and societal costs and no assurance of improved public safety (Gopnik, 2012). As a result, many jurisdictions now set a cutoff whereby individuals with smaller amounts either are not subject to the same legal penalties (e.g., they are charged with a less serious offense category) or are diverted rather than sentenced (e.g., to a drug education program rather than prison).

The typical child pornography possession offender is similar in some respects to the typical drug possession offender: Both groups have committed nonviolent offenses and will lose degrees of freedom in any efforts to lead a crime-free life after long periods of incarceration. I am not arguing that there should not be criminal sanctions for child pornography possession that might include imprisonment. But the sanctions should be proportionate, make the best use of limited criminal justice resources, and assign a higher priority to offenders who produce or actively distribute child pornography than to those who possess child pornography only or passively distribute it. Other distinctions that might be worth considering in law enforcement decisions include the age of the depicted minors (prepubescent or pubescent children vs. underage teens) and the use of commercial child pornography sites, which create a financial incentive for the production of new content. For solicitation crimes, contact-driven offenders should be given a much higher priority over fantasy-driven offenders, even though the latter group is more likely to engage with undercover police officers in online forums.

Police face many challenges in responding to online offending. The first challenge is in training to achieve sufficient technological competence and then in keeping up with new developments in relevant technologies, including distribution methods, security, encryption, and so forth. I remember one investigator, for example, telling me about a technologically savvy suspect who hid a wireless hard drive that contained the child pornography content within a wall. Only an on-site search of the computer allowed investigators to detect the hard drive.

A related challenge is being effective in detecting and engaging with suspects. One reason that technologically naive or unsophisticated offenders are more likely to be caught is that they are the most likely to be detected by less sophisticated policing methods (Jenkins, 2001). Only a technologically savvy investigative team is likely to detect the most technologically savvy offenders; thus, there is an ongoing arms race. Applied research about online technologies and police investigation methods is needed.

Prentky et al. (2010) analyzed 254 messages between offenders and undercover police officers for keywords, rated according to sexual content. Content analysis revealed that suspects were usually the first to use a special keyword and the first to ask about age and to share their own age; they also used 30% more keywords than did the undercover officers. Undercover officers used twice as many text messaging abbreviations (presumably to reflect the use of these abbreviations among the youths they are mimicking). Suspects had more misspellings, and this tendency increased as the suspect believed he was engaging the minor and making "progress" in the sexual solicitation. The use of keywords and keywords with higher ratings went up as a chat continued. These results on the language used by online suspects may be useful in shaping undercover practices, as proactive investigations, raising the perceived presence of law enforcement online, become part of a comprehensive response to the problem of Internet-facilitated sexual offending.

Another challenge for law enforcement is information sharing and international collaboration, given that online offending—like the Internet itself—is not bound by legal jurisdictions. This includes sharing information about child pornography images, individual suspects, and networks of suspects. Recall the examples from Chapter 1 of extraordinary investigative breaks that helped identify large groups of networked suspects and that identified child victims depicted in child pornography. Sher (2007) described the origins of the Child Exploitation Tracking System (CETS), beginning with an e-mail from Paul Gillespie, a Toronto police officer at the time, expressing his frustration about child pornography issues to Microsoft CEO Bill Gates. Unexpectedly, Gates acted on the e-mail and directed the head of Microsoft Canada to assist. CETS has now been implemented across multiple jurisdictions and countries, allowing police officers to share information internationally. The Kids Internet Safety Alliance is involved in rolling out CETS and training police officers in conducting online investigations (http://www. kinsa.net).[2] Other evidence of international collaboration includes the formation of the Virtual Global Taskforce and the Interpol section on child exploitation.

Sher (2007) also described how the National Center for Missing and Exploited Children (NCMEC) developed the Child Recognition Identification System, which uniquely identifies child pornography images using MD-5 hash values, a kind of digital fingerprint of unique photographs. NCMEC has also been involved in the development of PhotoDNA by Microsoft, now implemented in Facebook, the largest social network in the world in 2012; it is also beginning to be used by other major technology providers. Last, Sher (2007) described Operation Hamlet, which targeted a technologically sophisticated ring of child pornography offenders who had committed child sexual abuse on demand and engaged in real-life meetings to share victims (pp. 81–87). The international investigation eventually identified two-dozen offenders, accounting for more than 100 child victims. Sher (2007) compared and contrasted the processes and outcomes of this investigation with those of Landslide Productions in the late 1990s to support his thesis that police are getting better at coordinating their efforts and better at technology and that pursuing identification of child victims can be better than trying to chase child pornography–only suspects.

What is the primary purpose of online offender investigations? Some police services, such as the Toronto Police Service, have focused on victim identification, a mandate that is shared by NCMEC (Sher, 2007). If this is the primary purpose, then production offenders should be the top priority. Possession offenders may have images that could lead to victim identification, but the signal-to-noise ratio is likely to be poor because many if not most of the images they have sought online are already known. Once the investigation has determined that the possession offender has no child victims of his or her own, either historically or concurrently, then prioritization by risk and by victim identification would dictate moving on to a new case.

CORPORATE PARTNERS

Automation of new image detection, and therefore victim identification, may expedite forensic analysis for this particular purpose. Technologies such as PhotoDNA, with NCMEC's expertise, could greatly aid this purpose.

---

[2]Disclosure: I was previously on the advisory board of the Kids Internet Safety Alliance.

Police services can now use PhotoDNA or a modification of PhotoDNA to automatically search large child pornography collections (sometimes totaling millions of images) and flagging those that are already known (http://www. microsoft.com/presspass/presskits/photodna). The software can also generate reports about this known content in terms of age and gender distributions and other useful details. The forensic analysts could then focus on images that are not already known to PhotoDNA, thereby reducing the time and energy involved in producing an analysis for each new case.

CHILD PROTECTION

An abiding theme throughout this book is the preoccupation of policy-makers, professionals, and the public about the risk of harm to children, whether from being sexually exploited or abused in the production of child pornography, from being sexually solicited online, or from being victims of contact sexual offenses (see Appendix 8.1). Given the increase in criminal justice and clinical cases involving online offending, there will be concomitant increases in child protection referrals because of online offending. For example, if someone is charged with online child pornography or solicitation and resides or works with children, either his own or his partner's, there will be questions about child safety.

There is little empirical research on the potential impacts of involvement in child pornography, beyond anecdotal reports of trauma, distress, and anxiety stemming from the direct exploitation or abuse, the knowledge that images might be viewed by many people, and the knowledge that the images might later be used by offenders to facilitate solicitation or contact sexual offenses (e.g., Masha Allen's testimony before Congress, mentioned in Chapter 1). Sharon Cooper (2012) described how child pornography victims she has seen clinically report experiencing severe anxiety that someone may recognize them after viewing child pornography images. Solicitation victims may also worry that suggestive or embarrassing images, texts, or other recordings they shared could be used to blackmail them (recall the sad story of Amanda Todd from Chapter 1).

It is not clear how well the research on child sexual abuse victims may help us understand the impact of online victimization. The experience of sexual victimization is idiosyncratic and highly variable, depending on many risk and resilience factors. One potentially important difference between online and offline sexual offending is the knowledge that any images are likely to persist and might be viewed by thousands of individuals. There is no opportunity for closure in the way that pursuing legal action or reconciliation with the perpetrator might allow.

An unintended consequence of American law is that child pornography victims can continue to be reminded of their images: A federal law requires victims (or parents or guardians if still below the age of 18) to be notified every time their image comes up in a legal proceeding, so that they have the option of pursuing civil action and seeking financial compensation from the offender if convicted. Unless the victim opts out, they will receive these notices in perpetuity (Crime Victims' Rights Act of 2004; Crime Control Act of 1990). Does this knowledge empower victims and provide them with an opportunity to pursue civil redress from offenders who have used their images? Does this knowledge harm victims, reminding them again and again that the images continue to circulate online?

PREVENTION

I have emphasized several times in this book that the number of undetected online offenders greatly exceeds those who are detected. A simple comparison of the number of Internet protocol (IP) addresses (not quite number of users, because a single individual might have multiple IP addresses) with the number of identified cases illustrates this point (Prichard, Watters, & Spiranovic, 2011; Steel, 2009; U.S. Department of Justice, 2010). This is stated not to dishearten readers or those engaged in this battle with child pornography online but to make it clear that the clinical, social service, and criminal justice communities can only do so much to address the problem; there are only so many police, child protection workers, and clinicians available. Even though their resources are growing—though this is no guarantee at this time of fiscal strain in 2012—they cannot grow quickly enough to keep up with the current trends. Tough decisions need to be made about how dollars will be spent. Specialized services are required for higher-risk offenders, but what about the many low-risk offenders being captured? What about the many offenders who are likely to remain undetected? There is a tremendous need for different prevention efforts to respond to this problem. (See Appendix 8.2.)

Social Marketing

Organizations such as Stop It Now! (http://www.stopitnow.org) do not offer treatment, but they do provide a directory service, online resources, and a confidential, toll-free number for individuals who are concerned about their sexual interests or behavior involving children or for family members or others who have suspicions about someone they know. Adopting a public health approach, the aims of Stop It Now! are prevention, education, and outreach. Another benefit is the relatively low cost of such interventions. The Stop It Now! model has been exported to the United Kingdom, the Netherlands, and Australia.

One possibly inherent (and major) disadvantage of the social marketing and outreach approach is that the highest risk individuals—those who have an antisocial orientation and who already engage in contact sexual offending—are probably the least likely to seek self-help options. Another disadvantage is that follow-up data will not be available to evaluate the efficacy of these services. Nonetheless, outreach efforts ranging in resource intensity from croga.org (website maintenance) to Stop It Now (hotline and advocacy) to Dunkelfeld (outreach plus clinical service delivery) are all potential parts of a comprehensive response to the problem of online offending, with treatment reserved for higher risk offenders who have been detected.

Peer Advocacy Groups for Minor-Attracted Persons

B4UACT is a nonprofit organization founded by a coalition of minor-attracted persons and mental health professionals in Maryland, to provide confidential access to services and information for minor-attracted persons concerned about stigma and isolation (www.b4uact.org). A relatively new website, with the somewhat unfortunate name of Virtuous Pedophiles, was recently launched by two pedophilic men as an online support forum for other self-identified pedophiles who want to live a crime-free life (www.virped.org). Critical questions for advocacy groups are their ability to reach previously unidentified individuals and their impact on the subsequent behavior and quality of life of minor-attracted persons and self-identified pedophiles or hebephiles.

EDUCATION

I have already described some of the prevention efforts that exist, including self-help resources that are online (e.g., croga.org), outreach efforts such as Stop It Now!, and free and confidential treatment for help-seeking individuals through the Dunkelfeld Prevention Project. Another major avenue is parent and youth education about online risks and safety measures to prevent sexual solicitations or to prevent youths from responding positively to solicitations. There is a wide range of parent and teacher resources available, but most of these have not been empirically validated. Unfortunately, there is a strong sense of déjà vu for much of the educational content: Educational resources tend to emphasize "stranger danger," referring to "online predators" who target young children, lie about their motives, and use innocent revelations of personally identifying information to identify potential abduction and rape victims (see the Myths and Realities section in Chapter 3 and the Recapitulation section in Chapter 7).

The available research on solicitation offending has suggested that such education campaigns would be much more likely to be effective if they focused on vulnerable youths, emphasized the potential negative consequences of engaging in sexual interactions with adult men or sharing sexually suggestive or explicit images, and education about ways to respond to online solicitations. Emphasizing stranger danger runs the risk of unnecessarily alarming low-risk youths and their parents and encouraging overconfidence among youths who may not consider the person with whom they are interacting to be a stranger because they have chatted online. More research on the dynamics of statutory sexual offending could contribute a great deal to these educational campaigns, with the additional benefits of better understanding offline statutory offenses as well. For at-risk adults, Wolak, Finkelhor, Mitchell, and Ybarra (2008) suggested increasing awareness of existing laws, emphasizing social norms, and addressing the sexual and relationship factors that are also at play in statutory sexual offending.

An excellent and comprehensive example of online resources is Netsmartz411, an initiative of the National Center for Missing and Exploited Children and its corporate and foundation partners. The website (http://www. netsmartz.org) presents clear, succinct answers to questions parents might have about a variety of online problems, including online solicitation but also cyberbullying and other online behaviors. Netsmartz411 is part of the Netsmartz Workshop, which also has information for children ages 5 to 17, parents or guardians, educators, and law enforcement professionals. The site is well designed, with interactive animations and games. Yet the site does use the word *predators* in the link for tweens to information about online safety (as of February 10, 2012). Does this language scare or put off some youths or their parents or guardians? Does it provide a false sense of security to tweens, given that they might be solicited by older adolescents or young adults whom they already know or get to know online?

Wolak, Finkelhor, Mitchell, and Ybarra (2008) made helpful general suggestions for educational prevention campaigns: (a) Avoid descriptions of problems that emphasize young children, violence, or deception; (b) focus on adolescents rather than parents; (c) be clear about why sex with adults is problematic in terms of adolescent outcomes, social norms, and the law; (d) target at-risk youths; and (e) pay attention to the constellation of risky online behaviors.

Tsim (2006) reported on an uncontrolled evaluation of an educational presentation by a police officer to students. The comparison group was composed of students who did not happen to be present on the day of the presentation by police officer. Youths who received the presentation showed significant pre–post changes in potentially risky behaviors after a 6-month follow-up. However, it was not clear from the results presented whether the comparison group showed any change in the same direction, which suggests that other factors influenced online behavior. Also, school attendance may be related to risk-related characteristics because more vulnerable youths may also be more likely to skip classes. Finally, there was a high nonparticipation rate. A systematic evaluation, with teens randomly assigned to receive the information or not, with follow-up, would be valuable to the understanding of the impacts of these kinds of efforts.

Thus far I have focused on online solicitation. Other education is needed to address the problem of self-produced child pornography by youths. Some youths are not aware that "sexting" is illegal and could lead to criminal prosecution, over and above the social and personal consequences if the images are distributed more widely. A starting point for campaigns to address sexting is the established, successful campaigns to reduce risky sexual behavior that can lead to STDs or unwanted pregnancy (Kirby, 2002). As reviewed in Chapter 3, several studies have identified risky Internet behaviors to pay attention to in identifying vulnerable children and youths and to target in interventions. More research on other vulnerability factors—in terms of developmental history, personality, attitudes, and beliefs—would be helpful in this regard.

Parent engagement and education is critical. A consistent theme in surveys of children and youths regarding their online activities is the lack of parental supervision (e.g., Webwise, 2006). The United Kingdom Children's Council on Internet Safety (2010) reviewed U.K. research and found that youths who are online spend more than an hour on the Internet each day, often without parental supervision. Parents who would not think of letting their children, especially younger children, leave their home without knowing where they go and who they are with do not know what their children do online or who they interact with. The gap may exist because parents did not grow up with these technologies and are less comfortable with them. Supervision will be even more challenging given the increasing use of portable devices such as smartphones and tablets.

SITUATIONAL CRIME PREVENTION

In criminology, routine activities theory proposes that crimes are more likely to occur when there is a suitable target, lack of a capable guardian, and a motivated potential offender (Felson, 1987). Situational crime prevention works by making crime targets less attractive and by increasing effective guardianship through techniques such as *hot spot policing* (focusing police on high crime hotspots on the basis of quantitative analysis of crime data) and *target hardening* (e.g., putting in better lights, locks, and security cameras; Wortley & Smallbone, 2006). In the context of online sexual offending against minors, hot spot policing might include proactive investigations in potentially higher density online "locations." Target hardening can be achieved through parent and child education and widespread implementation of filtering and blocking software (see Hunter, 2000; Marcum, 2007; Marcum, Higgins, & Ricketts, 2010). A monitored section of the Internet for children would protect them, just as monitored playgrounds and parks can protect their physical safety and security.

The central premise of situational crime prevention is that a great deal of crime, including sexual crime, is opportunistic. This is true even when individuals might be highly motivated to commit the crimes, such as antisocial pedophiles who are interested in child pornography and sex with children. Everyone is sensitive to their environment. Thus, any physical or other changes to the environment that make crime more difficult can have significant effects on crime. In the context of car theft, for example, parking in higher traffic, well-lit areas, locking doors and windows, installing alarms, removing valuables, and using steering wheel locks can reduce risk. In online offending, an example of situational crime prevention is the development of PhotoDNA by Microsoft Research and Hany Farid of Dartmouth College, with initial large-scale implementation on Facebook, the world's largest social network with over 800 million users at the time this was written (http://www.microsoft.com/en-us/news/presskits/photodna/).

Target Hardening

Every unique digital file can be identified by a unique hash value. Resizing, renaming, or otherwise modifying an image file results in a new hash value, so it is difficult to determine whether a modified image file matches one that is already known. PhotoDNA is a relatively new technology that provides robust hashing of image files, which means that even modified child pornography images can be identified automatically by the software. This software can then be used to match new images uploaded on a photo-sharing service with a set of known child pornography images in a database maintained by NCMEC. The software runs automatically in the background, so that no person views the image, to protect user privacy. (It would also be practically impossible for human review of uploaded images given the amount of traffic involved.) The software algorithm determines only whether the image is likely to be child pornography, without recording or knowing anything about the image. The comparison is made on the basis of metadata about the image.

The potential benefit of the PhotoDNA technology is that it will impede the distribution of child pornography images, especially if PhotoDNA technology is adopted by other major file-sharing platforms. Knowledge that images can be detected and then accounts suspended and law enforcement notified could greatly reduce the avenues available for distribution by increasing the effectiveness of online guardianship. One can imagine other situational crime prevention strategies (e.g., Schell, Martin, Hung, & Rueda, 2006). For example, Taylor and Quayle (2008) suggested pop-up messages when using search terms connected to child pornography images to serve as warnings and to dissuade less committed seekers. Two other strategies are discussed next.

Safer Surfing

A variety of programs are available to concerned parents or guardians to filter and monitor online activity for children and younger adolescents. Prentky et al. (2010) compared 11 leading filter programs and found that all blocked specific websites and scanned e-mails, but none of them monitored instant message and peer-to-peer network activity, even though young people are heavy users of these platforms, a great deal of online solicitation might take place through instant messaging, and much online child pornography traffic takes place on peer-to-peer networks. Technologies are needed to address these gaps. Other reviews suggest that these programs are only moderately effective.

Offender Tracking

A federal law in the United States requires offenders to disclose any Internet identifiers, including e-mail addresses and user registration information for various sites (Adam Walsh Child Protection and Safety Act of 2006). This does not prevent, of course, an identified offender from creating a new anonymous e-mail address or creating new accounts rather than using existing accounts. Offenders who remain under supervision can be monitored using different software programs available for Internet-ready devices. The challenges here are publicly available computers, pay-to-go mobiles, and various technologies that allow one to hide surfing, create truly anonymous e-mail, and encrypt files.

Internet Architecture

Online offending is facilitated by several aspects of the Internet's architecture as it has evolved from its origins as a robust communication network for military and academic purposes. Decisions made by Internet pioneers, in line with their political and philosophical views, are becoming "locked in" (to use Lanier's, 2010, description), even though it is not intrinsic to the way that the Internet operates. To be more specific, a central tenet of the dominant Internet culture is that online activity should be anonymous, with maximum privacy and minimum regulation and oversight. (I am sympathetic to this as someone with some libertarian values who does not want his digital data accessed without permission.) Certainly, anonymity may have protected political dissidents, whistleblowers, and others, and privacy is a central concern of all people in the offline as well as online worlds (although see Morozov, 2011). But an anonymous, highly private Internet also creates a target-rich space for online sexual offending and other criminal conduct. Is this price worth paying?

Imagine instead what online life would be like if one could not login without verifiable identification—for example, by using a registered government-issued ID or credit card. We would lose a great deal of perceived freedom and privacy, even with legal and other regulations in place. In return, we would gain in terms of security and safety. An analogy can readily be drawn to the real world. Most readers of this book are free to travel and interact with whom we wish, but we are required to have identification when we cross national borders, and we are expected to follow the law. Subject to legal protections, we can be stopped and if there is probable cause, interrogated and searched. This is an inconvenience and undoubtedly irritates true libertarians, but it is an accepted hassle.

I am not a proponent of verified identification, but I am raising these issues to suggest that the Internet can play a huge, perhaps defining, role in online sexual offending and antisocial and criminal behavior online more generally (including the irritations of spam, flame-wars, and callow stupidity). If society is truly concerned about combating online crime, particularly online crime involving children, then some unorthodox thinking is needed. Adults might well resist verified identification for themselves but might accept restrictions for children in their care. What about a separate Internet space that requires verified identification for children to log in? Only minors and appointed, identity-authenticated guardians could surf within this protected world, with much closer monitoring and some restrictions on activities. This could greatly reduce unwanted exposure to pornography and sexual solicitations by adults.

CELIBATE PEDOPHILES

Some self-identified pedophiles have claimed they are celibate (i.e., they engage in no sexual activity with children), but little research evidence is available on celibate pedophiles; most of the published research has focused on detected online or contact offenders. Pedophiles who refrain from any illegal activity are unlikely to be studied outside of anonymous surveys (an exception is Fedoroff, Smolewska, Selhi, Ng, & Bradford, 2001). Of the 155 self-identified pedophiles or hebephiles studied by Neutze et al. (2011) in the Dunkelfeld Project, 27% had been inactive in the past 6 months, meaning that they reported no use of pornography and no sexual contacts with children during that time period. None had been inactive during their lifetime, however. Eighteen men provided only partial information on their lifetime history. Of the remaining 137 men, 42 had used child pornography, 45 had committed contact offenses without concomitant use of pornography, and 50 had used child pornography and committed contact sexual offenses. In other words, two thirds of the sample with complete lifetime history information had used child pornography. This was a selected sample of help-seeking individuals, however, and one would imagine that a celibate pedophile who was not distressed by his sexual interests in children would not have contacted the Dunkelfeld Project and thus would not be represented in the sample.

Combined with the contact offending history data examined by Seto et al. (2011) among identified online offenders, these studies have suggested that a sizable number of pedophiles do not have sexual contacts with children, though most have some involvement with child pornography. Can pedophiles be entirely abstinent, eschewing even their preferred child pornography? For those who cannot, Malamuth and Huppin (2007) raised the controversial idea of legalizing or decriminalizing virtual child pornography for low-risk individuals with no known history of contact sexual offending. Such pornography would not involve the exploitation or abuse of any real children. With the increasing realism of images produced by digital technologies (e.g., the film *Avatar*), such content could become a viable alternative to content depicting real children. Assuming no negative effects of viewing child pornography—a tenuous assumption if you agree with my speculations in Chapter 6—could society tolerate this idea, especially if it might prevent some pedophiles from acting on their sexual interests in real life?

More broadly, for the sake of greater child safety, could society come to view pedophilia and hebephilia more sympathetically, as mental disorders that are distinct from the criminal sexual behaviors associated with these sexual preferences, to provide more support and treatment? I am somewhat encouraged by a recent spate of online media stories that tackle the fear, anger, and stigma of pedophilia, including sympathetic posts by Dan Savage, a well-known sex and love advice columnist (thestranger.com/seattle/SavageLove?oid=12927907) and by recent online columns by Cord Jefferson (gawker.com/5541037/born-this-way-sympathy-and-science-for-those-who—want-to-have-sex-with-children) for Gawker.com and Tracy Clark-Flory for Salon.com (salon.com/2012/07/01/meet_pedophiles_who_mean_well).

APPENDIX 8.1
VICTIM IMPACT OF ONLINE EXPLOITATION

There are few data on the impacts of online victimization. For online solicitation victims, it might be possible to extrapolate from the literature on the effects of contact sexual offenses for those who are younger or who were threatened or forced into sexual activity. Though effects can vary greatly, influenced by individual resilience factors and by the nature and circumstances of the sexual abuse, the net effect is negative (Rind, Tromovitch, & Bauserman, 1998). For older adolescents who agreed to the sexual relationship (but who are not legally able to consent), the effects are less clear because little is available about their counterparts, that is, statutory sexual offense victims.

There is some limited research on child pornography victims, beyond the anecdotal reports of Masha Allen and a publicly distributed victim impact statement by "Amy," whose abuse was memorialized in the Misty series. Burgess, Hartman, McCausland, and Powers (1984) found that children who had been exploited for a year or longer through child pornography had more clinical symptoms. Terr (1990) described a case example of a young girl, age 5, who was photographed when she was between the ages of 15 and 18 months by the husband of her day care provider. The photographs depicted her nude with an erect penis in the image. The perpetrator was subsequently convicted of sexual offenses against children in the day care center. The girl experienced anxiety and distress, crying every day on the way to day care, drawing pictures of naked people, and avoiding her father, especially when her diaper was being changed.

Some data from offline child pornography victims are cited in Svedin, Back, and Barnen (1996). Svedin et al. reported on the impacts for 10 child pornography victims (five boys and five girls) from two offline child pornography investigations from a review of the court documents. These 10 children could be split into two groups, one containing five girls and two boys who were exploited by a family member or someone who was close to the victim's family, and the other consisting of the remaining three boys, who were exploited by a male stranger. All of the children in the former group came from average family backgrounds, whereas the children in the latter group came from troubled families. The unrelated perpetrators in the first group were trusted by the family and were often quite involved with the victims—for example, as an occasional babysitter or sports coach. Children were typically victimized years ago; the exploitation ranged from one occasion to over 8 years. All were sexually exploited and in most cases had been sexually abused, including masturbation and oral and attempted or completed anal sex. It is therefore impossible to determine what effects could be attributed to the sexual abuse versus the recordings of the abuse. Two girls were photographed while sleeping.

The nonperpetrating parents had no suspicion about the sexual offending and were shocked when they found out (Svedin et al., 1996). None of the children disclosed the sexual abuse until they were questioned as part of an official investigation. It is not clear how well the children were doing before the offenses were committed. Children in the first group seemed fine and there was no evidence of problems during the sexual exploitation, whereas the children in the second group showed serious behavior problems, including mental health involvement and problems at school. Without methodological controls, however, it is not clear how many of these difficulties could have been attributed to their already troubled family lives or to the experiences they went through. All of the children experienced stress and psychological symptoms after the crimes came to light, including feelings of shame, self-blame, and anger toward the perpetrator. Children in the first group seemed to be doing well after the criminal trials ended, whereas all three boys in the second group continued to have serious difficulties. Some of the boys later questioned their sexual identity, and five of the seven children who completed the Child Behavior Checklist reported obsessions with sexual thoughts.

Quayle, Erooga, Wright, Taylor, and Harbinson (2006) suggested that very young children may do better because they are less recognizable as adults and because they may be less aware of what has happened and therefore less likely to experience shame, guilt, fear, or anger as a result of any sexual exploitation or abuse that occurred. These authors suggested there are four levels of victim involvement: (a) being photographed without knowledge, (b) being sexually abused and photographed surreptitiously, (c) being sexually abused and openly photographed, and (d) being sexually abused, openly photographed, and actively involved in the child pornography offending—for example, in selecting other children to be pornographically photographed. A reasonable hypothesis is that different levels of involvement might lead to different outcomes for victims, with more negative outcomes for those at higher levels of involvement.

Weiler, Haardt-Becker, and Schulte (2010) conducted surveys and interviews with a wide range of professionals who counseled victims of sexual exploitation or abuse. A total of 245 child pornography victims (197 girls and 48 boys) were seen by these professionals between June 2000 and June 2005, with an additional 280 cases in which child pornography involvement was suspected but not known to have occurred.[3] According to the survey results, rather than the interviews with a more self-selected subsample of par-

---

[3]There could have been overlap of cases across professionals (e.g., if someone went to one clinician in 2001 and a different clinician in 2004).

ticipants, only a small number of the children (15 girls and five boys) knew that their images had been placed online. Six of these girls and all of these boys had seen the images online themselves. Many professionals reported that these known child pornography victims suffered from feelings of shame, guilt, fear, or disgust. However, all of the children were being seen for treatment after referral from the courts or from social service agencies, and so it is not known how many child pornography victims might not show these negative effects. Also, in all of these cases, production of child pornography co-occurred with contact sexual abuse (isolating the effects of involvement in child pornography would require matched comparisons with sexual abuse victims on relevant measures). Making inference even more challenging and complicated, some professionals stated that the children had been multiply abused or mistreated. It is heartbreaking that some of the children stated that the child pornography offender was the only person who took any interest in them. The specific impact of online distribution was not known because Weiler et al. did not compare the small group who knew their images were placed online with child pornography victims who were unsure or who knew that the images were not shared with others.

The most common reason the professionals cited for lack of disclosure by child victims was guilt and fear of the perpetrator. It is unclear how accurate this explanation is, given that we have to rely on clinical perceptions for this information. For example, all of the professionals thought the existence of child pornography images necessarily led to distress, which is not necessarily true (and could be iatrogenic, unfortunately, in creating the same expectations among their child clients). Data were available for 118 perpetrators. The majority (90%) were adult men who knew the victim. The most common category was "father," followed by "male friend of the family."

The effects of online victimization are an important area for research, because we want to determine the scope and magnitude of any effects of online victimization to design better interventions for victims. For child pornography in particular, it is also important from a policy perspective. Legally, possessors of child pornography can receive sentences comparable to production offenders or even contact sexual offenders (Hamilton, 2012). One legal argument has been that possessors of child pornography revictimize children depicted in the images because the knowledge that such images are being used as stimuli for fantasy and masturbation, and perhaps even to groom potential victims, is assumed to be distressing, as is the idea that someone might recognize a depicted child from those images. Thus, it is argued that the children depicted in child pornography are not only directly harmed by the person who produced the content but also by subsequent users. Whether this is true has not been empirically examined and needs to be if the argument of revictimization is to be made.

Such research would be complicated to conduct because in many cases the child has also been directly sexually abused during the production of the content. It has also been difficult to identify victims, and even with the prioritization of efforts (e.g., by the Toronto Police Service, National Center for Missing and Exploited Children) to identify victims who have been or are being sexually abused, it is difficult to disentangle the effects of sexual abuse and the effects of sexual exploitation as a result of child pornography. One study design could compare different groups: (a) children who had not been victims of online or offline sexual offenses, (b) children who had been photographed for child pornography and were not aware at the time, (c) children who were aware they had been pornographically photographed, (d) children who had been photographed and sexually abused, and (e) children who had been sexually abused without any photography. Controlling for background factors as best as possible, comparing the fourth and fifth groups would tell us about the impact of being photographed, in addition to being sexually abused. Comparing the first group to the second and third groups would tell us about the effects of being depicted in child pornography and whether knowing at the time that one was being photographed had an impact.

APPENDIX 8.2
MORE UNINTENDED CONSEQUENCES

There is controversy about the practice of some law enforcement officials in naming suspects before criminal conviction for child pornography offenses. An example is described in Sher's (2007) book about James LeCraw, who claimed he accessed only adult pornography when he was caught up in an investigation of subscribers to Landslide Productions (see Chapter 2). The charges were subsequently withdrawn, but he lost his job and friends, became depressed, and committed suicide on July 19, 2004. The suicide toll was perhaps most serious in the United Kingdom, with 35 men known to have killed themselves after being publicly identified in child pornography investigations (Sher, 2007). In some cases, the investigations may be started because of electronic evidence that is subsequently shown to be the result of hacking or other outside interference. For example, many suspects investigated as part of the police operations arising from the Landslide Productions case turned out to have been the victims of credit card fraud; their online information was hacked and their credit cards were used, without their knowledge, to pay for access to illegal pornography. Even if the person is subsequently found guilty, is the risk of that person's death enough to justify deterrence, bringing forward unknown victims, or other purposes of naming suspects before criminal conviction?

Is it always necessary to remove suspects from the home or to take children into the custody of child protection authorities? What about the unintended consequences on the offender's partner and children as a result of long sentences and then placement on a sex offender registry? Though uncommon, there is evidence that offenders identified on publicly accessible registries in the United States have been targets of vandalism, harassment, assault, and even homicide (Levenson & Cotter, 2005). Is sentencing proportionate to the harm that is caused and the risk of future harm through further offending?

9

CONCLUSIONS AND
FUTURE DIRECTIONS

WHO ARE ONLINE OFFENDERS

Our understanding of online sexual offending has grown quickly in the past 10 years. Research has begun to address fundamental questions about the characteristics of offenders, their motivations, and the risk they pose to offend again, either online or through contact sexual offenses. Some attention is beginning to be paid to etiological models and treatment as well, because existing sex offender treatment approaches are modified to deal with this increasing population of offenders in clinical and criminal justice settings. Outcome data are not yet available to guide clinicians on what works to reduce recidivism.

The research on characteristics and motivations suggests that we are dealing with different, albeit overlapping, populations of offenders: child pornography offenders, solicitation offenders, and contact sex offenders. There are individuals who engage in more than one of these criminal offenses, but

http://dx.doi.org/10.1037/14191-010
Internet Sex Offenders, by M. C. Seto

they are the minority. Indeed, these populations differ systematically in terms of offender characteristics, risk to reoffend, and criminogenic needs. The available data challenge the notion that child pornography is a gateway to contact sexual offending. When detected, many child pornography offenders are found to have committed contact offenses, but a substantial number have no known contact offenses (Seto, Hanson, & Babchishin, 2011). Moreover, relatively few child pornography offenders go on to commit a contact sexual offense postadjudication.

The most contrary evidence comes from the limited data on the timing of child pornography and contact sexual offenses. These studies suggest that when someone has committed both child pornography and contact offending, the contact offending typically occurred first. This may change, however, as more research is conducted and offenders are increasingly likely to have grown up with Internet access. On average, child pornography offenders in research samples are in their 30s, so many were already adults when online child pornography became more available. In contrast, younger adult offenders arrested now likely saw their first online pornography as young adolescents.

OFFENDER CHARACTERISTICS

As Wolak (2011) reported, more child pornography offenders were age 25 or younger in the 2009 National Juvenile Online Victimization Project, which suggests that we will begin to see a demographic surge in the numbers of adolescent and young adult online offenders in the next 5 to 10 years. These individuals grew up with the Internet and thus may have accessed child pornography before ever engaging in sexual contacts with young children. One could therefore predict that future studies will find that, among dual offenders, child pornography use tends to precede contact offending. This still does not support the idea that there is a causal relationship, however.

I think the most parsimonious explanation is that pedophilia and hebephilia explain the majority of cases of child pornography and of contact sexual offending against prepubescent and pubescent children. A pedohebephilic individual who is sufficiently antisocial to overcome the social and legal prohibitions against sex with a child is likely to engage in both forms of offending. A pedohebephilic individual who is low in antisocial tendencies may engage in child pornography offending but is unlikely to commit contact offenses. Finally, a pedohebephilic individual who is high in self-control, low in sex drive, and living a life with strong family, social, and community ties may not act illegally at all. This does not mean an entirely abstinent life because this last group of pedophilic individuals may still fantasize and masturbate about sex with children or may view legal images of children that they find to be sexually arousing (e.g., images of children in underwear or swimsuits), but it does not mean criminality.

Less is known about online solicitation offenders, but the existing evidence suggests they are similar to statutory sexual offenders, who are themselves a poorly understood offender population. These offenders are predominantly nonparaphilic; those who approach younger adolescents might be hebephilic, but by and large solicitation and statutory offenders are unlikely to be pedophilic or hebephilic. Instead, they appear to be adult men, typically young men under the age of 30, who are interested in sexually maturing or mature adolescents who are under the legal age of consent. Speculatively, the primary motivation for solicitation—whether offline or online—and statutory sexual offending is that approaching vulnerable adolescents increases sexual opportunities because such adolescents are more likely to be receptive to sexual advances than more experienced older adolescents and adult peers. The youths are less cognitively, emotionally, and socially developed, and relatively speaking, the adults are more impressive than same-aged peers because they have some money and afford access to adult status symbols (e.g., legal purchase of alcohol, owning a motor vehicle), even if the adults are not particularly impressive compared with other young adult men. There is some antisociality among these perpetrators that allows them to overcome personal and social inhibitions against engaging in illegal and socially sanctioned behavior.

We know almost nothing about other forms of online offending, including involvement with other illegal pornography (e.g., violent pornography, depictions of bestiality), sexual solicitations of adults that lead to sexual assaults, online behaviors that topologically resemble real-life offending such as exhibitionism and voyeurism, and the use of online technologies to facilitate juvenile prostitution, juvenile sex tourism, and sex trafficking. Given the increasing political attention to these topics, I expect the next big wave of online offending research will address these questions.

RISK TO REOFFEND

Accumulating evidence suggests that, on average, child pornography offenders are at low risk to commit contact sexual offenses in the future. We do not yet have data on the risk of recidivism posed by online solicitation offenders or by other types of online offenders. Some online offenders have already committed contact offenses, and a small minority will do so in the future, just as a small number will commit further child pornography offenses. However, the base rates for any sexual recidivism are relatively low after several years of opportunity, particularly for those with no known history of contact sexual offending (Eke, Seto, & Williams, 2011; Seto & Eke, 2005; Seto et al., 2011). These results belie the idea that online offenders necessarily pose a grave risk of sexually offending against children. Some do, of course, because any group of offenders is expected to be heterogeneous with regard to risk. Empirically based risk assessment is needed to identify those who do pose such a risk. Valid information about risk can then influence decision making throughout the clinical or criminal justice processes, from investigation to prosecution to sentencing to treatment and supervision. Information about risk is also critical for designing prevention campaigns and setting legal and social policy directions.

Research on risk factors has suggested that online sexual offending is orderly. The same kinds of risk factors that have been empirically validated in follow-up studies of contact sex offenders, and offenders more generally, are predictive of new offenses among online offenders. These variables include offender age, criminal history, and substance use problems (Eke et al., 2011; Eke & Seto, 2012). Specific to sexual offending, indicators of sexual deviance—self-reported sexual interest in children and ratio of boy-to-girl child pornography content—are also predictors of contact and child pornography recidivism, respectively.

INTERVENTION

A tough social and legal question is how we should respond to identified online offenders if they are at low risk to offend again. I realize sentencing should not be determined solely on risk posed by the offender; sentencing should also reflect society's rejection of the proscribed conduct and provide justice to the children who were exploited in the production of the content. Nonetheless, all other things being equal, the most severe sentences should be reserved for higher risk online offenders, in accordance with principles of justice, efficient use of resources, and the risk principle in corrections. Ideally, lower risk individuals would be responsive to proactive efforts such as those of Stop It Now! and the Dunkelfeld Project in Germany, wherein at-risk individuals are targeted for intervention before they commit online (or offline) sexual offenses.

Our knowledge about effective treatment and other forms of intervention lags what we know about risk and clinical need assessment. This is typical, because it takes time to implement and then evaluate treatment programs. However, there is a danger that modified or new programs are being implemented widely without sufficient empirical traction. Only systematic evaluations—ideally, methodologically rigorous evaluations using random assignment to different intervention conditions—will really tell us what affects treatment targets in the desired direction and, in the longer run, what reduces recidivism. The low recidivism rates observed so far suggest that these evaluations would require large samples followed for long periods of time. The research comparing online and contact offenders and evaluating dynamic risk factors helps identify potential treatment targets, in line with the need principle from corrections research (Andrews & Bonta, 2010). Of particular interest are sexual self-regulation and intimacy deficits, but other targets might include more generally compulsive online behavior. The risk principle says that the most intensive interventions should be reserved for higher risk online offenders.

UNANSWERED QUESTIONS

I have already identified many unexamined or unanswered questions in this volume. Given the relative newness of attention to online sexual offending, it is not surprising that there are many avenues for further research. (I have never met a researcher who did not think there was a need for more research.) Additional questions involve long-term risk to reoffend, best assessment and treatment technologies for online offenders, and changes in characteristics and motivations of online offending as demographic shift continues. Most youths are online, and it is increasingly likely that their first exposure to pornography or first sexual interactions (e.g., sexual chat) may take place online. This represents perhaps the largest unregulated social quasi-experiment. What is the impact of this widespread and potentially intense early exposure to pornography and to nonphysical sexual interactions?

We need to know more about forms of online offending that are not currently the focus of law enforcement efforts and that therefore remain untracked, including online exhibitionism and voyeurism. Most of the attention has been on child pornography and then solicitations of minors, but minors are also at risk of these forms of criminal behavior, as are adults. It is possible, for example, that minors are more likely to be exposed to by an adult stranger than they are to be sexually solicited and invited to meet in person. The current focus on online solicitation misses the potential distress that younger or more vulnerable minors might experience as a result of online exhibitionism in addition to the simple nuisance effect. Though there are examples of individuals who are criminally charged after being discovered for surreptitiously taking photographs, the prevalence of so-called upskirt or voyeur sites suggests this activity is significant (Ogas & Gaddam 2011).

There are not enough resources to deal with child pornography and solicitation offending, and realistically, there never will be enough resources despite large investments in law enforcement. What else can be done to address these problems? The involvement of Internet service providers (ISPs) and other industry players is critical. There is a tension between privacy and freedom and between security and safety online, but there are things that can be done.

UNIVERSALITY

As with the sexual offender and general offender literatures, much of the research comes from teams based in industrialized jurisdictions. Relatively little is known about online sexual offending outside of Canada, the United States, Western Europe, Australia, and New Zealand.[1] As mentioned in Chapter 1, many countries do not specifically have laws that prohibit child pornography (though some do through existing obscenity legislation). Many countries do not have laws for online solicitation either, so individuals may not face legal penalties for online sexual solicitations unless they meet in person and commit a conventional sexual offense.

The Internet's reach is global, yet we know little about online criminality, including online sexual offending, in non-Westernized countries. Internet usage is high in Asia overall, driven by the affluent countries, and is increasing quickly elsewhere. As of November 2011, there were an estimated two billion Internet users on our planet: Asia had the largest proportion of users (44% of world users) compared with Europe (23%), North America (13%), Latin America (10%), and Africa (6%), according to the Internet World Stats (Internetworldstats.com/stats). Though Asia has the largest proportion of Internet users, most of the research on Internet-facilitated sexual offending has been conducted in North America and Western Europe (Rainie, 2010). We know almost nothing about online sexual offending in Asian countries. Are there ethnic–cultural factors that may influence online offending and its repercussions? There has been much discussion about the permissive (in some ways) pornography culture in Japan, where adult men can openly read manga (graphic comic books) depicting sex with minors, sexual violence, and other atypical sexual content. Yet the sexual crime rates in Japan are low compared with Western countries. Are Asians (and other non-Caucasians) disproportionately unlikely to be involved in online sexual offending? Does the disproportionate representation of Caucasians among Canadian, American, and English samples translate to cross-country comparisons of different ethnic groups?

---

[1]Or, at least, little is published in English language sources; it is possible that researchers are examining online offending and presenting and publishing in non-English languages. These studies did not come up in my wide-ranging searches, however.

TECHNOLOGY

Over the approximately 3 years it took me to write this book, device use has begun to shift from a personal desktop or laptop computer to truly mobile platforms in the form of smartphones and tablets. These third-generation technologies offer high-speed Internet access, high-quality audio and video processing, and cheap memory storage. The near future is likely to bring hobbyist 3-D image and video effects, more realistic rendering of computer-generated persons, and virtual reality technologies. History tells us that these new technologies will quickly be adapted for pornographic and other sexual purposes, as previous technologies have in the past. What will be the impacts of these new technologies on online sexual offending?

I have described in several places the kinds of technological arms races that are taking place in response to online offending. In the previous chapter, I talked about the example of Microsoft's PhotoDNA initiative, which allows photo-sharing services to block the uploading of known child pornography images, to make distribution more difficult.[2] One can imagine the impact of PhotoDNA in other venues, for example, as a universal filter on peer-to-peer file-sharing systems or as a law enforcement tool to expedite the processing of large child pornography seizures (http://bit.ly/Ioeh1m). By rapidly identifying known images and automating reports of the content depicted in known child pornography images, forensic analysts can focus only on new images, to aid in victim identification and further expand the PhotoDNA database.

FINAL COMMENTS

International law and cooperation is evolving to address the global problem of online sexual offending, as demonstrated by the Virtual Global Taskforce in policing, United Nations efforts, and nongovernmental organizations such as ECPAT International[3] and the International Center for Missing and Exploited Children. At the same time, the intentional decentralization of the Internet, where digital data are usually not stored in any single location and is often not under the control of any single individual or group, means effective legal and social control of child pornography is

---

[2]Child pornography images are taken down as soon as possible, but an account that is only up for a number of hours still provides a means for anonymous users to share significant amounts of content. Any photo-sharing site or file-sharing service is vulnerable, and thus PhotoDNA can have a huge impact on situational crime prevention if it is implemented widely.
[3]ECPAT is a global network of approximately 80 groups around the world dedicated to eliminating the commercial sexual exploitation of children (http://www.ecpat.net).

unlikely unless the infrastructure of the Internet itself is changed. Individuals can currently access the Internet with perceived anonymity. Government or other oversight is fiercely resisted and allegations of privacy invasion are fiercely prosecuted. Moreover, the United Nations recently suggested (La Rue, 2011) that access to the Internet is a human right, given the role it plays in the free exchange of information, particularly in nondemocratic regimes (although see Morozov, 2011).

I would personally be unhappy with such a radical change in the online world. But it would be possible to greatly reduce the prevalence of Internet-facilitated sexual offending, and other Internet-facilitated crime and antisocial behavior, if the Internet were more vigorously regulated. There is a cultural battle between the increasing governmental regulation of the Internet and civil liberty advocates. The Attorney General's National Strategy Report (U.S. Department of Justice, 2010) notes that there is no federal law or regulation requiring ISPs to retain information for a particular length of time, which could be invaluable to law enforcement investigations. Indeed, 61% of investigators surveyed in 2009 reported that they had a case that had been impeded because ISP data had not been retained; 47% had to end an investigation as a result. Memory is cheap, so these data could be retained and turned over with court order, but it would be an unpopular law. However, ISPs already have a legal obligation to report any child pornography they discover. Ultimately, addressing online sexual offending means a larger engagement with these broader issues about the Internet, lawful regulation, and civil liberties.

Why Online Sexual Offending

At this time, online sexual offending seems to be primarily a first-world problem. On the basis of what we know so far about numbers and risk of direct exploitation or harm to children, the focus on online child pornography and solicitation offending is a luxury that the rest of the world cannot yet afford. The rest of the world struggles with more basic concerns about child labor, child slavery, and child sexual exploitation and abuse by domestic offenders, sex traffickers, and sex tourists.[4] It is no surprise, then, that most online sex crime cases have been identified in Canada, the United States,

---

[4]For more information, see http://www.justice.gov/criminal/ceos/citizensguide/citizensguide_trafficking. html and sextourism.net. NGOs such as ECPAT International have documented cases of individuals traveling to countries such as Thailand, Cambodia, Brazil, the Dominican Republic, India, and Sri Lanka to have sex with minors. The U.S. Attorney General (U.S. Department of Justice, 2010) specifically names countries in Southeast Asia, Latin America, and Eastern Europe in his National Strategy report.

Western Europe, and Australia. Yet much of the child pornography production and commercial sexual exploitation involves second-world countries; for
example, underage girls are trafficked for prostitution into Western Europe
or North America from poorer countries in Eastern Europe, Asia, and South
America. The response to online offending can be seen as part of a broader
movement against sexual exploitation and abuse of any kind. It can also be
seen as part of a broader movement recognizing that first-world nations have
a moral obligation to care about the impact of their actions on less developed
countries (e.g., worker conditions in China and other places where our goods
are produced). Put in this broader context, human rights is a universal issue.

It is hard to escape the conclusion that a major impetus for the investment of resources in combating online sexual offending is a moral one. The
ideas that someone is sexually interested in children and wants to view child
pornography, that someone masturbates and fantasizes to that content, that
someone is a pedophile, are abhorrent to many. I understand this moral reaction, and I understand why the public and politicians want to target online
sexual offenders. But these policy choices can have unintended consequences.
They can further drive pedophilia and hebephilia underground, away from
potential help to prevent sexual offending; they divert resources from the
still ongoing problems of direct sexual exploitation and abuse, and they are
changing the face of the Internet and of society, as laws and regulations are
implemented that affect online privacy and activity in the name of protecting children. How can we reconcile our moral outrage at the recognition that
sexual exploitation or abuse has been digitally memorialized, as I described
in the Introduction to this volume, with the realization that such individuals
are unlikely to sexually reoffend and cause further harm? I believe that inef-
ficiency, ineffectiveness, and injustice will fill the gap between what we know
and what we believe in setting policy and practice if empirical evidence does
not lead our responses. It is my hope that this book has provided an objective,
balanced, and comprehensive overview of what we know about online sexual
offending, to inform policy and practice in coming years.

RESOURCE A:
JUVENILE PROSTITUTION, TRAFFICKING, AND SEX TOURISM

JUVENILE PROSTITUTION

Juvenile prostitution involves minors exchanging sex for money, food, or drugs. The average age of entry is during adolescence (McClanahan, McClelland, Abram, & Teplin, 1999; Potterat, Rothenberg, Muth, Darrow, & Phillips-Plummer, 1998). A common story is that an adolescent turns to prostitution (or is forced into it) because they have run away from home or are kicked out by a parent or guardian and have few other options to financially support themselves (Bittle, 2002; Cusick, 2002). It is rare for runaway or throwaway (kicked out by their parent or guardian) children to leave home before the age of 12; in fact, approximately two thirds of runaway or throwaway children leave home between the ages of 15 and 17 (Hammer, Finkelhor, & Sedlak, 2002). Hammer et al. (2002) found that only a small proportion (1%) of runaway or throwaway children ended up involved in prostitution, with a total of 1,700 prostitution cases out of 38,600 children who were identified in their study to be at risk of sexual exploitation or harm.

Juvenile prostitution in Canada or the United States is unlikely to be associated with pedophilia or hebephilia. Younger children are occasionally involved but usually only as a result of parent or guardian involvement. For example, Faller (1991) found that 16 of the 48 multi-incest families she studied had allegedly used a child within the family for the production of child pornography or for juvenile prostitution. Inciardi (1984) described cases of young girls under the age of 12 who were pimped by a parent. There are also recent online examples, including mothers who allow their children to be pornographically photographed or who provide sexual access to their children in exchange for money or drugs or to maintain a relationship with an adult man who is sexually interested in both her and the children.

There has been a shift in recent years toward seeing juvenile prostitution as a child protection rather than delinquency or social services problem (Mitchell, Finkelhor, & Wolak, 2010). Mitchell and her colleagues (2010) surveyed law enforcement agencies about juvenile prostitution cases and distinguished three types of cases: (a) youths working on their own, including runaways or homeless youths as well as youths who were living at home but earning money through prostitution on the side; (b) youths working under third parties such as pimps or brothel owners, which included owners of escort services, massage parlors, and strip clubs; and (c) conventional child sexual abuse cases, where the perpetrator gave money or gifts of value to the youth to maintain his or her silence.

Almost all of the juvenile prostitution cases involved female youths, with most ranging in age from 14 to 17; only 11% of the prostituted youths were under the age of 14. Solo youths were more likely to be male (23%) and teenaged than were third-party cases, though this finding was limited by the amount of missing information for solo youth cases. Child sexual abuse cases were also more likely to involve male youths (22%), and more of these cases (23%) involved persons under age 14. Excluding child sexual abuse cases, most prostitution (98%) involved exchanging sex for money, though there were some cases involving the exchange of sex for alcohol or drugs or a place to stay. The Internet was involved in only a minority of cases, presumably through online advertisements or profiles.

JUVENILE SEXUAL TRAFFICKING

Some prostitutes are trafficked for commercial sexual purposes, either from other parts of the country or internationally. Much of the discussion of sexual trafficking has focused on international trafficking of women and children from less affluent "source" countries to more affluent "destination" countries. Malarek (2004), for example, has written about trafficking of Eastern European women to Canada and the United States.

ECPAT International has also documented sex trafficking, whereby minors are moved both within countries and across countries to provide workers for commercial sex businesses such as strip clubs and massage parlors. Advocates have aptly described many of these minors as modern-day slaves because they are bought and sold, are not paid for their work, and are not free to leave. Broad sociopolitical factors such as poverty; birth rate; the social roles of children, especially girls; and organized crime play roles. Gray, Gourley, and Paul (1996, as cited in Lim, 1998) estimated that 40% of the child prostitutes they studied were sold by their own families, and 15% were sold by "friends." Parents may wittingly or unwittingly (e.g., if they are deceived that their child would work as a servant) participate in this activity. An example of willing parental participation is the Thai practice of *tok khiew* for girls from relatively poorer northern villages. A girl's parents are given a loan when the girl reaches the age of 9 or 10, and they are given more money when she turns 12 or 13. She then has to work as a prostitute to pay off this loan (see Flamm, 1996, as cited in Lim, 1998). The girl is expected to obey her parents and can still get married and live a conventional life on returning to the village. The routes for the Southeast Asian traffic into southern Thailand were described by Lim (1998) and include girls from the hill tribes of northern Thailand, Cambodia, Laos, and Myanmar.

Nongovernmental agencies such as ECPAT USA (http://ecpatusa.org; an American member of the ECPAT network) and the Thorn Foundation (http://wearethorn.org) have begun drawing attention to the problem of domestic trafficking—that is, the movement of women and minors from one area of the United States to another for prostitution purposes (see also Sher, 2011). Mitchell, Jones, Finkelhor, and Wolak (2011) analyzed data from the National Juvenile Online Victimization Project, focusing on cases of commercial sexual exploitation that were facilitated by the Internet. Cases (total number was 106) were uncommon, as with juvenile prostitution investigations more generally, suggesting that this is not a high priority for law enforcement (therefore, few cases are investigated) or that the problem is not as large as some have argued.

Mitchell et al. (2011) distinguished between two types of Internet-facilitated commercial sexual exploitation of children (prostitution/trafficking or child pornography). Approximately a third involved the use of the Internet to advertise or purchase sexual access to minors or to child pornography that the offender produced. The remaining majority of cases involved the use of the Internet to sell or purchase child pornography that the offender did not produce himself. Sale of child pornography was uncommon, representing only 10% of the child pornography distribution cases. This is consistent with anecdotal observations that commercially produced child pornography content is rare (M. Collins, 2012; United Nations Office on Drugs and Crime, 2010). Instead, much of the child pornography that is available online is amateur-produced and freely traded. Money is being made from this form of child exploitation but in modest amounts.

As with other online offender samples from the National Juvenile Online Victimization Project and from other studies, almost all offenders in these commercial cases of child sexual exploitation were male, older (40 years old or older), and predominantly Caucasian. They had diverse educational and occupational backgrounds, however, and approximately one fifth (21%) were married at the time of their arrest. The minority who profited from child pornography production were younger, more likely to be African American, less likely to have finished high school, and less likely to be employed full time. Those who profited also had more extensive criminal histories and were more likely to produce child pornography themselves and offend with others. The authors concluded that these results indicate targeting profiteers would result in the arrest of a more antisocial and exploitative group of offenders. Most of the few female offenders in this study were in the for-profit group.

Data were also available on the sexually exploited minors for a subset of cases in Mitchell et al. (2011). As in the previous study by Mitchell, Finkelhor, and Wolak (2010) on juvenile prostitution, the majority of Internet-facilitated victims were female (82%) and between the ages of 13 and 17 (71%). Twenty-one percent were between the ages of 6 and 12. In slightly more than half the cases (53%), offenders were family relatives or acquaintances such as neighbors, relatives of friends, or trusted adults such as teachers or leaders of a youth organization.

There is evidence of organized crime involvement in juvenile prostitution and trafficking for commercial sexual purposes. Prostitution can be more profitable and is lower risk than other organized crime activities such as drug or firearms trafficking. In his National Strategy report, the United States Attorney General noted the existence of pimping circuits and networks across the United States, where prostituted minors are transported to different cities as "fresh faces" and for special events such as major sports games (United States Department of Justice, 2010). It is not clear, however, how large this organized crime involvement is and how the Internet and related technologies might play a role in this crime.

JUVENILE SEX TOURISM

Sex tourism involves travel by adults to locations where they can more freely engage in sexual contacts with minors because the laws or law enforcement is less stringent (e.g., in countries with insufficient policing resources or where corruption allows tourists to pay their way out of trouble). Sex tourism is related to juvenile prostitution because the minors (or, more likely, their pimps) are being paid for sex, and it is related to sexual trafficking because many prostitutes are trafficked in the countries that are best known for sex tourism. Child pornography can be involved as well, as when tourists travel to locations to take images and videos of children in sexual situations or to record their own sexual interactions with children.

Like almost all other forms of commerce, the Internet is playing a role in child sex tourism. Though it is more difficult to find now, there was a time when information about sex tours could be found in publicly accessible sites. It is likely still the case that information can be found through private chat rooms and the darker corners of the online landscape. This can be contrasted with sex tourism pre-Internet. For example, Lloyd (1976) described a cheaply produced travel guide called *Where the Young Ones Are* that listed places across the United States where male youths involved in prostitution could be found. This appears to have been a real guide; O'Brien (1983) investigated the guide and found that the Los Angeles sites listed were known by local police to be prostitution hot spots. Pre-Internet, this guide would have been difficult to obtain; one would have to know where to get a copy and would then have to be careful about hiding the guide, a physical object. In the Internet era, however, such information can be posted and accessed surreptitiously.

It is hard to find solid data on the extent and nature of juvenile sex tourism. Many political and social policy estimates exist, but the bases for many of these estimates are dubious. For example, Lim (1998) pointed out that ECPAT International had estimated in 1992 that there might be 200,000 to 800,000 child prostitutes in Thailand, an unlikely estimate given that those high numbers would mean approximately a quarter of the entire population of Thai minors was involved in prostitution. The government estimated the number of child prostitutes as 13,000, with approximately 10% being boys, whereas a national commission that was independent of the Thai government put the estimated number at 30,000. This range of values points out the problem of relying on guesstimates, especially from advocacy groups or others who have reasons to make a problem seem larger (or smaller) than it really is.

Focusing on Southeast Asia, Bruce (1996, as cited in Lim, 1998) studied 2,626 women and girls rescued by Malaysian police between 1986 and 1990 and found that half were under the age of 18, with the rest between the ages of 18 and 21. The sample was relatively young because of how they were identified. Lim (1998) also cited a 1992 survey of Indonesian prostitutes working in a large brothel and found that 10% were below age 17; 20% of adult prostitutes had begun working before age 17. Lim reported a survey suggesting that one fifth of prostitutes surveyed in a brothel reported starting between ages of 13 and 15. Gray et al. (1996, as cited in Lim, 1998) reported that at least one third of commercial sex workers were between the ages of 12 and 17 in a major survey of Phnom Penh and 11 Cambodian provinces. Sinha (1996, as cited in Lim, 1998) reported that a quarter of prostitutes are minors, many beginning before the age of 15.

Bruce (1996, as cited in Lim, 1998) reported that 2% of 685 bar workers (hostesses and bar-based prostitutes) were 15 years old or younger at the time they were surveyed; most were likely to be adolescents, because one would expect few young children to be in bars frequented by foreign tourists. This is not to suggest that child prostitution did not exist; instead, it would be invisible in bars popular with foreign tourists. Of the bar workers, 15% were under age 18, but the mean age was 20. Eleven percent of the workers reported engaging in their first sex work at or before the age of 15. The age distributions suggested to Bruce that there was a high degree of turnover, with some adolescents starting and leaving within a year.

There are several caveats regarding the research reported here. Younger girls are uncommon or may not be reached by rescue efforts. It is also hard to know ages precisely in jurisdictions with poor institutional record keeping, and estimating age by appearances can be challenging, especially where malnutrition can greatly affect physical maturation (Rosenbloom & Tanner, 1998; Stathopulu, Huse, & Canning, 2003). Nonetheless, these studies suggest that minors (persons under age 18) are involved in the domestic and international sex trade.

RESOURCE B:
ASSESSMENT OF ONLINE OFFENDERS

The increasing numbers of online offenders seen in clinical and criminal justice settings means there is increasing demand for assessments to understand the online offending behaviors and to identify risk to reoffend and the needs that might be the targets of treatment or supervision. In this appendix, I make some recommendations for how to proceed. I do not list specific measures because I have already done so in an appendix to my 2008 book, because the research is fast-moving enough that new measures are expected to supplant my recommendations, and because there are no well-validated specific measures yet for online sexual behavior and online offending parameters.

The literature reviewed in this book has suggested that a sound basis for a clinical evaluation of an online offender would cover the following domains, assessed through interviews, questionnaires, review of collateral information, and objective assessment measures:

- *Sexual development*, including early exposure to sex or pornography, sexual abuse, sexual onset (sexual feelings, masturbation, partnered sex), pornography use (age, frequency, type), sexual partner history, and sexual interests.
- *Antisocial behavior*, including early conduct problems, undetected delinquency, nonsexual misbehavior, and criminal history.
- *Online behavior*, including total time spent online; involvement with legal online pornography, particularly with paraphilic content; other online sexual behavior (sexual chat, casual liaisons); involvement in online sex forums; and familiarity with privacy and security measures.
- *Online offending*, including involvement with child and other illegal pornography, images of young children or images of boys, frequency of use, context (e.g., masturbation while viewing), sexual solicitations of minors, and use of online technologies to commit other kinds of sexual offenses, such as hiring juvenile prostitutes, engaging in juvenile sex tourism, and committing sexual offenses against adults.
- *Risk to reoffend*, including adaptations of actuarial risk measures developed for conventional sex offenders such as the Static–99 or Risk Matrix 2000 and dynamic risk measures such as the Stable–2007 (see Chapter 7).
- *Treatment readiness and offense pathway(s)* (see Chapter 8).

Interviews are the most efficient way to capture all of this information, whereas questionnaires are helpful for gathering information about more sensitive topics such as sexual history. Because of self-report biases, collateral information is important to obtain, including forensic analyses of digital pornography content and online behavior; objective assessments of sexual interests such as phallometric testing, which involves the measurement of sexual arousal to different kinds of sexual stimuli in the laboratory; and interviews with other persons (e.g., family members regarding developmental history and spouse regarding sexual behavior; see Kalmus & Beech, 2005).

RESOURCE C: TREATMENT

As described in more detail in Chapter 8, existing treatment approaches are mostly based on modifications of treatment components from the relapse prevention, addictions, and more general criminological literature. Much research on both sexual and nonsexual offenders has suggested that treatments will be most effective when they meet the risk, need, and responsivity principles articulated by Andrews and Bonta (2010), with interventions titrated to risk to reoffend (risk principle), aimed at dynamic risk factors that can be changed through intervention (need principle), and responsive to the individual's learning style and circumstances (responsivity principle). Other intervention research shows that offender interventions are most effective when they are concrete, problem-focused, and pragmatic. Effect sizes are not large, unfortunately, but even small reductions in recidivism can lead to meaningful impacts on victimization rates and the other costs of offending. Evaluations are essential to demonstrate efficacy (whether treatments can reduce reoffending in principle) and effectiveness (whether treatments can reduce reoffending in practice in real world settings when training can be suboptimal, treatment fidelity can drift, and where resources are more limited). On the basis of the literature on effective offender treatment, an evidence-based treatment approach would likely involve

- treatment streaming on the basis of a comprehensive assessment of the individual's motivations for online offending, offending pathway(s), motivation to change, capacity to participate in treatment, and risk to reoffend;
- a preparatory phase to increase motivation to change;
- cognitive–behavioral treatment to increase self-regulation skills, sexual and nonsexual, emphasizing the classic learning techniques of modeling, role play, and rehearsal;
- behavioral treatment to increase voluntary control of paraphilic sexual arousal (pedophilia, hebephilia, exhibitionism, voyeurism, sadism) if this is identified as a treatment need;
- booster sessions to maintain gains and to provide after care as the individual leaves treatment; and
- titrated supervision focusing on dynamic risk factors identified in initial and follow-up assessments, including paraphilic

sexual arousal, substance use, access to children, and access to the Internet.

Given the relatively low recidivism rates that have been observed so far, it is likely that many online offenders do not require treatment. Instead, sentencing and supervision may be sufficient. Given limited resources, treatment programs should be reserved for higher risk online offenders.

RESOURCE D:
GLOSSARY OF TECHNICAL TERMS

actuarial: In the forensic context, this refers to a class of risk assessment measures that combine empirically supported risk factors in an algorithmic way (e.g., through explicit scoring and weighing schemes) to produce a probabilistic estimate of the likelihood that someone will reoffend. For contact sex offenders, the most widely used and validated actuarial risk measure is the Static–99 (see http://www.static99.org).

anime: A Japanese style of animation that often features adult themes. It is a feature in online sexual offense investigations because some child pornography offenders have images or videos of animated (hand-drawn or computer-generated) depictions of children in sexual situations. Such content can still be indicative of sexual interest in children, even though it might not meet the jurisdiction's legal definition of child pornography.

antisociality: A term used by me and a number of colleagues to refer to a broad constellation of traits associated with persistent antisocial and criminal behavior. Antisociality involves antisocial attitudes and beliefs (e.g., views tolerant of sexual offenses involving children), antisocial personality traits such as impulsivity and callousness, and cognitive sets (e.g., a tendency to view the world as selfish or hostile).

area under the curve (AUC):   An index of diagnostic or prediction accuracy, ranging from 0.50 (chance) to 1.00 (perfect). The AUC value can be interpreted as the proportion of a randomly selected recidivist would have a higher score than a randomly selected non-recidivist.

chat room: A generic term that can be used to describe any online platform that allows interactive communications between users, including message boards on which users can simultaneously post to different ongoing discussions, instant messaging, and graphical environments, as in multiplayer gaming sites. Interactive communication is a feature in many online technologies, including social networking sites and some peer-to-peer networks.

Combating Paedophile Information Networks in Europe (COPINE):   An influential early research project on online child pornography. The COPINE scale was developed to rank child pornography content by severity; a modified version of this scale is part of the sentencing guidelines in the United Kingdom. The COPINE Project developed the croga.org site, and its large database of child pornography images is now managed by Interpol.

computer-generated imagery (CGI):   Imagery that is increasingly realistic (as demonstrated by Hollywood-produced blockbuster films) and already used to create virtual pornography that does not involve real persons.

grooming: In the literature on sexual offending, this refers to deliberate tactics used to gain the trust and cooperation of children for sexual purposes—for example, to convince them to participate in child pornography activities, engage in sexual chat, or to meet in real life (if they met online) to engage in sexual activity.

hebephilia: Clinically and scientifically defined as a sexual attraction to pubescent children—that is, children who are showing some signs of pubertal development such as breast budding, genital changes, and the development of axillary hair, but who are clearly not physically mature. Can be distinguished from *pedophilia*, a sexual attraction to prepubescent children (i.e., children who are not showing any signs of pubertal development). Hebephilia does not refer to sexual attraction to older adolescents who appear to be physically mature and who could be mistaken by naive observers to be 18 or older.

instant messaging: Real-time exchange of messages between device users, which could include instant messaging software but also instant messaging or chat features in social networks and other platforms. More broadly, this could include text messages sent by mobile phone.

Internet protocol (IP) address: A unique number assigned to each networked device that uses the Internet protocol to communicate with other devices. The Internet protocol in turn is the main protocol for communicating data packets across networks. The IP address can be fixed for a particular device or, as when someone signs onto the Internet through a local number, be dynamically assigned for a single session. Thus, an individual user accessing child pornography at different times can be responsible for multiple IP addresses associated with this activity by logging on using different devices or by signing on at different times through the same Internet service provider.

Internet service provider (ISP): The first point of contact for most people when accessing the Internet from home, workplace, or other location. Someone with broadband access to the Internet at home, for example, pays a fee to a cable or telecom company for that access.

morphing: The use of digital image editing software to seamlessly transition from one image to another. Also used to describe the combination of multiple images to create a new seamless image, for example, when someone digitally edits a known child's face onto the body of an unknown child depicted in child pornography or when an image of an adult model is digitally altered to resemble a minor.

pedophilia: Clinically and scientifically defined as a sexual attraction to prepubescent children—that is, children who are not showing any signs of pubertal development. Can be distinguished from *hebephilia*, a sexual attraction to pubescent children (i.e., children who are showing some signs of pubertal development such as breast budding, genital changes, and the development of axillary hair but who are clearly not physically mature).

peer-to-peer (P2P) network: These networks allow each computer device to act as either a client (e.g., requesting files) or server (e.g., providing files) for other computers on the network. Each computer, called a *node*, can therefore share files or tasks without a central server organizing the activity. P2P networks are popularly used to share music and other media files, often, though not exclusively in pirated form, including pornography. Child pornography is available through P2P networks.

search engine: A software program or interface for retrieving files or other data, especially from the Internet.

sexting: The sending of sexually explicit text or images, primarily between mobile phones. Sexually explicit images of a minor could constitute child pornography, such that a 16-year-old girl who sent a nude image of herself to her same-aged boyfriend could be charged with production and distribution of child pornography, and her boyfriend could be charged with possession.

sexual deviance: Along with *deviant sexual interests*, refers to persistent and recurrent sexual interests that are statistically rare, are maladaptive in the evolutionary sense, and that contravene social norms. In the context of this book, sexual deviance refers to *pedophilia* (interest in prepubescent children), *hebephilia* (interest in pubescent children), *exhibitionism* (interest in exposing one's genitals to unsuspecting strangers), *voyeurism* (interest in watching unsuspecting strangers undress or engage in other normally private activities), *sadism* (interest in causing suffering or humiliation), and *biastophilia* (interest in coercive sex, i.e., sex with nonconsenting persons).

social networking: An online platform that facilitates social networking among users who share real-life connections, interests, or backgrounds. Users create a profile that can be accessed by others. At the time this entry was written, the most well-known and popular social networking sites in North America included Facebook, Google+, and LinkedIn. The popularity of social networking sites waxes and wanes with momentum (more popular sites become even more popular because the opportunities for networking exponentially increase), user features, and shifting concerns about privacy and how user data will be used.

REFERENCES

Abbey, A., Zawacki, T., & McAuslan, P. (2000). Alcohol's effects on sexual perception. *Journal of Studies on Alcohol, 61*, 688–697.

Abel, G. G., Becker, J. V., Cunningham-Rathner, J., Mittelman, M., & Rouleau, J. L. (1988). Multiple paraphilic diagnoses among sex offenders. *The Bulletin of the American Academy of Psychiatry and the Law, 16*, 153–168.

Abel, G. G., Becker, J. V., Mittelman, M., Cunningham-Rathner, J., Rouleau, J. L., & Murphy, W. D. (1987). Self-reported sex crimes of nonincarcerated paraphiliacs. *Journal of Interpersonal Violence, 2*, 3–25. doi:10.1177/088626087002001001

Abel, G. G., Gore, D. K., Holland, C. L., Camp, N., Becker, J. V., & Rathner, J. (1989). The measurement of the cognitive distortions of child molesters. *Annals of Sex Research, 2*, 135–153.

Abel, G. G., Huffman, J., Warberg, B., & Holland, C. L. (1998). Visual reaction time and plethysmography as measures of sexual interest in child molesters. *Sexual Abuse: A Journal of Research and Treatment, 10*, 81–95.

Abma, J. C., Martinez, G. M., Mosher, W. D., & Dawson, B. S. (2004). *Teenagers in the United States: Sexual activity, contraceptive use, and childbearing, 2002.* Retrieved from http://www.cdc.gov/nchs/data/series/sr_23/sr23_024.pdf

Adam Walsh Child Protection and Safety Act of 2006, H.R. 4472, 109 Cong. U.S.C. §16.911 et. seq. (2006).

Ahlers, C. J., Schaefer, G. A., Mundt, I. A., Roll, S., Englert, H., Willich, S. N., & Beier, K. M. (2011). How unusual are the contents of paraphilias? Paraphilia-associated sexual arousal patterns in a community-based sample of men. *Journal of Sexual Medicine, 8*, 1362–1370. doi:10.1111/j.1743-6109.2009.01597.x

Ahlmeyer, S., Heil, P., McKee, B., & English, K. (2000). The impact of polygraphy on admissions of victims and offenses in adult sexual offenders. *Sexual Abuse: A Journal of Research and Treatment, 12*, 123–138.

Alexy, E. M., Burgess, A. N., & Baker, T. (2005). Internet offenders: Traders, travelers, and combination trader–travelers. *Journal of Interpersonal Violence, 20*, 804–812. doi:10.1177/0886260505276091

Allan, M., Grace, R. C., Rutherford, B., & Hudson, S. M. (2007). Psychometric assessment of dynamic risk factors for child molesters. *Sexual Abuse: A Journal of Research and Treatment, 19*, 347–367.

Allen, M., D'Alessio, D., & Brezgel, K. (1995). A meta-analysis summarizing the effects of pornography. II: Aggression after exposure. *Human Communication Research, 22*, 258–283. doi:10.1111/j.1468-2958.1995.tb00368.x

Allen, M., D'Alessio, D., & Emmers-Sommer, T. M. (2000). Reaction of criminal sexual offenders to pornography: A meta-analytic summary. In M. Roloff (Ed.), *Communication Yearbook 22* (pp. 139–169). Thousand Oaks, CA: Sage.

Allen, M., Emmers, T. M., Gebhardt, L., & Giery, M. A. (1995). Exposure to pornography and acceptance of rape myths. *Journal of Communication, 45*, 5–26. doi:10.1111/j.1460-2466.1995.tb00711.x

Allen, M., Emmers-Sommer, T., D'Alessio, D., Timmerman, L., Hanzal, A., & Korus, J. (2007). The connection between the physiological and psychological reactions to sexually explicit materials: A literature summary using meta-analysis. *Communication Monographs, 74*, 541–560. doi:10.1080/03637750701578648

American Psychiatric Association. (2000). *Diagnostic and statistical manual of mental disorders* (4th ed., text rev.). Washington, DC: Author.

American Psychiatric Association. (2012). *DSM–5 development.* Retrieved from http://www.dsm5.org/Pages/Default.aspx

Anderson, C. (2012). *The impact of pornography on children, youth, and culture.* Holyoke, MA: NEARI Press.

Anderson, C. A., Berkowitz, L., Donnerstein, E., Huesmann, R. L., Johnson, J., Linz, D., . . . Wartella, E. (2003). The influence of media violence on youth. *Psychological Science in the Public Interest, 4*, 81–110.

Anderson, C. A., & Bushman, B. J. (2002, March 29). The effects of media violence on society. *Science, 295*(5564), 2377–2379. doi:10.1126/science.1070765

Andrews, D. A., & Bonta, J. (2010). *The psychology of criminal conduct* (5th ed.). Cincinnati, OH: Anderson.

Anonymous. (1890). *When a child loves and when one hates: A tale of birch and bed by a gentleman.* [Privately printed and distributed.] Kinsey Institute, Bloomington, IN.

Anonymous. (1898). *Private letters from Phyllis to Marie, or the art of child-love, or the adventures and experiences of a little girl.* [Privately printed and distributed.] Kinsey Institute, Bloomington, IN.

Aos, S., Lieb, R., Mayfield, J., Miller, M., & Pennucci, A. (2004). *Benefits and costs of prevention and early intervention programs for youth.* Olympia, WA: Washington State Institute for Public Policy.

Aos, S., Phipps, P., Barnoski, R., & Lieb, R. (2001). *The comparative costs and benefits of programs to reduce crime: Version 4.0.* Olympia, WA: Washington State Institute for Public Policy.

Ariès, P. (1962). *Centuries of childhood: A social history of family life.* New York, NY: Knopf.

Ashcroft v. Free Speech Coalition, 535 U.S. 234 (2002).

Association for the Treatment of Sexual Abusers. (2010). *Statement supporting the use of randomized control trials for the evaluation of sex offender treatment.* Retrieved from http://www.atsa.com/statement-supporting-use-randomized-control-trials-evaluation-sexual-offender-treatment

Association for the Treatment of Sexual Abusers. (2011). *Risk assessment.* Retrieved from http://www.atsa.com/risk-assessment

Atkinson, J. L. (1996). Female sex offenders: A literature review. *Forum on Corrections Research, 8*(2), 39–42.

Baartz, D. (2008). *Australians, the Internet and technology—Enabled child sex abuse: A statistical profile* (Research report). Canberra, Australia: Australian Federal Police.

Babchishin, K. M. (2012, September). *Internet sex offenders: Reviewing research findings and their Implications for policy and practice.* Invited workshop presented at the 12th International Association for the Treatment of Sexual Abusers (IATSO) conference, Berlin, Germany.

Babchishin, K. M., Hanson, R. K., & Hermann, C. A. (2011). The characteristics of online sexual offenders: A meta-analysis. *Sexual Abuse: A Journal of Research and Treatment, 23,* 92–123. doi:10.1177/1079063210370708

Bader, S. M., Schoeneman-Morris, K. A., Scalora, M. J., & Casady, T. K. (2008). Exhibitionism: Findings from a Midwestern police contact sample. *International Journal of Offender Therapy and Comparative Criminology, 52,* 270–279. doi:10.1177/0306624X07307122

Bagley, C. (2003). Diminishing incidence of Internet child pornographic images. *Psychological Reports, 93,* 305–306.

Baker, N. (1992). *Vox.* New York, NY: Vintage.

Banse, R., Schmidt, A. F., & Clarbour, J. (2010). Indirect measures of sexual interest in child sex offenders: A multimethod approach. *Criminal Justice and Behavior, 37,* 319–335. doi:10.1177/0093854809357598

Barbaree, H. E., Langton, C. M., Blanchard, R., & Cantor, J. M. (2009). Aging versus stable enduring traits as explanatory constructs in sex offender recidivism: Partitioning actuarial prediction into conceptually meaningful components. *Criminal Justice and Behavior, 36,* 443–465. doi:10.1177/0093854809332283

Barbaree, H. E., & Marshall, W. L. (1991). The role of male sexual arousal in rape: Six models. *Journal of Consulting and Clinical Psychology, 59,* 621–630. doi:10.1037/0022-006X.59.5.621

Barbaree, H. E., Seto, M. C., Langton, C. M., & Peacock, E. J. (2001). Evaluating the predictive accuracy of six risk assessment instruments for adult sex offenders. *Criminal Justice and Behavior, 28,* 490–521. doi:10.1177/009385480102800406

Barbaree, H. E., Seto, M. C., & Maric, A. (1997). *Sex offender characteristics, response to treatment, and correctional release decisions at the Warkworth Sexual Behaviour Clinic* (Research Report 1997-73). Ottawa, Ontario, Canada: Ministry of the Solicitor-General and Correctional Service of Canada.

Barlow, J. P. (1996). *A declaration of the independence of cyberspace.* Retrieved from https://projects.eff.org/~barlow/Declaration-Final.html

Barnett, G. D., Wakeling, H. C., & Howard, P. D. (2010). An examination of the predictive validity of the Risk Matrix 2000 in England and Wales. *Sexual Abuse: A Journal of Research and Treatment, 22,* 443–470. Doi: 10.1177/1079063210384274.

Bartosh, D. L., Garby, T., Lewis, D., & Gray, S. (2003). Differences in the predictive validity of actuarial risk assessments in relation to sex offender type. *International Journal of Offender Therapy and Comparative Criminology, 47,* 422–438. doi:10.1177/0306624X03253850

Bates, A., & Metcalf, C. (2007). A psychometric comparison of Internet and non-Internet sex offenders from a community treatment sample. *Journal of Sexual Aggression, 13,* 11–20. doi:10.1080/13552600701365654

Becker, J. V., & Stein, R. M. (1991). Is sexual erotica associated with sexual deviance in adolescent males? *International Journal of Law and Psychiatry, 14,* 85–95. doi:10.1016/0160-2527(91)90026-J

Beier, K. M., Neutze, J., Mundt, I. A., Ahlers, C. J., Goecker, D., Konrad, A., & Schaefer, G. A. (2009). Encouraging self-identified pedophiles and hebephiles to seek professional help: First results of the Berlin Prevention Project Dunkelfeld (PPD). *Child Abuse & Neglect, 33,* 545–549. doi:10.1016/j.chiabu.2009.04.002

Bernard, F. (1985). *Paedophilia: A factual report.* Rotterdam, The Netherlands: Enclave Press.

Bhuller, M., Havnes, T., Leuven, E., & Mogstad, M. (2011). *Broadband Internet: An information superhighway to sex crime?* (Discussion Paper No. 5675). Retrieved from http://ftp.iza.org/dp5675.pdf

Bickley, J. A., & Beech, A. R. (2002). An investigation of the Ward and Hudson pathways model of the sexual offense process with child abusers. *Journal of Interpersonal Violence, 17,* 371–393. doi:10.1177/0886260502017004002

Bingham, C. R., & Crockett, L. J. (1996). Longitudinal adjustment patterns of boys and girls experiencing early, middle, and late sexual intercourse. *Developmental Psychology, 32,* 647–658. doi:10.1037/0012-1649.32.4.647

Bittle, S. (2002). *Youth involvement in prostitution: A literature review and annotated bibliography* (Research Report 2001-13e). Research and Statistics Division, Department of Justice Canada.

Blanchard, R. (2009). Reply to letters regarding *Pedophilia, Hebephilia, and the DSM–V. Archives of Sexual Behavior, 38,* 331–334. doi:10.1007/s10508-008-9427-9

Blanchard, R. (2010a). The *DSM* diagnostic criteria for pedophilia. *Archives of Sexual Behavior, 39,* 304–316. doi:10.1007/s10508-009-9536-0

Blanchard, R. (2010b). The fertility of hebephiles and the adaptationist argument against including hebephilia in *DSM–5* [Letter to the editor]. *Archives of Sexual Behavior, 39,* 817–818. doi:10.1007/s10508-010-9610-7

Blanchard, R. (2010c). The specificity of victim count as a diagnostic indicator of pedohebephilia [Letter to the editor]. *Archives of Sexual Behavior, 39,* 1245–1252. doi:10.1007/s10508-010-9659-3

Blanchard, R., Klassen, P., Dickey, R., Kuban, M. E., & Blak, T. (2001). Sensitivity and specificity of the phallometric test for pedophilia in nonadmitting sex offenders. *Psychological Assessment, 13,* 118–126. doi:10.1037/1040-3590.13.1.118

Blanchard, R., Kolla, N. J., Cantor, J. M., Klassen, P. E., Dickey, R., Kuban, M. E., & Blak, T. (2007). IQ, handedness, and pedophilia in adult male patients stratified by referral source. *Sexual Abuse: A Journal of Research and Treatment, 19,* 285–309.

Blanchard, R., Kuban, M. E., Blak, T., Klassen, P. E., Dickey, R., & Cantor, J. M. (2012). Sexual attraction to others: A comparison of two models of alloerotic responding in men. *Archives of Sexual Behavior, 41*(1), 13–29. doi:10.1007/s10508-010-9675-3

Blanchard, R., Lykins, A. D., Wherrett, D., Kuban, M. E., Cantor, J. M., Blak, T., . . . Klassen, P. E. (2009). Pedophilia, hebephilia, and the *DSM–V*. *Archives of Sexual Behavior, 38*, 335–350. doi:10.1007/s10508-008-9399-9

Boas, G. (1966). *The cult of childhood*. London, England: Warburg.

Boeringer, S. (1994). Pornography and sexual aggression: Associations of violent and nonviolent depictions with rape and rape proclivity. *Deviant Behavior, 15*, 289–304. doi:10.1080/01639625.1994.9967974

Bogaert, A. F. (2001). Personality, individual differences, and preferences for sexual media. *Archives of Sexual Behavior, 30*, 29–53. doi:10.1023/A:1026416723291

Bonta, J., Law, M., & Hanson, R. K. (1998). The prediction of criminal and violent recidivism among mentally disordered offenders. *Psychological Bulletin, 123*, 123–142. http://dx.doi.org/10.1037//0033-2909.123.2.123

Bonta, J., Pang, B., & Wallace-Capretta, S. (1995). Predictors of recidivism among incarcerated female offenders. *Prison Journal, 75*, 277–294.

Bonta, J., Zinger, I., Harris, A., & Carrière, D. (1998). The dangerous offender provisions: Are they targeting the right offenders? *Canadian Journal of Criminology, 40*, 377–400.

Borduin, C. M., Schaeffer, C. M., & Heiblum, N. (2009). A randomized clinical trial of multisystemic therapy with juvenile sexual offenders: Effects on youth social ecology and criminal activity. *Journal of Consulting and Clinical Psychology, 77*, 26–37. doi:10.1037/a0013035

Bourke, M. L., & Hernandez, A. E. (2009). The "Butner Study" redux: A report of the incidence of hands-on child victimization by child pornography offenders. *Journal of Family Violence, 24*, 183–191. doi:10.1007/s10896-008-9219-y

Bradford, J. M., Boulet, J., & Pawlak, A. (1992). The paraphilias: A multiplicity of deviant behaviours. *Canadian Journal of Psychiatry/La Revue canadienne de psychiatrie, 37*, 104–108.

Briere, J., & Runtz, M. (1989). University males' sexual interest in children: Predicting potential indices of "pedophilia" in a non-forensic sample. *Child Abuse & Neglect, 13*, 65–75. doi:10.1016/0145-2134(89)90030-6

Briggs, P., Simon, W. T., & Simonsen, S. (2011). An exploratory study of Internet-initiated sexual offenses and the chat room sex offender: Has the Internet enabled a new typology of sex offender? *Sexual Abuse: A Journal of Research and Treatment, 23*, 72–91.

Brown, I. A. (1997). Theoretical model of behavioral addictions applied to offending. In J. E. Hodge, M. McMurran, & C. R. Hollin (Eds.), *Addicted to crime?* (pp. 13–65). New York, NY: Wiley.

Brown, J. D., L'Engle, K. L., Pardun, C. J., Guang, G., Kenneavy, K., & Jackson, C. (2006). Sexy media matter: Exposure to sexual content in music, movies, television and magazines predicts Black and White adolescents' sexual behavior. *Pediatrics, 117,* 1018–1027. doi:10.1542/peds.2005-1406

Brown, S. L., St. Amand, M. D., & Zamble, E. (2009). The dynamic prediction of criminal recidivism: A three-wave prospective study. *Law and Human Behavior, 33,* 25–45. doi:10.1007/s10979-008-9139-7

Budin, L. E., & Johnson, C. F. (1989). Sex abuse prevention programs: Offenders' attitudes about their efficacy. *Child Abuse & Neglect, 13,* 77–87. doi:10.1016/0145-2134(89)90031-8

Burgess, A. W., Carretta, C. M., & Burgess, A. G. (2012). Patterns of federal Internet offenders: A pilot study. *Journal of Forensic Nursing, 8,* 112–121. doi:10.1111/j.1939-3938.2011.01132.x

Burgess, A. W., Hartman, C., McCausland, M., & Powers, P. (1984). Impact of child pornography and sex rings on child victims and their families. In A. W. Burgess (Ed.), *Child pornography and sex rings* (pp. 111–126). Lexington, MA: Lexington Books.

Burton, D. L. (2000). Were adolescent sexual offenders children with sexual behavior problems? *Sexual Abuse: A Journal of Research and Treatment, 12,* 37–48.

Buschman, J., & Bogaerts, S. (2009). Polygraph testing Internet offenders. In D. T. Wilcox (Ed.), *The use of the polygraph in assessing, treating and supervising sex offenders: A practitioner's guide* (pp. 113–128). Hoboken, NJ: Wiley.

Buschman, J., Wilcox, D., Krapohl, D., Oelrich, M., & Hackett, S. (2010). Cybersex offender risk assessment: An exploratory study. *Journal of Sexual Aggression, 16,* 197–209. doi:10.1080/13552601003690518

Buss, D. M. (1994). *The evolution of desire: Strategies of human mating.* New York, NY: Basic Books.

Buss, D. M., & Schmitt, D. P. (1993). Sexual strategies theory: An evolutionary perspective on human mating. *Psychological Review, 100,* 204–232. doi:10.1037/0033-295X.100.2.204

Cantor, J. M., Blanchard, R., Robichaud, L. K., & Christensen, B. K. (2005). Quantitative reanalysis of aggregate data on IQ in sexual offenders. *Psychological Bulletin, 131,* 555–568. doi:10.1037/0033-2909.131.4.555

Canwest News Service. (2009). Ontario police crack down on child pornography. *Canada.com.* Retrieved from www.canada.com/ottawacitizen/news/story.html?id=392a7d0f-e5dc-4e5b-b163-ef34711a9994&k=79268

Carey, C. (2008). Modeling collecting behavior: The role of set completion. *Journal of Economic Psychology, 29,* 336–347. doi:10.1016/j.joep.2007.08.002

Carnes, P. (1983). *Out of the shadows: Understanding sexual addiction.* Center City, MN: Hazelden.

Carnes, P., Delmonico, D., Griffin, E., & Moriarty, J. (2007). *In the shadows of the Net* (2nd ed.). Center City, MN: Hazelden.

Carpentier, M. Y., Silovsky, J. F., & Chaffin, M. (2006). Randomized trial of treatment for children with sexual behavior problems: Ten-year follow-up.

Journal of Consulting and Clinical Psychology, 74, 482–488. doi:10.1037/0022-006X.74.3.482

Center for Sex Offender Management. (2007). *Female sex offenders.* Retrieved from http://csom.org/pubs/female_sex_offenders_brief.pdf

Chagigiorgis, H., Michel, S., Laprade, K., Ahmed, A. G., & Seto, M. C. (2011). *Assessing short-term, dynamic changes in risk: The predictive validity of the Brockville Risk Checklist.* Manuscript submitted for publication.

Child Exploitation and Obscenity Act (1985), 18 U.S.C. § 2422

Child Protection Act (1984). H.R. 3635—98th Congress. Retrieved from http://www.govtrack.us/congress/bills/98/hr3635

Chivers, M. L., & Bailey, J. M. (2005). A sex difference in features that elicit genital response. *Biological Psychology, 70,* 115–120. doi:10.1016/j.biopsycho.2004.12.002

Chivers, M. L., Rieger, G., Latty, E., & Bailey, J. M. (2004). A sex difference in the specificity of sexual arousal. *Psychological Science, 15,* 736–744. doi:10.1111/j.0956-7976.2004.00750.x

Chivers, M. L., Seto, M. C., Lalumière, M. L., Laan, E., & Grimbos, T. (2010). Agreement of self-reported and genital measures of sexual arousal among men and women: A meta-analysis. *Archives of Sexual Behavior, 39,* 5–56. doi:10.1007/s10508-009-9556-9

Choo, K. R. (2009). *Online child grooming: A literature review on the misuse of social networking sites for grooming children for sexual offences* (Research and Public Policy Series No. 103). Retrieved from http://www.aic.gov.au/publications/current%20series/rpp/100-120/rpp103.aspx

Chou, C., & Hsiao, M. C. (2000). Internet addiction, usage, gratification, and pleasure experience: The Taiwan college student's case. *Computers & Education, 35,* 65–80. doi:10.1016/S0360-1315(00)00019-1

Chow, E. W. C., & Choy, A. L. (2002). Clinical characteristics and treatment response to SSRI in a female pedophile. *Archives of Sexual Behavior, 31,* 211–215. doi:10.1023/A:1014795321404

Clarke, R., & Knake, R. K. (2010). *Cyber war: The next threat to national security and what to do about it.* New York, NY: Ecco.

Cohen, M. N. (1996). *Lewis Carroll: A biography.* New York, NY: Vintage.

Collins, M. (2012, February). *Federal child pornography offenses.* Retrieved from http://www.ussc.gov/Legislative_and_Public_Affairs/Public_Hearings_and_Meetings/20120215-16/Testimony_15_Collins.pdf

Collins, R. L., Elliott, M. N., Berry, S. H., Kanouse, D. E., Kunkel, D., Hunter, S. B., & Miu, A. (2004). Watching sex on television predicts adolescent initiation of sexual behavior. *Pediatrics, 114,* e280–e289. doi:10.1542/peds.2003-1065-L

Condy, S. R., Templer, D. I., Brown, R., & Veaco, L. (1987). Parameters of sexual contact of boys with women. *Archives of Sexual Behavior, 16,* 379–394. doi:10.1007/BF01541421

Connolly, J. M., Slaughter, V., & Mealey, L. (2004). The development of preferences for specific body shapes. *Journal of Sex Research, 41,* 5–15. doi:10.1080/00224490409552209

Conte, J., Wolf, S., & Smith, T. (1989). What sexual offenders tell us about prevention strategies. *Child Abuse & Neglect, 13,* 293–301. doi:10.1016/0145-2134(89)90016-1

Cooper, A. (1998). Sexuality and the Internet: Surfing its way into the new millennium. *Cyberpsychology & Behavior, 1,* 24–28. doi:10.1089/cpb.1998.1.187

Cooper, A. (2002). *Sex and the Internet: A guidebook for clinicians.* New York, NY: Brunner-Routledge.

Cooper, A., Delmonico, D. L., Griffin-Shelley, E., & Mathy, R. M. (2004). Online sexual activity: An examination of potentially problematic behaviors. *Sexual Addiction & Compulsivity, 11,* 129–143. doi:10.1080/10720160490882642

Cooper, A., Galbreath, N., & Becker, M. (2004). Sex on the Internet: Furthering our understanding of men with online sexual problems. *Psychology of Addictive Behaviors, 18,* 223–230. doi:10.1037/0893-164X.18.3.223

Cooper, A. J., Swaminath, S., Baxter, D., & Poulin, C. (1990). A female sex offender with multiple paraphilias: A psychologic, physiologic (laboratory sexual arousal) and endocrine case study. *Canadian Journal of Psychiatry/La Revue Canadienne de Psychiatrie, 35,* 334–337.

Cooper, S. W. (2012, February). *The impact on children who have been victims of child pornography.* Retrieved from ussc.gov/Legislative_and_Public_Affairs/Public_Hearings_and_Meetings/20120215-16/Testimony_15_Cooper.pdf

Cortoni, F., & Marshall, W. L. (2001). Sex as a coping strategy and its relationship to juvenile sexual history and intimacy in sexual offenders. *Sexual Abuse: A Journal of Research and Treatment, 13,* 27–43.

Cox Communications. (2007). *Teen Internet Safety Survey, Wave II.* Retrieved from http://ww2.cox.com/wcm/en/aboutus/datasheet/takecharge/archives/2007-teen-survey.pdf?campcode=takecharge-archive-link_2007-survey_0511

Craven, S., Brown, S. J., & Gilchrist, E. (2006). Sexual grooming: A review of the literature and theoretical considerations. *Journal of Sexual Aggression, 12,* 287–299. doi:10.1080/13552600601069414

Crépault, C., & Couture, M. (1980). Men's erotic fantasies. *Archives of Sexual Behavior, 9,* 565–581. doi:10.1007/BF01542159

Crime Control Act, 42 U.S.C. § 10607 (1990).

Crime Victims Rights Act, 18 U.S.C. § 3771 (2004).

Criminal Code Act 1995 s 474.26, 474.27

Criminal Code of Canada. R.S.C., 1985, C-46, s. 172.1.

Crossman, L. L. (1995). Date rape and sexual aggression by college males: Incidence and the involvement of impulsivity, anger, hostility, psychopathology, peer influence and pornography use. *Dissertation Abstracts International: Section B. Sciences and Engineering, 55*(10-B), 4640.

Cusick, L. (2002). Youth prostitution: A literature review. *Child Abuse Review, 11,* 230–251. doi:10.1002/car.743

Darroch, J. E., Landry, D. J., & Oslak, S. (1999). Age differences between sexual partners in the United States. *Family Planning Perspectives, 31,* 160–167. doi:10.2307/2991588

Dauvergne, M., & Turner, J. (2010). Police-reported crime statistics in Canada, 2009 (Catalogue No. 85-002-X). Retrieved from statcan.gc.ca/pub/85-002-x/2010002/article/11292-eng.htm

Davis, R. A. (2001). A cognitive–behavioral model of pathological Internet use. *Computers in Human Behavior, 17,* 187–195. doi:10.1016/S0747-5632(00)00041-8

Dean, M. (2012). The story of Amanda Todd. *The New Yorker.* Retrieved from http://www.newyorker.com/online/blogs/culture/2012/10/amanda-todd-michael-brutsch-and-free-speech-online.html

Deardorff, J., Gonzales, N. A., Christopher, F. S., Roosa, M. W., & Millsap, R. E. (2005). Early puberty and adolescent pregnancy: The influence of alcohol use. *Pediatrics, 116,* 1451–1456.

DeClue, G. (2009). Should hebephilia be a mental disorder? A reply to Blanchard et al. *Archives of Sexual Behavior, 38,* 317–318. doi:10.1007/s10508-008-9422-1

DeLong, R., Durkin, K. F., & Hundersmarck, S. (2010). An exploratory analysis of the cognitive distortions of a sample of men arrested in Internet sex stings. *Journal of Sexual Aggression, 16,* 59–70. doi:10.1080/13552600903428235

Denov, M. S. (2003). The myth of innocence: Sexual scripts and the recognition of child sexual abuse by female perpetrators. *Journal of Sex Research, 40,* 303–314. doi:10.1080/00224490309552195

Des Sables, L. (1976). Résultats d'une enquête auprès d'un groupe de pedérastes [Results of an inquiry with a group of pederasts]. *Arcadie, 276,* 650–657.

Des Sables, L. (1977). Résultats d'une enquête auprès d'un groupe de pedérastes [Results of an inquiry with a group of pederasts]. *Arcadie, 277,* 35–45.

De Young, M. (1988). The indignant page: Techniques of neutralization in the publications of pedophile organizations. *Child Abuse & Neglect, 12,* 583–591. doi:10.1016/0145-2134(88)90076-2

Diamond, M., Jozifkova, E., & Weiss, P. (2011). Pornography and sex crimes in the Czech Republic. *Archives of Sexual Behavior, 40,* 1037–1043. doi:10.1007/s10508-010-9696-y

Diamond, M., & Uchiyama, A. (1999). Pornography, rape and sex crimes in Japan. *International Journal of Law and Psychiatry, 22,* 1–22. doi:10.1016/S0160-2527(98)00035-1

Dines, G. (2008). Childified women: How the mainstream porn industry sells child pornography to men. In S. Olfman (Ed.), *The sexualization of childhood* (pp. 121–142). Westport, CT: Praeger.

Dishion, T. J., McCord, J., & Poulin, F. (1999). When interventions harm: Peer groups and problem behavior. *American Psychologist, 54,* 755–764.

Document: Victim impact statement of girl in Misty series. (2009, October 25). *PilotOnline.com*. Retrieved from http://hamptonroads.com/2009/10/document-victim-impact-statement-girl-misty-series

Donovan, J. E., & Jessor, R. (1985). Structure of problem behavior in adolescence and young adulthood. *Journal of Consulting and Clinical Psychology, 53*, 890–904. doi:10.1037/0022-006X.53.6.890

Doren, D. M. (2002). *Evaluating sex offenders: A manual for civil commitments and beyond.* Thousand Oaks, CA: Sage.

Doren, D. M. (2004). Toward a multidimensional model for sexual recidivism risk. *Journal of Interpersonal Violence, 19*, 835–856. doi:10.1177/0886260504266882

D'Ovidio, R., Mitman, T., El-Burki, I. J., & Shumar, W. (2009). Adult–child sex advocacy websites as social learning environments: A content analysis. *International Journal of Cyber Criminology, 3*, 421–440.

Dowdell, E. B., Burgess, A. W., & Flores, J. R. (2011). Online social networking patterns among adolescents, young adults, and sexual offenders. *The American Journal of Nursing, 111*, 28–36. doi:10.1097/01.NAJ.0000399310.83160.73

Dreznick, M. T. (2003). Heterosocial competence of rapists and child molesters: A meta-analysis. *Journal of Sex Research, 40*, 170–178. doi:10.1080/00224490309552178

Durkin, K. F., & Bryant, C. D. (1999). Propagandizing pederasty: A thematic analysis of the online exculpatory accounts of unrepentant pedophiles. *Deviant Behavior, 20*, 103–127. doi:10.1080/016396299266524

Duwe, G. (2012). Can Circles of Support and Accountability (COSA) work in the United States? Preliminary results from a randomized experiment in Minnesota. *Sexual Abuse: A Journal of Research and Treatment.* Advance online publication. doi:10.1177/1079063212453942

Duwe, G., & Freske, P. J. (2012). Using logistic regression modeling to predict sexual recidivism: the Minnesota Sex Offender Screening Tool–3 (MnSOST–3). *Sexual Abuse: A Journal of Research and Treatment, 24*, 350–377. doi:10.1177/1079063211429470

Eke, A. W., & Seto, M. C. (2012). Risk assessment of online offenders for law enforcement. In K. Ribisl & E. Quayle (Eds.), *Internet child pornography: Understanding and preventing on-line child abuse* (pp. 148–168). Devon, England: Willan.

Eke, A. W., Seto, M. C., & Williams, J. (2011). Examining the criminal history and future offending of child pornography offenders: An extended prospective follow-up study. *Law and Human Behavior, 35*, 466–478. http://dx.doi.org/10.1007/s10979-010-9252-2

Elliott, I. A., & Ashfield, S. A. (2011). The use of online technology in the offence processes of female child molesters. *Journal of Sexual Aggression, 17*, 92–104. doi:10.1080/13552600.2010.537379

Elliott, I. A., & Beech, A. R. (2009). Understanding online child pornography use: Applying sexual offender theory to Internet offenders. *Aggression and Violent Behavior, 14*, 180–193. doi:10.1016/j.avb.2009.03.002

Elliott, I. A., Beech, A. R., Mandeville-Norden, R., & Hayes, E. (2009). Psychological profiles of Internet sex offenders: Comparisons with contact sexual offenders. *Sexual Abuse: A Journal of Research and Treatment, 21*, 76–92.

Elo, I. T., King, R. B., & Furstenberg, F. F. (1999). Adolescent females: Their sexual partners and the fathers of their children. *Journal of Marriage and the Family, 61*, 74–84. doi:10.2307/353884

Endrass, J., Urbaniak, F., Hammermeister, L. C., Benz, C., Elbert, T., Laubacher, A., & Rossegger, A. (2009). The consumption of Internet child pornography and violent sex offending. *BMC Psychiatry, 9*, 43. doi:10.1186/1471-244X-9-43

Estes, R. J., & Weiner, N. A. (2005). The commercial sexual exploitation of children in the United States. In S. W. Cooper, R. J. Estes, A. P. Giardino, N. D. Kellogg, & V. I. Vieth (Eds.), *Medical, legal, and social science aspects of child sexual exploitation: A comprehensive review of pornography, prostitution, and Internet crimes* (pp. 95–128). St. Louis, MO: G. W. Medical. doi:10.3886/ICPSR03366.v1

Faller, K. C. (1991). Polyincestuous families: An exploratory study. *Journal of Interpersonal Violence, 6*, 310–322. doi:10.1177/088626091006003004

Farrington, D. P., Piquero, A. R., & Jennings, W. G. (in press). *Offending from childhood to late middle age: Recent results from the Cambridge Study in Delinquent Development*. New York, NY: Springer.

Faust, E., Renaud, C., & Bickart, W. (2009, October). *Predictors of re-offense among a sample of federally convicted child pornography offenders*. Paper presented at the 28th Annual Conference of the Association for the Treatment of Sexual Abusers, Dallas, TX.

Fedoroff, J. P., Smolewska, K., Selhi, Z., Ng, E., & Bradford, J. M. W. (2001, July). *Victimless pedophiles*. Poster presented at the annual meeting of the International Academy of Sex Research, Montréal, Canada.

Felson, M. (1987). Routine activities and crime prevention in the developing metropolis. *Criminology, 25*, 911–932. doi:10.1111/j.1745-9125.1987.tb00825.x

Festinger, L. (1957). *A theory of cognitive dissonance*. Evanston, IL: Row, Peterson.

Finkelhor, D. (1984). *Child sexual abuse*. New York, NY: Free Press.

Finkelhor, D., & Jones, L. (2006). Why have child maltreatment and child victimization declined? *Journal of Social Issues, 62*, 685–716. doi:10.1111/j.1540-4560.2006.00483.x

Finkelhor, D., & Ormrod, R. (2004). *Child pornography: Patterns from NIBRS* (Juvenile Justice Bulletin No. NCJ 204911). Washington, DC: United States Department of Justice, Office of Justice Programs, Office of Juvenile Justice and Delinquency Prevention.

Finkelhor, D., Ormrod, R., & Chaffin, M. (2009). *Juveniles who commit sexual offenses against minors* (Juvenile Justice Bulletin No. NCJ 227763). Retrieved from http://www.ncjrs.gov/pdffiles1/ojjdp/227763.pdf

Finkelhor, D., Ormrod, R. K., Turner, H. A., & Hamby, S. L. (2005). Measuring poly-victimization using the JVQ. *Child Abuse & Neglect, 29*, 1297–1312. doi:10.1016/j.chiabu.2005.06.005

Firestone, P., Kingston, D. A., Wexler, A., & Bradford, J. M. (2006). Long-term follow-up of exhibitionists: Psychological, phallometric, and offense characteristics. *The Journal of the American Academy of Psychiatry and the Law, 34*, 349–359.

Flanigan, C. M. (2003). Sexual activity among girls under age 15: Findings from the National Survey of Family Growth. In B. Albert, S. Brown, & C. M. Flanigan (Eds.), *14 and younger: The sexual behavior of young adolescents* (pp. 57–63). Washington, DC: National Campaign to Prevent Teen Pregnancy.

Fortin, F., & Roy, J. (2007). Cybérpedophilie: profiles d'amateur de pédopornographie. [Cyberpedophilia: Profiles of users of child pornography.] In M. St-Yves & M. Tanguay (Eds.), *Psychologie des entrevues d'enquête: De la recherce a la pratique* [The psychology of investigative interviews: From research to practice] (pp. 465–502). Québec, Canada: Éditions Yvon Blais.

Fottrell, J. M., Debrota, S., & Hakes, F. (2012). Statement for the record of James M. Fottrell, Steve Debrota, and Francey Hakes, Department of Justice, before the United States Sentencing Commission Hearing on the Child Pornography Guidelines. Retrieved from http://www.ussc.gov/Legislative_and_Public_Affairs/Public_Hearings_and_Meetings/20120215-16/Testimony_15_Hakes_DeBrota_Fottrell.pdf

Franklin, K. (2009). The public policy implications of "hebephilia": A response to Blanchard et al. [Letter to the editor]. *Archives of Sexual Behavior, 38*, 319–320. doi:10.1007/s10508-008-9425-y

Franklin, K. (2010). Hebephilia: Quintessence of diagnostic pretextuality. *Behavioral Sciences and the Law, 28*, 751–768. doi:10.1002/bsl.934

Frei, A., Erenay, N., Dittmann, V., & Graf, M. (2005). Paedophilia and the Internet—A study of 33 convicted offenders in the Canton of Lucerne. *Swiss Medical Weekly, 135*, 488–494.

Freund, K. (1990). Courtship disorder. In W. L. Marshall, D. R. Laws, & H. E. Barbaree (Eds.), *Handbook of sexual assault: Issues, theories, and treatment of the offender* (pp. 195–207). New York, NY: Plenum Press.

Freund, K., Watson, R., & Rienzo, D. (1988). The value of self-reports in the study of voyeurism and exhibitionism. *Annals of Sex Research, 1*, 243–262.

Fromuth, M. E., & Burkhart, B. R. (1987). Childhood sexual victimization among college men: Definitional and methodological issues. *Violence and Victims, 2*, 241–253.

Fromuth, M. E., Burkhart, B. R., & Jones, C. W. (1991). Hidden child molestation: An investigation of adolescent perpetrators in a nonclinical sample. *Journal of Interpersonal Violence, 6*, 376–384. doi:10.1177/088626091006003009

Fulda, J. S. (2002). Do Internet stings directed at pedophiles capture offenders or create offenders? And allied questions. *Sexuality & Culture: An Interdisciplinary Quarterly, 6*, 73–100.

Fulda, J. S. (2007). Internet stings directed at pedophiles: A study in philosophy and law. *Sexuality & Culture, 11*, 52–98. doi:10.1007/BF02853935

Galbreath, N. W., Berlin, F. S., & Sawyer, D. (2002). Paraphilias and the Internet. In A. Cooper (Ed.), *Sex and the Internet: A guidebook for clinicians* (pp. 187–205). Philadelphia, PA: Brunner-Routledge.

Gallagher, B. (2007). Internet-initiated incitement and conspiracy to commit child sexual abuse (CSA): The typology, extent and nature of known cases. *Journal of Sexual Aggression, 13*, 101–119. doi:10.1080/13552600701521363

Gannon, T., Terriere, R., & Leader, T. (2012). Ward and Siegert's pathways model of child sexual offending: A cluster analysis evaluation. *Psychology, Crime & Law, 18*, 129–153. doi:10.1080/10683160903535917

Garber, J., & Hollon, S. D. (1991). What can specificity designs say about causality in psychopathology research? *Psychological Bulletin, 110*, 129–136. doi:10.1037/0033-2909.110.1.129

Gelber, A. (2009). *Response to "A Reluctant Rebellion"* [Letter from United States Department of Justice, Criminal Division]. Retrieved from justice.gov/criminal/ceos/downloads/ReluctantRebellionResponse.pdf

Gibson, W. (1984). *Neuromancer*. New York, NY: Ace.

Gigerenzer, G., Todd, P. M., & the ABC Group. (1999). *Simple heuristics that make us smart*. New York, NY: Oxford University Press.

Gillespie, A. (2010). Legal definitions of child pornography. *Journal of Sexual Aggression, 16*, 19–31. doi:10.1080/13552600903262097

Glasgow, D. (2010). The potential of digital evidence to contribute to risk assessment of Internet offenders. *Journal of Sexual Aggression, 16*(1), 87–106. doi:10.1080/13552600903428839

Glasgow, D. (2012). The importance of digital evidence in internet sex offending. In K. Ribisl & E. Quayle (Eds.), *Internet child pornography: Understanding and preventing on-line child abuse* (pp. 171–187). Devon, England: Willan.

Glitter jailed over child porn. (1999, November 12). *BBC News*. Retrieved from http://news.bbc.co.uk/2/hi/uk_news/517604.stm

Good Lives Model. (2011). *The good lives model of offender rehabilitation: A strengths based approach*. Retrieved from http://www.goodlivesmodel.com/glm/Home.html

Goode, A. (2011, November 4). Life sentence for possession of child pornography spurs debate over severity. *The New York Times*. Retrieved from http://www.nytimes.com/2011/11/05/us/life-sentence-for-possession-of-child-pornography-spurs-debate.html

Gopnik, A. (2012, January 30). The caging of America. *The New Yorker*. Retrieved from newyorker.com/arts/critics/atlarge/2012/01/30/120130crat_atlarge_gopnik

Gordon, W. M. (2002). Sexual obsessions and OCD. *Sexual and Relationship Therapy, 17*, 343–354. doi:10.1080/1468199021000017191

Granic, I., & Lamey, A. V. (2000). The self-organization of the Internet and changing modes of thought. *New Ideas in Psychology, 18*, 93–107. doi:10.1016/S0732-118X(99)00039-2

Graupner, H. (2000). Sexual consent: The criminal law in Europe and overseas. *Archives of Sexual Behavior, 29*, 415–461. doi:10.1023/A:1001986103125

Green, R. (2010). Sexual preference for 14 year olds as a mental disorder: You can't be serious!! [Letter to the editor]. *Archives of Sexual Behavior*. doi:10.1007/s10508-010-9602-7

Greenberg, D. M., Bradford, J., & Curry, S. (1995). Infantophilia—A new subcategory of pedophilia? A preliminary study. *The Bulletin of the American Academy of Psychiatry and the Law, 23,* 63–71.

Greenfield, L. A. (1997). *Sex offenses and offenders: An analysis of data on rape and sexual assault* (Bulletin No. NCJ. 163392). Washington, DC: Bureau of Justice Statistics.

Grosskopf, A. (2009). *A qualitative enquiry into the nature of online interactions captured by Internet based police investigations involving paedophiles who engage male children.* (Unpublished master's thesis). Charles Sturt University, Goulburn, Australia.

Hall, G. C. N., & Hirschman, R. (1991). Toward a theory of sexual aggression: A quadripartite model. *Journal of Consulting and Clinical Psychology, 59,* 662–669. doi:10.1037/0022-006X.59.5.662

Hamilton, M. (2012). The child pornography crusade and its net widening effect. *Cardoza Law Review, 33*(1). Retrieved from papers.ssrn.com/sol3/papers.cfm?abstract_id=1914496

Hammer, H., Finkelhor, D., & Sedlak, A. J. (2002). *Runaway/thrown-away children: National estimates and characteristics* (Bulletin No. NCJ196469). Washington, DC: Office of Juvenile Justice and Delinquency Protection.

Hansen, M. (2009, June 1). A reluctant rebellion. *ABA Journal.* Retrieved from abajournal.com/magazine/article/a_reluctant_rebellion

Hanson, R. K., Bourgon, G., Helmus, L., & Hodgson, S. (2009). The principles of effective correctional treatment also apply to sexual offenders: A meta-analysis. *Criminal Justice and Behavior, 36,* 865–891. doi:10.1177/0093854809338545

Hanson, R. K., & Bussière, M. T. (1998). Predicting relapse: A meta-analysis of sexual offender recidivism studies. *Journal of Consulting and Clinical Psychology, 66,* 348–362. doi:10.1037/0022-006X.66.2.348

Hanson, R. K., Gordon, A., Harris, A. J. R., Marques, J. K., Murphy, W., Quinsey, V. L., & Seto, M. C. (2002). First report of the Collaborative Outcome Data Project on the effectiveness of treatment for sex offenders. *Sexual Abuse: A Journal of Research and Treatment, 14,* 169–194.

Hanson, R. K., & Harris, A. J. R. (2000). Where should we intervene? Dynamic predictors of sexual assault recidivism. *Criminal Justice and Behavior, 27,* 6–35. doi:10.1177/0093854800027001002

Hanson, R. K., Harris, A. J. R., Scott, T.-L., & Helmus, L. (2007). *Assessing the risk of sexual offenders on community supervision: The Dynamic Supervision Project* (User Report 2007-05). Ottawa, Ontario, Canada: Public Safety Canada.

Hanson, R. K., & Morton-Bourgon, K. (2004). *Predictors of sexual recidivism: An updated meta-analysis* (Catalog No. PS3-1/2004-2E-PDF). Ottawa, Ontario, Canada: Public Safety and Emergency Preparedness Canada.

Hanson, R. K., & Morton-Bourgon, K. (2005). The characteristics of persistent sexual offenders: A meta-analysis of recidivism studies. *Journal of Consulting and Clinical Psychology, 73,* 1154–1163. doi:10.1037/0022-006X.73.6.1154

Hanson, R. K., & Morton-Bourgon, K. E. (2009). The accuracy of recidivism risk assessments for sexual offenders: A meta-analysis of 118 prediction studies. *Psychological Assessment, 21,* 1–21. doi:10.1037/a0014421

Hanson, R. K., & Scott, H. (1996). Social networks of sexual offenders. *Psychology, Crime & Law, 2,* 249–258. doi:10.1080/10683169608409782

Hanson, R. K., Steffy, R. A., & Gauthier, R. (1993). Long-term recidivism of child molesters. *Journal of Consulting and Clinical Psychology, 61,* 646–652. doi:10.1037/0022-006X.61.4.646

Hanson, R. K., & Thornton, D. (2000). Improving risk assessments for sex offenders: A comparison of three actuarial scales. *Law and Human Behavior, 24,* 119–136. doi:10.1023/A:1005482921333

Harmon-Jones, E., & Mills, J. (Eds.). (1999). *Cognitive dissonance: Progress on a pivotal theory in social psychology.* Washington, DC: American Psychological Association. doi:10.1037/10318-000

Harris, A. J. R., & Hanson, R. K. (2004). *Sex offender recidivism: A simple question* (Corrections User Report No. 2004-03). Ottawa, Ontario, Canada: Public Safety Canada.

Harris, A. J. R., Phenix, A., Hanson, R. K., & Thornton, D. (2003). *Static-99 coding rules: Revised 2003.* Ottawa, Ontario, Canada: Public Safety Canada.

Harris, G. T., & Rice, M. E. (1996). The science in phallometric testing of male sexual interest. *Current Directions in Psychological Science, 5,* 156–160. doi:10.1111/1467-8721.ep11512355

Harris, G. T., & Rice, M. E. (2007). Adjusting actuarial violence risk assessments based on aging or the passage of time. *Criminal Justice and Behavior, 34,* 297–313. doi:10.1177/0093854806293486

Harris, G. T., Rice, M. E., Quinsey, V. L., & Chaplin, T. C. (1996). Viewing time as a measure of sexual interest among child molesters and normal heterosexual men. *Behaviour Research and Therapy, 34,* 389–394. doi:10.1016/0005-7967(95)00070-4

Hart, S. D., & Logan, C. (2011). Formulation of violence risk using evidence-based assessments: The structured professional judgment approach. In P. Sturmey & M. McMurran (Eds.), *Forensic case formulation* (pp. 81–106). Chichester, England: Wiley-Blackwell.

Hartman, C. R., Burgess, A. W., & Lanning, K. V. (1984). Typology of collectors. In A. W. Burgess & M. L. Clark (Eds.), *Child pornography and sex rings* (pp. 93–109). Toronto: Lexington.

Hathaway, S. R., McKinley, J. C., Butcher, J. N., Dahlstrom, W. G., Graham, J. R., Tellegen, A., & Kaemmer, B. (1989). *The Minnesota Multiphasic Personality Inventory 2: Manual for administration and scoring.* Minneapolis, MN: University of Minnesota Press.

Hayes, E., & Middleton, D. (2006). *Internet sexual offending treatment programme (i-SOTP): Theory manual.* Westminster, England: National Offender Management Service.

Heil, P., Ahlmeyer, S., & Simons, D. (2003). Crossover sexual offenses. *Sexual Abuse: A Journal of Research and Treatment, 15*, 221–236.

Helmus, L. (2009). *Re-norming Static-99 recidivism estimates: Exploring base rate variability across sex offender samples* (Master's thesis). Available from ProQuest Dissertations and Theses database. (UMI No. MR58443)

Helmus, L., Hanson, R. K., Babchishin, K. M., & Mann, R. E. (2012). Attitudes supportive of sexual offending predict recidivism: A meta-analysis. *Trauma, Violence, and Abuse.* Advance online publication. doi:10.1177/1524838012462244

Helmus, L., Hanson, R. K., Thornton, D., Babchishin, K. M., & Harris, A. J. R. (2012). Absolute recidivism rates predicted by Static-99R and Static-2002R sex offender risk assessment tools vary across samples: A meta-analysis. *Criminal Justice and Behavior, 39*, 1148–1171. doi:10.1177/0093854812443648

Henry, O., Mandeville-Norden, R., Hayes, E., & Egan, V. (2010). Do Internet-based sexual offenders reduce to normal, inadequate and deviant groups? *Journal of Sexual Aggression, 16*, 33–46. doi:10.1080/13552600903454132

Herbenick, D., Schick, V., Reece, M., Sanders, S., & Fortenberry, J. D. (2010). Pubic hair removal among women in the United States: Prevalence, methods and characteristics. *Journal of Sexual Medicine, 7*, 3322–3330. doi:10.1111/j.1743-6109.2010.01935.x

Herman-Giddens, M. E., Slora, E. J., Wasserman, R. C., Bourdony, C. J., Bhapkar, M. V., Koch, G. G., & Hasemeier, C. M. (1997). Secondary sexual characteristics and menses in young girls seen in office practice: A study from the Pediatric Research in Office Settings Network. *Pediatrics, 99*, 505–512. doi:10.1542/peds.99.4.505

Hill, A., Briken, P., & Berner, W. (2006). Pornographie im Internet—Ersatz oder Anreiz fuer sexuelle Gewalt? [Pornography on the Internet—Substitute or stimulus for sexual violence?] In J. Eschemann (Ed.), *Stiftung Deutsches Forum fuer Kriminalpraevention: Internet-Devianz* [German Forum for Criminal Prevention: Internet Deviance] (pp. 113–134). Berlin, Germany: Bundesverwaltungsamt.

Hinduja, S., & Patchin, J. W. (2008). Personal information of adolescents on the Internet: A quantitative content analysis of MySpace. *Journal of Adolescence, 31*, 125–146. doi:10.1016/j.adolescence.2007.05.004

Hines, D., & Finkelhor, D. (2007). Statutory sex crime relationships between juveniles and adults: A review of social scientific research. *Aggression and Violent Behavior, 12*, 300–314. doi:10.1016/j.avb.2006.10.001

Holt, T. J., Blevins, K. R., & Burkert, N. (2010). Considering the pedophile subculture on-line. *Sexual Abuse: A Journal of Research and Treatment, 22*, 3–24.

Howard, P., Francis, B., Soothill, K., & Humphreys, L. (2009). *OGRS 3: The revised Offender Group Reconviction Scale* (Ministry of Justice Research Summary 7/09). Retrieved from http://eprints.lancs.ac.uk/49988/1/ogrs3.pdf

Howitt, D. (1995). Pornography and the paedophile: Is it criminogenic? *British Journal of Medical Psychology, 68*, 15–27. doi:10.1111/j.2044-8341.1995.tb01810.x

Hudson, S. M., Ward, T., & McCormack, J. C. (1999). Offense pathways in sexual offenders. *Journal of Interpersonal Violence, 14,* 779–798. doi:10.1177/088626099014008001

Hughes, D., Gibson, S., Walkerdine, J., & Coulson, G. (2006). Is deviant behaviour the norm on peer-to-peer file sharing networks? *IEEE Distributed Systems Online, 7*(2). Retrieved from http://ieeexplore.ieee.org/xpls/abs_all.jsp?arnumber=1610578

Hughes, D. M. (2000). "Welcome to the rape camp": Sexual exploitation and the Internet in Cambodia. *Journal of Sexual Aggression, 6,* 29–51. doi:10.1080/13552600008413308

Hunt, S. A., & Kraus, S. W. (2009). Exploring the relationship between erotic disruption during the latency period and the use of sexually explicit material, online sexual behaviors, and sexual dysfunctions in young adulthood. *Sexual Addiction & Compulsivity, 16,* 79–100. doi: 10.1080/10720160902724228

Hunter, C. (2000). Social impacts: Internet filter effectiveness testing over- and underinclusive blocking decisions of four popular web filters. *Social Science Computer Review, 18,* 214–222. doi:10.1177/089443930001800209

Imhoff, R., Schmidt, A. F., Nordsiek, U., Luzar, C., Young, A. W., & Banse, R. (2010). Viewing time effects revisited: Prolonged response latencies for sexually attractive targets under restricted task conditions. *Archives of Sexual Behavior, 39,* 1275–1288. doi:10.1007/s10508-009-9595-2

Inciardi, J. (1984). Little girls and sex: A glimpse at the world of the "baby pro." *Deviant Behavior, 5,* 71–78. doi:10.1080/01639625.1984.9967632

International Center for Missing and Exploited Children. (2010). *Child pornography: Model legislation & global review* (6th ed.). Retrieved from icmec.org/en_X1/icmec_publications/English__6th_Edition_FINAL_.pdf

International Labour Organization. (2006). *Commercial sexual exploitation of children and adolescents: The ILO's response.* Retrieved from ilo.org/ipecinfo/product/download.do?type=document&id=9150

Investigating and Preventing Criminal Electronic Communications Act of 2012 (Bill C-30).

Jackson, R. L., & Hess, D. T. (2007). Evaluation for civil commitment of sex offenders: A survey of experts. *Sexual Abuse: A Journal of Research and Treatment, 19,* 425–448.

Jacobs, R., & Albert, T. (2008, August). *Ethnicity, Internet adoption and use of online services.* Paper presented at the annual meeting of the Association for Education in Journalism and Mass Communication, Chicago, IL.

Jenkins, P. (1998). *Moral panic: Changing concepts of the child molester in modern America.* New Haven, CT: Yale University Press.

Jenkins, P. (2001). *Beyond tolerance: Child pornography on the Internet.* New York, NY: New York University Press.

Jespersen, A. F., Lalumière, M. L., & Seto, M. C. (2009). Sexual abuse history among adult sex offenders and non-sex offenders: A meta-analysis. *Child Abuse & Neglect, 33,* 179–192. doi:10.1016/j.chiabu.2008.07.004

Johnson v. United States, 528 F. 3d 1318, No. 08-6925 (2008).

Jones, L., & Finkelhor, D. (2001). *The decline in child sexual abuse cases* (Bulletin No. NCJ 184741). Washington, DC: Office of Juvenile Justice and Delinquency Prevention.

Jung, S., Ennis, L., Stein, S., Choy, A. L., & Hook, T. (in press). Child pornography possessors: Comparisons with contact and non-contact sex offenders. *Journal of Sexual Aggression*. doi:10.1080/13552600.2012.741267

Jung, S., Ennis, L. P., & Malesky, L. A. (2012). Internet sex offending seen through three theoretical lenses. *Deviant Behavior, 33*, 655–673. doi:10.1080/01639625.2011.636726

Jung, S., & Stein, S. (2012). An examination of judicial sentencing decisions in child pornography and child molestation cases in Canada. *Journal of Criminal Psychology, 2*, 38–50. doi:10.1108/20093821211210486

Juvonen, J., & Gross, E. F. (2008). Extending the school grounds? Bullying experiences in cyberspace. *The Journal of School Health, 78*, 496–505. doi:10.1111/j.1746-1561.2008.00335.x

Kafka, M. P. (1997). A monoamine hypothesis for the pathophysiology of paraphilic disorders. *Archives of Sexual Behavior, 26*, 343–358. doi:10.1023/A:1024535201089

Kafka, M. P., & Hennen, J. (2003). Hypersexual desire in males: Are males with paraphilias different from males with paraphilia-related disorders? *Sexual Abuse: A Journal of Research and Treatment, 15*, 307–321.

Kahneman, D. (2011). *Thinking, fast and slow.* New York, NY: Farrar, Straus & Giroux.

Kalmus, E., & Beech, A. R. (2005). Forensic assessment of sexual interest: A review. *Aggression and Violent Behavior, 10*, 193–218. doi:10.1016/j.avb.2003.12.002

Kaufman, K. L., Hilliker, D., Lathrop, P., Daleiden, E., & Rudy, L. (1996). Sexual offenders' modus operandi: A comparison of structured interview and questionnaire approaches. *Journal of Interpersonal Violence, 11*, 19–34. doi:10.1177/088626096011001002

Kaufman, K. L., Hilliker, D. R., & Daleiden, E. L. (1996). Subgroup differences in the modus operandi of adolescent sexual offenders. *Child Maltreatment, 1*, 17–24. doi:10.1177/1077559596001001003

Kaufman, K. L., Holmberg, J. K., Orts, K. A., McCrady, F. E., Rotzien, A. L., Daleiden, E. L., & Hilliker, D. R. (1998). Factors influencing sexual offenders' modus operandi: An examination of victim-offender relatedness and age. *Child Maltreatment, 3*, 349–361. doi:10.1177/1077559598003004007

Kennedy, H. G., & Grubin, D. H. (1992). Patterns of denial in sex offenders. *Psychological Medicine, 22*, 191–196. doi:10.1017/S0033291700032840

Kilpatrick, A. C. (1986). Some correlates of women's childhood sexual experiences: A retrospective study. *Journal of Sex Research, 22*, 221–242. doi:10.1080/00224498609551302

Kingston, D. A., Fedoroff, P., Firestone, P., Curry, S., & Bradford, J. M. (2008). Pornography use and sexual aggression: The impact of frequency and type of pornography use on recidivism among sexual offenders. *Aggressive Behavior, 34,* 341–351. doi:10.1002/ab.20250

Kingston, D. A., & Malamuth, N. M. (2011). Problems with aggregate data and the importance of individual differences in the study of pornography and sexual aggression: Comment on Diamond, Jozifkova, and Weiss (2010). *Archives of Sexual Behavior, 40,* 1045–1048. doi:10.1007/s10508-011-9743-3

Kingston, D. A., Malamuth, N. M., Fedoroff, P., & Marshall, W. L. (2009). The importance of individual differences in pornography use: Theoretical perspectives and implications for treating sexual offenders. *Journal of Sex Research, 46,* 216–232. doi:10.1080/00224490902747701

Kingston, D. A., Yates, P. M., & Firestone, P. (2012). The self-regulation model of sexual offending: Relationship to risk and need. *Law and Human Behavior, 36,* 215–224. doi:10.1007/s10979-011-9287-z

Kirby, D. (2002). *Do abstinence-only programs delay the initiation of sex among young people and reduce teen pregnancy?* Retrieved from: thenationalcampaign.org/resources/pdf/pubs/abstinence_only.pdf

Koenig, L. J., Doll, L. S., O'Leary, A., & Pequegnat, W. (Eds.). (2004). *From child sexual abuse to adult sexual risk: Trauma, revictimization, and intervention.* Washington, DC: American Psychological Association. doi:10.1037/10785-000

Krone, T. (2004). Typology of online child pornography offending. *Trends and Issues in Crime and Criminal Justice* (Research Report No. 279). Retrieved from http://aic.gov.au/documents/4/F/8/%7B4F8B4249-7BEE-4F57-B9ED-993479D9196D%7Dtandi279.pdf

Krone, T. (2005). International police operations against online child pornography. *Trends and Issues in Crime and Criminal Justice* (Research Report No. 296). Retrieved from http://www.aic.gov.au/documents/3/C/E/%7B3CED11B0-F3F4-479C-B417-4669506B3886%7Dtandi296.pdf

Kroner, D. G., & Loza, W. (2001). Evidence for the efficacy of self-report in predicting nonviolent and violent criminal recidivism. *Journal of Interpersonal Violence, 16,* 168–177. doi:10.1177/088626001016002005

Krueger, R. B., Kaplan, M. S., & First, M. B. (2009). Sexual and other Axis I diagnoses of 60 males arrested for crimes against children involving the Internet. *CNS Spectrums, 14,* 623–631.

Kuhle, L., Konrad, A., & Beier, K. M. (2011, November). *Variability in sexual preference and use of sexually explicit and nonexplicit images of children.* Paper presented at the 30th Annual Conference of the Association for the Treatment of Sexual Abusers, Toronto, Ontario, Canada.

Kutchinsky, B. (1973). The effect of easy availability of pornography on the incidence of sex crimes: The Danish experience. *Journal of Social Issues, 29,* 163–181. doi:10.1111/j.1540-4560.1973.tb00094.x

Kutchinsky, B. (1991). Pornography and rape: Theory and practice? Evidence from crime data in four countries where pornography is easily available. *International Journal of Law and Psychiatry, 14,* 47–64. doi:10.1016/0160-2527(91)90024-H

Lalumière, M. L., Harris, G. T., Quinsey, V. L., & Rice, M. E. (2005). *The causes of rape: Understanding individual differences in the male propensity for sexual aggression*. Washington, DC: American Psychological Association. doi:10.1037/10961-000

Lalumière, M. L., & Quinsey, V. L. (1996). Sexual deviance, antisociality, mating effort, and the use of sexually coercive behaviors. *Personality and Individual Differences, 21,* 33–48. doi:10.1016/0191-8869(96)00059-1

Lam, A., Mitchell, J., & Seto, M. C. (2010). Lay perceptions of child pornography offenders. *Canadian Journal of Criminology and Criminal Justice, 52,* 173–201. doi:10.3138/cjccj.52.2.173

Lamb, M. (1998). Cybersex: Research notes on the characteristics of the visitors to online chatrooms. *Deviant Behavior, 19,* 121–135. doi:10.1080/01639625.1998.9968079

Lane, E. (1977). Arab poets of Andalusia. In W. Leyland (Ed.), *Orgasms of light: The Gay Sunshine anthology* (p. 11). San Francisco, CA: Gay Sunshine Press.

Lang, R. A., & Frenzel, R. R. (1988). How sex offenders lure children. *Annals of Sex Research, 1,* 303–317.

Langan, P. A., Schmitt, E. L., & Durose, M. R. (2003). Recidivism of sex offenders released from prison in 1994 (Report No. NCJ198281). Retrieved from bjs.ojp.usdoj.gov/content/pub/pdf/rpr94.pdf

Langevin, R., & Curnoe, S. (2004). The use of pornography during the commission of sexual offenses. *International Journal of Offender Therapy and Comparative Criminology, 48,* 572–586. doi:10.1177/0306624X03262518

Langevin, R., Curnoe, S., Fedoroff, P., Bennett, R., Langevin, M., Peever, C., . . . Sandhu, S. (2004). Lifetime sex offender recidivism: A 25-year follow-up study. *Canadian Journal of Criminology and Criminal Justice, 46,* 531–552. doi:10.3138/cjccj.46.5.531

Långström, N., & Seto, M. C. (2006). Exhibitionistic and voyeuristic behavior in a Swedish national population survey. *Archives of Sexual Behavior, 35,* 427–435. doi:10.1007/s10508-006-9042-6

Langton, C. M. (2003). Contrasting approaches to risk assessment with adult male sexual offenders: An evaluation of recidivism prediction schemes and the utility of supplementary clinical information for enhancing predictive accuracy. *Dissertation Abstracts International, 64*(4-B), 1907.

Langton, C. M., Barbaree, H. E., Seto, M. C., Peacock, E. J., Harkins, L., & Hansen, K. T. (2007). Actuarial assessment of risk for reoffense among adult sex offenders: Evaluating the predictive accuracy of the Static-2002 and five other instruments. *Criminal Justice and Behavior, 34,* 37–59. doi:10.1177/0093854806291157

Lanier, J. (2010). *You are not a gadget: A manifesto.* New York, NY: Knopf.

Lanning, K. V. (2001). *Child molesters: A behavioral analysis* (4th ed.). Washington, DC: Office of Juvenile Justice and Delinquency Prevention. Retrieved from http://www.missingkids.com/en_US/publications/NC70.pdf

La Rue, F. (2011). Report of the Special Rapporteur on the promotion and protection of the right to freedom of opinion and expression. Retrieved from http://www2. ohchr.org/english/bodies/hrcouncil/docs/17session/A.HRC.17.27_en.pdf

Laulik, S., Allam, J., & Sheridan, L. (2007). An investigation into maladaptive personality functioning in Internet sex offenders. *Psychology, Crime & Law, 13,* 523–535. doi:10.1080/10683160701340577

Laws, D. R., Hudson, S. M., & Ward, T. (Eds.). (2000). *Remaking relapse prevention with sex Offenders: A sourcebook.* Thousand Oaks, CA: Sage.

Leander, L., Christianson, S. A., & Granhag, P. A. (2008). Internet-initiated sexual abuse: Adolescent victims' reports about on- and off-line sexual activities. *Applied Cognitive Psychology, 22,* 1260–1274. doi:10.1002/acp.1433

Leary, M. G. (2010). Sexting or self-produced child pornography? The dialogue continues—Structured prosecutorial discretion within a multidisciplinary response. *Virginia Journal of Social Policy and the Law, 17,* 486-566.

Lebailly, H. (1999). C. L. Dodgson and the Victorian cult of the child *The Carrollian. The Lewis Caroll Journal, 4,* 3–31.

Leclerc, B., Beauregard, E., & Proulx, J. (2008). Modus operandi and situational aspects in adolescent sexual offences against children: A further examination. *International Journal of Offender Therapy and Comparative Criminology, 52,* 46–61. doi:10.1177/0306624X07300271

Leclerc, B., Proulx, J., Lussier, P., & Allaire, J.-F. (2009). Offender–victim interaction and crime event outcomes: Modus operandi and victim effects on the risk of intrusive sexual offences against children. *Criminology, 47,* 595–618. doi:10.1111/j.1745-9125.2009.00151.x

Lee, A. F., Li, N.-C., Lamade, R., Schuler, A., & Prentky, R. A. (2012). Predicting hands-on child sexual offenses among possessors of Internet child pornography. *Psychology, Public Policy, and Law, 18,* 644–672. doi:10.1037/a0027517

Leitenberg, H., & Saltzman, H. (2000). A statewide survey of age at first intercourse for adolescent females and age of their male partner: Relation to other risk behaviors and statutory rape implications. *Archives of Sexual Behavior, 29,* 203–215. doi:10.1023/A:1001920212732

Lenhart, A., Ling, R., Campbell, S., & Purcell, K. (2010). *Teens and mobile phones.* Retrieved from pewInternet.org/~/media//Files/Reports/2010/PIP-Teens-and-Mobile-2010-with-topline.pdf

Letourneau, E. J., Henggeler, S. W., Borduin, C. M., Schewe, P. A., McCart, M. R., Chapman, J. E., & Saldana, L. (2009). Multisystemic therapy for juvenile sexual offenders: 1-year results from a randomized effectiveness trial. *Journal of Family Psychology, 23,* 89–102. doi:10.1037/a0014352

Levenson, J. S., Brannon, Y., Fortney, T., & Baker, J. (2007). Public perceptions about sex offenders and community protection policies. *Analyses of Social Issues and Public Policy, 7,* 137–161.

Levenson, J. S., & Cotter, L. P. (2005). The effect of Megan's Law on sex offender reintegration. *Journal of Contemporary Criminal Justice, 21*, 49–66. http://dx.doi.org/10.1177/1043986204271676

Lewis, M. (2011). *Memoirs of an addicted brain: A neuroscientist examines his former life on drugs*. Toronto, Ontario, Canada: Doubleday Canada.

Lim, L. L. (1998). *The sex sector: The economic and social bases of prostitution in Southeast Asia*. New York, NY: United Nations International Labor Office.

Lipsey, M. W. (1998). What do we learn from 400 research studies on the effectiveness of treatment with juvenile delinquents? In J. McGuire (Ed.), *What works: Reducing reoffending—Guidelines from research and practice* (pp. 63–77). London, England: Wiley.

Lloyd, R. (1976). *For money or love: Boy prostitution in America*. New York, NY: Vanguard Press.

Long, M. L., Alison, L. A., & McManus, M. A. (2012). Child pornography and likelihood of contact abuse: A comparison between contact child sexual offenders and non-contact offenders. *Sexual Abuse: A Journal of Research and Treatment*. Advance online publication. doi:10.1177/1079063212464398

Lösel, F., & Schmucker, M. (2005). The effectiveness of treatment for sexual offenders: A comprehensive meta-analysis. *Journal of Experimental Criminology, 1*, 117–146. doi:10.1007/s11292-004-6466-7

Loughlin, J., & Taylor-Butts, A. (2009). Child luring through the Internet (Report No. 85-002-X). Ottawa, Ontario, Canada: Statistics Canada. Retrieved from statcan.gc.ca/pub/85-002-x/2009001/article/10783-eng.htm

Lounsbury, K., Mitchell, K. J., & Finkelhor, D. (2011). *The true prevalence of "sexting."* Durham, NH: University of New Hampshire. Retrieved from unh.edu/ccrc/pdf/Sexting%20Fact%20Sheet%204_29_11.pdf

Lundy, J. P. (1994). Behavior patterns that comprise sexual addiction as identified by mental health professionals. *Sexual Addiction & Compulsivity, 1*, 46–56. doi:10.1080/10720169408400027

MacDonald, W. M. (1973). *Indecent exposure*. Springfield, IL: Charles Thomas.

Magaletta, P. R., Faust, E., Bickart, W., & McLearen, A. M. (2012). Exploring clinical and personality characteristics of adult male Internet-only child pornography offenders. *International Journal of Offender Therapy and Comparative Criminology*. Retrieved from http://ijo.sagepub.com/content/early/2012/11/21/0306624X12465271

Malamuth, N. M., Addison, T., & Koss, M. (2000). Pornography and sexual aggression: Are there reliable effects and can we understand them? *Annual Review of Sex Research, 11*, 26–91.

Malamuth, N. M., & Huppin, M. (2007). Drawing the line on virtual child pornography: Bringing the law in line with the research evidence. *New York University Review of Law and Social Change, 31*, 773–827.

Malamuth, N. M., Linz, D., Heavey, C., Barnes, G., & Acker, M. (1995). Using the confluence model of sexual aggression to predict men's conflict with women: A

10-year follow-up study. *Journal of Personality and Social Psychology, 69*, 353–369. doi:10.1037/0022-3514.69.2.353

Malamuth, N. M., & Pitpitan, E. V. (2007). The effects of pornography are moderated by men's sexual aggression risk. In D. E. Guinn (Ed.), *Pornography: Driving the demand for international sex trafficking?* (pp. 125–143). Los Angeles, CA: Captive Daughters Media.

Malarek, V. (2004). *The Natashas: The new global sex trade.* Toronto, Ontario, Canada: Penguin Canada.

Malesky, L. A. (2007). Predatory online behavior: Modus operandi of convicted sex offenders in identifying potential victims and contacting minors over the Internet. *Journal of Child Sexual Abuse, 16*, 23–32. doi:10.1300/J070v16n02_02

Malesky, L. A. Jr., & Ennis, L. (2004). Supportive distortions: An analysis of posts on a pedophile Internet message board. *Journal of Addictions & Offender Counseling, 24*, 92–100. doi:10.1002/j.2161-1874.2004.tb00185.x

Mancini, C., Reckdenwald, A., & Beauregard, E. (2012). Pornographic exposure over the life course and the severity of sexual offenses: Imitation and cathartic effects. *Journal of Criminal Justice, 40*, 21–30. doi:10.1016/j.jcrimjus.2011.11.004

Manlove, J., Moore, K., Liechty, J., Ikramullah, E., & Cottingham, S. (2005). *Sex between young teens and older individuals: A demographic portrait.* Retrieved from http://www.childtrends.org/Files/StatRapeRB.pdf

Mann, R. E., Hanson, R. K., & Thornton, D. (2010). Assessing risk for sexual recidivism: Some proposals on the nature of psychologically meaningful risk factors. *Sexual Abuse: A Journal of Research and Treatment, 22*, 191–217.

Marcum, C. (2007). Are we protecting our youth online? An examination of programs keeping youth safe and analysis of policy vacuum. *International Journal of Cyber Criminology, 1*, 198–212.

Marcum, C. D., Higgins, G. E., & Ricketts, M. L. (2010). Potential factors of online victimization of youth: An examination of adolescent online behaviors utilizing routine activity theory. *Deviant Behavior, 31*, 381–410. doi:10.1080/01639620903004903

Marques, J. K., Nelson, C., Alarcon, J.-M., & Day, D. M. (2000). Preventing relapse in sex offenders: What we have learned from SOTEP's experimental treatment program. In D. R. Laws, S. M. Hudson, & T. Ward (Eds.), *Remaking relapse prevention with sex offenders: A sourcebook* (pp. 321–340). Thousand Oaks, CA: Sage.

Marques, J. K., Wiederanders, M., Day, D. M., Nelson, C., & van Ommeren, A. (2005). Effects of a relapse prevention program on sexual recidivism: Final results from California's Sex Offender Treatment Evaluation Project (SOTEP). *Sexual Abuse: A Journal of Research and Treatment, 17*, 79–107.

Marshall, W. L., & Barbaree, H. (1988). The long-term evaluation of a behavioral treatment program for child molesters. *Behaviour Research and Therapy, 26*, 499–511. doi:10.1016/0005-7967(88)90146-5

Marshall, W. L., Cripps, E., Anderson, D., & Cortoni, F. A. (1999). Self-esteem and coping strategies in child molesters. *Journal of Interpersonal Violence, 14*, 955–962. doi:10.1177/088626099014009003

Marshall, W. L., & Marshall, L. E. (2007). The utility of the Random Controlled Trial for evaluating sexual offender treatment: The gold standard or an inappropriate strategy? *Sexual Abuse: A Journal of Research and Treatment, 19,* 175–191.

Marshall, W. L., Marshall, L. E., Serran, G. A., & O'Brien, M. D. (Eds.). (2011). *Rehabilitating sexual offenders: A strengths based approach.* Washington, DC: American Psychological Association. doi:10.1037/12310-000

Marshall, W. L., Serran, G. A., & Cortoni, F. A. (2000). Childhood attachments, sexual abuse, and their relationship to adult coping in child molesters. *Sexual Abuse: A Journal of Research and Treatment, 12,* 17–26.

Martellozzo, E. (2010). *Policing online child sexual abuse. A case study of the London Metropolitan Police.* Kingston, England: Kingston University.

Martellozzo, E., Nehring, D., & Taylor, H. (2010). Online child sexual abuse by female offenders: An exploratory study. *International Journal of Cyber Criminology, 4,* 592–609.

Maruna, S., & Mann, R. (2006). Fundamental attribution errors? Re-thinking cognitive distortions. *Legal and Criminological Psychology, 11,* 155–177. doi:10.1348/135532506X114608

Matsuzawa, Y. K. (2009). *MMPI-2 characteristics of Internet sex offenders* Unpublished doctoral dissertation, Pepperdine University, Malibu, CA.

Maxfield, M. G., & Widom, C. S. (1996). The cycle of violence: Revisited six years later. *Archives of Pediatrics and Adolescent Medicine, 150,* 390–395.

McCarthy, J. A. (2010). Internet sexual activity: A comparison between contact and non-contact child pornography offenders. *Journal of Sexual Aggression, 16,* 181–195. doi:10.1080/13552601003760006

McClanahan, S. F., McClelland, G. M., Abram, K. M., & Teplin, L. A. (1999). Pathways into prostitution among female jail detainees and their implications for mental health services. *Psychiatric Services, 50,* 1606–1613.

McGee, L., & Newcomb, M. D. (1992). General deviance syndrome: Expanded hierarchical evaluations at four ages from early adolescence to adulthood. *Journal of Consulting and Clinical Psychology, 60,* 766–776. doi:10.1037/0022-006X.60.5.766

McGrath, R. J., Cumming, G. F., Burchard, B. L., Zeoli, S., & Ellerby, L. (2009). *Current practices and emerging trends in sexual abuser management: The Safer Society 2009 North American Survey.* Brandon, VT: Safer Society Press.

McLaughlin, J. F. (2000). *Cyber child sex offender typology.* Retrieved from http://web.archive.org/web/20040205045423/http://www.ci.keene.nh.us/police/Typology.html

McManus, M., Long, M. L., & Alison, L. (2011). Child pornography offenders: towards an evidenced-based approach to prioritizing the investigation of indecent image offences. In L. Alison & L. Rainbow (Eds.), *Professionalizing offender profiling* (pp. 178–188). Oxon, England: Routledge.

McMaster, L. E., Connolly, J., Pepler, D., & Craig, W. M. (2002). Peer to peer sexual harassment among early adolescents. *Development and Psychopathology, 14,* 91–105. doi:10.1017/S0954579402001050

McPhail, I. V. (2010). *Implicit and explicit emotional congruence with children in sexual offenders against children: A multi-method examination and cumulative meta-analysis*. Unpublished master's thesis, Carleton University, Ottawa, Ontario, Canada.

McWhaw, A. (2011). *Child pornography offender classification: Determining if online child pornography offenders constitute a unique sub-population of sex offenders using the predictive items of the Static-2002*. Unpublished master's thesis, University of Ottawa, Ottawa, Ontario, Canada.

Mehta, M. D. (2001). Pornography in Usenet: A study of 9,800 randomly selected images. *CyberPsychology & Behavior, 4*, 695–703. doi:10.1089/109493101753376641

Mehta, M. D., Best, D. & Poon, N. (2002). Peer-to-peer sharing on the Internet: An analysis of how Gnutella networks are used to distribute pornographic material. *Canadian Journal of Law and Technology, 1*(1). Retrieved from http://cjlt.dal.ca/vol1_no1/articles/01_01_MeBePo_gnutella.pdf

Merdian, H. L., Curtis, C., Thakker, J., Wilson, N., & Boer, D. P. (2011). The three dimensions of online child pornography offending. *Journal of Sexual Aggression*. doi:10.1080/13552600.2011.611898

Michel, J.-B., Shen, Y. K., Aiden, A. P., Veres, A., Gray, M. K., The Google Books Team, . . . Aiden, E. L. (2011, January 14). Quantitative analysis of culture using millions of digitized books. *Science, 331*(6014), 176–182. doi:10.1126/science.1199644

Middleton, D. (2009). Internet sex offenders. In A. Beech, L. Craig, & K. Browne (Eds.), *Assessment and treatment of sex offenders: A handbook* (pp. 199–215). London, England: Wiley.

Middleton, D., Elliott, I. A., Mandeville-Norden, R., & Beech, A. R. (2006). An investigation into the application of the Ward and Siegert pathways model of child sexual abuse with Internet offenders. *Psychology, Crime & Law, 12*, 589–603. doi:10.1080/10683160600558352

Middleton, D., Mandeville-Norden, R., & Hayes, E. (2009). Does treatment work with Internet sex offenders? Emerging findings from the Internet Sex Offender Treatment Programme (i-SOTP). *Journal of Sexual Aggression, 15*, 5–19. doi:10.1080/13552600802673444

Miner, M. H., Coleman, E., Center, B. A., Ross, M., & Rosser, B. R. S. (2007). The Compulsive Sexual Behavior Inventory: Psychometric properties. *Archives of Sexual Behavior, 36*, 579–587. doi:10.1007/s10508-006-9127-2

Ministry of Justice. (n.d.). *Internet Sex Offender Treatment Programme (i-SOTP)*. Retrieved from http://www.ynyprobation.co.uk/files/i-SOTP.pdf

Mishna, F., McLuckie, A., & Saini, M. (2009). Real-world dangers in an online reality: A qualitative study examining online relationships and cyber abuse. *Social Work Research, 33*, 107–118.

Mishra, S., & Lalumière, M. L. (2009). Is the crime drop of the 1990s in Canada and the USA associated with a general decline in risky and health-related behaviors? *Social Science & Medicine, 68*, 39–48. doi:10.1016/j.socscimed.2008.09.060

Mitchell, K. J., Finkelhor, D., Jones, L., & Wolak, J. (2010). Use of social networking sites in online sex crimes against minors: An examination of national incidence and means of utilization. *Journal of Adolescent Health, 47*, 183–190. doi:10.1016/j.jadohealth.2010.01.007

Mitchell, K. J., Finkelhor, D., & Wolak, J. (2001, June 20). Risk factors for and impact of online sexual solicitation of youth. *JAMA, 285*(23), 3011–3014. doi:10.1001/jama.285.23.3011

Mitchell, K. J., Finkelhor, D., & Wolak, J. (2007). Online requests for sexual pictures from youth: Risk factors and incident characteristics. *Journal of Adolescent Health, 41*, 196–203. doi:10.1016/j.jadohealth.2007.03.013

Mitchell, K. J., Finkelhor, D., & Wolak, J. (2010). Conceptualizing juvenile prostitution as child maltreatment: Findings from the National Juvenile Prostitution Study. *Child Maltreatment, 15*, 18–36. doi:10.1177/1077559509349443

Mitchell, K. J., Finkelhor, D., Wolak, J., & Jones, L. M. (2010). Growth and change in undercover online child exploitation investigations in the U.S., 2000 to 2006. *Policing & Society, 20*, 416–431. doi:10.1080/10439463.2010.523113

Mitchell, K. J., Jones, L. M., Finkelhor, D., & Wolak, J. (2011). Internet-facilitated commercial sexual exploitation of children: Findings from a nationally representative sample of law enforcement agencies in the United States. *Sexual Abuse: A Journal of Research and Treatment, 23*, 43–71.

Mitchell, K. J., Wolak, J., & Finkelhor, D. (2005). Police posing as juveniles online to catch sex offenders: Is it working? *Sexual Abuse: A Journal of Research and Treatment, 17*, 241–267.

Mitchell, K. J., Wolak, J., & Finkelhor, D. (2007). Trends in youth reports of unwanted sexual solicitations, harassment and unwanted exposure to pornography on the Internet. *Journal of Adolescent Health, 40*, 116–126. doi:10.1016/j.jadohealth.2006.05.021

Moffitt, T. E. (1993). Adolescence-limited and life-course-persistent antisocial behavior: A developmental taxonomy. *Psychological Review, 100*, 674–701. doi:10.1037/0033-295X.100.4.674

Mohr, J., Turner, R. E., & Jerry, M. B. (1964). *Pedophilia and exhibitionism: A handbook.* Toronto, Ontario, Canada: University of Toronto Press.

Monahan, J. (1981). *Predicting violent behavior: An assessment of clinical techniques.* Beverly Hills, CA: Sage.

Moore, R., Lee, T., & Hunt, R. (2007). Entrapped in the web? Applying the entrapment defense to cases involving online sting operations, *American Journal of Criminal Justice, 32*(1–2), 87–98.

Morahan-Martin, J., & Schumacher, P. (2000). Incidence and correlates of pathological Internet use among college students. *Computers in Human Behavior, 16*, 13–29.

Morozov, E. (2011). *The Net delusion: The dark side of Internet freedom.* New York, NY: PublicAffairs. doi:10.1017/S1537592711004026

Motiuk, L., & Vuong, B. (2002). *Homicide, sex, robbery and drug offenders in federal corrections: An end-of-2001 review.* Ottawa, Ontario, Canada: Correctional Service of Canada.

Motiuk, L. L., & Brown, S. (1993). *Survival time until suspension for sex offenders on conditional release* (Research Report No. 31). Ottawa, Ontario, Canada: Research and Statistics Branch, Correctional Service Canada.

Motivans, M., & Kyckelhahn, T. (2007). Federal prosecution of child sex exploitation offenders, 2006. *Bureau of Justice Statistics Bulletin* (Report No. NCJ 219412). Washington, DC: Bureau of Justice Statistics.

Moultrie, D. (2006). Adolescents convicted of possession of abuse images of children: A new type of adolescent sex offender? *Journal of Sexual Aggression, 12,* 165–174. doi:10.1080/13552600600823670

Nathan, D., & Snedeker, M. (2001). *Satan's silence: Ritual abuse and the making of a modern American witch hunt.* New York, NY: Basic Books.

The National Campaign to Prevent Teen and Unplanned Pregnancy. (2008). Retrieved from thenationalcampaign.org/sextech/PDF/SexTech_Summary.pdf

Neidigh, L. W., & Tomiko, R. (1991). The coping strategies of child sexual abusers. *Journal of Sex Education & Therapy, 17,* 103–110.

Neutze, J., Seto, M. C., Schaefer, G. A., Mundt, I. A., & Beier, K. M. (2011). Predictors of child pornography offenses and child sexual abuse in a community sample of pedophiles and hebephiles. *Sexual Abuse: A Journal of Research and Treatment, 23,* 212–242. doi:10.1177/1079063210382043

Ng, E. M. L. (2002). Pedophilia from the Chinese perspective. *Archives of Sexual Behavior, 31,* 491.

Nicholas, S., Kershaw, C., & Walker, H. (2007). *Crime in England and Wales 2006/2007.* London, England: Home Office. Retrieved from http://webarchive. nationalarchives.gov.uk/20110218135832/http://rds.homeoffice.gov.uk/rds/ pdfs07/hosb1107.pdf

Nielssen, O., O'Dea, J., Sullivan, D., Rodriguez, M., Bourget, D., & Large, M. (2011). Child pornography offenders detected by surveillance of the Internet and by other methods. *Criminal Behaviour and Mental Health, 21,* 215–224. doi:10.1002/ cbm.809

O'Brien, S. (1983). *Child pornography.* Dubuque, IA: Kendall/Hunt.

O'Carroll, T. (1980). *Paedophilia: The radical case.* Retrieved from ipce.info/host/ radicase

O'Connell, R. (2003). *A typology of child cybersexploitation and online grooming practices.* Preston, England: University of Central Lancashire. Retrieved from http:// image.guardian.co.uk/sys-files/Society/documents/2003/07/24/Netpaedoreport. pdf

O'Connor, C. (2005). Child pornography and the Internet—A statistical review. *Australian Police Journal, 59,* 190–199.

Ogas, O., & Gaddam, S. (2011). *A billion wicked thoughts: What the world's largest experiment reveals about human desire*. New York, NY: Dutton.

O'Halloran, E., & Quayle, E. (2010). A content analysis of a "boy love" support forum: Revisiting Durkin and Bryant. *Journal of Sexual Aggression, 16*, 71–85. doi:10.1080/13552600903395319

Olver, M. E., Wong, S. C. P., Nicholaichuk, T., & Gordon, A. (2007). The validity and reliability of the Violence Risk Scale—Sexual Offender Version: Assessing sex offender risk and evaluating therapeutic change. *Psychological Assessment, 19*, 318–329. doi:10.1037/1040-3590.19.3.318

Oosterbaan, D. (2005, May). Meeting the law enforcement challenges of online child victimization in the United States. In M. Eisen & R. Owens (Chairs), *Symposium on Online Child Exploitation*. Symposium conducted at the meeting of University of Toronto Centre for Innovation Law and Policy, Toronto, Ontario, Canada.

Oosterbaan, D., & Ibrahim, A. (2009). *Report to LEPSG on the "Global Symposium for Examining the Relationship Between Online and Offline Offenses and Preventing the Sexual Exploitation of Children."* Washington, DC: U.S. Department of Justice. Retrieved from http://www.iprc.unc.edu/G8/FinalReport.pdf

Osborn, J., Elliott, I., Middleton, D., & Beech, A. (2010). The use of actuarial risk assessment measures with UK Internet child pornography offenders. *Journal of Aggression, Conflict and Peace Research, 2*, 16–24. doi:10.5042/jacpr.2010.0333

Otto, R. K., & Douglas, K. S. (Eds.). (2009). *Handbook of violence risk assessment*. New York, NY: Routledge.

Pakhomou, S. M. (2006). Methodological aspects of telephone scatologia: A case study. *International Journal of Law and Psychiatry, 29*, 178–185. doi:10.1016/j.ijlp.2005.09.005

Palmer, T. (2011, June). *Online offending behaviour—Implications for child protection and the best interests of the child*. Paper presented at the Harm In The Digital Playground Conference of the Ontario Association of Children's Aid Societies, Toronto, Ontario, Canada.

Paul, B., & Linz, D. G. (2008). The effects of exposure to virtual child pornography on viewer cognitions and attitudes toward deviant sexual behavior. *Communication Research, 35*, 3–38. doi:10.1177/0093650207309359

Peter, J., & Valkenburg, P. M. (2006). Adolescents' exposure to sexually explicit online material and recreational attitudes toward sex. *The Journal of Communication, 56*, 639–660. doi:10.1111/j.1460-2466.2006.00313.x

Peter, T. (2009). Exploring taboos: Comparing male- and female-perpetrated child sexual abuse. *Journal of Interpersonal Violence, 24*, 1111–1128. doi:10.1177/0886260508322194

Petersen, J. L., & Hyde, J. S. (2010). A meta-analytic review of research on gender differences in sexuality: 1993 to 2007. *Psychological Bulletin, 136*, 21–38. doi:10.1037/a0017504

Pithers, W. D., Marques, J. K., Gibat, C. C., & Marlatt, G. A. (1983). Relapse prevention: A self-control model of treatment and maintenance of change for sexual aggressives. In J. Greer and I. R. Stuart (Eds.), *The sexual aggressor: Current perspective on treatment* (pp. 214–239). New York, NY: Van Nostrand Reinhold.

Plaud, J. J. (2009). Are there "hebephiles" among us? A response to Blanchard et al. *Archives of Sexual Behavior, 38*, 326–327. doi:10.1007/s10508-008-9423-0

Potterat, J. J., Rothenberg, R. B., Muth, S. Q., Darrow, W. W., & Phillips-Plummer, L. (1998). Pathways to prostitution: The chronology of sexual and drug abuse milestones. *Journal of Sex Research, 35*, 333–340. doi:10.1080/00224499809551951

Prentky, R., Burgess, A., Dowdell, E. B., Fedoroff, P., Malamuth, N., & Schuler, A. (2010). *A multi-prong approach to strengthening Internet child safety*. Needham, MA: Justice Resource Institute.

Prentky, R. A., Knight, R. A., & Lee, A. F. S. (1997). Risk factors associated with recidivism among extrafamilial child molesters. *Journal of Consulting and Clinical Psychology, 65*, 141–149. doi:10.1037/0022-006X.65.1.141

Price, M., Gutheil, T. G., Commons, M. L., Kafka, M. P., & Dodd-Kimmey, S. (2009). Telephone scatologia: Comorbidity and theories of etiology. *Psychiatric Annals, 31*, 226–232.

Prichard, J., Watters, P. A., & Spiranovic, C. (2011). Internet subcultures and pathways to the use of child pornography. *Computer Law & Security Review, 27*, 585–600. doi:10.1016/j.clsr.2011.09.009

Prosecutorial Remedies and Other Tools to end the Exploitation of Children Today (PROTECT) Act of 2003, S. 151 (2003).

Protecting Children From Internet Pornographers Act of 2011, H.R. 1981.

Protection of Children and Prevention of Sexual Offences (Scotland) Act 2005.

Proulx, J., McKibben, A., & Lusignan, R. (1996). Relationships between affective components and sexual behaviours in sexual aggressors. *Sexual Abuse: A Journal of Research and Treatment, 8*, 279–289.

PublicResourceOrg. (2009, June 6). *Special needs offenders: FCI Butner sex offender treatment program (Part 1, Tape 1 of 2)* [Video file]. Retrieved from http://www.youtube.com/watch?v=k2Ogdifmw4k

Quayle, E. (2008). Online sex offending: Psychopathology and theory. In D. R. Laws & W. T. O'Donohue (Eds.), *Sexual deviance* (2nd ed., pp. 439–458). New York, NY: Guilford Press.

Quayle, E., Erooga, M., Wright, L., Taylor, M., & Harbinson, D. (2006). *Only pictures? Therapeutic work with Internet sex offenders*. Dorset, England: Russell House.

Quayle, E., & Jones, T. (2011). Sexualized images of children on the Internet. *Sexual Abuse: A Journal of Research and Treatment, 23*, 7–21.

Quayle, E., & Taylor, M. (2002). Child pornography and the Internet: Perpetuating a cycle of abuse. *Deviant Behavior, 23*, 331–362. doi:10.1080/01639620290086413

Quayle, E., & Taylor, M. (2003). Model of problematic Internet use in people with sexual interest in children. *CyberPsychology & Behavior, 6*, 93–106. doi:10.1089/109493103321168009

Quinn, B. (2012, September 28). Jimmy Savile alleged to have abused girls as young as 13. *The Guardian*. Retrieved from http://www.guardian.co.uk/tv-and-radio/2012/sep/28/jimmy-savile-abused-girls-alleged

Quinsey, V. L., Coleman, G., Jones, B., & Altrows, I. (1997). Proximal antecedents of eloping and reoffending among mentally disordered offenders. *Journal of Interpersonal Violence, 12*, 794–813. doi:10.1177/088626097012006002

Quinsey, V. L., Harris, G. T., Rice, M. E., & Cormier, C. A. (2006). *Violent offenders: Appraising and managing risk* (2nd ed.). Washington, DC: American Psychological Association. doi:10.1037/11367-000

Quinsey, V. L., Skilling, T. A., Lalumière, M. L., & Craig, W. (2004). *Juvenile delinquency: Understanding individual differences*. Washington, DC: American Psychological Association. doi:10.1037/10623-000

Rainie, L. (2010). *Internet, broadband, and cell phone statistics*. Pew Internet & American Life Project. Retrieved from http://www.pewinternet.org/Reports/2010/Internet-broadband-and-cell-phone-statistics.aspx

Ray, J. V., Kimonis, E. R., & Donoghue, C. (2010). Legal, ethical, and methodological considerations in the Internet-based study of child pornography offenders. *Behavioral Sciences & the Law, 28*, 84–105. doi:10.1002/bsl.906

Ray, J. V., Kimonis, E. R., & Seto, M. C. (in press). Personality and behavioral correlates of child pornography use in a community sample. *Sexual Abuse: A Journal of Research and Treatment*.

Reijnen, L., Bulten, E., & Nijman, H. (2009). Demographic and personality characteristics of Internet child pornography downloaders in comparison to other offenders. *Journal of Child Sexual Abuse, 18*, 611–622. doi:10.1080/10538710903317232

Renaud, P., Joyal, C., Stoleru, S., Goyette, M., Weiskopf, N., & Birbaumer, N. (2011). Real-time functional magnetic imaging-brain-computer interface and virtual reality. promising tools for the treatment of pedophilia. *Progress in Brain Research, 192*, 263–272. doi:10.1016/B978-0-444-53355-5.00014-2

Ribisl, K., & Quayle, E. (Eds.). (2012). *Internet child pornography: Understanding and preventing on-line child abuse*. Devon, England: Willan.

Rice, M. E., Harris, G. T., Lang, C., & Cormier, C. A. (2006). Violent sex offenses: How are they best measured from official records? *Law and Human Behavior, 30*, 525–541.

Riegel, D. L. (2004). Effects on boy-attracted pedosexual males of viewing boy erotica [Letter to the editor]. *Archives of Sexual Behavior, 33*, 321–323. doi:10.1023/B:ASEB.0000029071.89455.53

Rind, B., Tromovitch, P., & Bauserman, R. (1998). A meta-analytic examination of assumed properties of child sexual abuse using college samples. *Psychological Bulletin, 124*, 22–53. doi:10.1037/0033-2909.124.1.22

R. Kelly to be tried on child pornography charges. (2007, August 2). *CNN.com*. Retrieved from http://www.cnn.com/2007/SHOWBIZ/Music/08/02/pornography.rkelly.reut/index.html?eref=rss_topstories

Rosenbloom, M. L., & Tanner, J. (1998). Misuse of Tanner puberty stages to estimate chronological age. *Pediatrics, 102*, 1494. doi:10.1542/peds.102.6.1494

Sabina, C., Wolak, J., & Finkelhor, D. (2008). The nature and dynamics of Internet pornography exposure for youth under 18. *CyberPsychology & Behavior, 11*, 691–693. doi:10.1089/cpb.2007.0179

Salter, D., McMillan, D., Richards, M., Talbot, T., Hodges, J., Bentovim, A., . . . Skuse, D. (2003, February 8). Development of sexually abusive behaviour in sexually victimised males: A longitudinal study. *The Lancet, 361*(9356), 471–476. doi:10.1016/S0140-6736(03)12466-X

Santtila, P., Mokros, A., Hartwig, M., Varjonen, M., Jern, P., Witting, K., . . . Sandnabba, N. K. (2010). Childhood sexual interactions with other children are associated with lower preferred age of sexual partners including sexual interest in children in adulthood. *Psychiatry Research, 1–2*, 154–159. doi.org/10.1016/j.psychres.2008.10.021

Savage, D. (2012, March 7). Another gold-star pedophile. *Savage Love* [Web log message]. Retrieved from http://www.thestranger.com/seattle/SavageLove?oid=12927907

Schell, B. H., Martin, M. V., Hung, P. C. K., & Rueda, L. (2006). Cyber child pornography: A review paper of the social and legal issues and remedies—And a proposed technological solution. *Aggression and Violent Behavior, 12*, 45–63. doi:10.1016/j.avb.2006.03.003

Schild, M. (1988). The irresistible beauty of boys: Middle Eastern attitudes about boy-love. *Paidika: The Journal of Paedophilia, 1*, 37–48.

Schneider, J. P. (2000). Effects of cybersex addiction on the family: Results of a survey. *Sexual Addiction & Compulsivity, 7*, 31–58. doi:10.1080/10720160008400206

Schram, D., & Milloy, C. (1995). *Community notification: A study of offender characteristics and recidivism* (Research Report 95-10-1101). Olympia, WA: Washington State Institute for Public Policy.

Schwartz, J. (2010, February 2). Child pornography and an issue of restitution. *The New York Times.* Retrieved from https://www.nytimes.com/2010/02/03/us/03offender.html?_r=1#articleBodyLink

Schwartz, M. F., & Masters, W. H. (1994). Integration of trauma-based, cognitive, behavioral, systemic and addiction approaches for treatment of hypersexual pair-bonding disorder. *Sexual Addiction & Compulsivity, 1*, 57–76. doi:10.1080/10720169408400028

Seigfried, K. C., Lovely, R. W., & Rogers, M. K. (2008). Self-reported online child pornography behavior: A psychological analysis. *International Journal of Cyber Criminology, 2*, 286–297.

Serran, G. A., & Marshall, L. E. (2006). Coping and mood in sexual offending. In W. L. Marshall, Y. M. Fernandez, L. E. Marshall, & G. A. Serran (Eds.), *Sexual offender treatment: Controversial issues* (pp. 109–124). London, England: Wiley.

Seto, M. C. (1992). A review of anxiety and sexual arousal in human sexual dysfunction. *Annals of Sex Research, 5*, 33–43. doi:10.1177/107906329200500102

Seto, M. C. (2001). The value of phallometry in the assessment of male sex offenders. *Journal of Forensic Psychology Practice, 1*, 65–75. doi:10.1300/J158v01n02_05

Seto, M. C. (2003). Interpreting the treatment performance of sex offenders. In A. Matravers (Ed.), *Managing sex offenders in the community: Contexts, challenges, and responses* (pp. 125–143). London, England: Willan.

Seto, M. C. (2005). Is more better? Combining actuarial risk scales to predict recidivism among adult sex offenders. *Psychological Assessment, 17*, 156–167. doi:10.1037/1040-3590.17.2.156

Seto, M. C. (2008). *Pedophilia and sexual offending against children: Theory, assessment, and intervention.* Washington, DC: American Psychological Association. doi:10.1037/11639-000

Seto, M. C. (2009, October). *"A picture is better than a thousand words": What do we know about child pornography offenders?* Plenary address presented at the 28th annual conference of the Association for the Treatment of Sexual Abusers, Dallas, TX. Slides retrieved from http://www.atsa.com/sites/default/files/ConfHO2009Seto.pdf

Seto, M. C. (2010). Child pornography use and Internet solicitation in the diagnosis of pedophilia [Letter to the editor]. *Archives of Sexual Behavior, 39*, 591–593. doi:10.1007/s10508-010-9603-6

Seto, M. C. (2012). Is pedophilia a sexual orientation? *Archives of Sexual Behavior, 41*, 231–236. doi:10.1007/s10508-011-9882-6

Seto, M. C., & Barbaree, H. E. (1995). The role of alcohol in sexual aggression. *Clinical Psychology Review, 15*, 545–566. doi:10.1016/0272-7358(95)00033-L

Seto, M. C., & Barbaree, H. E. (1997). Sexual aggression as antisocial behavior: A developmental model. In D. Stoff, J. Breiling, & J. D. Maser (Eds.), *Handbook of antisocial behavior* (pp. 524–533). New York, NY: Wiley.

Seto, M. C., Cantor, J. M., & Blanchard, R. (2006). Child pornography offenses are a valid diagnostic indicator of pedophilia. *Journal of Abnormal Psychology, 115*, 610–615. doi:10.1037/0021-843X.115.3.610

Seto, M. C., & Eke, A. W. (2005). The future offending of child pornography offenders. *Sexual Abuse: A Journal of Research and Treatment, 17*, 201–210.

Seto, M. C., & Fernandez, Y. M. (2011). Dynamic risk groups among adult male sexual offenders. *Sexual Abuse: A Journal of Research and Treatment, 23*, 494–507. doi:10.1177/1079063211403162

Seto, M. C., & Hanson, R. K. (2011). Introduction to Special Issue on Internet-facilitated sexual offending. *Sexual Abuse: A Journal of Research and Treatment, 23*, 3–6. doi:10.1177/1079063211399295

Seto, M. C., Hanson, R. K., & Babchishin, K. M. (2011). Contact sexual offending by men arrested for child pornography offenses. *Sexual Abuse: A Journal of Research and Treatment, 23*, 124–145.

Seto, M. C., Harris, G. T., Rice, M. E., & Barbaree, H. E. (2004). The Screening Scale for Pedophilic Interests and recidivism among adult sex offenders with child victims. *Archives of Sexual Behavior, 33,* 455–466. doi:10.1023/B:ASEB.0000037426.55935.9c

Seto, M. C., Hermann, C. A., Kjellgren, C., Priebe, G., Svedin, C. G., & Långström, N. (2013). *Viewing child pornography: Correlates in a representative community sample of young men.* Manuscript submitted for publication.

Seto, M. C., Kjellgren, C., Priebe, G., Mossige, S., Svedin, C. G., & Långström, N. (2010). Sexual victimization and sexually coercive behavior: A population study of Swedish and Norwegian male youth. *Child Maltreatment, 15,* 219–228. doi:10.1177/1077559510367937

Seto, M. C., & Lalumière, M. L. (2001). A brief screening scale to identify pedophilic interests among child molesters. *Sexual Abuse: A Journal of Research and Treatment, 13,* 15–25. doi:10.1177/107906320101300103

Seto, M. C., & Lalumière, M. L. (2010). What is so special about male adolescent sexual offending? A review and test of explanations using meta-analysis. *Psychological Bulletin, 136,* 526–575. doi:10.1037/a0019700

Seto, M. C., Lalumière, M. L., & Kuban, M. (1999). The sexual preferences of incest offenders. *Journal of Abnormal Psychology, 108,* 267–272. doi:10.1037/0021-843X.108.2.267

Seto, M. C., Lalumière, M. L., & Quinsey, V. L. (1995). Sensation seeking and males' sexual strategy. *Personality and Individual Differences, 19,* 669–675. doi:10.1016/0191-8869(95)00101-B

Seto, M. C., Maric, A., & Barbaree, H. E. (2001). The role of pornography in the etiology of sexual aggression. *Aggression and Violent Behavior, 6,* 35–53. doi:10.1016/S1359-1789(99)00007-5

Seto, M. C., Marques, J. K., Harris, G. T., Chaffin, M., Lalumière, M. L., Miner, M. H., . . . Quinsey, V. L. (2008). Good science and progress in sex offender treatment are intertwined: A response to Marshall and Marshall (2007). *Sexual Abuse: A Journal of Research and Treatment, 20,* 247–255.

Seto, M. C., Reeves, L., & Jung, S. (2010). Motives for child pornography offending: The explanations given by the offenders. *Journal of Sexual Aggression, 16,* 169–180. doi:10.1080/13552600903572396

Seto, M. C., Wood, J. M., Babchishin, K. M., & Flynn, S. (2012). Online solicitation offenders are different from child pornography offenders and lower risk contact sexual offenders. *Law and Human Behavior, 36,* 320–330.

Sexual Exploitation of Children Act (1978). 18 USC § 2251.

Shaffer, H. J. (1994). Considering two models of excessive sexual behaviors: Addiction and obsessive-compulsive disorder. *Sexual Addiction & Compulsivity, 1,* 6–18. doi:10.1080/10720169408400024

Sheehan, V., & Sullivan, J. (2010). A qualitative analysis of child sex offenders involved in the manufacture of indecent images of children. *Journal of Sexual Aggression, 16,* 143–167. doi:10.1080/13552601003698644

Sheffield, C. (1989). The invisible intruder: Women's experiences of obscene phone calls. *Gender & Society, 3*, 483–488. doi:10.1177/089124389003004006

Sheldon, K., & Howitt, D. (2008). Sexual fantasy in paedophile offenders: Can any model explain satisfactorily new findings from a study of Internet and contact sexual offenders? *Legal and Criminological Psychology, 13*, 137–158. doi:10.1348/135532506X173045

Sher, J. (2007). *One child at a time: The global fight to rescue children from online predators.* Toronto, Ontario, Canada: Random House Canada.

Sher, J. (2011). *Somebody's daughter: The hidden story of America's prostituted children and the battle to save them.* Chicago, IL: Chicago Review Press.

Shim, J. W., Lee, S., & Paul, B. (2007). Who responds to unsolicited sexually explicit materials on the Internet? The role of individual differences. *CyberPsychology & Behavior, 10*, 71–79. doi:10.1089/cpb.2006.9990

Silverman, J. G., Raj, A., Mucci, L. A., & Hathaway, J. E. (2001, August 1). Dating violence against adolescent girls and associated substance use, unhealthy weight control, sexual risk behavior, pregnancy, and suicidality. *JAMA, 286*(5), 572–579. doi:10.1001/jama.286.5.572

Sit down with a molestation survivor [Transcript]. (January 18, 2006). In *Nancy Grace*. Retrieved from http://transcripts.cnn.com/TRANSCRIPTS/0601/18/ng.01.html

Smallbone, S., Marshall, W. L., & Wortley, R. K. (2008). *Preventing child sexual abuse: Evidence, policy and practice.* Devon, England: Willan.

Smith, A. (2007). *Teens and online stranger contact.* Retrieved from pewInternet.org/PPF/r/223/report_display.asp

Specter, A., & Hoffa, L. (2012). A quiet but growing judicial rebellion against harsh sentences for child pornography offenses—Should the laws be changed? *The Champion, 33*(6). Retrieved from nacdl.org/champion.aspx?id=22897

Spielhofer, T. (2010). *Children's online risks and safety: A review of the available evidence.* Retrieved from media.education.gov.uk/assets/files/pdf/c/childrens%20online%20risks%20and%20safety%20nfer%202010.pdf

Stabenow, T. (2011). A method for careful study: A proposal for reforming the child pornography guidelines. *Federal Sentencing Reporter, 24*, 108–136. doi:10.1525/fsr.2011.24.2.108

Stack, S., Wasserman, I., & Kern, R. (2004). Adult social bonds and use of Internet pornography. *Social Science Quarterly, 85*, 75–88. doi:10.1111/j.0038-4941.2004.08501006.x

Stathopulu, E., Huse, J. A., & Canning, D. (2003). Difficulties with age estimation of Internet images of South-East Asian girls. *Child Abuse Review, 12*, 46–57. doi:10.1002/car.781

Steel, C. M. (2009). Child pornography in peer-to-peer networks. *Child Abuse & Neglect, 33*, 560–568. doi:10.1016/j.chiabu.2008.12.011

Steele, C. M., & Josephs, R. A. (1990). Alcohol myopia: Its prized and dangerous effects. *American Psychologist, 45*, 921–933. doi:10.1037/0003-066X.45.8.921

Suler, J. (2004). The online disinhibition effect. *CyberPsychology & Behavior, 7*, 321–326. doi:10.1089/1094931041291295

Sullivan, J., & Beech, A. R. (2003). Are collectors of child abuse images a risk to children? In A. MacVean & P. Spindler (Eds.), *Policing paedophiles on the Internet* (pp. 11–20). London, England: The New Police Bookshop.

Surjadi, B., Bullens, R., van Horn, J., & Bogaerts, S. (2010). Internet offending: Sexual and non-sexual functions within a Dutch sample. *Journal of Sexual Aggression, 16*, 47–58. doi:10.1080/13552600903470054

Svedin, C. G., Back, K., & Barnen, R. (1996). *Children who don't speak out: About children being used in child pornography.* Stockholm, Sweden: Radda Baren.

Tannahill, R. (1980). *Sex in history.* New York, NY: Stein & Day.

Taylor, M., Holland, G., & Quayle, E. (2001). Typology of paedophile picture collections. *The Police Journal, 74*, 97–107.

Taylor, M., & Quayle, E. (2003). *Child pornography: An Internet crime.* New York, NY: Brunner-Routledge.

Taylor, M., & Quayle, E. (2008). Criminogenic qualities of the Internet in the collection and distribution of abuse images of children. *The Irish Journal of Psychology, 29*, 119–130. doi:10.1080/03033910.2008.10446278

Templeman, T. L., & Stinnett, R. D. (1991). Patterns of sexual arousal and history in a "normal" sample of young men. *Archives of Sexual Behavior, 20*, 137–150. doi:10.1007/BF01541940

Terr, L. (1990). *Too scared to cry: Psychic trauma in childhood.* New York, NY: Basic Books.

Tewksbury, R. (2005). Collateral consequences of sex offender registration. *Journal of Contemporary Criminal Justice, 21*, 67–81. doi:10.1177/1043986204271704

Thomas, F., Renaud, F., Benefice, E., De Meeüs, & Geugan, J.-F. (2001). International variability of ages at menarche and menopause: Patterns and main determinants. *Human Biology, 73*, 271–290.

Thornton, D., Mann, R., Webster, S., Blud, L., Travers, R., Friendship, C., & Erikson, M. (2003). Distinguishing and combining risks for sexual and violent recidivism. *Annals of New York Academy of Sciences, 989*, 225–235. http://dx.doi.org/10.1111/j.1749-6632.2003.tb07308.x

Tomak, S., Weschler, F. S., Ghahramanlou-Holloway, M., Virden, T., & Nademin, M. E. (2009). An empirical study of the personality characteristics of Internet sex offenders. *Journal of Sexual Aggression, 15*, 139–149. doi:10.1080/13552600902823063

Trevethan, S., Crutcher, N., & Moore, J.-P. (2002). *A profile of federal offenders designated as dangerous offenders or serving long-term supervision orders* (Research report). Ottawa, Ontario, Canada: Correctional Service of Canada. Retrieved from http://www.csc-scc.gc.ca/text/rsrch/reports/r125/r125-eng.shtml

Tromovitch, P. (2009). Manufacturing mental disorder by pathologizing erotic age orientation: A comment on Blanchard et al. *Archives of Sexual Behavior, 38*, 328. doi:10.1007/s10508-008-9426-x

Troup-Leasure, K., & Snyder, H. (2005). *Statutory rape known to law enforcement* (Juvenile Justice Bulletin No. NCJ 208803). Washington, DC: Office of Juvenile Justice and Delinquency Prevention.

Tsim (2006). *Internet safety education: Information retention among middle school aged children*. San Jose, CA: San Jose State University Press.

United Kingdom Children's Council on Internet Safety. (2010). *Children's online risks and safety: A review of the available evidence* (Research report). Retrieved from http://media.education.gov.uk/assets/files/pdf/c/childrens%20online%20risks%20and%20safety%20nfer%202010.pdf

United Nations Office on Drugs and Crime. (2010). *The globalization of crime: A transnational organized crime threat assessment*. Vienna, Austria: Author. Retrieved from unodc.org/documents/data-and-analysis/tocta/TOCTA_Report_2010_low_res.pdf

U.S. Department of Education. (2011). *Student reports of bullying and cyber-bullying: Results from the 2007 School Crime Supplement to the National Crime Victimization Survey*. Washington, DC: Author. Retrieved from http://nces.ed.gov/pubs2011/2011316.pdf

U.S. Department of Justice. (2010). *The National Strategy for Child Exploitation Prevention and Interdiction: A report to Congress*. Washington, DC: Author. Retrieved from http://www.justice.gov/psc/docs/execsummary.pdf

U.S. Sentencing Commission. (2009). *The history of the child pornography guidelines* (Research report). Retrieved from http://www.ussc.gov/Research/Research_Projects/Sex_Offenses/20091030_History_Child_Pornography_Guidelines.pdf

U.S. v. Comstock, 551 F. 3d 274, No. 08-1224 (2009).

U.S. v. Dost. 636 F. Supp. 828 (S.D. Cal. 1986).

van Naerssen, A. (1991). Man–boy lovers: Assessment, counseling, and psychotherapy. *Journal of Homosexuality, 20*, 175–187. doi:10.1300/J082v20n01_11

Vega, V., & Malamuth, N. (2007). The role of pornography in the context of general and specific risk factors. *Aggressive Behavior, 33*, 104–117. doi:10.1002/ab.20172

von Dornum, D. D. (2012, February). *Written statement before the United States Sentencing Commission Public Hearing on Child Pornography Sentencing*. Retrieved from http://www.ussc.gov/Legislative_and_Public_Affairs/Public_Hearings_and_Meetings/20120215-16/Testimony_15_vonDornum.pdf

Wakeling, H. C., Howard, P., & Barnett, G. (2011). Comparing the validity of the RM2000 scales and OGRS3 for predicting recidivism by Internet sexual offenders. *Sexual Abuse: A Journal of Research and Treatment, 23*, 146–168.

Wall, G. K., Pearce, E., & McGuire, J. (2011). Are internet offenders emotionally avoidant? *Psychology, Crime & Law, 17*, 381–401. doi:10.1080/10683160903292246

Walters, G. D. (2006). Risk-appraisal versus self-report in the prediction of criminal justice outcomes: A meta-analysis. *Criminal Justice and Behavior, 33*, 279–304. doi:10.1177/0093854805284409

Ward, T., Polaschek, D., & Beech, A. R. (2006). *Theories of sexual offending*. Chichester, England: Wiley.

Ward, T., & Siegert, R. J. (2002). Toward and comprehensive theory of child sexual abuse: A theory knitting perspective. *Psychology, Crime & Law, 8*, 319–351. doi:10.1080/10683160208401823

Webb, L., Craissati, J., & Keen, S. (2007). Characteristics of Internet child pornography offenders: A comparison with child molesters. *Sexual Abuse: A Journal of Research and Treatment, 19*, 449–465. doi:10.1007/s11194-007-9063-2

Webster, S., Davidson, J., Bifulco, A., Gottschalk, P., Caretti, V., Pham, T., . . . Craparo, G. (2012). *Final report: European Online Grooming Project*. Retrieved from http://www.natcen.ac.uk/media/843993/european-online-grooming-project-final-report.pdf

Webwise. (2006). *Survey of children's use of the Internet*. Retrieved from http://www.webwise.ie/Webwise2006Survey.pdf

Weiler, J., Haardt-Becker, A., & Schulte, S. (2010). Care and treatment of child victims of child pornographic exploitation (CPE) in Germany. *Journal of Sexual Aggression, 16*, 211–222. doi:10.1080/13552601003759990

Werner, E. E. (1993). Risk, resilience, and recovery: Perspectives from the Kauai Longitudinal Study. *Development and Psychopathology, 5*, 503–15. http://dx.doi.org/10.1017/S095457940000612X

Wheeler, D. L. (1997). The relationship between pornography usage and child molesting. *Dissertation Abstracts International: Section A. The Humanities and Social Sciences, 57*(8-A), 3691.

White, J. L., Moffitt, T. E., & Silva, P. A. (1989). A prospective replication of the protective effects of IQ in subjects at high risk for juvenile delinquency. *Journal of Consulting and Clinical Psychology, 57*, 719–724. doi:10.1037/0022-006X.57.6.719

Whittle, H., Hamilton-Giachritsis, C., Beech, A., & Collings, G. (2012). A review of online grooming: Characteristics and concerns. *Aggression and Violent Behavior*. doi:10.1016/j.avb.2012.09.003

Whitty, M. T. (2003). Pushing the wrong buttons: Men's and women's attitudes toward online and offline infidelity. *CyberPsychology and Behavior, 6*, 569–579. doi:10.1089/109493103322725342

Who star cautioned over child porn. (2003, December 19). *CNN.com*. Retrieved from http://edition.cnn.com/2003/WORLD/europe/05/07/uk.townshend/index.html

Widom, C. S., & Ames, M. A. (1994). Criminal consequences of childhood sexual victimization. *Child Abuse & Neglect, 18*, 303–318. doi:10.1016/0145-2134(94)90033-7

Wilson, G. D., & Cox, D. N. (1983). *The child-lovers: A study of paedophiles in society*. London, England: Peter Owen.

Winters, J., Christoff, K., & Gorzalka, B. B. (2010). Dysregulated sexuality and high sexual desire: Distinct constructs? *Archives of Sexual Behavior, 39*, 1029–1043. doi:10.1007/s10508-009-9591-6

Witt, P. H. (2010). Assessment of risk in Internet child pornography cases. *Sex Offender Law Report, 11*, 1–16.

Witt, P. H., Merdian, H. L., Connell, M., & Boer, D. P. (2010). Assessing parental risk in parenting plan (child custody) cases involving Internet sexual behavior. *Open Access Journal of Forensic Psychology, 2*, 116–136.

Wolak, J. (2011, October). *What we know (and don't know) about Internet sex offenders*. Paper presented at the annual meeting of the Association for the Treatment of Sexual Abusers, Toronto, Ontario, Canada. Retrieved from atsa.com/sites/default/files/ConfHO2011Wolak.pdf

Wolak, J. (2012). *Statement to the U.S. Sentencing Commission public hearing on federal child pornography offenses: Findings about sentencing from a national survey of local, state and federal law enforcement agencies*. Retrieved from: http://www.ussc.gov/Legislative_and_Public_Affairs/Public_Hearings_and_Meetings/20120215-16/Testimony_15_Wolak.pdf

Wolak, J., & Finkelhor, D. (2011). *Sexting: A typology*. Durham, NH: Crimes against Children Research Center.

Wolak, J., Finkelhor, D., & Mitchell, K. (2004). Internet-initiated sex crimes against minors: Implications for prevention based findings from a national study. *The Journal of Adolescent Health, 35*, 11–20. doi:10.1016/j.jadohealth.2004.05.006

Wolak, J., Finkelhor, D., & Mitchell, K. (2008). Is talking online to unknown people always risky? Distinguishing online interaction types in a national sample of youth Internet users. *CyberPsychology & Behavior, 11*, 340–343. doi:10.1089/cpb.2007.0044

Wolak, J., Finkelhor, D., & Mitchell, K. J. (2005). *Child-pornography possessors arrested in Internet-related crimes: Findings from the National Juvenile Online Victimization study*. Retrieved from unh.edu/ccrc/pdf/jvq/CV81.pdf

Wolak, J. Finkelhor, D., & Mitchell, K. J. (2009). *Law enforcement responses to online child sexual exploitation crimes: The National Juvenile Online Victimization Study, 2000 & 2006*. Retrieved from unh.edu/ccrc/pdf/LE_Bulletin_final_Dec_09.pdf

Wolak, J., Finkelhor, D., & Mitchell, K. J. (2011). Child pornography possessors: Trends in offender and case characteristics. *Sexual Abuse: A Journal of Research and Treatment, 23*, 22–42.

Wolak, J., Finkelhor, D., & Mitchell, K. J. (2012). How often are teens arrested for sexting? Data from a national sample of police cases. *Pediatrics, 129*, 4–12. doi:10.1542/peds.2011-2242

Wolak, J., Finkelhor, D., Mitchell, K. J., & Jones, L. M. (2011). Arrests for child pornography production: Data at two time points from a national sample of U.S. law enforcement agencies. *Child Maltreatment, 16*, 184–195. doi:10.1177/1077559511415837

Wolak, J., Finkelhor, D., Mitchell, K. J., & Ybarra, M. L. (2008). Online "predators" and their victims: Myths, realities, and implications for prevention and treatment. *American Psychologist, 63*, 111–128. doi:10.1037/0003-066X.63.2.111

Wollert, R. (2012). *The implications of recidivism research and clinical experience for assessing and treating federal child pornography offenders: Written testimony presented to the U.S. Sentencing Commission.* Retrieved from http://www.ussc.gov/Legislative_and_Public_Affairs/Public_Hearings_and_Meetings/20120215-16/Testimony_15_Wollert_2.pdf

Wollert, R., Cramer, E., Waggoner, J., Skelton, A., & Vess, J. (2010). Recent research (*N* = 9,305) underscores the importance of using age-stratified actuarial tables in sex offender risk assessments. *Sexual Abuse: A Journal of Research and Treatment, 22,* 471–490. doi:10.1177/1079063210384633

Wollert, R., Waggoner, J., & Smith, J. (2012). Federal Internet child pornography offenders—Limited offense histories and low recidivism rates. In B. K. Schwartz (Ed.), *The sex offender* (Vol. 7; pp. 2-1–2-21). Kingston, NJ: Civic Research Institute.

Wood, J. M., Seto, M. C., Flynn, S., Wilson-Cotton, S., & Dedmon, P. (2009, October). *Is it "just" pictures? The use of polygraph with Internet offenders who deny abusive sexual contact.* Poster presented at the 28th Annual Conference for the Association of the Treatment of Sexual Abusers, Dallas, TX.

World Health Organization. (2010). *International statistical classification of diseases and related health problems* (10th rev.). Retrieved from http://apps.who.int/classifications/icd10/browse/2010/en

Wortley, R., & Smallbone, S. (Eds.). (2006). *Situational prevention of sexual offenses against children.* Devon, England: Willan.

Yates, P., Prescott, D., & Ward, T. (2010). *Applying the good lives and self-regulation models to sex offender treatment: A practical guide for clinicians.* Brandon, VT: Safer Society Press.

Yates, P. M., & Kingston, D. A. (2006). Pathways to sexual offending: Relationship to static and dynamic risk among treated sexual offenders. *Sexual Abuse: A Journal of Research and Treatment, 18,* 259–270.

Ybarra, M. L., Espelage, D. L., & Mitchell, K. J. (2007). The co-occurrence of Internet harassment and unwanted sexual solicitation victimization and perpetration. *Journal of Adolescent Health, 41,* S31–S41. doi:10.1016/j.jadohealth.2007.09.010

Ybarra, M. L., & Mitchell, K. (2008). How risky are social networking sites? A comparison of places online where youth sexual solicitation and harassment occurs. *Pediatrics, 121,* e350–e357. doi:10.1542/peds.2007-0693

Ybarra, M. L., & Mitchell, K. J. (2005). Exposure to Internet pornography among children and adolescents: A national survey. *CyberPsychology & Behavior, 8,* 473–486. doi:10.1089/cpb.2005.8.473

Ybarra, M. L., Mitchell, K. J., Hamburger, M., Diener-West, M., & Leaf, P. J. (2011). X-rated material and perpetration of sexually aggressive behavior among children and adolescents: Is there a link? *Aggressive Behavior, 37,* 1–18. doi:10.1002/ab.20367

Yee, N., Bailenson, J. N., & Ducheneaut, N. (2009). The Proteus effect: Implications of transformed digital self-representation on online and offline behavior. *Communication Research, 36,* 285–312. doi: 10.1177/0093650208330254

Young, K. (2005). Profiling online sex offenders, cyber-predators, and pedophiles. *Journal of Behavioral Profiling, 5*, 1–18.

Young, S. (1997). The use of normalization as a strategy in the sexual exploitation of children by adult offenders. *Canadian Journal of Human Sexuality, 6*, 285–295.

Zander, T. K. (2009). Adult sexual attraction to early-stage adolescents: Phallometry doesn't equal pathology. *Archives of Sexual Behavior, 38*, 329–330. doi:10.1007/s10508-008-9428-8

Zgoba, K., Witt, P., Dalessandro, M., & Veysey, B. (2008). *Megan's Law: Assessing the practical and monetary efficacy* (Report on grant award 2006-IJ-CX-0018). Washington, DC: National Institute of Justice.

Zillman, D., & Bryant, J. (1998). Pornography's impact on sexual satisfaction. *Journal of Applied Social Psychology, 18*, 438–453. doi:10.1111/j.1559-1816.1988.tb00027.x

Zimring, F. E. (2006). *The great American crime decline.* Oxford, England: Oxford University Press. doi:10.1093/acprof:oso/9780195181159.001.0001

INDEX

Antisociality, *continued*
  in motivation–facilitation model of
      sexual offending, 127, 128, 129
  as offender characteristic, 158–159
  and pathways model of sexual
      offending, 238–239
  as risk factor for offenders, 196,
      202, 210
Apparently normal offenders, 163
Approach-automatic pathway to sexual
      offending, 237, 238
Approach-explicit pathway to sexual
      offending, 237
Arabic literature, child pornography
      in, 39
Arrests
  of adolescents for sexting, 68–69
  for child pornography offenses,
      51–53
Ashcroft v. Free Speech Condition, 63
Ashfield, S. A., 16–17
Asia, online sexual offending in, 268
Assault, online solicitation and, 95
Association for the Treatment of Sexual
      Abusers (ATSA), ix, 199,
      229, 241
Attitudes
  about women, 175
  offense-supportive. *See* Offense-
      supportive attitudes and beliefs
Attitudes supportive of sexual assault
      domain (Stable–2000), 200
Australia, child pornography and solici-
      tation laws in, 14
Availability, of online child pornogra-
      phy, 42–43
Avalanche (operation), 22, 54
Avoidant-active pathway to sexual
      offending, 236–237
Avoidant-passive pathway to sexual
      offending, 236, 238
Axis I psychopathology, 85

Babchishin, K. M., 89, 139–148, 150,
      151, 153, 159, 161, 180–181,
      183, 190n5, 194
Back, K., 257
Backpage.com, 32, 104
Bader, S. M., 112
Bagley, C., 43

Bail, 204–206
Barbaree, H. E., 126
Bare-backing, 100
Barely legal genre, 92
Barely Legal series, 34
Barnen, R., 257
Barnes, G., 174
Bar workers, 277–278
Barlow, John Perry, 13
Bates, A., 19, 140, 141
Beauregard, E., 179
Becker, M., 123
Beech, A., 213
Beech, A. R., 117–120, 141, 143, 163,
      165, 212, 237–238
Behavioral problems, of victims, 258
Beier, K. M., 21n5, 27, 141, 142na, 155,
      186–187, 214, 232
Beliefs, offense-supportive.
      See Offense-supportive
      attitudes and beliefs
Berner, W., 79, 176
Best, D., 42
Bhuller, M., 173
Biastophilia, 63
Bickart, W., 159, 204
Bickley, J. A., 237–238
BitTorrent, 21
Blanchard, R., 29n7, 141, 146, 152, 184
Blevins, K. R., 31, 59
Boer, D., 86–87, 213
Boeringer, S., 173
Bogaert, A. F., 48, 177
Bogaerts, S., 156–157
Bonta, J., 234, 281
Bourgon, G., 235
Bourke, M. L., 181–183, 215, 229
Boychat, 42n2, 57, 59, 60
Boy-lovers, 59
Boy moments, 60
Boy predator group (pathways model),
      120
Bradford, J. M., 112, 174–175
Briggs, P., 84–86, 91, 100
Briken, P., 79, 176
Brown, I. A., 121
Brown, J. D., 191–192
Browsers (offender typology), 79, 164
Bryant, C. D., 57, 58
Bryant, J., 175–176

Budin, L. E., 106–107
Bullens, R., 156–157
Bulten, E., 141, 142na
Burgess, A. W., 75, 257
Burkert, N., 31, 59
Burkhart, B. R., 27
Burton, D. L., 161
Buschman, J., 154
Butner Federal Correctional Institution
    Sex Offender Treatment Program,
    229–230
Butner Study Redux, 181, 182, 215–216
Byers, Matthew, 218–219

Cambodia, sex tourism in, 277
Canada
    age of consent, 96
    child pornography investigations, 54
    child pornography laws, 14
    juvenile prostitution, 273
    legal definition of child pornography,
        37–38
    prevalence of child pornography, 19
    recorded crime, 171–172
    sentencing of offenders, 243–244
    sexual trafficking of women to, 274
    solicitation laws, 24, 54
    virtual child pornography, 63
Cantor, J. M., 29, 141, 152, 184
Carey, C., 132
Carroll, Lewis, 39
Casady, T. K., 112
Casual sex, interest in, 145
Caucasian sex offenders, 146–147
Celibate pedophiles, 255–256
Centre for Addiction and Mental
    Health, Toronto, 229
CETS. *See* Child Exploitation Tracking
    System
CGI. *See* computer-generated imagery
Charité hospital, Berlin, 232
Chat rooms, 81–82, 283
Child, legal definition of, 37
Child and Family Services Act
    (Ontario provincial law), 233
Child exploitation, 18, 22
Child Exploitation and Obscenity
    Section, 14
Child Exploitation and Online
    Protection Center, 245

Child Exploitation Tracking System
    (CETS), 246–247
Childhood sexual abuse, 23
Child pornography, 37–57
    aggregate-level analysis on, 170–172
    availability of online, 42–43
    best-known series of, 3–4
    cathartic effect of, 178–179
    characteristics of children in, 45–46
    content of, 44–47
    defining, 23, 37–38
    distribution of, 253–254
    effects of, 176–177
    as gateway crime, 187–188
    history of, 38–40
    international laws against, 13–15
    Internet's effect on, 40–42, 44
    and juvenile sexual trafficking, 275
    law enforcement response to
        possession of, 245
    laws against, 23–24
    legal definition of, 37–38
    and online paraphilic adult
        pornography, 64–65
    in online sexual offending, 3–5
    and online solicitation, 87–93
    online solicitation offenders' use of, 79
    in pedohebephilia subculture, 57–62
    in pedophilia/hebephilia diagnosis,
        28–29
    policing efforts against, 53–54
    preferred vs. nonpreferred, 223
    prevalence of, 18–22, 48–50
    pseudo, 34
    relapse prevention approach, 227
    and sexting by adolescents, 66–69
    and technology, 12–13, 44
    trends in, 50–53
    victim identification in, 4–5
    victims of, 257–259
    virtual, 63, 256
Child pornography offenders
    adolescent, 133–134
    antisociality of, 158–159
    arousal patterns of, 151
    characteristics of, 264–265
    collecting pathology of, 132
    conditional release of, 204–206
    contact offenses by, 203–204,
        264–266

Child pornography offenders, *continued*
    continuum of culpability for, 55–56
    intelligence of, 146
    mandatory minimum sentencing of,
        242
    motivations of, 155–157
    online solicitation offenders vs.,
        86–87, 143
    pedophilia by, 151, 154
    pre-Internet vs. current, 130–131
    problematic Internet use by, 121–122
    risk factors for, 202–207
    risk measures for, 207–211
    risk of recidivism for, 194, 214
    selection effects in studies of, 137–139
    sentencing of, 243–244
    sexual addiction/compulsivity view
        of, 123–125
    sexual deviance of, 153–155
    sexual recidivism by, 194–195,
        265–266
    typology of, 162–165
    undetected, 183–184
Child protection
    and intervention, 248–249
    and juvenile prostitution, 273–274
    and risk assessment priorities,
        220–223
Child Protection Act (1984), 23
Child Recognition Identification
    System, 247
Children. *See also specific groups*
    characteristics of child pornography
        victims, 45–46
    emotional identification with, 118,
        119, 149–150
Children's Council on Internet
    Safety, 252
Child sexual exploitation, 275–276
Child welfare agencies, 23
Chinese literature, child pornography
    in, 39
Choy, A. L., 159, 194–195
Christianson, S. A., 72–73
Christoff, K., 125
Clark-Flory, Tracy, 256
Clinical functioning, problematic
    Internet use and, 122
Closet collectors, 163
Cloud storage, of child pornography, 43

Cognitions, of solicitation offenders, 83
Cognitive behavioral model of
    problematic Internet use, 121
Cognitive dissonance, 149
Cognitive distortions, 57–58, 130
Collecting pathology, 132
Collectors, 163, 165
Collins, R. L., 191–192
Combating Paedophile Information
    Networks in Europe (COPINE),
    14, 46, 231, 283
Commercial collectors, 163
Commercial exploitation offenders, 163
Commercial production of child
    pornography, 56
Communal traders, 163
Community management, 244
Compulsive Sexual Behavior Inventory,
    124
Compulsivity view of online sexual
    offending, 124–125
Computer-generated imagery (CGI),
    63, 283
Conditional release, 204–206
Confluence models, 177, 188
Congruence, pathways model and,
    118, 119
Congruence with children, 149–150
Connell, M., 213
Contact-driven offenders, 84–87,
    129, 166
Contact sex offenders
    antisociality of, 158–159
    intelligence of, 146
    interventions for, 226–228
    online offenders vs., 120, 140–143,
        166–167
    risk assessment for, 195–201
    sentencing of, 91, 243–244
    sexual abuse history of, 160
Contact sexual offending, 169–189
    cathartic effect of child pornography
        on, 178–179
    child pornography as gateway crime
        to, 187–188
    by child pornography offenders,
        203–204, 264
    by exhibitionists, 112
    and online offender policies,
        188–189

Digital evidence of sexual offending, 22–23, 222–223
Digital technologies, 44
Dines, G., 34
Direct victimization offenders, 163
Displacement function, of pornography, 172
Distal events, with problematic Internet use, 121
Distorted sexual scripts, in pathways model, 118, 119
Distress, depictions of, 46
Distribution, of child pornography, 55
Distributors (offender typology), 164
Dittmann, V., 155
Dodgson, Charles, 39
Doll, L. S., 161
Domestic sexual trafficking, 274, 275
Don Juanism, 124n2
Donoghue, C., 139
Donovan, J. E., 158
Dost test, 23–24
D'Ovidio, R., 57
Dowdell, E. B., 75, 76
Drug enforcement, 245
DSM–5. *See Diagnostic and Statistical Manual of Mental Disorders*, 5th ed.
DSM–IV–TR. *See Diagnostic and Statistical Manual of Mental Disorders*, 4th ed., text rev.
Dual offenders, 22, 180–188
    in group specificity studies of offender characteristics, 142na
    online offenders without contact histories vs., 184–188
    Static–99 measure for, 202–203
    undetected online offenders as, 183–184
Dunkelfeld Prevention Project, 155, 232–233, 250, 256, 266
Durkin, K. F., 57, 58, 83
Duwe, G., 241
Dynamic risk factors, 89, 199–201, 212
Dysphoric mood, 86
Dysregulated sexuality, 125

Eastern Europe, sexual trafficking in, 274
ECPAT International, 269n3, 274, 276n2, 277

ECPAT USA, 275
Educational level of online offenders, 146
Educational presentations, 250–252
Egan, V., 163, 167
Ego-dystonic behavior, 124–125
Ego-syntonic behavior, 124–125
Eke, A., 3, 7, 17, 46, 55, 180, 203–207, 209, 245
El-Burki, I. J., 57
Electronic Frontier Foundation, 12
Elliott, I., 16–17, 117–120, 140, 141, 143, 163, 212, 213
Emmers-Sommer, T. M., 173
Emotional dysregulation, in pathways model, 118, 119
Emotional identification with children, 118, 119, 149–150
Empathy, 150
Endrass, J., 205
Ennis, L., 59, 159, 194–195
Entrepreneurial offenders, 164
Erenay, N., 155
Erooga, M., 258
Erotophilia, 48
Espelage, D. L., 77
Ethnicity of online offenders, 146–147
Etiological models of online sexual offending, 117–131
    for adolescent offenders, 133–135
    collecting pathology in, 132
    common features of, 129–131
    and hypersexuality disorder, 126
    motivation–facilitation model, 126–129
    pathways model of contact offending, 118–120
    problematic Internet use in, 120–122
    relationship effects in, 122–123
    sex-as-coping model, 125–126
    sexual addiction or compulsivity view, 123–125
Evidence-based treatment approach, 281–282
Excitation transfer, 176
Exhibitionism, 46, 63, 111–112
    and obscene telephone calling, 113
    online, 203, 267
Experimental sexting, 68

Kraus, S. W., 173–174
Krone, T., 20, 81, 83, 163, 164
Krueger, R. B., 88, 90, 122, 126
KX series, 4
Kyckelhahn, T., 18, 158

Lalumière, M. L., 129, 161
Lamb, M., 79–81, 84, 94, 164
Landslide Productions, 22, 54, 205,
    247, 261
Lang, R. A., 106
Langevin, R., 79
Lanning, K. V., 46–47, 60, 132, 163
Laulik, S., 121–122, 177
Law enforcement. *See also* Police
    arrests of adolescents for sexting by,
        68–69
    child pornography investigations by,
        21–22, 42
    efforts against child pornography by,
        53–54
    international collaboration of,
        247–248
    interventions by, 244–247
    naming of suspects by, 261
    offender identification by, 137–138
    priorities of, 115
    recidivism study by, 206–207
    reporting of statutory sexual
        offending to, 96–97
    resources for investigations by, 23
    and transjurisdictional nature of
        online sexual offending, 25
Laws
    child pornography, 40
    international, 13–15, 269–270
    on online sexual offending, 7–8,
        13–15, 23–25
Leader, T., 120
Leaf, P. J., 175
Leander, L., 72–73
LeCraw, James, 261
Lee, A. F., 185–186
Lee, T., 114
Leuven, E., 173
Levenson, J. S., 22
Libertarianism, Internet, 61–62
Liddell, Alice, 39
Lim, L. L., 275, 277
Linz, D., 174

Linz, D. G., 191
Lloyd, R., 277
London Metropolitan Police, 83
Loneliness, 150
Long, M. L., 245
Longitudinal studies of contact sexual
    offending, 174–175
Lords, Traci, 92
Lounsbury, K., 66
Lovely, R. W., 48–49
Lucy Faithfull Foundation, 231
Lundy, J. P., 124n2
Luring, 34–35. *See also* Online
    solicitation
Lusignan, R., 126

MacDonald, W. M., 112
Magaletta, P. R., 159
Malamuth, N. M., 63, 172, 174, 177,
    190, 191, 256
Malarek, V., 274
Malaysia, sex tourism in, 277
Malesky, L. A., 59, 90, 107, 108
Mancini, C., 179
Mancuso, Matthew, 4
Mandatory minimum sentencing,
    221, 242–243
Mandatory reporting obligations, 233
Mandeville-Norden, R., 19, 118–120,
    141, 143, 163, 167
Mann, R. E., 147, 196–197
Marques, Janice, 227
Marriage status, of online offenders,
    147
Marshall, L. E., 227
Marshall, W. L., 125, 150, 227
Martellozzo, E., 16, 83
Masters, W. H., 124
Match.com, 104
Matsuzawa, Y. K., 141
Maxfield, M. G., 160
McCarthy, J. A., 151, 185, 187–188
McCausland, M., 257
McCormack, J. C., 236
McGarry, Bill, 4
McGuire, J., 150
McKibben, A., 126
McLaughlin, J. F., 164
McLearen, A. M., 159
McManus, M. A., 245

McPhail, I. V., 150
McWhaw, A., 146, 154, 159
Media attention, 17–20
Mehta, M. D., 42
Merdian, H. L., 86–87, 213
Metcalf, C., 19, 140, 141
Microsoft, 246–247
Middle school students, attempted
        online solicitation of, 75
Middleton, D., 19, 118–120, 141, 213,
        230, 231, 238
Misty series, 4, 257
Mitchell, K. J., 51–53, 55, 66–68, 77,
        84, 85, 92–96, 99–100, 110, 114,
        174, 175, 183, 188, 216, 251,
        273–276
Mitman, T., 57
Mobile phones, sexting with, 69
Mogstad, M., 173
Monahan, J., 195, 197
Mood problems, 158
Moore, R., 114
Morally indiscriminate offenders,
        164, 165
Morphing, 284
Mosaic browser, 11
Motivans, M., 18, 158
Motivation–facilitation model of sexual
        offending, 126–129, 199
    assessment and intervention based
        on, 130
    and individual differences in
        pornography effects, 177, 188
    and offender characteristics, 166
    and risk–recidivism paradox, 214
Motivations
    of offenders, 91–92, 155–157
    offender typology based on, 165
    of online solicitation offenders,
        101–102
Motivation to change, 230, 235–239
Moultrie, D., 133–134
Multiple dysfunctions, in pathways
        model, 119
Mundt, I. A., 21n5, 141, 142na, 155,
        186–187, 214
Mutual reinforcement, of offense-
        supportive attitudes/beliefs,
        60–61
Myspace, 109

Nademin, M. E., 142
Naivety, of online solicitation victims,
        95–96
National Campaign to Prevent Teen
        and Unplanned Pregnancy, 25, 66
National Center for Missing and
        Exploited Children (NCMEC),
        x, 56, 247, 251, 253
National Center for Supercomputing
        Applications, 11
National Incident-Based Reporting
        System (NIBRS), 97, 99
National Juvenile Online Victimization
        (NJOV) Project
    arrests for Internet sexual crimes in, 19
    child pornography research in, 46,
        50–53, 55, 90, 183, 216
    commercial sexual exploitation in, 275
    cyberbullying in, 77
    grooming tactics in, 79
    offender characteristics in, 264
    online solicitation research in, 90, 93
National Report on Child Exploitation, 213
National Strategy report (U.S. Attorney
        General), 270, 276
National Survey of Family Growth, 97
National Telecommunications and
        Information Administration, 147
NCMEC. See National Center for
        Missing and Exploited Children
Need principle of correctional rehabili-
        tation, 234–235, 281
Negative affect, 125–126
Nehring, D., 16
Netsmartz411, 251
Neuromancer (Gibson), ix
Neutze, J., 21n5, 141, 142na, 155,
        186–187, 214, 256
New Jersey, 69
NIBRS (National Incident-Based
        Reporting System), 97, 99
Nielssen, O., 138
Nijman, H., 141, 142na
Noncontact offense history, in
        Static–99, 203
Nonpreferred child pornography, 223
Nonsecure collectors, 164
Non-Westernized countries, 268
Not Real People (NRP) stimulus set, 63
Nymphomania, 124n2

probability vs. severity of, 215–217
and pseudo child pornography, 34
and pseudo online luring, 34–35
pubertal status in, 35–36
public reactions to, 6–7, 17–20
and sex tourism, 31–32
and sexual trafficking, 31–32
solicitation in, 5–6
technology used in, 12–13, 269
transjurisdictional nature of, 25
universality of, 268
Online solicitation, 71–102
characteristics of vulnerable youths,
108–110, 265
child pornography and, 87–93
descriptive studies of, 79–84
examples of offenses, 72–73
fantasy vs. contact-driven, 84–87
future research directions, 101–102
grooming tactics, 78–79, 106–107
incidence of, 73–74
international laws against, 13–15
international scope of, 76–77
myths about, 93–96
offline vs., 77–78
in online sexual offending, 5–6
and paraphilic behavior, 111–113
prevalence of, 74–76
prevention of, 250–252, 254–255
and sexual offenses against adults,
103–105
and statutory sexual offending,
96–101
Online solicitation offenders
arousal patterns of, 151, 152
characteristics of, 84, 265
child pornography offenders vs.,
86–87, 143
child pornography use by, 79
contact offenses by, 183
grooming tactics of, 78–79, 106–107
motivations for, 101–102
police entrapment of, 114–115
risk factors for, 202
selection effects in studies of, 138
typology of, 165–166
Online surveys of sexual offenders, 139
Online victimization, impact of,
248–249, 257–260
Online voyeurism, 203, 267

Ontario, child pornography investigations
in, 54
Ontario Association of Children Aid
Societies, x
Operation Avalanche, 22, 54
Operation Fairplay, 43
Operation Hamlet, 247
Operation Ore, 17, 22, 54
Operation Roundup, 43
Operation Snowball, 22, 54
Ore (operation), 17, 22, 54
Organized crime, 276
Ormrod, R. K., 112
Osborn, J., 213
Out of the Shadows (Lundy), 124n2
Overtly sexual exchanges, 81

P2P networks. *See* Peer-to-peer (P2P)
networks
Paedophila, 28. *See also* Pedophilia
Palmer, Tink, x
Paraphilia-related disorders, 85–86, 125
Paraphilic adult pornography, 64–65
Paraphilic behavior, 46, 155
online vs. offline, 111–113
and technology, 63–64
Parents
engagement of, 252
juvenile prostitution involving, 273
juvenile sex trafficking involving,
274–275
online activity monitoring by, 92–93
Parole, 204–206
Passive distributors, 55
Patchin, J. W., 109
Pathways model of sexual offending
adapting, for online offending,
118–120
and motivation to change, 236–239
Paul, B., 191
Pearce, E., 150
Pedohebephilia, 57–62
child pornography and diagnosis
of, 29
effects of, 60–62
and offender characteristics,
264–265
prevalence of, 28–31
themes in, 58–60
Pedophile collectors, 163

ABOUT THE AUTHOR

Michael C. Seto, PhD, received his doctorate in psychology from Queen's University in Kingston, Canada. He is a registered clinical psychologist and the director of forensic rehabilitation research for the Royal Ottawa Health Care Group's Integrated Forensic Program. He also has adjunct professorship appointments in psychology and/or psychiatry at four accredited universities: the University of Toronto, Ryerson University, Carleton University, and the University of Ottawa. Dr. Seto has published extensively on pedophilia, child pornography, sexual offending, violence risk assessment, and mentally disordered offenders and regularly presents at scientific meetings and professional workshops on these topics. He recently authored a well-reviewed book on pedophilia and sexual offending against children, *Pedophilia and Sexual Offending Against Children: Theory, Assessment, and Intervention*, published by the American Psychological Association in 2008. Further information is available from his LinkedIn profile: http://ca.linkedin.com/in/mcseto. You can follow him on Twitter @MCSeto.